The World Order
Socialist Perspectives

Edited by
RAY BUSH, GORDON JOHNSTON and DAVID COATES

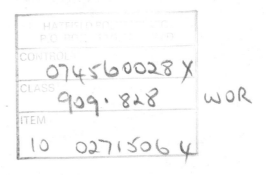
Polity Press

First published 1987 by Polity Press in association with Basil Blackwell.

Editorial Office:
Polity Press, Dales Brewery, Gwydir Street, Cambridge CB1 2LJ, UK

Basil Blackwell Ltd
108 Cowley Road, Oxford OX4 1JF, UK

Basil Blackwell Inc.
432 Park Avenue South, Suite 1503, New York, NY 10016, USA

British Library Cataloguing in Publication Data

The world order : socialist perspectives.
1. History, Modern — 1945-
I. Bush, Ray   II. Johnston, Gordon, 1952-
III. Coates, David
908.82'8   D840

ISBN 0-7456-0028-X
ISBN 0-7456-0029-8 Pbk

Library of Congress Cataloging in Publication Data

The World order.

Includes index.
1. World politics—1945-   . I. Bush, Ray.
II. Johnston, Gordon, 1952-. III. Coates, David.
D843.W645 1987   327'.0904   86-30341
ISBN 0-7456-0028-X
ISBN 0-7456-0029-8 (pbk.)

Typeset in 10/11pt CG Times by System 4 Associates, Buckinghamshire
Printed in Great Britain by
Billing & Sons, Ltd. Worcester

This book is dedicated to the memory of
Judy Kimble (1952–1976):
friend, and staunch opponent of
oppression and racism.

Contents

Notes on Contributors   viii

Introduction *Ray Bush, Gordon Johnston and David Coates*   1

Part One Character of the World Order   5

1 From Fordism to Reaganism   7
    The Crisis of American Hegemony in the 1980s
    Mike Davis

2 The Soviet Bloc   26
    Ernest Mandel

3 Ups and Downs   43
    The Fortunes of the West European and Japanese Economies
    since 1945
    John Harrison and David Bavar

4 The New International Division of Labour   65
    Ankie Hoogvelt

5 The Crisis in the Third World   87
    Morris Szeftel

6 The Arms Race and the Cold War   141
    Dan Smith

Part Two Conflict and Change in the World Order   169

7 The Third Great Revolution   171
    The Experience of Revolutionary Socialism in China
    Gordon White

8 The Middle East in International Perspective   201
    Problems of Analysis
    Fred Halliday

9 The United States and Central America   221
    Nora Hamilton

10 Southern Africa   256
    The Struggle Ahead
    Ray Bush and Lionel Cliffe

Bibliography   288

Index   294

Notes on Contributors

David Bavar is a freelance writer living in London.

Ray Bush is a lecturer in Politics at the University of Leeds. He has published in the area of African Politics and is currently researching the Politics of Famine.

Lionel Cliffe has worked on African issues for 30 years. He is a founder – editor of the *Review of African Political Economy*. He has worked in and published on the Horn, Tanzania, Kenya, Zambia and Zimbabwe as well as general issues of peasant politics and liberation struggles. He is currently Senior lecturer in Politics at the University of Leeds.

David Coates is Senior Lecturer and currently Head of Department of Politics, University of Leeds. He has written extensively on politics and capitalism in Britain and on problems of socialist strategy. His recent publications include *The Context of British Politics* and (edited with John Hillard) *The Economic Decline of Modern Britain*.

Mike Davis is a member of the editorial collective of the *New Left Review*. He is the author of *Prisoners of the American Dream* (1986).

John Harrison is Senior Lecturer in Economics at Thames Polytechnic. He is author of *Marxist Economics for Socialists*, co-author, with Andrew Glyn, of *The British Economic Disaster*, and with Philip Armstrong and Andrew Glyn of *Capitalism Since World War II*. He is also Series Editor of *Arguments for Socialism*.

Fred Halliday is Professor of International Relations at the London School of Economics. He studied at the University of Oxford, the School of Oriental and African Studies, London and the LSE, and was for a number of years a member of the Editorial Board of *New Left Review*. Since 1974 he has been a Fellow of the Transnational Institute, Amsterdam and Washington. His books include: *Arabia Without Sultans* (1974), *Iran: Dictatorship and Development* (1978), with Maxine Molyneux, *The Ethiopian Revolution* (1982) and *The Making of the Second Cold War*, 2nd edn, (1986).

Nora Hamilton is Associate Professor, Department of Political Science, University of Southern California. She has researched in and published extensively on Latin and Central American politics. She is an editor of *Latin American Perspectives*. Her recent publications include *The Limits of State Autonomy: Post Revolutionary Mexico*, and (edited with Timothy Harding) *Modern Mexico: State, Economy and Social Conflict*.

Ankie M. M. Hoogvelt is a lecturer in the Department of Sociological Studies, University of Sheffield, where she teaches courses in Third World Studies and in Transnational Corporations. She is author of *The Sociology of Developing Societies*, and of *The Third World in Global Development*.

Gordon Johnston is Senior Lecturer in Politics at Leeds Polytechnic. He is co-editor (with David Coates) of *Socialist Arguments* and *Socialist Strategies* and (with David Coates and Ray Bush) *A Socialist Anatomy of Britain*.

Ernest Mandel has for 40 years been a leading member of the Fourth International. He was a member of the Economic Studies Commission of the Belgian T.U.C. (FGTB) 1954–1963 and since 1972 Professor at the Free University of Brussels. He has written many books and pamphlets on Marxism and contemporary political developments in the world order. These writings include, *Marxist Economic Theory, Late Capitalism, Revolutionary Marxism Today, Trotsky: A Study in the Dynamic of his Thought, The Second Slump*.

Dan Smith is a Vice-Chairperson of CND and a former Chairperson (1981–2) of END. He is author of *The Defence of the Realm in the 1980s* (1980), co-author of *The War Atlas* and *The Economics of Militarism* (both 1983) and co-editor of *Protest and Survive* (1980). As D. W. Smith he is author of two crime novels – *Father's Law* (1986) and *Serious Crimes* (1987). He is also a member of the Alternative Defence Commission.

Morris Szeftel was born in Zambia and taught at the University of Zambia before joining the Department of Politics at the University of Leeds. He is a member of the editorial board of *The Journal of Southern African Studies* and reviews editor of *The Review of African Political Economy*. He has co-edited the 1984 issue of ROAPE on 'Resistance and Resettlement in Southern Africa' and a 1985 issue on 'War and Famine in Africa' and is co-author of *The Dynamics of the One Party State in Zambia* (1984). He is presently working on a number of projects concerned with the post-colonial state in the third world, relations between state and capital, and politics and class formation in Zambia.

Introduction

RAY BUSH, GORDON JOHNSTON AND DAVID COATES

The world which surrounds us is fraught with the most appalling social and economic inequalities, military tensions and economic instabilities. People are going hungry and thousands are starving in a world which is capable of providing goods in plenty, and in which significant minorities enjoy higher standards of living than the world has ever seen before. But the productivity of the twentieth-century world economy has produced neither peace nor stability. On the contrary, that productive capacity and potential has been developed inside a world order dominated by intense military, economic and ideological conflict between power blocs and between individual nation states; and one in which the rhythms of economic expansion and recession, political domination and popular resistance have generated and continue to generate a number of crisis points and issues on which we need to take a view and on which we need to act. The threat of nuclear war will not go away unless we do act. Nor will famines vanish from Africa and elsewhere unless action is taken there and in the key centres of power in the advanced industrial world. We sit in such a centre of power. But what view should we take of the world order which surrounds us and how are we to act within it?

This book is an attempt by socialists to help bring together some of the information necessary for the creation of informed action by the left. In what follows, various contributors will explain the nature of the current international order: the present revitalized American imperialism, the new international division of labour, the character of the Soviet bloc and the different dimensions of political and economic turmoil in the Third World. The topics they will discuss are complex and controversial: the contributors are not all in total agreement in the analyses they offer. But they share a commitment to moving beyond the bland assertion – so common on the left – that the ills of the world order derive in some simple and obvious way from capitalism. There is nothing simple and obvious about the economic, social and political forces shaping the contemporary world: and what contributors have done, in their various ways, is to provide a map of these forces.

The world order has been determined in large part by the accumulation of capital in the United States, Japan and Western Europe and it is with these cases that our analysis begins. Mike Davis is concerned in chapter 1 to establish the internal changes that have recently occurred in the US political economy, and to see why the American electorate chose to confirm in office an administration which is busy trying to claw the US back to a position of global dominance; one which contemplates nuclear holocaust and regularly destabilizes democratically elected regimes in its own 'backyard' and beyond; one which is steadfast in its opposition to socialist reconstruction and struggles for national liberation; and one which uses its economic might to tie impoverished Third World countries to western technology and its own military superiority.

John Harrison and David Bavar also recognize (in chapter 3) the importance which patterns of capital accumulation have had for post-war reconstruction in Western Europe and Japan, but they stress too the way in which the post-war reaffirmation of capitalism in those areas met significant amounts of working-class resistance. They then chart the interplay of capital and labour in the rhythm of boom and slump in the economies of America's major political allies.

In chapter 2, Ernest Mandel examines the importance of the Bolshevik revolution in 1917 and then the liberation of Eastern Europe at the closing stages of World War II, in creating a bulwark against global capitalist expansion. He explains how the eastern bloc has developed and assesses how effective it has been in providing a counterbalance to US imperialism. He also asks if the Soviet Union is itself imperialist and in what respects, if any, its social system differs from the capitalism of the west? In raising these questions Mandel introduces a further layer of analysis which reminds us of the complex system of relations underpinning the current world order. His is an analysis of post-war reconstruction which needs to be read alongside that provided by Dan Smith (in chapter 6) who highlights the interplay of internal contradictions within the United States and the Soviet Union and of external interactions between these superpowers, in order to explain the arms race and the Cold War. For Smith, the arms race has its own dynamic which may outweigh at different times the more general economic and social processes which underpin it; and in arguing that, Smith shifts the weight of emphasis away from the class forces stressed by Davis, Harrison and Mandel, to emphasize instead the logic of military and civilian complexes and inter-state relationships.

Ankie Hoogvelt documents in great detail in chapter 4 the contradictory processes which the internationalization of capital since 1945 has established, both on superpowers and underdeveloped capitalist countries alike. The world economy since the war has been plagued by conflict. The early chapters explain this conflict as the product of internal crises of capital accumulation resulting from working-class opposition and falling rates of profit, the restrictions placed on the movement of new investment by the emergence of Soviet spheres of influence after 1945, and struggles by workers and peasants in the Third World. But these restrictions on the profitability of capital have also resulted from the patterns of international-ization of capital itself. It is this added dimension of the contemporary world order that Hoogvelt presents in chapter 4. She asks what exactly is meant by the much-used term 'the new international division of labour'. Has this division of labour become a way of reducing economic crises in the capitalist heartland by the export of capital and enterprise overseas? Why has the new international division of labour become the catchword of the 1980s for so many concerned with development issues, and how real is the movement of resources to parts of the world hitherto ignored by capital or exploited solely for raw material extraction?

Crucial to Hoogvelt's analysis is the *uneven* character of the movement of investment from the west to the south and east – not only in terms of quantity but also in terms of quality – the precise type and form of investment. She shows that the assembly 'sweat' shops of Taiwan, the Philippines and elsewhere have done little to promote conditions for autonomous industrialization promised by protagonists of a new international economic order. This theme is extended by Morris Szeftel in chapter 5, in which he discusses the crises facing much of the Third World and takes us into the underdeveloped countries to explain the nature of local patterns of class formation and domination in Africa and elsewhere. How have political actors in those countries created their own basis for power? To what degree have they been subject to local peasant and working-class resistance and how far have they been subordinated by international agencies such as multinational corporations, the World Bank and the International Monetary Fund?

It is only when we are equipped with this final layer of analysis that we can adequately grasp the multifaceted nature and complexity of the current world order. It is an order which is not simply structured around the current aggressive and chauvinistic actions of the United States. It is an order constructed around patterns of capitalist accumulation and crises in the west and north, Soviet dominance of an eastern bloc, and the independent although often subordinate actions of ruling elites and classes in the underdeveloped countries in the southern parts of the globe.

Part II of this book lays out some of the key points at which struggles for greater autonomy from both local elites and international subordination are currently taking place. It begins with an assessment of the Chinese Revolution in 1949, and with contemporary developments in communist China. Gordon White in chapter 7 describes China after 1949 as another model of non-capitalist economic development in the Third World, and he reminds us of China's impact on the Soviet Union. Chapter 7 places recent developments in China within the context of the 1949 revolution and debates within the Communist Party of China and Communist Party of the Soviet Union over the strategy and possibility of building socialism in an underdeveloped non-industrial society.

Chapter 8 is an examination by Fred Halliday of current conflicts in the Middle East. He explains the ongoing turmoil in Lebanon, Iran and Iraq, as well as the struggle for Palestine, by placing them in the particular histories of the different Middle Eastern countries, and in the manner of their insertion into the world economy. A similar approach is also taken by Nora Hamilton in her discussion in chapter 9 on the United States and Central America. She documents changing styles of imperialist intervention in Central America and reminds us that US intervention in the Caribbean basin dates back to the start of the nineteenth century, from which time we can also identify local 'clients' of US business willing to repress the democratic aspirations of peasants and workers in what Reagan today calls his 'backyard'.

In the concluding chapter on southern Africa, Ray Bush and Lionel Cliffe document the ascendency of South Africa in the region, and analyse the nature of that country's economic and political power. They detail how the apartheid state structure has been erected and what modifications have recently been made. They also look at the politics of different movements struggling for the liberation of South Africa and at attempts which have been made by countries in the region to disengage from the Pretoria regime. Crucial also to their analysis is an understanding of the position which the more aggressive American imperialism has taken with regard to southern Africa. This has been reflected in the US government's simultaneous call for the withdrawal of Cuban troops from Angola – as a premise to independence for Namibia – while Washington openly courts, and funds, Savimbi's terrorist movement in southern Angola and South Africa's occupation of that country, which is the very reason for the presence of Cuban advisers.

Although we do not necessarily share all the views expressed in this collection, we believe that it highlights very clearly the background and character of the present world order. Together the contributors provide a guide to the contemporary reassertion of US hegemony, the Cold War crisis and political and economic trauma in parts of the Third World. Taken as a whole, their essays help to identify the present character and nature of the international order, the major social forces which dictate that order and the location and source of its central contradictions. We hope this information will be of value to readers attempting to identify more fully what is going on in the trouble spots of the world, to recognize who and what are the progressive forces at work there, to see how to begin to relate socialist politics at home to those wider progressive struggles. The complexities of the world order – and the scale of the problems it generates – are a major barrier to its successful transformation by the left: and so often struggles in one place fail for lack of support elsewhere from other radicals and socialists who lack the knowledge of what is going on in other areas. Such knowledge is not a guarantee of effective left-wing politics, but the continuation of the present ignorance will certainly guarantee its absence. A powerful left will need to be an informed one: and it is our hope that in a modest way, this volume helps to provide some elements of that information.

Part One

Character of the World Order

1

From Fordism to Reaganism
The Crisis of American Hegemony in the 1980s

MIKE DAVIS

The post-war world has been dominated politically by American military power and economically by the weight of American-inspired production systems and markets: and the key to much of the contemporary world crisis lies in the erosion of these political and economic bases of American domination. To understand what is now going on, we need to look at the character of US power and politics: externally, in its relations to the rest of the capitalist world, and internally, at the changing nature of the US economy, class structure and political forces. In fact, the key to understanding the character of American foreign policy now lies in the interplay of those internal and external forces in the post-war years. The purpose of this article is to lay out – in a necessarily highly schematic way – the contradictions of that interplay: to take us from Fordism to Reaganism.

Atlantic 'Ultra-Imperialism'?

The post-war era of world American domination was inaugurated by a 'revolution from above' between 1945 and 1950 which reconstructed the power of the European bourgeoisies along a new axis of liberalism and interdependency congruent with US global power, while simultaneously purging and fragmenting the European labour movement. The crucial precondition for this transforma-tion, was the unique techno-military advantage attained by the United States in the summer of 1945. The great historical contingency of the atomic bomb was joined to the more predictable results of the full-scale mobilization of the productive forces of the giant American economy (which *doubled* its capacity between 1940 and 1944), and to American exemption from the main brunt of combat against the Nazi war machine. Hiroshima marked the beginning of the 'American Century': from 8 August 1945 all constraints on power-sharing in the post-war world – as they had been deliberated by the Allied triumverate at Yalta – were swept away by a vision of total American domination. Military integration under the slogan of collective security preceded and quickened the interpenetration of

the major capitalist economies. In an almost concentric accretion around the central
fortress of the national-security state, successive presidential initiatives and
'doctrines' – responding to the shifting geo-political storm centres of revolution
and nationalist insurgency – erected an interlocking structure of military alliances
and nuclear trip-wires. From the Chapultepec Pact of 1945 – which created a
Western Hemisphere military alliance – to the Manila Pact of 1954 – which created
the South East Asian Treaty Organization (SEATO) – a single network began to
link together the outposts and continents, imperial and mercenary, in 40 countries,
to their ultimate headquarters in the basement of the White House.

It was only within the framework of bourgeois stability guaranteed by this
nuclear imperialism that the old Wilsonian project of the 'liberalization' of
European (and now, also, Japanese) capitalism was actually accomplished in the
early Cold War years. It is important to recall that, apart from the brief and
unstable interlude between 1918 and 1933, the post–1945 period was the first
time in which parliamentary democracy, based upon a universal franchise, became
the norm in Western European history (the Iberian fascist states, of course,
remaining significant exceptions). Before then two insuperable obstacles had inter-
posed themselves in the path of a democratic stabilization. First was the relative
weight and militancy of the local labour movements. Second was the persistence
of much of the sociological and political structure of late absolutism. Time and
again a weakened bourgeoisie, incapable of founding its own mass parties or
reconciling its own internal differentiations, allied itself with a persistent aristo-
cracy – often supported by an ultramontane peasantry or ruined *Mittelstand* –
to overthrow democratic structures seemingly too conducive to radical or reformist
labour movements. This fragility of European political capitalism was directly
related to the meagreness of the 'welfare surplus' available as a resource for class
conciliation. The latter, in turn, was an expression of the general underdevelopment
of coherent capitalist relationships of production and consumption – the prevalence
of pre-capitalist agriculture, strength of *rentier* strata, inefficient and cartelized
heavy industries, mass underconsumptionism, and so on.

An American project to intervene in the reshaping of European capitalism was
first elaborated during World War I as part of the Wilson administration's attempt
to merchandize 'democratic war aims' to the sceptical American and weary Allied
publics. Although Wilson ultimately failed to sell the League of Nations to German
or Irish-American voters in his own party, his encouragement of a US *private*
capitalist offensive in Europe was more successful; and this first crusade to
mobilize Americanism as a countervailing world ideology to Bolshevism was
sustained, after the signing of the Dawes Plan, through the brief but extra-
ordinary Weimar boom of 1925–9 which prefigured many of the ideological and
political relationships of the 1950s. With American loans putting German workers
back to work there was an uninhibited and naive celebration of all things American
– a euphoria about the brave new world across the Atlantic. However with the
collapse of the American economy in 1929 – largely as a result of the all too
successful anti-labour offensive of 1919–23, which halved the American Federation of Labor's membership and froze mass incomes – the temporary honeymoon
of German social democracy and the export sector of German industry also broke
down: brutal home-grown idylls replaced the flirtation with jazz and Ford cars.

The American intervention in Western Europe after 1945 was of a qualitatively different character from the twenties, and focused far more directly on the overriding structural problems of containing radical labour (without destroying labour reformism *per se*) and of creating a mass electoral support for bourgeois domination. This latter problem was largely resolved through the creation of a new European political current, 'Christian Democracy', in an alliance after 1943 between the Holy See and the White House. The success of Christian democracy in becoming the largest single political bloc in Western Europe, was, however, more than the sum of its endorsements from the Pope, the President or frightened capitalists. Particularly in the first post-war years when the movement had to compete vigorously against popular communist and socialist alternatives, Christian democracy, supported with US aid, undertook its own programme of pre-emptive, anti-radical reform: with especially striking results in Italian agriculture, but also in Germany and France in the creation of corporatist mechanisms of industrial relations. The famous troika of Schumann, Adenauer and De Gasperi could claim to represent a unique synthesis of rural populism, anti-communism, ultra-montanism and economic modernism.

If Christian democracy thus provided the previously absent mass electoral base for capitalist dominance in the parliamentary state, it was still a majoritarian current only in parts of the countryside and amongst the traditional petty-bourgeoisie. The left still overwhelmingly commanded the Western European working classes, and the wartime experience of common resistance to fascism had encouraged hopes of continued socialist–communist coooporation and the reunification of the European trade-union movement. The second prong, therefore, of the US offensive to 'liberalize' post-war Europe was the struggle, not just against the communists, but against labour unity and strength in any form. Throughout the allied zones of occupation in Germany, left social democrats, as well as communists, were purged from their positions, local 'united fronts' outlawed, and strikes forbidden. Armed with wads of money and official support, the American Federation of Labor (and later the Congress of Industrial Organizations as well, following the expulsion of its own left-led unions) played a crucial role in subverting trade-union solidarity. Only after thus fragmenting European trade unionism could the Christian Democrats, Gaullists and Americans move to the next stage of excluding the communists from the right of participation in Western European government. The great confrontation of the winter of 1947/8, culminating in the Marshall Plan, the first Berlin Crisis and the defeat of the French miners' strike, was the founding moment, so to speak, of the North Atlantic Treaty Organization's state system. With the communists and left-socialists ostracized from coalition politics, and with the trade-union movements irreparably divided, the structure was created for a relatively stable competition of Christian democratic, Gaullist and right-wing social democratic parties. Although local electoral alignments ranged from the volatility of the Fourth Republic to the monolithicism of Italian Christian Democracy, there was a sanitized pluralism within the conditions of an implicit loyalty oath to NATO, the Cold War, and the atomic bomb.

Without equally far-reaching transformations in European capitalism, however, this state system might have proven as short-lived and crisis-torn as its Versailles predecessor. What precisely distinguished the nature of the 1950s recovery from the ephemeral Weimar boom was that, alongside the secondary role of US capital, there were radical transformations in the very composition of European capital.

After 1945 the American corporate and financial establishment redirected European economic development away from cartelism and colonialism to auto-centred growth based on consumer-durable consumption within an integrated European domestic market. This Americanization of the European economy involved a recomposition of internal power within the European bourgeoisies which marginalized the classical *rentier*/colonial and protectionist/heavy-industry blocs. Its economic pre-conditions were given by the Korean War boom and the formation of the European Iron and Steel Community; its political pre-condition was the emergence of a 'growth coalition', with intimate American ties, which linked together leading cliques of all the NATO parties. The result was the creation of a European economy of mass production and of mass consumption – in a word – the creation of European 'Fordism'.

In summary, we may say that the temporary American economic and military *supremacy* at the end of World War II was transformed into a more durable US *hegemony* only because American power was simultaneously deployed for counter-revolutionary ends (to break up the threat of a unitary European labour movement) and for bourgeois revolutionary purposes (to liberalize and restructure European political economy). As a result the axis of the world market economy shifted from inter-imperialist rivalries between semi-self-sufficient monetary–colonial blocs to inter-metropolitan exchange based on the generalization of Fordism in Europe, America and Japan.

The Economic Underpinnings of American Power

It was above all, the growth of the domestic US economy in the 1950s and 1960s that provided sustained momentum to the international system as a whole, allowing the European and Japanese economies to reconstruct their productive forces on US mass-assembly principles and to achieve the recovery 'miracles' of the late 1950s. The American economy was only able to fulfil this happy function because its insertion into the world economy was uniquely assymetrical. On the one hand, its absolute contribution to world trade and investment was sufficiently large to produce dynamizing demand and supply effect. On the other hand, compared to the rest of the economies in the Organization for Economic Cooperation and Development (OECD), it was relatively self-sufficient: until 1970 only 7 per cent of the US gross national product circulated in the world market. The United States was therefore able to flexibly accommodate to the increasing shares of Western Europe and Japan in world manufacturing trade. Unlike earlier mercantile–colonial eras, American economic domination was not founded on a rigid pre-eminence in world trade but on the maintenance of robust conditions of accumulation within the domestic economy.

There have been two primary mechanisms of post-war domestic growth in the United States: a 'wage-led' dynamic of mass consumption, and a 'tax-led' dynamic of sectoral/regional expansion.

The first pattern of accumulation was based on the full circuiting of rising productivity, profits and wages via multi-annual collective bargaining and a super-liquid domestic credit system supported by federal home loans and tax relief for mortgages. Previously, during the first great consumer-durable boom of the

1920s, the majority of the semi-skilled industrial working class remained trapped in poverty-level incomes, unable to participate in the hoopla of car and house buying. In this sense, incipient Fordism was defeated by the very success of the open-shop 'American plan' which destroyed unionism and blocked wage advance. It took the decade-long struggle of the new industrial unions to force the way for union recognition and the codification of a dynamic wage system – in the collective bargaining agreements of the late 1940s – that synchronized mass consumption to labour productivity. In this fashion, perhaps a quarter of the US population – especially ethnic-white semi-skilled workers and their families – were raised to previously middle-class or skilled-worker norms of house owner-ship and credit purchase during the 1950s. Another quarter to one-third of the population, including most blacks and all agricultural labourers, remained outside the boom, constituting that 'other America' which rebelled in the 1960s.

This continuous transformation of the American working class's conditions of life and the correlative expansion of the primary, high-wage labour market were complexly coordinated with the *second* engine of post-war accumulation in the United States: *the formation of the Sunbelt*. Between the beginning of World War II and the end of the Vietnam War, an astonishing revolution in the sectoral and regional structures of American capitalism was achieved with the rapid urbanization and industrialization of the Pacific slope, Texas and parts of the non-cotton south. We describe this industrial revolution in the old hinterland as 'tax-led' because federal fiscal transfers, secured by the political power of the south and west, were the prime movers in the creation of the Sunbelt. By the end of the Vietnam War boom a Sunbelt urban–industrial region had emerged roughly equal in income and output to the older industrial area of the United States, but distinguished from it by very different accumulation conditions.

For example, the Sunbelt tends to be energy-rich, land-extensive, relatively non-union and with significantly lower social overheads on a local government level. Its economy is founded on the sectoral predominance of science-based industries (aerospace and electronics) primary products, and amenities (tourism, retirement and recreation); the north still retains most of the older heavy and consumer-durable industries. Correlatively, mass-production workers still con-stitute a crucial component of the 'Frostbelt' social structure, while the south and west are characterized by the segmentation of the labour forces into unusual concentrations of technical scientific workers on one side, and very low-wage primary and tertiary sector workers on the other. In the ex-plantation south, where millions of tenants and share-croppers were displaced by farm mechanization, the black rural poor bore the brunt of emigration to the northern inner-city areas being evacuated by suburb-bound white workers. In aggregate terms the Sunbelt was able to export its poverty northwards while simultaneously shifting the margin of tax expenditure southwards: the downtowns of Cleveland and Newark withered while the suburbs of San Diego and Houston bloomed.

In general, it is possible to say that the economic macrodynamics of American hegemony, as maintained for over 30 years by a unified imperial military and state system, came close to fulfilling the popular clichés of the Americanization of Europe and the Californization of America. The creeping trend towards the equalization of income levels between the United States and the Euro-industrial heartland, as well as between the major regions of the United States itself, was an incipient reality by the time of the crest in the long post-war boom in the early 1970s. Meanwhile, *within* the United States, the Vietnam War boom accelerated capital formation and income growth throughout the southeast and the southwest. Between 1969 and 1974 per capita income in southern metropolitan areas increased from 93 to 98 per cent of the national average, and by the 1980 census it was actually superior. The overall regional differentials, which in 1940 had ranged from .65 for the south to 1.15 for the Pacific Coast, had shrunk by the end of the 1970s to a total discrepancy, from lowest to highest, of only .15.

Along with this tendency for wage and productivity levels to come together within the Fordist core of the world economy there has also been a trend towards the *relative saturation* of the consumer-durable markets which have been the primary engines of the coordinated expansion of metropolitan capitalism. The significance of this threshold within the history of world capitalism, and specifically for the system of accumulation under US hegemony, is similar to the coming to an end of the great age of international railroad construction, under the aegis of British *rentier* capitalism, in the 1905–12 period. Like this earlier watershed, which produced the deep economic malaise that prefaced World War I, the Fordist crisis of the 1970s has brought with it a series of profound structural consequences:

1. It raised metropolitan energy consumption to a level incompatible with the artificially low, even depreciating, international oil prices. The oil shocks which inevitably ensued challenged the entire structure of existing capitalization, based as it was on super-cheap energy, and led to the depreciation of large quantities of existing plant and technology. Apart from the quasi-fictional transfers of income to the Organization of Petroleum Exporting Countries (OPEC), rising oil prices also induced a restructuring of profit-distribution processes within 'core' capital itself: US oil majors, for instance, suddenly were awash with one-third of total US corporate profits, while many manufacturing sectors were in acute liquidity crises. Although the shifts in the energy-price substructure of manufacturing costs certainly benefitted the most technologically advanced, energy-conservative goods-producers, their principal result was to spectacularly strengthen *metropolitan* finance and *rentier* interests at the expense of the productive economy as a whole.
2. The explosive growth of privatized consumption in the 1960s imposed unprecedented strains on the fiscal resources available to sustain the collective infrastructure (e.g. roads, new schools, suburban services, etc.) of that privatized consumption. Public spending and taxes thus increasingly became a terrain of division between suburbanized workers and middle strata, on one hand, and inner-city workers and non-waged poor on the other. Runaway inflation, with its perverse distributional effects and illusions (e.g. working-class home-owners are simul-taneously victims of higher property taxes and benficiaries of inflated equities), polarized further these consumption-defined locations, tempting the stronger or more advantaged sections of the working class to abandon class solidarism for inter-class blocs of the 'haves' formed against the collective 'have-nots'.
3. The consumer-durable industries and some of their primary supplies have reacted, in classic fashion, to market-saturation and growing foreign competition by undertaking the rationalization of existing capacity. The historic originality of the present rationalization movement is that it has taken the form of the creation of genuine world industries. Allowing part of their domestic plant to close down

and rust away, multinationals have shifted amortization funds overseas to the strategic handful of countries whose political regimes maintain the combination of literate skilled labour and low wages. The result is not further branch production for local markets, but the emergence of integrated international assembly-lines in the auto, tyre, appliance, pharmaceutical and electronic component industries – all financed by burgeoning offshore capital markets.

4. The relative diminution of the previously dynamic regional and national differences within the 'core' galvanized the search in the 1970s for new capital-goods markets in the industrializing 'semi-periphery'. Ironically, it was the staggering accumulation of 'stateless' dollars, arising from the US trade deficit and the OPEC price explosion, that provided the fuel for the 'debt-led' industrial boom which swept the American, Mediterranean and East Asian borderlands from 1976 to 1980. This longest and giddiest of individual post-war booms was based on the export of metropolitan debts, magically recycled by the international banking system as credit-money, to newly industrializing countries whose future export growth was, in turn, pledged as collateral. Built into this amazing circle of growth via metamorphosed indebtedness was the virtual certainty that a recession in the core would produce rampant, negative multiplier effects in the over-investing semiperiphery.

Thus the maturation of Fordism, under American hegemony, has produced a structure of crisis that simultaneously interlaces contradictions at the levels of the composition of capital, the composition of labour, the balance of class forces, the international division of labour and the relative autonomy of the world financial system. In a general way, all these 'crises within the crisis', which demand specific analyses, can be synthetically coalesced into the question of the crisis's 'solution'. Current debate, as well as the simple logic of the analytic categories already adduced, suggest two alternative or combined paths for the resumption of long-term capital accumulation on a world scale and in continuity with the structures of the preceding phase. First is the possibility of extending mass production and consumption into the belt of urban societies on the borderlands of the core. Second is the possibility of internally broadening the Fordist productivity and demand dynamic within the metropolitan societies to encompass the tertiary sectors.

If the earlier hypothesis has been accepted that American hegemony has provided the dynamic structural coherence for the diffusion of Fordism within Europe and America, then the question of the character and prospects of the present crisis of that hegemony must be related to the potential capacity of the American imperial role to ensure the transition to these new forms of global accumulation. Is the United States capable of carrying out yet a second capitalist revolution to make Mexico and South Korea advanced consumer societies, and/or to 'reindustrialize' itself around the dynamism of a new 'educational–medical complex' linked to a shorter working-life?

The answer is clearly no. American hegemony has become increasingly incompatible with the requisite restructuring of capital accumulation on a world scale. But before considering the political fields of force and of interests that impeded such transformations – or, even, their visualization as strategies within the ambit of imperial politics – it is first essential to briefly examine some of the failed legacy of the sixties: Kennedy's Marshall Plan for the Western Hemisphere and the rebellion of the 'other America'. It is these antecedent class struggles, interacting with the maturation of Fordist economic patterns, that have reshaped political alliances in ways that preclude successful systemic reform.

The Alliance that Failed

Until 1980 there had been a discernible rotation in power between alternative concepts of US hegemony espoused by the Republicans and the Democrats, within the broad parameters of the general Cold War Atlanticism embraced by a bipartisan congressional majority. Republican administrations had tended to advocate a more 'custodial' concept of hegemony, while the Democrats had urged 'sweepingly offensive' strategies. Thus Republican regimes tended to emphasize a reliance on strategic air power (rather than US groundforce commitments), the reduction of imperial overheads (like foreign aid), and the utility of more traditional balances of power. The Democrats, on the other hand, urged aggressive military Keynesianism, simultaneously combining economic expansion and domestic reform with trade liberalization, pre-emptive counter-insurgency and accelerated spending on strategic weapons. In other words, whereas Republicanism (despite Dullesian slogans about 'roll-back') was more concerned with cost-conscious management of the imperial status quo and the protection of home-market industry, the Democratic Party – allying both organized labour and key internationalist factions of capital – offered ambitious schemes for dynamizing and expanding the economic and military supports of hegemony.

The period from the Bay of Pigs to the Tet Offensive witnessed the most spectacular attempt to apply the Democratic 'maximum' programme of expansion, reform and repression. While the 'New Economics' supposedly fine-tuned the domestic economy towards full employment and economic growth, the 'Grand Design' (led by the 1963 Trade Expansion Act and the Kennedy GATT Round) enticed European capitalism to accept junior partnership in a completely liberalized (and Americanized) world market. The Peace Corps and development assistance were sent out to win hearts and minds, while the Green Berets shot away less tractable obstacles to 'modernization' – the favourite buzzword of the Kennedy gang. McNamara, announcing the era of omnicompetent 'flexible response', launched the biggest arms race in history. Finally, the War on Poverty at home, and the Alliance for Progress in the Latin American backyard, were patterned after the model of Marshall Aid to create millions of new, anti-communist mass consumers.

It is sobering to recall how much of this over-arching programme was immediately buried in the imperialist debacle in Southeast Asia; or, more strongly, how much of it has been recently exhumed and repackaged as the last word in Republicanism. Yet if military Keynesianism – once the bane of Eisenhower's conservative budget-balancers – has been reborn as Reaganomics, it is equally striking how complete has been the putrefication of international New Dealism or domestic egalitarianism. It is not merely that the slogans are slightly out-of-date, it is rather, and more profoundly, that the projects which they embody are no longer imaginable pretensions of late-imperial America.

To take the Alliance for Progress first: following the precedent of Truman's 'revolution from above' in Western Europe, the Kennedy administration elaborated a hemispheric Marshall Plan in which the United States promised to inject £20 billion in aid into Latin America. The idea was that the *Alianza*, so ceremoniously launched in 1961, would unite Latin America's reforming anti-communists in a grand coalition for growth and stabilized bourgeois democracy – as an answer to the challenge of the Cuban revolution. But, as Fidel Castro observed at the time, 'you can put wings on a horse, but it won't fly.' Within the first 18 months of the *Alianza* there were five coups against constitutional governments; only two countries (Mexico and Venezuela) bothered to propose credible agrarian reforms; giant US corporations vehemently protested at the subversive illusions cultivated by the *Alianza's* official propaganda, and Washington only disbursed two-thirds of the initial aid package. The 'vital centre' mythologized by the Kennedy people, seemed scarcely to exist South of the Rio Grande; or, rather, where it did, as in the Dominican Republic in 1965 with Bosch's mildly social-democratic movement, the Marines were sent in to crush it.

By blowing populists and social democrats out of the water, the United States has perpetuated a system of class relations that is incompatible with elementary reform or stable democracy. Democracy in present-day Latin America has become an essentially *revolutionary* goal which only a revolutionary left – steeled to the enormity of protracted, brutal struggle – can realistically achieve. In this sense, the cautious *apertuaras* are guided elections being attempted by some of the more hard-pressed military regimes are misleading: the current debt bondage of the major Latin American industrial economies, and the draconian austerity which this enforces, can only ensure a more explosive, and, thus, intolerably subversive, relationship between democratic rights and social demands. It is thus highly likely that the unfolding process of repoliticalization in the Southern Cone, including Brazil, will produce a new cycle of militant mass mobilization, reactionary violence, and new Yankee interventions. Even the exceptional 'democracies' of Mexico and Venezuela, now that their internal regulative mechanisms of growth and cooptation have been overruled by IMF rules, may see a sharp class polarization.

In a period when Euro-Communism has become practically defunct, the Arab left destroyed, and Asian capitalism (with the exception of the Philippines) stabilized, the massive, deep and continuing process of popular radicalization in Latin America and the Caribbean has truly become *the* spectre which haunts American imperialism. The situation, of course, is all the more significant in that the classical ideological relations of American hegemony are inverted: instead of the allure of capitalist 'democracy', here capitalism has cancelled democracy. Likewise, the miracle economies of the 1970s – Brazil, Mexico and Venezuela – stand more exposed in the nakedness of their dependency upon immiseration and super-exploitation. No *deus ex machina*, acting in the higher self-interest of the world capitalist system, is available to restructure the rigid barriers of class relations, congealed around comprador accumulation models, that block further dynamic integration of the semi-industrial economies of Latin America (or, for that matter, of Turkey, Egypt, Indonesia or Thailand) into an OECD-type growth scenario.

Thus, at least under the specific form of American hegemony, the extension of democratic capitalism and the Fordist dynamic to the semi-periphery has become largely unimaginable. Yet at the same time the core economies and their borderlands are becoming implicated in dense new patterns of labour mobility

and interdependent production. Nowhere is this overlapping and interpenetration
of economies so far advanced, or so entirely driven by raw accumulation processes,
than in North America, where the US Sunbelt has thrust southward, into Mexico
and the Caribbean Basin. This socio-economic upheaval is a principal expression
of a new, more malign accumulation logic taking hold in the US economy, which
is simultaneously – in its integration of millions of new workers – incorporating
the Latin American dialectic of permanent revolution into the very heart of
American domestic politics.

The New Rich and the New Poor

Unlike the ill-fated *Alianza*, the War on Poverty has generally been adjudged
at least a partial success. By 1976, for instance, it was estimated that the ranks
of the poor, a quarter of the nation in 1960, had been reduced to a residual
12 per cent – a reduction in relative poverty roughly comparable to that achieved
in the aftermath of New Deal and World War II. In the latter case, as we have
seen, the Fordist integration of the semi-skilled industrial workforce gave a
sustained impetus to the economy. The War on Poverty, however, did not provide
the same positive catalyst to accumulation as the Wagner Act and the rise of the
CIO. Indeed, official poverty statistics disguise some of the most important and
harrowing facts about the trend of the contemporary American political economy:

1. The 'victory' in the War on Poverty is largely an artifact of income transfers
within the working class which leave structural employment situations intact. Begin
to remove these federal income supports, as Reagan has recently done, and the
original 1960 level of officially designated poverty reappears. Despite the long
sixties boom, the private economy failed to generate 'decent' jobs for the millions
of former farm tenants and labourers displaced to the central cities in the 1950s
and early 1960s. Above all, the economy has failed to integrate black male
workers, whose participation rate in the labour force (a key index of structural
unemployment) has declined from nearly 80 per cent in 1945 to barely 50 per
cent today. A generation after the first march on Washington for 'jobs and
freedom', black unemployment remains double that of whites, while black poverty
is three times more common. Sixty per cent of employed black males (and
50 per cent Hispanics) are concentrated in the lowest-paid jobs.
2. Official poverty figures, with their ludicrously low standards of subsistence,
hide massive and rapidly increasing numbers of the *working poor*. At least a third
of the 100-million-strong labour force consists of wage-earners trapped in a
low-wage ghetto slightly above the official poverty line. Lest it be imagined that
poverty is primarily a by-product of the stagnation of employment, it should be
emphasized that during the crisis-ridden 1970s new jobs were being created at
twice the rate of the three previous decades – 20 million in all. But millions of
these new jobs (and millions created between 1975 and 1981 in particular) were
for women. As women's labour-force participation doubled between 1955 and
1981, their relative earnings declined from 65 per cent of the male average to
59 per cent. One-third of full-time women workers earned less than $7,000 in
1980. Thus poverty is being mass produced, not only through the relative exclusion

of Third-World men, but especially through the dynamic incorporation of women into burgeoning low-wage sectors of the economy. Low-wage employment, far from being a mere 'residue' or 'periphery' of the economy, has become its growth-pole.

What happened in the 1970s was the emergence of a new regime of accumulation which might be called *overconsumptionism*. This has little to do with the sumptuary habits of the very rich, whose wasteful profligacy with yachts and mansions is an incomparably smaller social problem than their control over the global means of production. Rather, by overconsumptionism, we wish to indicate the increasing social subsidization of a sub-bourgeois *mass* layer of managers, professionals, new entrepreneurs and *rentiers* who – in the absence of the countervailing force of an authentically populist or social-democratic challenge in the early seventies – have been overwhelmingly successful in profiteering from both inflation and expanded state spending. Of course, an unusually large middle strata has been a permanent feature of the twentieth-century US social landscape. What is new is the way in which the development of a large tertiary sector in the economy has been harnessed as a redistributive mechanism for an expanded managerial–professional strata as well as a frontier of accumulation for new entrepreneurs. The old charmed circle of the poor getting richer as the rich get richer is being superceded by the trend of poorer poor and richer rich as the proliferation of low-wage jobs simultaneously enlarges an affluent market of non-producers and new bosses.

It is clear that a major difference between the class structures of the advanced capitalist countries is the size and composition of their middle strata. France, Italy and Japan, for instance, are characterized by the persistence of the *old middle classes* of peasants, independent shopkeepers and artisans. The social weight of these groups is the result of deliberate political subsidization. Because these strata are indispensable supports for the ruling bourgeois parties (Gaullists, Christian democrats and liberal democrats) enabling them to form majority coalitions, their economic positions have been artificially stabilized by massive state intervention. In the United States, on the other hand, the *new middle class* of professionals, salaried managers, franchise-holders and technicians is 23.8 per cent of the labour-force (1976/7) – a higher proportion than any country except Sweden. Since the US state sector, even with the military included, is not relatively larger than other major capitalist countries, what accounts for this unusually large new middle strata? The answer includes a multiplicity of causes, such as the unusually large relative size of the research establishment and of public higher education as well as the headquartering of so much transnational production in the United States. More important, however is the enormous quota of positions associated with the super-vision of labour, the organization of capital and the conduct of the sales effort. In per capita terms, the United States is monumentally overstaffed with line managers and foremen (twice as many as Japan), lawyers (twice as many as England), salesmen (twice as many as France) and retailers (twice as many as West Germany). Meanwhile, the old middle class in the United States – at 8.5 per cent relatively the smallest of all advanced industrial countries – has suddenly started to grow again. The 75-year secular decline in the percentage of self-employment was dramatically reversed in the findings of the 1980 census. Although groups like family farmers are still shrinking, both relatively and absolutely, there has been a vast incease in small entrepreneurs and independent professions. In fact, private-sector tertiary employment growth has been most rapid in four broad sectors: health-care, business services, fast food and personal services. In each of these sectors it is possible to discern specific dynamics of low-wage employment combined with specific forms of overconsumptionism.

In Europe the success of the trade-union offensives of the 1967–73 period, and thereby the dual expansion of wages and welfare, has imposed a direct constraint on capital – especially in lieu of further expansion of international trade or the world market. In the United States, on the other hand, in the absence of any comparably generalized trade-union offensive, and with falling real blue-collar wages over the last decade, it is probably more accurate to account much of the problem of corporate profitability and of the 'fiscal crisis of the state' to the success of the economic and political offensives of the new managerial, entrepreneurial and *rentier* strata. Given the present disproportionate power of the overconsumptionist 'coalition' in American politics, however, the detonation of all the latent contradictions between big capital and the new middle strata, between the goods-producing and service economies, is unlikely. Although medical insurance, for instance, now comprises a larger cost of auto-making than raw steel, it is more expedient for General Motors to squeeze the unions on 'peripherals' than to directly launch a swingeing assault on the oligopolistic power of doctors. Although innumerable clashes of an ordinary kind will continue to take place at the various legislative levels between the myriad sectoral lobbies, the larger pattern of interest formation in the 1970s has unified corporate capital and most of the new middle strata in a strategy of cost-displacement toward the working and unwaged poor. In other words, the massive reproduction of the non-union, low-wage service economy imposes costs on the traditional industrial core that are compensated by corporate offensives against both the established unions and state social spending. The struggle to maintain corporate profits in a period of rising *rentier* incomes and professional salaries is transformed into new pressures on wages and unionization.

Finally, it is necessary to consider two of the most important trends of the future – the expansion of high-technology manufacturing and the growth of a trans-national border economy – in relationship to the over-consumptionist regime of accumulation. First there has been a great ballyhoo that the burgeoning 'hi-tech' sector – including semiconductors, computers, telecommunications, aircraft, laboratory equipment, data processing, software, pharmaceuticals and so on – will be a compensatory source of high-wage job creation. However, detailed projections prepared for the Bureau of Labor Statistics indicate that the 'hi-tech' part of the American economy – conceived in the broadest definition – will generate over the next decade less than half as many new jobs as the number of old manufacturing jobs (approximately two million) eliminated by the 1980–2 recession. At present 'hi-tech' comprises only 3 per cent of the workforce and fewer than a third of the new jobs it will provide will be for engineers, scientists or technicians: most will be for old-fashioned semi-skilled operatives and traditional managers. Unlike previous scientific and technological revolutions which created large numbers of compensatory new jobs in the manufacture of the new technologies themselves, the immediate feedback effect of microelectronic technology into microelectronic manufacture – through, amongst other things, increasing robotization – is so great that new job creation is much attentuated and certainly incapable, by itself, of reversing the trends towards low-wage service employment. Moreover, the consequences of the incorporation of the new technologies into the tertiary sector – especially their impact on productivity – must be offset against the broad substitutability of cheap labour. Ultimately, whether 'good' technical jobs or 'bad' menial jobs are created in a given occupational/technological interface will have more to do with the balance of class power than with any inherent logic of technological change.

The emerging border economy is a primary reason why it is possible to make the judgement that the 'overconsumptionist' trends we have outlined are truly coalescing into a new social structure of accumulation. As the rapidly industrializing, urbanizing Sunbelt converts Mexico and the entire circum-Caribbean region into its own 'domestic' hinterland, the social crisis of Latin America becomes inextricably linked to the overconsumptionist transformation of the US economy. For example, unlike the guest workers of Europe who can be more or less repatriated at governmental will, the flow of 'undocumented workers' across the Rio Grande (or the Pacific) is part of an irreversible process of the structural assimilation of economies and labour markets. With almost 50 per cent of its workforce unemployed or underemployed, Mexico provides an almost infinite labour-reserve army for the US Sunbelt.

In Los Angeles alone an estimated one-and-a-half million 'undocumented' workers provide a perfectly elastic labour supply for every kind of personal service, sweated manufacturing or other menial task. Meanwhile the entire border zone has become an integrated economy of twin cities – one rich, one poor – from San Diego/Tijuana to Brownsville/Matamoros. The accelerated formation of this borderlands economic system since the late sixties, including the role of extra-economic coercion supplied by the daily terror of the immigration police, has become absolutely integral to the new accumulation patterns characterized by coordinated expansion of low-wage employment and middle-strata affluence. As labour markets are irreversibly transnationalized, their segmentation is simultaneously reinforced. The neo-colonial logic of Sunbelt capitalism thus assures that there is no way to redress the problem of low-wage exploitation without also dealing with the roots of hyper-unemployment and underdevelopment in Mexico and the Caribbean. Unexpectedly in the 1980s the domestic economic and political systems of American imperialism are becoming porous to the revolutionary crises of Latin America.

The Conservative Revolution

This epochal shift in the American economy during the 1970s from a Fordist to a tendentially underconsumptionist dynamic was politically catalysed by what might be called 'class struggles of a third kind', involving neither militant labour nor reactionary capital, but insurgent middle-strata. Compared to the 1960s, the social base of political mobilization during the 1970s was an inverse mirror-image. If the former decade was dominated by the mass civil rights movement, the new student left and their cognate liberation currents, then the 1970s were, without quite so much sound and fury, the decade of the revanchist middle classes. The election of Ronald Reagan in American politics became possible through two parallel displacements of popular power. First was the demobilization of the popular constituencies of the 1960s to the advantage of the middle-strata's suburban-based backlash in the 1970s. Second was the closure of the electorate in the seventies – via both alienated, popular self-disfranchisement and a fundamental restructuring of electoral processes – which dramatically increased the effective weight of the middle-strata and the corporations. In both ways the conservative 'revolution' of the early 1980s was, when finally achieved, more the result of prior exclusion and disorganization of the majority than of its conversion to a new ideological agenda.

The demobilization of the 1960s movements was brutally sudden and, to many survivors, still inexplicable. Although in all cases, including the unions, repression played a crucial role in disrupting mass organization (the black liberation movement being especially hard hit by J. Edgar Hoover's vicious operations) the decline of activism must be fundamentally ascribed to a combination of the new left's failure to unify around a radical *reformist* project, and the success of the old liberal establishment in rebounding to disorganize the grassroots through a selective absorption of its organizers. And as the new left disintegrated after 1968, the general trend, in both major political parties, was progressively towards the right. Some of this shift must be accounted by the massive corporate lobbying and campaign financing skilfully coordinated around a series of interlinked single-issue fronts (deregulation, accelerated depreciation, tax relief, anti-labour-law reform, and so on) by the Business Roundtable and other groups; but the revolutionary element was the increased intensity of middle-strata political mobilization. In a pattern which most recalls the emergence of the Progressive movement in the Republican Party at the turn of the century (which had also been a rebellion of new professional and business strata), a whole generation of young professionals, middle managers and new entrepreneurs entered local and state politics from the 1970s onward (in some cases from the failed Goldwater campaign of 1964).

This insurgency, which shook the middle class by its grassroots, was and is far broader than the nominal zealotry of the 'new right'. Although its general trajectory has been to act as the political agency of 'overconsumptionism', it has been tremendously variegated in its specific forms. A rudimentary typology of the myriad of local and national single-issue groups expressive of middle-strata activism would encompass at least three broad categories. First, there were thousands of local groups linked to the national campaigns to revive the Cold War and to support a new interventionism in the Middle East and Latin America. A second category of mobilization, overwhelmingly led by a suburban world view but also with significant working-class participation, was religious-based moral revanchism. The third genre of conservative grassroots movements is by far the most important in understanding the specific *raison d'être* of Reaganism as a politics of overconsumptionism. It encompasses the organized anti-busing groups, the proponents of local privatization (including the 'sagebrush rebellion' in the far west), landlords and realtors organizations (truly massive, with hundreds of thousands of ardent members organized to oppose rent-control and public housing) and, most importantly, the tax revolt groups of 1978–80 which forced 19 states to enact legislative or constitutional limits on property or income taxes. Rather than just transient forms of protest against minority-group demands, these mobilizations have reinforced the now dense infrastructure of local-interest representation and political influence which safeguards and perpetuates the position of the popular *nouveau riche*. Overrepresentation at the political level has allowed the establishment and consolidation of overconsumptionism at an economic level.

Through the rise of these new socio-economic protests, a broadly embracing politics of the 'haves' was coined which gave a political interpretation to stagflationary trends and conscripted part of the traditional New Deal coalition to the project of a radical restructuring of state spending in a more inegalitarian direction. Inflation, especially within the context of a weakly organized and highly segmented labour force, had tremendously disorganizing and centrifugal effects on the US working class and the cohesion of its economic interests. Thus despite partial indexation of transfer payments, the sectoral concentration of the highest commodity inflation rates in basic necessities ensured that the working poor were disproportionately affected. At the same time, working-class and middle-class homeowners – not to mention the ubiquitous number of small landlords in both categories – were often able to profiteer handsomely through inflated equities and land values. Overall in the 1970s, real disposable income increased by almost a quarter while real wages declined by a tenth: a discrepancy explained not only by the scale of relative transfers from wage-workers to the middle strata, but also by the widening wage differentials within the working class. While organized workers in basic industries and transportation bargained for parity or better with the cost of living (largely through so-called 'escalator clauses' and 'cost of living adjustments'), unorganized blue-collar workers and especially clericals suffered their biggest attrition of income in the twentieth century.

Thus the *subordinate* logic of the 'have rebellion', exemplified in the innumerable property owners and suburban residents' movements, was a defensive participation of skilled workers and the lower salariat in support of what they perceived to be their threatened prerogatives of social mobility and consumption (homeownership, superior suburban schools, nepotistic apprentice systems and so on). Faced with genuinely collapsing standards of living in other sections of the traditional white working class, these groups increasingly visualized themselves – even though their actual property values and wages may have been increasing until 1980 – as locked into a zero-sum rivalry with equality-seeking blacks and women.

The *superordinate* logic of the haves, on the other hand, was the *nouveau riche* desire to increase social inequality – indeed, to dynamically harness it to expand low-wage labour markets, reduce tax overheads and ensure a 'union-free environment'. Although the rhetoric of the various campaigns was vigorously anti-statist, the actual programmatic direction was towards a restructuring, rather than reduction, of state spending and intervention in order to enhance the frontiers of entrepreneurial and *rentier* opportunity, e.g. unfettered speculative real estate markets and rampant condominization, taxless capital gains on mineral and oil equities, transfer of tax resources from public to private education, privatization of state services, maximization of 'tax expenditures' (write-offs) for upper middle strata, lowering of minimum wage and abolition of health and safety standards for small businesses, deregulation and so on. General anti-busing, anti-tax, and anti-spending symbols were deployed in such ways as to service these more specific objectives, which, although they frequently coincided with the goals of the national corporate offensive as orchestrated through the Business Roundtable, remained essentially autonomous. Furthermore, this new constellation of propertied interests also diverged significantly from the historic 'old right' bloc of Midwestern manufacturing capital precisely in its reliance on big government (especially a bloated defence budget), a high-growth, even inflationary, economy and the fiscal transfer of resources to the Sunbelt (at the expense of older industries).

The convergent thrusts of this have rebellion and the new Cold War lobby were already recomposing the agenda of US politics well before Reagan won the Republican nomination. In fact, the real turning point was probably 1978 when Carter abandoned *détente* while congressional 'liberals' began to fall all over themselves in devising ingenious ways to transfer social spending to the Pentagon. Indeed, Reaganism in its triumphant form would probably have been impossible without the prefigurative context of the Carter administration's last year and a half. Similarly, Reagan's successes in pushing through his social spending cuts, his 1.5 trillion dollar defence five-year plan, and his tax cuts for the wealthy, would have also been unthinkable without, not only the open collusion of the renegade Democratic 'bollweevils', but also the more subtle complicity of a rightward moving Democratic leadership that adheres, albeit more 'moderately', to key parts of the Republican programme.

Reaganism and Democratic 'neo-liberalism' have come to overlap in four crucial regards that represent nothing less than a fundamental redrawing of the boundaries of US bourgeois politics:

1. *All* Democratic presidential candidates in 1984, with the honourable exceptions of George McGovern and Jessie Jackson, accepted the consensual principle of a massive arms build-up. They only differed with Reagan as to the particular efficiency of specific programmes and the rate of increase.

2. Most leading Democrats, except Kennedy, MacGovern and perhaps Cranston, have implicitly surrendered the struggle to defend the integrity of Great Society income and employment programmes targeted at blacks, women and the poor. They have retreated, instead, to a defence of the New Deal and Fair Deal legislation essential to the well-being of the skilled working-class strata. Ascendent Democratic ideologues openly contrast the beneficient calculus of the New Deal which was good for business ('rationalized capitalism', etc.) with the unaffordable extravagance of the Great Society ('eliminated incentives to create wealth', etc.). In effect, the most disadvantaged are virtually excluded from neo-liberal political discourse, which contracts around the maintenance of the entitlements of the 'have' sections of the working class in the face of the threat from the all-out union-busters and welfare-dismantlers; and even the Reagan administration is divided on this score.

3. It is universally accepted within both parties that only private capital can 'reindustrialize' America. The major difference between the parties is over the form of social subsidy best designed to encourage corporate investment: tax-cut 'trickle downs' versus a loose 'industrial policy'.

4. Finally, the Wilsonian rhetoric of universalistic, democratic capitalism – so central in the original extension of American hegemony and the creation of a US-dominated global consumer culture – has fallen on hard times. There is a broad, non-partisan acceptance of the necessity of using military power to counterbalance deficits in economic or political aspects of hegemony. Although 'pragmatic' Democrats shy away from the ideological rigidity of right-wing Republicanism, scarcely anyone has been prepared to challenge the Frankenstein-like backlash of national chauvinism which Carter created during the hostage crisis. There is no longer any soaring rhetoric about new *Alianzas* or Marshall Plans, and no presidential candidate speaks any longer of 'saving' the Third World. Future Democratic administrations – confronted with global revolt as a result of the current IMF-imposed depression – would primarily seek to rationalize the new Cold War, and not end it. Indeed, a Democrat might as easily grasp for the 'Grenada factor' as a Republican.

Inventing the US Left

'The Crisis', Gramsci observed, 'consists precisely in the fact that the old is dying and the new cannot be born.'[1] As I have tried to argue, the coherence of American hegemony has necessarily collapsed as Atlantic Fordism has reached the internal limits of expansion within the constraints of its own regulative structures. At the same time, the renewal of long-wave accumulation through a combination of world market expansion (via rising mass consumption in the newly industrial countries) and metropolitan market-deepening (via a 'socio-industrial complex') is blocked by the power of the social forces which have fattened on the inflationary cycle of the 1970s: the international bankers and oil *rentiers*, the Sunbelt millionaires and the expanded strata of the American *nouveau riche*.

As Marx showed in his famous example of the struggle for the ten-hour workday in the 1840s, the specific form of the restructuring undertaken by capital in crisis is determined not only by the nature of emergent productive forces (whether steam-engines or integrated circuits) but, especially, by the dominant form of the class struggle. Thus the rise of the new industrial unions in the thirties in the United States ultimately constrained capital to accept a Fordist growth path, although without ensuring a full-fledged welfare state. (In Western Europe, American-sponsored anti-radical reforms in the face of the communist challenge also secured a Fordist reconstruction; more solidaristic labour movements won a higher 'social wage' than in the United States.) Conversely, the revolt of the US middle classes in the 1970s (echoes of which have also been heard in Western Europe) has increasingly substituted an 'overconsumptionist' regime of accumulation allied to military hyper-expenditure and the accelerated exploitation of the North American borderlands.

A new, malignant regime of accumulation is coming into being in the United States based on low-wage labour, permanently high reservoirs of unemployment, and generally widened social differentials of every kind. Ronald Reagan is a morbid symptom of this deeper malaise. But it should be clear that this line of development was not preordained in some deep structural sense. On the contrary, it is partly a result of the far-from-inevitable failure of the movements in the 1960s to constitute a new popular Left. Of course, once this possibility was foreclosed by defeat it brought in its train an accumulation of after-effects: most strikingly, a devaluation of collective self-action amongst broad sectors of the American working class.

What evidence is there to suggest that Reaganism, by the very radicalism of its attacks on the social wage, is catalysing a reactive politicization of popular constituencies? In a recent article, only partially tongue in cheek, John Kenneth Galbraith has praised Reagan's inimitable genius from promoting black voter registration, widening the 'gender gap' and popularizing the Nuclear Freeze movement. Others have discerned the clear signs of a new 'liberal left' capable of reversing the rightward drift of Democratic Party policy and congressional performance. Yet, while welcoming the emergence of a distinctive female constituency in politics as well as the dramatic turnaround in minority voter participation, some realistic qualifications need to be entered about the preconditions for a revival of a popular left in the United States.

1.   Increased electoral participation and self-consciousness will probably not be sustainable without a great leap forward in self-organization and activism at the workplace and in the community. Certainly an electoral 'left' (whether hyphenated with liberalism or socialism) is unthinkable without the recreation of mass organization engaged in innumerable forms of struggle. As late as 1983 there was still a great disjuncture between the flurry of increased voter registration by blacks, hispanics and women, and the continuing low-level of mass resistance against Reagonomics and the new Cold War.
2.   Any revival of national left of left-liberal politics would obviously entail broad programmatic agreement between movements rooted in segmented sections of the working class and those representing specific interests of women and non-white (or non-Anglo) communities. Lately, most grassroots campaigns derived from the 'new politics' (which tend to be overwhelmingly white) have consciously focused on 'easy' unifying issues like rent control or progressive taxation that skirt the deep division within the working class. A national radical programme, however, could only resonate in South Texas or South Chicago, if it vigorously tackled the 'hard' issues as well, like support for increased affirmative action and school integration. Moreover, existing 'white' left organizations might have to accept a process of political regroupment in which they did not play the leading role – or, even, the theoretical role.
3.   A new left of the late eighties and nineties would have to recognize that the boundaries of 'American' politics were increasingly just that. The irreversible, sometimes almost cataclysmic, process which is integrating the economies and workforces of North America from the Canal to the tundra is also creating an unprecedented kind of space – an informal common market – that poses a similar challenge to the United States left as that posed by Europe to the contemporary British left. In a situation where Puerto Rico is both New York and San Juan, where the auto industry is both Detroit and Windsor, and where San Diego and Tijuana have long ago merged into a single metropolitan system – 'American' solidarity and common action have already become organizing frameworks. Moreover, as the far right has instinctively recognized, the integral, dynamic 'borderlands' of the United States contain far more radical social chemistries than were ever concocted in any Berkeley heyday. If one could invest the most audacious – and, thus, possibly most realistic – future for socialist politics in the United States it would entail precisely some form of hemispheric internationalism.

Notes

1 Selections from the *Prison Notebooks of Antonio Gramsci*, edited by Quintin Hoare and Geoffrey Nowell-Smith (London, Lawrence & Wishart, 1971) p. 276.

2

The Soviet Bloc

ERNEST MANDEL

Historical and Political Origins

Since World War I, the capitalist system has entered a phase of historical decline. This manifests itself in the form of a nearly uninterrupted chain of violent explosions: two world wars; innumerable local wars; two major economic depressions, the second one of which is still far from being finished; many revolutions on all continents (ending either in victory or in defeat) and many violent counter-revolutions – mainly fascist dictatorships and military coups.

This decline of capitalism provides the possibility for socialism. But while the world is 'overripe' for socialism from an objective (socio-economic) point of view, the overthrow of capitalism is conditional upon the overthrow of bourgeois state power. This has to be a political act and is not and cannot be the automatic result of social and economic crisis. The success or failure of the socialist world revolution in turn depends upon the correlation of class forces, in which both objective and subjective factors (the level of class consciousness of the proletariat and the relative political efficiency of its leadership) play an essential role. This correlation of class forces differs from period to period and from country to country: it results from the particular history of each specific working class and each specific bourgeois state it faces, and not simply from general features of the capitalist mode of production and of bourgeois society. It follows that the conquest of power by the proletariat depends upon the uneven economic, social, political and cultural development of world capitalism. It cannot be simultaneous in all or even in the major countries of the world. The socialist world revolution takes the form of an interrupted and at the same time uninterrupted revolution. To put it another way: the process of *permanent* revolution implies not only continuity but also discontinuity. There would neither be a *process* nor a *permanence* of revolution if that revolution were to be simultaneous or near-simultaneous in all major countries.

The first successful socialist revolution occurred in Russia in October 1917. The possibility for this had been recognized as early as 1905 by Leon Trotsky and also partially by Kautsky and Rosa Luxemburg, whereas most Marxists had earlier denied that possibility. But if Russia was ripe for a socialist revolution it certainly was not 'ripe' for the building of a fully developed socialist society – which could not even be achieved in a single industrially advanced country, let alone a relatively backward one. This was also understood by Trotsky as early as 1905 and by all revolutionary Marxists, starting with Lenin and the Bolshevik leaders, as well as by all the leaders of other communist parties in 1918–23. The historical function of the Russian revolution, besides lifting Russia out of backwardness, was to give a decisive impulse to world revolution.

Indeed, revolutionary developments began to occur in Central Europe less than a year after October and November 1917. Socialist revolutions broke out in Finland, Germany, Austria, Hungary and incipiently in Italy. They were defeated in the 1919–23 period, essentially because of the inadequacy of working-class leadership, itself a function of the whole past history of the organized labour movement in these countries; the objective strength of the bourgeoisie in and by itself was insufficient to make defeats unavoidable. It was sufficient to prevent revolutions in countries like the USA, France and Britain, although the threat of the 'triple alliance strike' and then the General Strike of 1926, showed the vulnerability even of British bourgeois power before the strength of the working class.

The combination of the Russian victory and the Central European defeat of socialist revolution left the first workers' state isolated in an international capitalist environment. As Marxist theoreticians predicted, this had to lead to a failure of 'building socialism' in Russia. But what form would the failure take? In general, Marxists assumed that it would mean the restoration of capitalism in Russia. But like a successful socialist revolution, the overthrow of a workers' state by capitalism cannot be an essentially gradual or spontaneous process.It is a political act, realized by a specific social class through concrete political forces. It so happened that both the Russian and the international bourgeoisie were too weak after 1919, or even after 1923, to realize such a project. The Russian bourgeoisie had been decimated through the civil war it desparately launched against the Soviet Republic. The rich layer of peasants (kulaki), developing after 1923, while representing a serious economic threat through the New Economic Policy in Russia, was politically too scattered and too inept to constitute a serious challenge to the power of the Communist Party of the Soviet Union (CPSU). As for the European bourgeoisie, intent upon overthrowing the Soviet government, it was unable to break the resistance of the European working class – in the first place the British, French and German one – against the launching of a full-scale war against Soviet Russia in the 1917–29 period.

The balance of class forces which emerged from the 1917–23 period permitted the survival of the Soviet Union as a non-capitalist, post-revolutionary society. The impossibility of building a socialist classless society in Russia did not express itself through the restoration of capitalism. Rather, it expressed itself through a phenomenon of the *Thermidor* type.[1] There was a victorious *political* counter-revolution which expropriated the mass of the Russian working class from the direct exercise of political power in the 1921–7 period. But the essential economic conquests of the October revolution – the suppression of private ownership of the major means of production; the suppression of the commodity character of labour power; the insulation of the Soviet economy from the rule of the law of value, through the state monopoly of foreign trade; the possibility of planned economic growth based upon consciously chosen priorities – were conserved throughout the Soviet Thermidor, in just the way that the essential economic conquests of the great French revolution remained throughout Thermidor, Bonapartist rule and even Bourbon restoration.

The social agency of the Soviet Thermidor was the Soviet bureaucracy, a layer grown out of the gradual merging together of the full-time functionaries of the ruling party (party and trade-union apparatus), the functionaries of the Soviet state (economic, state and military hierarchy) and remnants of the Tsarist state apparatus and petty-bourgeois intelligentsia. This Soviet bureaucracy assured for itself increasing material privileges (essentially in the sphere of consumption) which it could, however, only guarantee and conserve on the basis of an increasing monopoly of power – political rule and economic administration. It had therefore to institutionalize the one-party system which took more and more the form of totalitarian control over all spheres of social life. It had to maintain the atomization of the working class. Any shake-up of one of these two pillars immediately threatened and continues to threaten both the rule and the privileges of the bureaucracy, as events in East Germany in 1953, Hungary in 1956, China in 1964–8, Czechoslavakia in 1968 and Poland in 1956 and 1980–1 have eloquently demonstrated.

The political difficulty which the Soviet bureaucracy faced inside the country – again similar to those with which the French Thermidorians were confronted after July 1794 – was the fact that ideology and tradition linger on long after the material conditions which give rise to them have disappeared. In other words: most Russian (and international) communists, among those accepting the leadership of the Stalin faction in the CPSU and the Comintern[2] still thought of themselves consciously as revolutionary communists, bent upon realizing world socialism, be it along a more twisting and indirect road than that projected by Lenin and Trotsky. The Soviet bureaucracy had therefore to maintain at least formally its allegiance to Marxism (rebaptised 'Marxism-Leninism' by Zinoviev first, Stalin and his successors later) and even to canonize Lenin, in order to stress its continuity with the October revolution. So it was not easy for the contemporary witnesses to understand the successive stages of the Soviet Thermidor, of the political counter-revolution with its innumerable implications also in the economic sphere.

This partial ideological continuity – partial because it implied an increasingly pragmatic–apologetic deformation of Marxist theory – was again not simply functional. It corresponded, and continues to correspond, to the specific nature of the Soviet bureaucracy as a social layer, which has not completely cut its umbilical cord with the Russian and international working class – and which, indeed, can be seen, be it on a very high level of abstraction, as an extremely privileged, remote and 'petty-bourgeoisified' layer *of* the working class, and not as a new ruling class with an entirely independent class ideology. This in turn reflects the specific nature of Soviet society, which is neither socialist, nor capitalist, nor a 'new class society'. It is a society in transition between capitalism and socialism, frozen by the bureaucratic dictatorship at that given intermediate stage of historical development, and which can make a decisive step forward towards socialism only through a new political revolution, restoring direct working-class power, combined with a socialist revolution in some key capitalist countries.

The particular 'twist' (deformation) of Marxist theory which reflected the Soviet

Thermidor most synthetically was the theory of the possibility of achieving the 'building of socialism in one country', popularized by Stalin in the 1924–7 period. All Russian communists – with the possible exception of a few extreme 'leftists' – agreed upon the necessity to fight for the survival of the Soviet state during the period separating it from an extension of the revolution to other countries. They therefore all agreed upon the necessity of *beginning* with the building of socialism nationally. Indeed, it was the left opposition around Trotsky and Preobrazhensky as early as 1923, then the united opposition around Trotsky, Zinoviev and Kamenev, who, against the Stalin–Bukharin bloc, stressed the need for an accelerated pace of planned industrialization, but not at the expense of the workers' standard of living, nor at the expense of the peasantry.

The theory of 'socialism in one country' did not simply express the need for accelerated industrialization in Russia, but a view of world politics – of the Soviet state and of the Comintern – which systematically subordinated the interests of the world revolution and of the international working class to the alleged need to consolidate the Soviet state, in reality to the specific social interests of the Soviet bureaucracy. The formation of the 'Soviet bloc' at the end of World War II is the direct result of that decisive 'turn' in CPSU policies (and those of the Soviet state and various 'national' communist parties). But so are the consequences of the constitution of that bloc, the so called 'socialist camp' – consequences which were unforeseen by the Soviet bureaucracy: the Tito–Stalin rift; the Sino–Soviet conflict, the collapse of the so-called 'world communist movement' and the workers' anti-bureaucratic revolutions in various Eastern European countries.

The Emergence and Nature of the 'Socialist Camp'

The survival of the Soviet state as non-capitalist made World War II at least in one essential aspect different from an imperialist war like World War I. While the inter-imperialist conflict had as its object the redistribution of the international spoils of imperialism between various great capitalist powers, any military conflict between the USSR and imperialist states had for its object the destruction of the social and economic structure of the Soviet Union and its transformation into a (semi)-colony of imperialism, which implied the restoration of private property in the USSR. This was evidently the object of the Nazi aggression against the Soviet Union.

But as Trotsky stressed in 1939–40, the opposite would also be true. Any durable move of the Soviet army beyond the August 1939 frontiers of the USSR, in as much as it would lead to durable occupation, was unavoidably linked to a trans-formation of property and production relations in the occupied territories and countries. The Soviet bureaucracy, not being a bourgeois class or a fraction of the international bourgeoisie, could not rule in the long run over any country without its assimilation to the USSR's specific social structures.

The successful counter-offensive of the Red Army after its victories at Stalingrad and Kursk in 1943, combined with the delays and partial failures of the invasion of occupied Europe by the western allies, led to a *de facto* military division of Europe at the end of World War II. It was not any 'sell out' by Roosevelt and Churchill at Yalta but the given military relationship of forces, i.e. the presence of either the Russian or the Anglo-American armies on the spot which – give and take some miles – determined that division, and the emergence of the 'Soviet bloc'.

All this was not the result of any long-term planning by the Soviet bureaucracy. It could have been upset by many developments. A victorious surge of the working class towards socialism in Italy, France, Greece and even Britain was possible in 1945 (in Italy probably up till 1948), in spite of the presence of western armies. Likewise, Stalin had not in advance decided upon letting his troops stay in all places where they had arrived in 1944–5 (in fact they withdrew not only from Finland and Austria and West Berlin, but also from Yugoslavia and Albania, with all the political consequences which flowed from these withdrawals). The precise social and political status of Europe (or at least several European countries) remained in the balance for several years. From the Prague coup of February 1948 though, the situation became largely settled. To the east of the Lübeck/Trieste line, capitalism was overthrown essentially by revolution from above, through military and bureaucratic moves by the Soviet bureaucracy, combined with various degrees of limited and strictly controlled mass mobilization. The only exception was Yugoslavia, where capitalism was suppressed through a classical process of mass popular permanent revolution. The national liberation struggle of the Yugoslav masses against the imperialist occupying forces and their stooges increasingly became combined with a radical social revolution, under the leadership of the Yugoslav Communist Party, which had consciously opted for that goal as early as May 1941.

In this way, the Soviet bloc emerged during the Cold War as a group of satellite countries (glacis) of the Soviet bureaucracy, in which the local communist parties governed, basing themselves upon Soviet military and repressive (police) power. This was mainly because they lacked any autonomous power basis in their own working class or peasantry for ruling without the umbrella of the Kremlin. But it was likewise so – as the Czechoslovak example of 1968–9 would dramatically illustrate – because the Soviet bureaucracy could not allow them to conquer such an autonomous basis. The so-called 'Breshnev doctrine of limited sovereignty' is the ideological expression of this 'extension' of the theory of 'socialism in one country' into the theory of the 'socialist camp under the leadership of the Soviet Union' – read: 'of the Soviet bureaucracy'.

One exception confirms the rule. The only communist party of Eastern Europe which had both a large independent social basis and its own independent instrument of rule was the Yugoslav Communist Party, which had come to power and established its own workers state at the head of a popular socialist revolution. Stalin tried to destroy both that independent state power (through attempts at establishing control by his agents over the Yugoslav army, the Yugoslav secret police and the leadership of the Yugoslav Communist Party apparatus) and the independent social basis of the Yugoslav Communist Party. These attempts failed in the 1947–50 period. As a result Yugoslavia emerged as the first workers state independent from the Soviet bureaucracy. China was to be the second.

The Kremlin's control over Eastern Europe – except Yugoslavia – was and remains in the first place political and military. When that political control (through the control over the leadership of the local communist parties (CPs) is broken, only naked military intervention can restore it, as the above-mentioned examples of workers uprisings confirm. But to recognize that the Kremlin controls Eastern Europe essentially through political and military means does not imply that economic ties are insignificant or secondary. The 'structural assimilation' of Eastern Europe to the USSR has two main features:

1.   These countries are cut off, as is the USSR, from any rule by the law of value through their 'disintegration' from the world market. But these are small countries, without any autonomous raw-material base, unable to go through a similar process of modernization and (or) accelerated industrialization on an essentially self-sufficient basis, as did the USSR. Their 'disintegration' from international capitalism was therefore linked to their subordination to prioritized foreign trade with the USSR. So the Comecon[3] emerged, side by side with the (political) Soviet bloc and the Warsaw Treaty military alliance.
2.   As these countries (ruled by 'national' privileged bureaucracies) embarked upon economic development, without being able to substitute mechanisms of workers' control and workers' self management for the suppressed mechanisms of the capitalist market economy, they have had by and large to imitate the pattern of bureaucratically centralized management of the economy which is prevalent in Soviet society (with some minor variants). There is no other way through which these bureaucracies can maintain, extend and consolidate their privileges, and the power which guarantees it.

Thereby, the non-socialist, non-capitalist, non-'new-class' nature of these societies rapidly asserts itself, exactly as in the Soviet Union. Like the Soviet Union, they are transitional societies between capitalism and socialism, frozen by a bureaucratic dictatorship at their given level of social development. But this similarity between Eastern bloc states is combined with important differences. In all these countries – always with the exception of Yugoslavia – communist rule appears in the eyes of the masses as foreign rule: 'local' CP leaders appear as satraps of the Kremlin. While national pride and even 'nationalism' up to a certain point bolsters the bureaucracy's rule in Russia, it is a powerful permanent source of challenge to the Kremlin's power in Eastern Europe. All kinds of indigenous social forces express this latent national rebelliousness: the Polish Catholic Church, the Czechoslovak *literati*, East German scientists and philosophers, Hungarian activists. Given the power of these sentiments, and the desperate need of the 'local' bureaucracy to find some autonomous power basis, and even modest political legitimacy of its own, these bureaucrats are periodically tempted to channel the call for national independence into specific political designs, sometimes of a more or less genuine 'reform communism' type (Gomulka, Dubček, and partially Kádár), sometimes of a purely demagogic nature (Ceauşescu).The margin of manoeuvre they actually have towards the Kremlin is very limited but it does exist. This is especially as tensions grow and tend to become cumulative inside the *bloc*; the Kremlin must consider in each case whether a limited and controllable 'autonomy' is not a lesser evil compared to repeated and politically more and more costly military interventions against open mass revolts.

The Stalinist-type mass purges of the working class (of the non-CP political and trade-union cadres as well as inside the CP itself) in Eastern Europe in 1947–53 never had the radical and monstrous consequences they had in the USSR in the two decades 1934–53. There were indeed radical reprisals against social democrats, independent trade-unionists, revolutionary oppositionists and local CP leaders (e.g. the show trials against Kostov in Bulgaria, Rajk in Hungary, Slansky in Czechoslavakia, Doce in Albania). But a core of working-class militants survived who prevented the labour movements' traditions and working-class traditions from being fundamentally destroyed in these countries, as they have been in the USSR. This in turn favoured a periodic resurgence of working-class militancy and action in various Eastern European countries, in the first place in Poland and Czechoslovakia.

Finally, while the major part of Eastern Europe's foreign trade is within the Soviet bloc, its 'disintegration' from the world market is less radical than that of the Soviet Union, both for historical reasons and because of conscious choices by the ruling bureaucracies, at least tolerated if not induced by the Kremlin itself. This fact, combined with a stronger 'western' tradition of the *intelligentsia* even inside the CP apparatus (with the possible exception of Bulgaria), makes these societies more susceptible to outside pressure than the USSR. That pressure is generally bourgeois and petty-bourgeois, but it can also be working-class whenever there are powerful working-class explosions in the capitalist countries, as with the influence of the French May of 1968 upon Czechoslovakia and Yugoslavia.

Social and Political Conflicts within 'Soviet Bloc' Countries

Social and political conflicts within the 'Soviet bloc' are a function of the social structures of these countries and of the specific way in which they are related to each other and to the capitalist countries. From a Marxist point of view, it does not make sense to 'see these conflicts emanating solely from a 'basic contradiction' between 'the socialist camp' and the 'imperialist camp'. This would be merely to extend the specific bureaucratic ideology of 'socialism in one country', i.e. an apology for the specific interests of the Soviet bureaucracy. It is closely linked with the idealist attempt to explain social conflicts not essentially by conflicting material *interests* but by conflicting *ideologies*, supposedly in stark opposition with the social nature and social interests of the people involved in these conflicts.

The Polish *Solidarnosc* movement is a striking illustration of these two basically different approaches to social conflicts inside the bloc. The 'campist' explanation is simple. As *Solidarnosc* is 'nationalist' 'anti-Russian', 'hostile to the (socialist) state', it can only be 'an agency of world imperialism' (mediated through the Catholic hierarchy and the Vatican). This becomes a simple syllogism, if not an axiom. But it leaves aside all elements of Marxist materialist analysis. Why would 10 million Polish workers, the overwhelming majority of the Polish working class (around 75% of it), let themselves be manipulated by class enemies, by people opposed to their elementary material interests, both immediate and historical ones, when for the first time for 30 years they were able to decide their social and political position? Their adherence to *Solidarnosc* was absolutely without coercion (comparison with the German *Arbeitsfront* or with company unions is absurd). They joined under great risk, including the risk of losing jobs if not going to jail. How could this be manipulation when inside *Solidarnosc* there was practically unlimited freedom of opinion and expression?

The Marxist/materialist explanation is exactly the opposite. Ten million Polish workers joined *Solidarnosc* because its basic demands expressed the *immediate* interests of the working class: a shorter work week; higher wages; the right to strike; and the right to join a trade-union organization independent from the state and from the bureaucratic factory bosses; the fight for greater equality in the distribution of goods and services. Simultaneously, *Solidarnosc* started to grope towards formulating the *historical* class interests of the Polish proletariat, be it in a more uneven, differentiated and contradictory way, under the weight of the tremendous discredit which 30 years of bureaucratic dictatorship has inflicted on all ideas and programmes presented as 'communist', 'Marxist' or even 'socialist'. That historical class interest was reached by the demand of generalized self-management by the workers (producers) in the economy and the state, i.e. a system with a pluralistic socialized socialist democracy: that was the concrete content of the formula 'self-managed republic'. While there was a lot of confusion on the relation between planning and the market or the concrete focus of political power there was not the slightest trend in favour of a restoration of private property in industry, banking or foreign trade, or in wholesale 'national' trade.

The basic social conflict behind the political struggle which opposed the mass of *Solidarnosc* to the state and the Party bosses was therefore not a conflict between 'imperialism' (or 'bourgeois ideology' or 'Catholic reactionaries') and socialism, but a conflict between the working class and the bureaucracy. *Mutatis mutandis* the same applies for the Hungarian revolution of 1956. The social and economic content of that struggle is the following: *who* determines – has the actual *power to determine* – the division of the social product between private consumption, public consumption and accumulation; the rhythm of growth of the product and the great proportions of the social surplus; the extent of surviving social inequality and its dynamics? The bureaucracy or the mass of the workers? In other words: who determines what is to be produced, how and to whom it is to be distributed?

This basic conflict does not occur in a complete void, neither nationally nor internationally. It is intertwined with the secondary conflicts which can roughly be described as follows:

1 That between the private owners of the means of production and distribution (peasants, tradespeople, self-employed in the service sector) on the one hand, and the bureaucracy (as well as sectors of the working class) on the other.
2 That between international capital and the bureaucratized workers states.
3 That inside the bureaucracy.
4 That between the 'national' bureaucracies, or sectors of them, and the Soviet bureaucracy (the conflict between the 'national' working classes and the Soviet bureaucracy is generally mediated through the basic conflict between the workers and the 'local' bureaucrats, except in extreme situations like the one of Czechoslovakia from August 1968 to March 1969, or Hungary immediately after November 1956).

We do not include in this list any 'class struggle between the proletariat and the bourgeoisie'. The reason for this omission is simple. There does not exist any bourgeois class of any significance in any 'bloc' country, except a petty-bourgeoisie and small layer of middle bourgeoisie, which are mentioned above. Private owners of the means of production, who hire and exploit tens, if not to say hundreds of wage-earners, have completely disappeared. It is therefore inaccurate to speak about a class struggle between capital and labour.

International capitalism only interferes with social conflicts inside the 'bloc' in a very contradictory yet significant way. The existence of a capitalist environment, with a higher standard of living and a higher level of average productivity of labour in the imperialist countries, exercises a constant pressure on society to 'imitate and catch up'. The borrowing of western technology and consumption patterns is a real obsession for the bureaucracy, for reasons of material self-interest (they want to enjoy the 'goodies' first of all themselves), and for reasons of political interest: they are firmly convinced that 'gulash communism', 'consumerism', i.e. the gradual spread of western consumer habits among the mass of the workers and peasants, is the best way to buy political peace – tolerance of the bureaucratic dictatorship by the people.

In that sense, far from being a stimulus for the 'restoration of capitalism', or a weapon of the 'class struggle of the bourgeoisie', increased east–west trade, increased 'Americanization' of consumption, increased depoliticization of the population, increased 'streamlining' of economic management, including a larger sector of 'market socialism', is seen by the bureaucracy as a means of consolidating and *stabilizing* its rule, not as a risk of destabilization. That's why the *bureaucracy* (and not the workers and the peasants) beg for and eagerly accept more western credits, stand for closer collaboration with the imperialist banks and even for gradual integration into the International Monetary Fund. As the Soviet bureaucracy itself is interested in the stability of bureaucratic rule in Eastern Europe, it tolerates and sometimes favours these moves, at least up to a certain limit.

But on the other hand, these objective pressures, and the bureaucracy's adaptation to them, unleashes processes of differentiation inside the bureaucracy (and in a secondary way, among the petty-bourgeoisie, including parts of the peasantry and some high-income layers of the working class) which do go in the direction of 'primitive accumulation of capital'. These are sustained by universal corruption and a gradual expansion of the 'grey' and 'black' market. This process of social and ideological differentiation is accompanied by periodic pressures from sectors of the bureaucracy – especially, but not only, technocrats at factory level – to push 'economic liberalization' ('market socialism') beyond a certain threshold, by 'increasing the rights of the managers', in the first place the right to fire workers. This again obviously favours the resurgence of pro-capitalist forces, especially inside the bureaucracy itself, on a much broader scale than among the peasants or the urban petty-bourgeoisie.

It is the interlocking of the inner-bureaucratic conflict with the opposition between international capitalism on the one hand and the bureaucratized workers state on the other hand which represents the main 'complement' to the basic conflict between the mass of the workers and the bureaucracy inside the camp.

The biggest constraint on that basic conflict is not the workers 'fear' of assisting a restoration of capitalism (which is still very remote, although not historically excluded), but the fear of intervention by the Soviet armed forces, i.e. the uneven development of workers' militancy in (some) of the Eastern European countries and in the USSR. Because of the repeated use of Soviet force to suppress workers' uprisings in Eastern Europe – East German workers in 1953, the Hungarian revolution in 1956, the Prague Spring of 1968 and the use of the Polish military to crush *Solidarnosc* in 1980–1 – it is very difficult for any East European workers to pose the question as to how to forge an anti-bureaucratic revolution without simultaneously asking: 'What do we do about the Soviet army?' This tends to place an irremovable obstacle on the road to the emancipation of East European workers, while the Soviet proletariat remains inactive. It does though create a specific problem which is very much alive among Eastern European oppositionists. It is a problem which has to be tackled frankly and openly, and was one of the key justifications for the 'strategy of the self-limited revolution' applied by all the political inspirators of *Solidarnosc*, from the Catholic hierarchy to the leaders of the Workers' Defence Committee (KOR).

Inner-bureaucratic conflicts cannot be reduced to straightforward conflicts of 'sectorial' material interests. They often concern differences of judgement on what policies are best for furthering the overall interests of the bureaucratic caste(s) as such. The conflict between those in favour of a radical denunciation of Stalin's crime, and those against any clear de-Stalinization, (conflicts which erupted around Khruschev's project before and after the 20th Congress of the CPSU) are an example of that type. In the same category can be placed the conflicts over military intervention in Poland in October 1956, over military intervention in Hungary in November 1956, over '*détente*' policies pushed beyond a certain limit.

Nevertheless the 'sectorial' conflicts are very real. The longer the bureaucracy rules, the more it becomes immovable at least in its highest layers, and the more hyper-centralized control tends to be eroded, each specific apparatus becoming more and more autonomous from the centre and following its own logic and peculiar interests in pursuing or proposing certain lines of action. In that sense, the following bureaucratic subgroups can be identified in the USSR and most other countries of the 'camp': the central party apparatus; the main regional Party apparatuses; the secret police apparatus; the military (officers' caste) apparatus; the central planning apparatus; the apparatus of the main 'economic' ministries; the central 'cultural' (scientific–literary–artistic) apparatus. There are, of course, interconnections between these apparatuses, as in the obvious interconnection between the 'ideology' department of the Party apparatus and the central 'cultural' apparatus.

Opposed to these centralized apparatuses, the bureaucracy at plant or *glavk* (group of enterprises, trusts, etc.) level does not form an institutionalized country-wide interknit network. But it has an informal network which can grow very powerful. In some countries of the 'camp', especially Poland, a vertical network arose, regrouping regional party bosses, industrial branch managers and sectors of the 'economic' ministries' bureaucracies, especially Gierek's personal fief in Silesia around the coal and steel enterprises.

Political and Economic Conflicts inside the 'Soviet Bloc'

The immediate origin of tensions and conflicts between the various 'Soviet bloc' countries originates in the way the 'bloc' was constituted: through military conquest and pressure by the Soviet army and political police, and by 'revolution from above'. This has led to virulent national opposition from the mass of the people of the 'bloc' countries (with the possible exception of Bulgaria) towards rule by local representatives or accomplices of a foreign hegemonic power, the Soviet Union.

This conflict has a deeper source. It reflects the usurpation of political power inside the Soviet Union itself by a privileged bureaucracy, which extended its rule beyond the original frontiers of the USSR in a specific form to further its particular self-interest. Soviet rule in Eastern Europe in the specific way in which the Kremlin exercises that rule is neither in the interest of the Soviet masses nor in the long-run interest of the Soviet state. It is rooted in the attempt to defend and extend the privileges and power of the Soviet bureaucracy as a particular social layer.

Because of that drive 'proletarian internationalism', corrupted and perverted by that bureaucracy's self-interest – first under Stalin, then under the various successors of Stalin – is turned into its opposite: great-Russian nationalism, 'Soviet' chauvinism, which then, by an irrestible internal dialectic, produces many forms of 'nationalism' in the various 'bloc' countries themselves. It is impossible to promote genuine proletarian internationalism without genuine internationalist practice. Essential to the latter is strict respect for the equality of status and right of self-determination of all nations, as well as strict application of international workers' solidarity towards all movements of emancipation of the exploited and the oppressed. Once this practice is replaced by *de facto* subordination of whole nationalities, and important sectors of the international working class, to specific interests of the Soviet bureaucracy, it is unavoidable that large sectors of the toiling masses in Eastern Europe (and not only there!) will view the 'proletarian internationalism' preached by the Kremlin as vacuous. They then reject it out of hand, and fall in turn heavily under the spell of 'local' nationalism – which at least has the advantage of being a 'nationalism of the oppressed', in contrast to the 'nationalism of the oppressor'.

But is this political oppression nothing but a prop for economic exploitation? Is the Soviet bloc, under a slightly different form, simply a colonial empire ruled by an 'imperialist superpower'? Although often asserted, this hypothesis is hard to sustain.

It is true that during the first years of Soviet occupation, forms of direct economic exploitation of some of the bloc countries did occur through, for example, the establishment of 'Soviet joint stock companies'. In East Germany, large-scale dismantling of industrial and transport equipment in the guise of war reparations took place. But after Stalin's death, essentially under the pressure of the East German workers' uprising of June 1953, this policy was abolished. Since the creation of the Comecon, economic interrelations between the Soviet bloc countries are based upon international trade, on the one hand, and the slowly evolving international specialization (division of labour) on the other hand. If we examine the concrete contents of these two forms of international economic relations we can note the obvious differences with the 'imperialism/semi-colonies' relationship which exists between capitalist imperialist countries and their neo-colonies.

In general, the trade between the USSR and its East European satellites takes the form of raw material exports by the USSR and manufactured goods exports by Eastern Europe, i.e. the exact opposite of the trade between imperialist states and semi-colonies. As this trade is conducted on the basis of world market prices (be it not annual but bi-annual averages or even five-years averages), and because world market terms of trade normally move against raw material exporting countries, we can't conclude that through foreign trade the USSR is 'exploiting' Eastern Europe – this leaves aside some special cases like the appropriation of uranium. Likewise, if there is a trend towards industrial specialization inside the Comecon, it has not at all taken the form of the USSR reserving for itself the output of advanced industrial or high technology goods. On the contrary, if anything, economic nationalism asserted itself through the attempts of practically each of the bloc countries to imitate the complete pattern of Soviet industrialization, each of them (most often uneconomically) building up its own steel industry, car industry and heavy machine industry, even where all raw materials had to be imported from thousands of miles away.

The balance-sheet is clear: no transfer of value occurs, on an aggregate basis, between Eastern Europe and the USSR, at the expense of the first and in favour of the second. This judgement is confirmed if one examines the dynamics of levels of industrialization and standards of living between the bloc countries and the USSR. During the last 20 years, the German Democratic Republic, Czechoslovakia and Hungary (possibly even Poland up till 1976) have grown quicker and increased the average level of consumption more than has the USSR. And the distance between Bulgaria and Rumania on the one hand and the USSR on the other has decreased, not increased.

Some argue in a much more indirect and sophisticated manner, that if Eastern Europe traded more with the west (and the Third World) and less with the USSR, it would have had a healthier economic development and it would have achieved a higher standard of living for the bulk of the population than in the straightjacket of the Comecon. Even if we granted the point, this does not constitute 'exploitation' in any sense of the word, but politically thwarted, lopsided growth. The argument could also be turned the other way around. If the USSR had sold all the raw materials (in the first place oil, gas and rarer metals) on the world market at current prices instead of selling them to Eastern Europe under somewhat preferential conditions, it would have gained more. In other words, the Comecon is not a source of additional income for the 'superpower'.

But the very argument of lopsided development, as compared with development inside the capitalist world market, is dubious. International capitalist development is characterized by cycles of growth and stagnation (regression). These impose rigid limits on long-term economic development. Furthermore, under the pressure of international competition, smaller countries, even imperialist ones, not to speak of the semi-industrialized ones, encounter increasing difficulties in developing or maintaining important branches of industry, especially in the field of advanced technology. To believe that, outside of Russia's 'hegemony', it would have been easier for the GDR, Czechoslovakia or Poland to have an advanced and successful electronics or computer industry, is to assume that countries like Spain, Holland, Belgium, Sweden, Denmark, Switzerland, Austria or Australia, have easily developed such industries, which they obviously have not. By and large one could rather argue the opposite: the Comecon 'umbrella' has enabled the bloc countries to get more long-term steady industrial growth, and certainly less economic up-heaval and less of the social misery associated with unemployment, than if they had been integrated in the world market, i.e. than if they had been capitalist countries.

We already stressed that Eastern Europe is more integrated in the capitalist world market than the USSR, but the latter is not totally disconnected from that market. In a more general way, partial commodity production survives inside the bloc, independently from its relations with the international economy too. This means that while the law of value does not rule these countries economies, it does *influence* them. This means that the bloc countries are subject to the severe fluctuations in the capitalist world economy. And at this point of the analysis, both the specific nature of their economy (society) and the specific nature of their interrelation is strikingly confirmed.

During the 1974–5 and 1980–2 recessions, neither the USSR nor Eastern Europe witnessed any absolute decline of industrial output, employment or income, as did all the imperialist (and for the early eighties, also all the semi-industrialized) countries. The only exception was Poland, for specific reasons which are linked with the Gierek regime's wreckless economic adventurism and waste. On the other hand, the more a post-capitalist country was integrated in the international capitalist economy, the harder it was hit by capitalist recessions, i.e. the more its rate of growth declined: much more in Poland, Hungary and Yugoslavia than in the USSR, the GDR, Bulgaria or Rumania.

This does not mean that bureaucratic rule over the bloc doesn't have any negative economic consequences and that the effects of the Kremlin's hegemony are economically and commercially neutral. On the basis of fraternal international cooperation, rooted in strict equality between nations and democratic self-managed planning open to the broadest public control and criticism, Eastern Europe and the USSR would certainly have known a much more harmonious, and probably (if the producers concerned wished so) a much more rapid economic development, with a much higher and better balanced standard of living (especially a smaller work load), than they have enjoyed up till now. This remains the materialist rationale for the anti-bureaucratic political revolution both in the USSR and Eastern Europe, leading to increased and not less cooperation between socialized economies (in the long run to the socialist United States of Europe and the Socialist World Federation).

From this line of analysis, one cannot conclude that economic development, thwarted and lopsided as it is by bureaucratic mismanagement, waste and caste egoism, on the international as well as on the national scale, would have been more harmonious or more advantageous for these countries if they had remained integrated in the world market and ruled by the law of value, i.e. if they had remained capitalist.

But the fact that there is no real exploitation of Eastern Europe by the Soviet bureaucracy does not imply that there are no real conflicts of economic interest between them. Neither does it imply that many (nor all) of these conflicts are automatically solved in the favour of the Soviet bureaucracy, because of its superior power and of the political dependence of the national bureaucracies upon the Kremlin. Those conflicts can turn around sudden shifts in pricing of import/export goods, sudden changes in guaranteed contingents to be delivered independently from price shifts on the world market. They can also turn around major problems of long-term economic (and commercial) strategy. The margins of manoeuvre in these fields for the national bureaucracies are larger than is generally assumed in the west. The bargaining and mutual bickering is very real. The basic reason for that state of affairs is the fact that the Kremlin gives absolute priority to political stability – and that when national explosions occur, in part at least triggered off by insufficient previous room for manoeuvre of the national rulers, the material price which Moscow then has to pay afterwards is much higher than it would have cost to make preventive concessions. In Hungary after 1956–7 and in Czechoslovakia after 1969, the Soviet bureaucracy had to give heavy economic subsidies to Kadar and Husak to enable them to buy peace from their rebellious peoples.

Cuba and Vietnam are special cases. Here, the economy, far from being exploited by the 'superpower', is permanently and heavily subsidized by the Soviet Union. In the case of Cuba, this subsidy is extremely high – which goes a long way to explain why Fidel Castro toes the Moscow line on most issues of foreign policy, notwithstanding his natural inclination and political instinct to the contrary.

Conflicts of a 'purely' local national character, which periodically arise inside the bloc, should be mentioned in passing, like the conflict around the Hungarian minority in Rumania, the Macedonian minority in Bulgaria, the German minority in Hungary, the Czech–Slovak tension in Czechoslovakia, the nationality conflicts inside Yugoslavia, and so on. But while bureaucratic rule, political oppression and sheer mismanagement certainly tend to postpone the solution of these conflicts, the point must again be made: these conflicts are much less violent and much less explosive than in the period previous to the abolition of capitalism in Central and Eastern Europe.

The 'Soviet' and Global Class Struggle

What has been the effect on the global class struggle of the expansion of power of the Soviet bureaucracy and of the emergence of the 'socialist camp'? It cannot be encompassed into a simple black-or-white formula. It is many-sided and very contradictory, reflecting in its own way the dual, contradictory nature of the Soviet bureaucracy itself.

The destruction of capitalism in Eastern Europe, but much more the relative military superiority gained by the Soviet armed forces at the end of World War II on the continent of Europe, have led to a shift in the international relationship of forces at the expense of imperialism. The 'American century', which Roosevelt and US imperialism strove to install at the end of that war, did not materialize. US and world imperialism's possibilities of manoeuvre on a world scale are limited and hampered by the increased power of the Soviet state.

This is especially true for the counter-revolutionary potential of imperialism. Given its historically confirmed tendency to launch counter-revolutionary aggressions against every important victorious (or even unfolding) social revolution in the world, this new constraint is of extreme importance. It is hard to deny that the consolidation of the Yugoslav and the Chinese revolutions, the survival of North Korea as a non-capitalist state, the victory of the Vietnamese revolution, the survival of the Cuban and the Nicaraguan revolutions, would have been much more difficult without the strength of the Soviet state.

The same applies to important national liberation movements which did not create victorious socialist revolutions. Without the Soviet counterweight against imperialism, Nasser's Egypt, the Algerian revolution, the emergence of India as a semi-industrialized country still dependent upon imperialism but definitely no more of a semi-colonial type, would have been very difficult to realize.

For both these historical developments after World War II, it is not only the objective weight of the Soviet bloc in world affairs but also concrete acts by the Soviet and allied governments (in the first place arms deliveries, in the case of Cuba also key economic help to break the US blockade) which played that objectively progressive role.

But even in these clearest of cases, the role of the Soviet bureaucracy was never unilaterally 'progressive'. In most if not all of the cited cases, the Soviet bureaucracy tried to restrain or even to prevent the upsurge of the revolutionary mass movements, either through direct advise and pressure, through the factions it controlled inside the CPs concerned (Yugoslavia, China, Vietnam), or through the local CPs counter-posed to the political organizations leading the revolutions or national liberation movements (India, Algeria, Cuba, Nicaragua). Certainly it tried to keep them from growing over into victorious socialist revolutions. The documentary and political evidence in that regard is indisputable. Likewise, the weight of the Kremlin was decisive in causing grave defeats of the revolution in all those Third World countries where the local CPs remained completely under its control (Iraq, Brazil, Bolivia, especially Chile). While its responsibility in the most tragic defeat of a revolution in the Third World – that of Indonesia, which lost almost one million lives – is less than that of the Mao bureaucracy, it is great indeed. So even the global balance-sheet of its role with regard to the Third World revolutionary movements is less uniform than might appear at first sight. Its general orientation towards 'revolution' by stages, 'blocs' with the 'national' bourgeoisie, 'non-capitalist and non-socialist paths of development', has caused tremendous ideological confusion and political havoc among two generations of 'Third World revolutionists, confusion and havoc which are by no means over, as the recent example of the Tudeh Party's attitude towards Khomeiny's 'Islamic revolution' tragically illustrates.

If the Soviet bloc's record is contradictory with regard to revolutions in the Third World, it is much clearer with regard to working-class struggles in the imperialist countries. Here, the negative consequences of the Soviet bureaucracy's consolidation of power after World War II far outweighs any objectively positive ones. This consolidation has in two ways heavily weighed against a victorious extension of socialist revolution in the west. In the first place, it has concretely imposed upon national CPs strategies and tactics of accepting the permanence of bourgeois rule and of class collaboration, which were decisive at least on five occasions (France in 1944–6, Italy in 1945–8, France in May 1968; Italy in 1969; Portugal in 1974–5; possibly also Spain 1975–6) for saving capitalism either from a long revolutionary crisis or even from its being overthrown. The case of Greece could be added to the list. The imposition of these neo-reformist strategies was not accidental. Nor was it essentially dogmatic or ideological. It was a clear application of the line of 'socialism in one country' extended to the line of giving priority to the diplomatic and military manoeuvres of the 'socialist camp' over any international extension of revolution. Indeed it was more than that. It was the result of a real deal with imperialism presented under the guise of 'peaceful coexistence': if you leave our rule over Eastern Europe unchallenged, we'll instruct the CPs not to challenge your rule over Western Europe.

In the second place, the consequences of bureaucratic dictatorship, repression and mismanagement in the USSR itself and in Eastern Europe have deeply tarnished the image of socialism in the eyes of a large sector of the working class in the metropolitan countries. It is not only 'imperialist anti-communist propaganda' (which was much more strident and vicious in the twenties and the thirties without having anything like the effects of today), but the social and political reality of the USSR, of Czechoslovakia, of Poland, which has created inside the western working class a deep disillusionment with socialism and communism as a desirable alternative to the evils of bourgeois society. The negative effects of this lack of alternative far outweigh any positive effects of the strength of the Soviet bloc in the west, as for example, the restraint it puts upon a rebirth of fascism in a country like West Germany. The gradual disintegration of the 'world communist movement', with major CPs (not only the Yugoslav and Chinese, but also the Italian, Japanese, Spanish, French and Mexican CPs) becoming publicly critical of Moscow, is a product of that phenomenon.

Of course, the global picture has to take account of a number of dimensions: it has to include the constant military pressure which imperialism continues to exercise upon the Soviet Union and other countries where capitalism has been abolished. This pressure does not depend upon the Kremlin's particular sins, although it is enhanced (made politically more acceptable to the masses in some imperialist countries) as a result of these sins (Afghanistan is an example to the point). It would be at least similar, if not stronger, if there were genuine socialist democracy and direct workers' power in the USSR and Eastern Europe. One should reject as largely mystifying the thesis of a parallel responsiblity of 'both superpowers' in the arms race following World War II, especially the nuclear arms race. Each new stage in that race has been initiated by imperialism. Imperialism, and imperialism alone, is driven by objective inner contradictions on that road – not the Soviet bureaucracy, for which participation in the arms race creates a more and more insuperable economic and political burden.

But there again the picture is not all white (or red) in favour of Moscow. While the responsibility for the suicidal nuclear arms race should be laid squarely at the feet of the imperialists, the way in which the Kremlin responded (and still responds) to that race has greatly helped imperialism in reducing the political price it would have to pay for this criminal course. By first defending the irresponsible doctrine of 'winning a nuclear war' (the Sokolovsky doctrine), then, even after abandoning it, still embarking upon a course of nuclear parity, the Soviet bureaucracy has lost occasion upon occasion to give a powerful impetus to the popular anti-war movement in the west and in Japan.

Again, this is not accidental. A privileged nationalist social layer like the Soviet bureaucracy fears any bold moves of mass mobilization against the 'right' of states, governments and army heads to decide upon military and foreign policies – because such a course making concrete gains in the west would inevitably stimulate similar modes in the east too. It prefers to negotiate and bargain with imperialism about the pace of nuclear rearmament rather than help the masses of the world to stop the march towards the Holocaust by direct action leading to unilateral nuclear disarmament and the undermining and overthrow of imperialist power.

The conservative, counter-revolutionary nature of the Soviet bureaucracy is clearly revealed in that example, as it likewise reveals to what point its policies conflict with the historic interests of the Soviet people and of a revolutionary defence of the Soviet Union.

The historical balance-sheet of 'campism' – by an extension of Stalinism – is that it doesn't pay from the point of view of the interests of the exploited and the oppressed the world over. In the long run, real proletarian internationalism, the right of masses of each nation to set their own course towards liberation irrespective of great power manoeuvres and interests, to move towards fraternal cooperation on the basis of strict equality, is more efficient. It is along that road that world revolution will eventually triumph. It is certainly only along that road that a real transcending of nation-state sovereignty, a real practical transcending of nationalism into a Socialist World Federation, can be progressively achieved. And without such a transcending of the nation state, the road towards nuclear annihilation remains wide open.

Notes

1   That period of the French Revolution (July 1794 – August 1795) in which the suppression of popular democratic forces heralded the beginnings of the political counter-revolution and the subsequent rise to power of Napoleon. The parallels between the character of the counter-revolutions in France and Russia was suggested by Trotsky and others in the 1920s and 1930s.
2   The Communist International established in 1919 to 'organize joint action by the proletariat of the different countries which pursue the one goal: the overthrow of capitalism, the establishment of the dictatorship of the proletariat and an international Soviet republic...' Dissolved in 1943.
3   Council for Mutual Economic Assistance, a multilateral economic and trade association, set up in 1949 by the Soviet Union and East European states, partly in response to establishment of OECD (Organisation for Economic Cooperation and Development). Membership now includes Cuba, Mongolia and Vietnam.

3

Ups and Downs
The Fortunes of the West European
and Japanese Economies since 1945

JOHN HARRISON AND D. BAVAR

The West European and Japanese economies have undergone several major changes of fortune since 1945. Initial dislocation and uncertainty gradually gave way to stability and rapid growth. By the mid–1950s, the greatest boom in history was underway. In the late 1960s, difficulties set in and profitability fell. Following the international crash of 1974–5, growth slowed dramatically, profits slumped further and mass unemployment entered the picture for the first time for a generation. No real recovery has yet occurred.

Both Japan and continental Europe did well against major rivals (most notably the USA) over the period as a whole. They outperformed most competitors in terms of output and productivity growth, shares of world trade and so on. Japan's success was nothing short of phenomenal. Forty years ago, it was hardly an industrial nation. Today, it is second only to the USA and has overtaken it in many sectors.

The key to differences in performance – both over time and between countries – lies in the rhythms of capital accumulation and class conflict. These interact in a complex, chicken-and-egg fashion. Indeed, this chapter is largely an attempt to chart the shifting contours of this dialectic. One of the main transmission mechanisms – from accumulation to class struggle and back again – is capitalist confidence. Industrial militancy damages confidence and hence investment. By providing jobs and the resources to raise living standards, accumulation often dampens down conflict. But only at a price – for by strengthening the labour movement, it helps tip the future balance of forces in the workers' favour.

Post-War Reconstruction and Boom

At the close of hostilities in 1945, Japan and continental Europe faced enormous hardship. Half the housing in many major Japanese cities lay in ruins. Food was in short supply. Millions of refugees were streaming across borders. Many were dying from starvation and disease. Corpses were a common sight on the streets of dozens of cities.

Millions of civilians regularly trekked out from the cities to the countryside to beg, barter or steal food. One Sunday in September 1945, a month after the end of hostilities, one million people left Tokyo in search of food from the peasantry. The scale of misery in Germany was compared to the middle ages.

The *Economist* in January 1946 summed up the overall situation well: 'the tragedy is vast. It may vary in intensity; the peasantry are reasonably well provided for and the rich can use the black market, but the poor urban population of Europe, perhaps a quarter of its 400 millions, are condemned to go hungry this winter. . .the plague spots are Warsaw, Budapest, Vienna, Northern Italy, the Ruhr, Berlin and most larger German towns. . .Greece and Holland are improving, but are still below subsistence. Paris and large towns of France face a new food crisis. . .'.

Few held high hopes for the future. As early as 1943 the well-known economist P. Samuelson anticipated a combination of the worst features of inflation and deflation, fearing that 'there would be ushered in the greatest period of unemployment and industrial dislocation which any economy has ever faced.'[1] This view was echoed by Schumpeter who remarked that 'the general point of view seems to be that capitalist method will be unequal to the task of reconstruction. . .the decay of capitalist society is very far advanced.'[2] Most prognoses ranged between the pessimistic and the catastrophic.

The internal situations in these nations were not the only sources of turmoil. The domination of imperialist countries over their colonies was called into question by an upsurge in national liberation struggles. Capitalism also confronted a new and ultimately hostile social system whose prestige had been enhanced by the war – that of the USSR. The relations *between* the advanced capitalist countries had also been violently shaken up. The USA had emerged as undisputed economic champion: its production half as big again as before the war. Output in Germany and Japan was running at only one-fifth or so of pre-war levels and exports at only one half.[3]

Contrary to immediate appearances, destruction of the physical wherewithal to produce was not the key problem. All the countries considered in this chapter ended the war with a larger labour force than at the beginning. Death and serious injuries were more than offset by a combination of natural population growth, massive influxes of refugees (8 million into West Germany from the east; 6 million into Japan from its dismantled empire) and increases in the proportion of women in waged work (everywhere except in West Germany).

Destruction of plant and machinery was heaviest in Japan, which lost about 30%. About 17.5% of Germany's capital stock was destroyed as was 10% in France and 8% in Italy. The United Kingdom sustained only negligible damage. But these losses were more than offset by feverish wartime investment. Table 3.1 presents the best available estimates for the net effect of these developments on the capital stock.

Reconversion to peacetime production posed fewer problems than many had feared. Machine tools proved remarkably versatile.

The damage was, of course, uneven; so important bottlenecks existed. Workers were short of food, factories starved of fuel. Transport was desperately unreliable. Destruction of bridges and much shipping had posed many problems by the end of the war. But, as events showed, these bottlenecks could be widened, and then eliminated, within a short space of time. Pre-war production levels were restored in the coal sector by 1947. The crop year 1947/8 saw food output in Northern and Western Europe back to pre-war levels. Even the German railway system was working smoothly again by 1946.

Table 3.1   Wartime changes in the stock of means of production[1]

	Percentage change	
	Machine tools	Total stock of fixed capital
UK	15	0
France	5	n.a.
Italy	40	0
Germany	50	20
Japan	25	0

Note:
1 Figures show percentage change between 1938 and 1945 and are only very approximate.
Source:
P. Armstrong, A. Glyn and J. Harrison, *Capitalism Since World War II* (London, Fontana, 1984).

Social and political difficulties proved far more deep-seated obstacles to economic recovery than did physical destruction and strategic bottlenecks. Capitalism, based on private ownership and the principle of production for profit, can function smoothly only if the bourgeoisie can exert effective authority, within both the factories and the country at large. In 1945, the bourgeoisie had lost effective control on the shop floor and within the state in most of the countries this chapter is concerned with.

Wartime mobilization had brought full – even 'overfull' – employment. Civilian employment had risen despite the enormous expansion of the armed forces. In the UK, trade-union membership rose from 6 to 8 million during the war. Unions had been encouraged to play a major role in executing wartime plans. But rationing and anti-strike agreements entered into by the leaderships had bottled up expec-tations. The release of demands and militancy at the end of hostilities could prove far more explosive than the host of German bombs still ticking undetected in the rubble. The situation was different in Germany and Japan. There the organized labour movement had been smashed years earlier. Everything had to be created anew. The state apparatus was in the hands of occupying forces, committed to capitalism and often initially welcomed as liberators, but also ill-equipped as peacetime administrators. Since the old bourgeois politicians were severely discredited by revelations of the role they played in the war, the capitalists were often as weak as the workers. Everything was up for grabs.

In Germany, the anti-fascist committees (Antifas) received short shrift from the occupying forces. Social-democratic leaders were wheeled back from exile to promote the free market and private entrepreneurial initiatives, alongside state participation in reconstruction and the control of key monopolies. In Italy and France, formidable mass resistance movements were led by the working class. Socialists and communists were universally recognized as the most dynamic part of the anti-fascist resistance. As the resistance movements emerged from the underground, radical reform programmes surfaced with them. Forces in France,

Italy and Germany demanded nationalization, reconstruction of basic industries and control over the distribution of necessities. Parties of all political persuasions united in support of national reconstruction programmes.

Even in the UK, where social disruption was on a smaller scale, grassroot demands for socialization were widespread. 1945 saw the election of the first majority Labour government.

The overall situation was clearly far from stable. Much would depend on the attitude taken by the enormously strengthened USA both towards its allies and the defeated powers. At one extreme, it could exploit its economic supremacy to the hilt. Alternatively, it could actively assist recovery abroad. The first course would involve minimizing aid and pressurizing Western Europe and Japan to allow full access for American goods. It would help boost US exports in the short run, but only at the risk of increasing instability within the capitalist bloc as a whole. The second option would involve massive aid and a tolerance towards restrictions on American imports. It could boost the system as a whole, offering expanded overall markets in future, but at the cost of aid payments, a short-term sacrifice of export possibilities, and the likelihood of serious competition to American industry in future.

For the first two post-war years, the USA opted for policies broadly in line with the first alternative. It made little or no attempt to stimulate economic recovery in Germany and Japan, the countries most directly under its control. Production grew steadily in France and Italy and the UK recovered rapidly. These differences in performance bred corresponding differences in the forms of working-class response.

In Germany, workers demanded direct intervention from the military occupation. In France and Italy the working class sought a direct role in policy and administration through involvement in government. In the UK hopes were pinned on the first ever majority Labour government. In Japan, poverty inevitably pushed wages to the forefront of working-class struggles. Issues of union recognition rapidly gave way to demands for improved pay and conditions. Struggles for workers' control and planning followed.

The forms of working-class offensive in turn shaped the responses of the authorities. As momentum gathered in Japan, the occupation administration intervened both to threaten and harass the fledgling movement and to shore up the bosses. Japanese workers, with a minimal history of organization, showed an enormous capacity for advanced forms of industrial struggle. But, on the political plane, the peasantry delivered a massive blow by voting Conservative in the wake of a land reform. The Socialist Party was enticed into coalition and the communists were isolated.

In Germany, the occupation initially followed a policy of massive deindustrialization under the pretext of demilitarization. Workers responded to this lack of concern for the appalling hardship they faced with sporadic industrial action, culminating in waves of strikes in 1947. The strikers demanded broad reconstruction measures, a halt to the dismantling of factories, land reform and effective administration of the distributive sector with workers' participation.

In Italy, the Communist Party opted for a broad popular front, in a coalition government under the banner of national unity. On the industrial front, a stalemate existed: workers were unable to secure advances in industrial democracy and employers were too weak to push through the widespread dismissals required to restore profitability in the context of low levels of capital utilization. In France, the Liberation brought political, and limited economic gains to the workers. The Communist Party exercised restraint until 1947 in exchange for a place in the government. But rank and file discontent with the moderation urged by the trade-union leaders soon proved too powerful to contain. The Communists withdrew from the coalition. Working-class gains were then gradually rolled back.

In the UK, the 1945–51 Labour government implemented most of its electoral programme of nationalization. This programme had long since replaced the objective of comprehensive planning with one of state takeover of longtime unprofitable industries. Compensation was generous. Whilst the welfare state was extended appreciably, living standards grew only slowly. Rank-and-file expectations were thwarted and strikes mushroomed.

In 1947, the USA changed its tack towards Europe and Japan. The Marshall Plan of that year committed the USA to provide aid for economic reconstruction for several years ahead. The recipients were to draw up plans mapping out a recovery path. The plans were poorly coordinated and the sums of aid money were barely greater than pre-1947 (although a greater proportion took the form of grants rather than loans). But the move did signal a new-found American commitment to the restoration of a healthy capitalist system within these countries. This encouraged the various regimes to push through measures to restore and cement bourgeois control.

The following years saw concentrated attacks on the workers in country after country. Deflationary financial policies, aimed at weakening the labour movement through unemployment, at stabilizing prices and at restoring capitalist confidence, were backed up with more direct attacks on the trade unions. The restoration of financial and social discipline eventually achieved was to lay the foundation for the phenomenal economic success of the 1950s and 60s.

The French general strike in the autumn of 1947 led to 80,000 army reservists being called up. A direct assault on the strikers and mass arrests forced an abandonment of the strike within one month. Divisions between the socialists and the communists led the socialist minority in the trade-union movement to split from the Confédération Générale du Travail (CGT – the main militant union grouping in France). A new union, *Force Ouvrière*, was established, with finance from the USA.

The breaking of the class stalement in Italy also involved splits in the main trade-union organization, dominated by the communists and socialists – the Confederazione Generale Italiana del Lavoro (CGIL). The Christian democrats created a parallel trade union, following the discovery of a fictitious CGIL insurrectionary plan. Again American money financed the split. In the UK under Labour, an anti-communist witch hunt was launched in the trade unions in response to the reorganized Cominform declaration of 1947, which embodied a much-hardened attitude towards the west.

The Japanese clamp-down was the most dramatic. A right to dismiss anyone, communist or not, who interfered with the normal management of enterprises was proclaimed by the Japanese League of Employment. This charter for a 'red purge' was legitimized by the occupation in 1950. More than 12,000 workers were dismissed, 11,000 from the private sector, 2,500 of whom were trade-union officials. The communist-dominated trade-union confederation, Sanbetsu, was smashed.

The capitalists combined this assault on the working class with a major currency readjustment. Under direct pressure from the American Treasury in September 1949, the UK devalued Sterling by 30%, France and Germany cut the dollar values of their currencies by just over 20% and Italy followed suit by nearly 10%. These realignments helped translate shop-floor gains for the capitalists into improved international competitiveness.

Table 3.2 Prices and exchange rates, end of 1949

index numbers pre-war=100	(1) Wholesale prices	(2) Dollar value of currency as percentage of pre-war value	Dollar wholesale prices (1)×(2) / 100
USA	200	100	200
UK	246	57	140
France	1,944	11	213
Germany	195	59	127
Italy	4,747	3	142
Japan	21,886	1	219

Source:
Bank for International Settlements, *Annual Report 1949–50*, pp. 95, 104, 154.

The stage was set for a period of successful capitalist expansion. The performance did not begin at once; the ravages of the last decade had hit capital hard and confidence was restored only slowly. But by the mid-1950s, a sustained boom was underway everywhere. It turned out to be by far and away the greatest boom in human history.

Table 3.3 Long-term growth 1820–1973

	Average annual percentage growth rates[1]			
	Output	Output per head of population	Stock of fixed capital	Exports
1820–1870	2.2	1.0	n.a.	4.0
1870–1913	2.5	1.4	2.9	3.9
1913–1950	1.9	1.2	1.7	1.0
1950–1973	4.9	3.8	5.5	8.6

Note:
1 Arithmetic averages of individual country figures.
Source:
Armstrong *et al.*, *Capitalism Since World War II*.

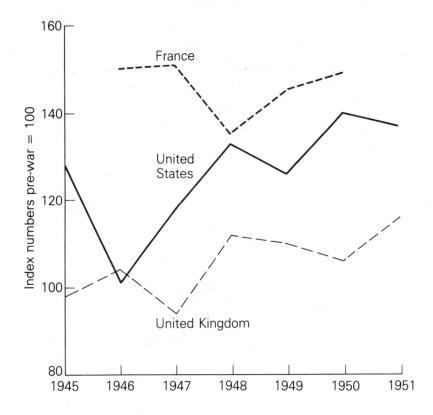

Figure 3.1 Profitability 1945–51[1]
Note: 1 Indices of the profit share with pre-war share (usually 1938) = 100
Source: Armstrong *et al.*, *Capitalism Since World War II*.

The quarter century between 1950 and 1975 saw more growth in manufacturing output in Western Europe and Japan than in the previous three-quarters of a century. Exports also grew rapidly, relative both to previous historical periods and to the performance of the major competitor, the USA.

Table 3.4 Growth of export volumes 1953–71

| | Average annual percentage growth rates | |
	1953–9	1959–71
USA	0.2	6.3
Germany	16.9	9.2
Japan	19.0	15.9

Source:
Armstrong *et al.*, *Capitalism Since World War II*.

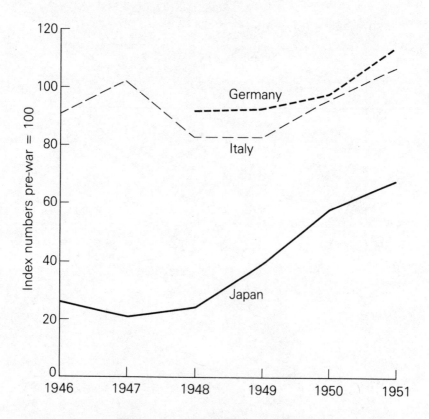

Figure 3.2 Profitability 1946–51[1]
Note: 1 Indices of the profit share with pre-war share (usually 1938) = 100
Source: Armstrong *et al.*, *Capitalism Since World War II*.

The boom was most dramatic in Japan. Exports trebled between 1949 and 1952 and the share of profits doubled. This crucial boost in profitability was possible as wages did not increase in line with increases in productivity. Some commentators argue that this was due to the oriental humbleness of Japanese workers. Others point more accurately to the systematic destruction of independent working-class organizations and their replacement by company unions. By the close of the fifties, militant trade unions had been literally eradicated in the private sector.

Not so in Western Europe. There the unparalleled economic strides made during the 'golden years' of the 1950s and 60s persuaded many observers that capitalism had changed fundamentally: that it had become a system capable of generating permanent, stable and rapid growth, of providing jobs for all, as well as decent, and constantly rising, living standards, whilst enshrining basic trade-union rights in law. Optimism bred political conformity as parties of both left and right reached a broad consensus on the way forward and agreed on the parameters within which to contest residual differences.

This agreed framework could have been promoted with the slogan 'towards a managed humanitarian capitalism'. Its main features were:

1   Acceptance of a mixed economy; that is, a capitalist economy with substantial state holdings.
2   Commitment by governments to ensure full employment by using 'Keynesian' techniques to boost spending, in order to provide jobs as necessary.
3   An extension of the welfare state.
4   Legal guarantees of workers' rights to exert an influence on conditions of employment. The most fundamental was the right to form trade unions. More developed variants incorporated representation on company-level decision-making bodies.
5   Regular government intervention to shape the pace and direction of economic development by means of indicative planning and industrial policy.

Whilst enthusiasm for the various features of the consensus varied both across the political spectrum and across countries, it was nevertheless fairly ubiquitous. A list of its major advocates in Western Europe would read like a roll call of post-war politicians: Macmillan, Adenauer, de Gaulle, Wilson and Brandt, to name but a handful. In the UK, commentators elided the names of the leading Tory politician, Butler, and the Labour leader, Gaitskell, to tag the consensus 'Butskellism'.

The notion of the mixed economy came to the fore with the election of the 1945 Labour government in the UK. Labour had long sought public ownership of certain basic industries which had 'failed the nation'. As early as 1934 it had drawn up a programme for the nationalization of these (fuel, power, transport, iron and steel) together with banking and land. Apart from banking and land these industries were all taken into public ownership after the war. Similar developments took place elsewhere. France nationalized more than the UK in the early post-war years.

The UK was also the first country to adopt an explicit commitment to the peacetime use of Keynesian techniques to maintain full employment. This was enshrined in the Beveridge Report of 1942. Other countries followed suit. However, the commitment was never seriously tested during the boom years. The pace of accumulation alone provided the jobs. Since governments averaged a more or less balanced budget, the boom was not sustained by expansionary deficits.

The ideal of a welfare state was well summarized in a wartime French resistance document which called for 'a complete plan of social security designed to secure the means of existence for all French men and women whenever they are incapable of providing such a means for themselves by working'.[4] Elements of such a system had existed since the 1880s, when the German Kaiser had announced, at Bismarck's behest, that 'the care of social ills must be sought not exclusively in the repression of the social democratic excesses, but simultaneously in the positive advancement of the welfare of the working masses.'[5] But the scale of welfare provision grew considerably during the boom. The proportion of output absorbed by government civil spending (excluding debt interest and subsidies) on average grew from 15% in 1952 to 24% in 1973. By the early 1970s, a typical continental European country was spending more than 20% of its total income on welfare provisions. The UK was devoting 17% to 18%, but Japan a mere 10%.

Over half the increases resulted from extended coverage (i.e. from more of the population gaining access to benefits).

Table 3.5   Growth of welfare spending in advanced capitalist countries in the 1960s

	As percentage of gross domestic product	Due to demographic changes[1]	coverage[2]
Education	1.1	0.0	0.6
Income maintenance	2.0	0.8	1.2
Health	1.9	0.1	1.1
Total	5.0	0.9	2.9

Notes:
1   The effect on spending of the changing age-structure of the population (old people, children).
2   The effect on spending of welfare schemes covering an increasing proportion of the population.
Source:
OECD, *Public Expenditure Trends* (Paris, OECD, 1976), table 7.

This development represented a significant transfer of resources to the more disadvantaged sectors of the population. But it hardly lived up to the aspirations of the French resistance. On standardized poverty figures (a percentage of national earnings based on the average of official national poverty standards) 7.5% of the British, as well as 3% of the West Germans lived in poverty in the early 1970s. Ironically, France was bottom of the league with 16%.

The union movement rebuilt itself in those Western European countries in which it had been smashed by fascism and war (notably Germany and Italy). It was generally recognized as a legitimate and powerful social force. Total membership in the advanced capitalist countries rose from 49 million in 1952 to 62 million in 1970. Regular wage negotiations, often annual, became the accepted norm. Japan was the exception. There, by the 1950s, the independent private-sector unions had been smashed and replaced by subservient pro-company 'social unions'. Since then, no major strike has taken place in large-scale private industry in Japan.

Workers' direct involvement in company decision-making made most formal headway in West Germany. There, the principle of 'co-determination' was a major preoccupation of the unions in the immediate post-war years. In the early 1950s, well over nine out of ten miners and metal workers voted to strike in order to win co-determination. Workers elected one third of the members of supervisory boards (half in the Steel and Coal industries) with the shareholders electing the rest and appointing a 'neutral' chair. Workers' Councils, elected by employees only, had the right to certain company information, to consult over certain issues (e.g.. dismissals and redundancies), to veto certain management decisions (e.g. transfers and job-classification changes) and to co-determine others (e.g. hours and implementation of pay scales).

In practice, workers' control has been far more constrained than these provisions suggest. Co-determination certainly seems to have done little for working conditions, even in the industries where the provisions are strongest: 'Exhausting physical effort, excessive heat, hazardous safety and health conditions has been far less the point of attention (and redress) than in American Steel industry and at least straight-time workers endure a high measure of personal coercion (speed-up in one word) by supervision!'[6] Other countries lagged well behind West Germany in this field. Management clings to its right to manage – and manage alone – more than to any other prerogative.

Indicative planning was taken furthest in France. It grew out of the 1945 Monnet Plan, which sought to coordinate the post-war reconstruction of six basic sectors. Civil servants and managers came together in Modernization Commissions to agree on plans for output and investment. Later variants employed increasingly sophisticated forecasts for overall economic growth and its sectoral implications.

Firms seem to have taken some account of the plans in the 1960s. A 1967 survey showed that 85 per cent of large companies knew of the forecast for their industry. But enthusiasm fell off later. By 1979 only 9 per cent of employers thought the plan very important. Other countries were generally unsuccessful in their attempts to import French methods. The 1964–70 UK Labour government's five year National Plan was abandoned when the outcome in early years made a laughing stock of the projected targets.

Industrial policy was pursued most forcefully in Japan. The Ministry of International Trade and Industry (MITI) opted to try to improve drastically the export performance of carefully selected industries; to pick and mould winners. It brought representatives of leading firms together, promoted 'rationalization plans' and exerted a strong influence on the direction of future development, not least by controlling access to low-interest government finance.

MITI-sponsored industries certainly registered remarkable successes. Shipbuilding, one of MITI's first ventures, became Japan's first miracle industry. By the early 1970s half the world's ships hit the high seas from the Japanese shipyards. Steel was the next candidate selected for the treatment. By 1977, Japan boasted 25 blast furnaces with 2 million tonnes or more capacity. The EEC ran 7 and the USA none. Under MITI's guiding hand, the Japanese automobile industry was also transformed from a handful of down-at-heel truck producers into the largest car exporter in the world. But Japan has had equally spectacular successes with sectors in which MITI has played little or no role. Examples include motorbikes, television sets, Hi Fi equipment and zips. Western European countries were unable to replicate MITI. Much of their industrial policy amounted to regional aid designed mainly, and often unsuccessfully, to influence industrial location.

It is one thing to describe the key elements of the consensus, but quite another to evaluate their importance. No one can be certain how the Japanese economy would have performed in the absence of MITI, or West Germany without co-determination. But some things are clear. None of these changes transformed the basic nature of capitalism. Its dynamic remained production for private profit. Nor did they render it permanently crisis free, as later events demonstrated forcefully. But there is little doubt that during the boom most people believed that these changes had transformed the system. By boosting capitalists' confidence, this belief may have contributed to maintaining boom conditions by stimulating investment.

Onset of Crisis

By the late 1960s, however, the success was increasingly shaky. Growing instability in Western Europe and Japan was part and parcel of a deepening crisis of the system as a whole, whose broader dimensions lie outside the scope of this chapter. Here we focus on the contribution of developments in these blocs to the unfolding of the overall process, and on ways in which the global crisis struck Western Europe and Japan differently from how it struck the USA. Four features stand out:

1. The underlying cause of the demise of the greatest boom in history is a major decline in profitability, the *raison d'être* of capitalism. By 1973, the profit rate for both corporate business as a whole and the crucial and sensitive manufacturing sector had fallen from its post-war peak by about one-third in each of the three major blocs.

But while similar in extent, the fall varied considerably in timing between North America, Western Europe, and Japan. The rot set in in Europe in 1960, the USA in the mid-sixties and in Japan in 1970. In the mid-sixties, a sharp rise in Japanese profitability was offsetting a sharp fall in the USA. In the late sixties, a brief rise in European profitability played a similar, though more muted, role; in the early seventies, a decline in Europe and a collapse in Japan dwarfed a minor recovery in the USA.

These divergencies were crucial both to the length of the boom and to the speed of its break-up. Once developments in the three major blocs ceased to counter-balance each other, the decline became precipitate. For the advanced capitalist countries as a whole, the profit rate fell by one fifth between 1968 and 1973.
2. The three blocs also grew at different rates during the boom. Europe outstripped the USA, and Japan left everyone else in the shade. This severely undermined American dominance, and weakened its hold over the international trade and payment system. The dollar crises of the late sixties were inevitable consequences.
3. Western Europe, alone amongst the major blocs, experienced a remarkable and surprisingly uniform hotting up of the industrial class struggle in the closing couple of years of the 1960s. Wave after wave of strikes won big wage rises, putting severe pressure on profits and prices.

May 1968 in France is the best-known example. Italy's 'hot Autumn' of 1969 had probably the greatest impact on subsequent economic developments. All were very destabilizing and nothing comparable occurred elsewhere. Strikes and money-wage rises in the USA in the early 1970s outran those of the 1960s, but the tempo began to increase earlier and the shifts were far less dramatic. In Japan, strikes remained fairly constant and low.

Finally, the oil crisis of the winter of 1973–4, which sparked off the 1974–5 crash and marks the watershed between the great boom and the mass unemployment to follow, had a far greater negative impact on Western Europe and Japan than on the USA. Japan lacks fossil fuels. It is almost entirely dependant on imported oil to meet its energy requirements; so its import bill shot up in the wake of what the Japanese call the 'oil shock'. The quadrupling of oil prices was simply a bad blow. There were no mitigating benefits.

Table 3.6　Weight of the US economy 1950–70

	Percentages	
	1950	1970
US share of output in advanced capitalist countries	58[1]	47
US share of capital stock in advanced capitalist countries	52[1]	45
US output per head of population in relation to		
United Kingdom	182	166
France	217	133
Germany	270	133
Italy	400	217
US manufacturing productivity in relation to		
United Kingdom	279	285
Germany	367	232
Japan	n.a.	272[3]
US share of manufacturing output (big 10)	62[2]	44[4]
US share of manufacturing exports (world)	33	16

Notes:
1　1952.
2　1953.
3　Using Roy's estimates of Japanese productivity relative to Germany.
4　1971.
Source:
Armstrong *et al.*, *Capitalism Since World War II*.

Table 3.7　The European wage explosions 1965–70

	Strikes[1]	Money wage[2]	Real wage[2]
France			
1965–7	2,569	5.8	2.9
1968–9	76,000[3]	11.0	5.4
Germany			
1966–8	147	5.6	3.3
1969–70	171	12.0	9.2
Italy			
1966–8	10,761	6.9	4.3
1969–70	29,356	11.3	7.3
UK			
1967–9	4,774	6.9	2.4
1970–1	12,265	12.0	3.9

Notes:
1　Thousands of days occupied in strikes, annual averages.
2　Average annual percentage change during the years shown.
3　Estimated by Kendall W. The Labour Movement in Europe (London, Allen Lane, 1975) p. 365.
Source:
Armstrong *et al.*, *Capitalism Since World War II*.

The USA, at the other extreme, has the capacity to satisfy its own oil requirements. It also possesses enormous deposits of shale oil and bituminous schists; extracting oil from these sources becomes increasingly economical as the price of oil soars. Western Europe falls between these two extremes, but West Germany, the major European rival to the USA, is closer to Japan than to Uncle Sam in this regard. Finally, the oil companies, whose profits rose from $3.9 billion US in 1972 to $12.1 billion in 1974, are almost all US owned.

The world economy began to crash in the summer of 1974. Industrial production in the advanced capitalist countries as a whole fell by 10% between July 1974 and April 1975. By the first half of 1975, output was 3.5% lower than 12 months earlier and international trade had fallen by 13%. It was the biggest peacetime crash since 1929.

The crash marked a major turning point in the fortunes of advanced capitalism. Since 1973, output has grown less than half as fast as in the 1960s. Had it grown as fast, then in 1985 the world would have been richer to the tune of considerably more than the combined annual production of West Germany and Japan.

Once again, developments in Europe and Japan differed from those in the USA. While output in the USA fell by 1.5% between 1973 and 1975, it remained more or less constant in Western Europe and rose by 1.5% in Japan. So the relative health of the productive sector in these latter blocs cushioned the adverse effects of a collapse in the USA on the system as a whole.

Table 3.8   Business profit rates 1968–75

			Percentages	
	Advanced capitalist countries	USA	Europe	Japan
1968	17.2	19.4	13.5	31.7
1973	13.6	14.8	11.3	19.6
1975	10.2	12.3	7.3	13.5

Source:
Armstrong *et al.*, *Capitalism Since World War II*.

Table 3.9   Manufacturing profit rates 1968–75

			Percentages	
	Advanced capitalist countries	USA	Europe	Japan
1968	23.6	28.9	14.8	46.0
1973	19.3	22.5	12.1	33.5
1975	11.6	16.7	7.9	10.4

Source:
Armstrong *et al.*, *Capitalism Since World War II*.

The most obvious and tragic effect of the sharp slow down has been the re-emergence, and seemingly remorseless growth, of mass unemployment in the heartlands of the system. Official unemployment figures seriously understate the real extent of joblessness, because of deficiencies in data collection and attempts by governments to 'massage' the figures downwards. Thus in the early eighties a third of all new job vacancies in Western Europe were filled by people not previously registered as unemployed. But the trends and *relative* levels displayed by the official data are probably fairly accurate.

Table 3.10   Unemployment rates 1973–83[1]

| | Percentages | | | |
	Advanced capitalist countries	USA	Japan	EEC
1973	3.4	4.8	1.3	3.0
1975	5.5	8.3	1.9	4.5
1980	5.6	7.0	2.0	6.0
1981	6.5	7.5	2.2	8.0
1982	7.9	9.5	2.4	9.3
1983[2]	8.4	9.8	2.7	10.1

Notes:
1   Adjusted by OECD to secure comparability between countries.
2   First nine months.
Source:
OECD, *Economic Outlook*, December 1983, table R.12.

Western Europe and Japan again display a different pattern to the USA. In Japan, the rate of increase of unemployment is fairly similar to that in the USA but the absolute level is far lower throughout. So, from the viewpoint of the system as a whole, Japan has acted to cushion the extent of mass unemployment, but has had little impact on its rising trend. Europe, on the other hand, began with a lower unemployment rate than the USA and now has a higher rate. So it has contributed more to the problem of rising joblessness, in a statistical sense at least, than have the other blocs.

Unemployment results from a mismatch between the numbers of job vacancies and of those seeking work. The number of people after jobs in turn depends on both the rate of growth of the population of working age and any changes in the proportion of that group seeking work. Once again, experiences in Western Europe and Japan differed from that in the USA.

The increase in the proportion of the adult population of working age seeking employment (the *participation rate*) was the net outcome of quite different trends for men and women. The male participation rate fell, mainly because men began to retire earlier. In Germany – the extreme case – the percentage of 60- to 64-year-old men in or seeking work dropped from 75 in 1970 to only 40 in 1979. Female participation rose enough to more than offset this decline. In our view, this shows the remarkable resilience of the shift in social attitudes towards, and especially by,

Table 3.11　Population, labour force and employment 1960–82

	Average annual percentage growth rates		
	1960–8	1968–73	1973–82
Population aged 15 to 64			
USA	1.6	1.8	1.6
EEC	0.6	0.5	0.7
Japan	2.0	1.1	0.8
Advanced capitalist countries	1.1	1.2	1.1
Labour force			
USA	1.7	2.2	2.3
EEC	0.1	0.5	0.7
Japan	1.4	1.0	0.9
Advanced capitalist countries	1.0	1.3	1.4
Employment			
USA	1.9	1.9	1.7
EEC	0.1	0.5	0.2
Japan	1.5	1.0	0.7
Advanced capitalist countries	1.1	1.2	0.8

Source:
OECD, *Historical Statistics*, 1960–81, tables 1.2, 1.3, 1.6; OECD *Employment Outlook*, tables 4 and 5.

Table 3.12　Participation rates in advanced capitalist countries 1960–82[1]

	1960	1968	1973	1979	1982
Total	69.7	68.1	68.5	70.2	70.4
Women	46.8	47.6	49.7	54.4	55.9
Men	93.5	89.5	87.8	86.2	85.2

Note:
1 Percentage of population aged between 15 and 64 who are in the labour force (employed or registered unemployed).
Sources:
OECD, *Historical Statistics*, 1960–81, tables 2.6, 2.7, 2.8; OECD, *Employment Outlook*, table 3.B.

women engaging in waged labour which occurred in the boom years. The New Right is fighting a losing battle in its attempt to drive women back into the home.

The leap in unemployment over the last decade hit different groups unevenly, and the impact has varied from bloc to bloc. Perhaps the most dramatic development has been an unparalleled jump in youth unemployment. Many governments have publicly agonized over the potential implications of this development. Its effect has been felt far more in Western Europe than elsewhere, and has given rise to much alarm. Belgium's labour minister has asked rhetorically, 'who can say when we will reach the point when the flames start?'[7]

For workers, unemployment has been the outstanding feature of the last decade. But capital has been more concerned with low profits. By 1981, business profitability in Japan stood at only 44% of its 1970 peak. Europe fared a little bit

Table 3.13   Youth unemployment rates 1973–82

| | Percentages of youth labour forces | |
	1973	1982[1]
USA	9.9	17.0
Japan	2.3	4.4
France	4.0	20.3
Germany	1.0	7.0[2]
Italy	12.6	27.4[2]
UK	3.3	19.8[2]

Notes:
1   Age 16 to 24.
2   1981.
Source:
OECD, *Labour Force Statistics*, 1970–81.

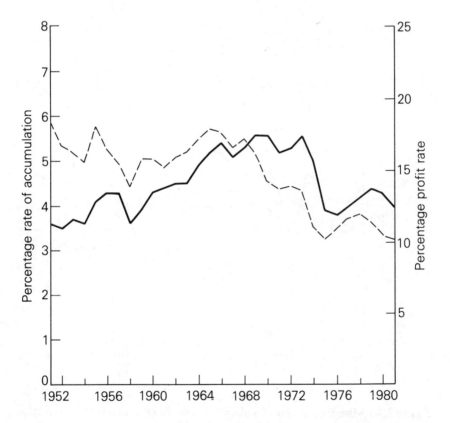

Figure 3.3   Business accumulation and profit rates in advanced capitalist countries 1951–81
Source: Armstrong *et al.*, *Capitalism Since World War II*.

better at 47% of the 1960 peak. This sharp decline in profitability is the key to the fall-off in accumulation which in turn explains lower economic growth and rising unemployment. Accumulation has fallen off far more in Western Europe and Japan than in the USA. By 1982, Japanese business accumulation had fallen to 5.7% per year, less than half the rate in the early seventies. In Western Europe, it was down from 5.5% per year to 3.1%. In the USA, by contrast, the 4% achieved in 1980 equalled the rate in the early seventies. It still stood at 3.2% in 1982.

The contrast is particularly great in manufacturing. By 1980, the rate of manufacturing accumulation in Western Europe and Japan had fallen to a half or less of that achieved in the 1960s. In the USA, it was running at double the 1960s rate and close to that achieved in Japan (double the rate in Western Europe). So, the late 1970s saw a depressed rate of accumulation in Japan and Western Europe putting a drag on the system as a whole.

Developments in the relative competitiveness of the three blocs are more complex. The crucial determinant of underlying, long-term changes in competitiveness is relative productivity growth. Despite a considerable slow-down, Japan and Western Europe run the USA ragged in this regard. In the context of a marked

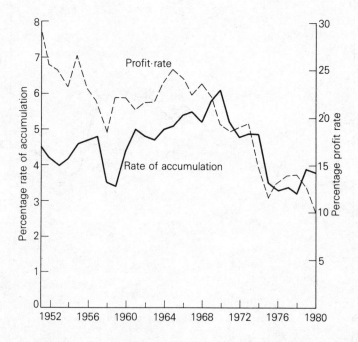

Figure 3.4 Manufacturing accumulation and profit rates in advanced capitalist countries 1951–80
Source: Armstrong *et al.*, *Capitalism Since World War II.*

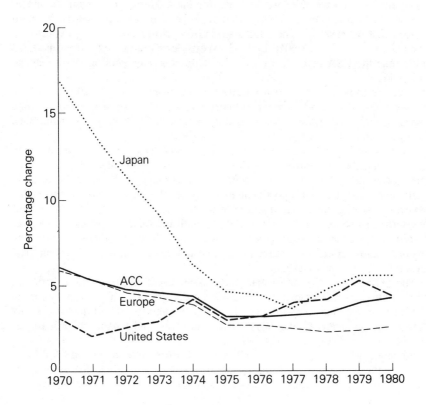

Figure 3.5 Manufacturing accumulation 1970–80[1]
Note: 1 Growth rate of gross fixed capital stock.
Source: Armstrong *et al.*, *Capitalism Since World War II*

Table 3.14   The productivity slowdown 1960–81

	Average annual percentage growth rates		
	Europe	Japan	USA
Manufacturing output per hour			
1960–73	5.7	10.5	3.4
1973–81	4.2	5.8	1.6
Gross domestic product per head			
1960–73	4.3	8.4	2.0
1973–81	1.9	2.9	0.1

Source:
Armstrong *et al.*, *Capitalism Since World War II.*

fall in the rate of growth of world trade in manufactures (down from an annual rate of 10.8% during the boom to one of 5.1% between 1973 and 1981), Western Europe lost out heavily. The EEC's share of world manufacturing exports fell from 67.5% in 1973 to 60% in 1981. West Germany had exported one-third more than the USA in 1973; by 1982 its share was only a couple of percentage points higher.

Over the same period, Japan's share shot up from 14.4% to 19.6%. Where as West Germany had exported almost two-thirds more manufactures than Japan in 1973, by 1980 Japan was only around 0.2% behind its main West European rival.

The rise in Japan's share was primarily a product of its rapid productivity growth, and hence improved competitiveness. But it was also essential to the stability of the system. Japan's import bill for primary products, and especially fuel, were boosted disproportionately to those of other countries during the seventies; selling more manufactures was the only viable solution. But neither Western Europe nor the USA were happy with the logic of events. They tried to resist the invasion of Japanese cars and videos. This response has been the major impetus behind a growth in protectionism (attempts to keep other countries' exports out of your markets).

The percentage of trade in manufactures covered by one or more forms of protectionist control rose from 13 in 1974 to 30 in 1982. The most important device employed has been the negotiation of 'voluntary' export quotas, usually (though by no means exclusively) between the EEC and Japan, which is cast as the *bête noire* of advanced capitalism.

So much for relations between Western Europe and Japan, and for those between these two blocs and the system as a whole. But what of developments between the classes within these two major blocs of capital accumulation?

Class Struggle and the End of the Post-war Boom

A number of trends are discernible. One is a reduction in industrial militancy on the part of workers. This is perhaps most apparent in Western Europe, which was rocked by wage explosions at the close of the sixties. But a similar downturn occurred in Japan too. Western European employers – desperate because faced with low profits, and yet emboldened by the decline in worker militancy – have opted to go on the offensive. They have tried among other things to force through changes in work practices, attacking staffing (often sexistly referred to as 'manning') levels. The basic aim is to try and reimpose a degree of authority over the work process sufficient to restore profitability, capitalist confidence and hence the basis for rapid and sustainable accumulation.

The cutting edge of their offensive has been directed towards imports of manufactures from Japan. They hope to eventually replace the importation of Japanese video recorders with Japanese management techniques. Ford has so far come the cleanest. It launched its assault on the western labour movement with the slogan 'After Japan'. The fact that the rate of profit remains low is the best indication that western employers have so far failed to achieve this objective.

Table 3.15 Days occupied in strikes 1953–82[1]

	1953–61	1962–6	1967–71	1972–6	1977–81	1982
Japan	45	25	19	21	5	2
France	41	32	350	34	23	26
Germany	7	3	8	3	8	0
Italy	64	134	161	200	151	192
UK	28	23	60	97	112	47

Note:
1 Average number of days per year occupied in strikes per 100 workers in industry and transport.
Source:
Employment Gazette, October 1963, October 1972, March 1983, March 1984.

This continuing stalemate is the key to recent political developments in Western Europe. The consensus politics of the long post-war boom have been radically undermined by the economic developments of the last decade. Certain parties of the right, most notably the British Conservatives under Thatcher, have responded by openly abandoning the Butskellite consensus in favour of nakedly pro-capitalist policies. Few workers' parties, and certainly none in power, have been as radical.

The main problem faced by social democrats anxious to retain the framework of post-war consensus politics is the erosion of the high profits which characterized the boom, and thereby gave spurious credence to the effectiveness of 'Keynesian' policies. All such parties which have come to power in Western Europe in the last decade have fallen foul of the new, changed circumstances. They have discovered that, try as hard as they may, it is impossible to juggle policies so as to remain within all the old, previously agreed parameters. That is a valuable lesson. New games mean breaking old rules. The question is always: which? Unfortunately, come the crunch (or even earlier) workers' parties have invariably opted to junk the 'rules' which benefited the workers, so as not to breach those which protected capital.

The only hope for the Western European labour movements (and our Japanese comrades) lies in an explicit reversal of these priorities. That alone could provide the material basis for a socialist transformation of society.

Summary and Prospects

Under capitalism, accumulation – and hence prosperity, employment and social stability – depends ultimately on capitalists' ability to exercise enough authority in the workplace to ensure smooth and profitable production. Focusing on this central relationship between the classes gives shape to the saga of the reconstruction, boom, crisis and stagnation of the West European and Japanese economies since 1945.

But, whilst the key to understanding the past, such a focus is no crystal ball when it comes to the future. In retrospect, history often seems inevitable. But at crucial points during the last 40 years, future prospects seemed highly uncertain. Post-war radicalism was contained and then defeated in Western Europe and Japan because capitalist forces ultimately proved equal to the task. Looking back, we can weigh up fairly accurately the strength and weaknesses of the combatants. But any contemporary assessment could only have been provisional. The strengths of the forces would be fully revealed only in the clash of events. The same is true today.

The relative stagnation of the last decade has been the product of a class stalemate. Capitalists have been unable to repeat their post-1947 achievements. Workers have been unable to restore full employment; any party elected on that platform has capitulated to the logic of capitalist crisis and opted for retrenchment, rather than break with the rules of the game.

This situation may persist for some time. 'Underperformance', like that of the last ten years, need not be unstable. New products and processes may promote steady if weak accumulation, despite idle capacity. Even modest productivity gains permit some rise in living standards for the employed, despite lengthening dole queues. Japan, and to a lesser extent the European powerhouse of West Germany, may be able to expand further at the expense of rivals.

Nevertheless, neither capitalists nor workers find the situation satisfactory. Sections of both are likely to intensify efforts to shift the balance of forces decisively in their favour.

Unsurprisingly, this process has proceeded furthest in the weakest of the West European economies – the UK. Thatcherism represents a radical – though to date unsuccessful – attempt to crush labour. The left of the British Labour Party and a section of the trade-union movement (notably the National Union of Miners leadership) have shown themselves unwilling to sacrifice workers' interests on the altar of capitalist logic. Such forces will be in the forefront of the struggle to build a viable socialist alternative to stagnation and decay.

Notes

1 P. Samuelson, 'Full Employment after the War', in S. Harris (ed.), *Post-war Economic Problems* (New York, McGraw-Hill, 1943), p. 51.
2 J. Schumpeter, 'Capitalism in the Post-war World', in Harris, *Post-war Economic Problems*, p. 120.
3 Unless otherwise stated, all data in this piece, including tables and charts, are taken from P. Armstrong, A. Glyn and J. Harrison, *Capitalism Since World War II: the making and breakup of the great boom* (London, Fontana, 1984), which also contains a more detailed exposition and defence of the analysis.
4 Quoted in Y. Saint-Jours, 'France', in P. Kohler and H. Zacher (eds), *The Evolution of Social Insurance 1881–1981* (London, Frances Pinter, 1982), p. 122.
5 Quoted in G. Rimlinger, *Welfare Policy and Industrialisation in Europe, America and Russia* (New York, Wiley, 1971), p. 144.
6 R. Herding *Job Control and Union Structure* (Rotterdam, Rotterdam University Press, 1972), pp. 329–30.
7 Quoted in the *Financial Times*, 17 January 1983.

4

The New International Division of Labour

ANKIE HOOGVELT

The term 'new international division of labour' has become current since the mid-1970s. It refers to the relocation of industrial production from the traditional centres of world industrial activity to new emerging centres. These centres are located in Southern Europe, in parts of Latin America and in parts of Southeast Asia; there are even a few emerging new centres in parts of Eastern Europe. These countries are now variously referred to as the newly industrializing countries, the newly industrialized countries or the semi-industrialized countries. As we shall see, together they form a second ring of industrial activity around the old centres, and testify to a widening circumference of an increasingly more integrated, more interdependent and yet more multi-polarizing world capitalist system.

The Newly Industrializing Countries

Whenever there is talk of a new phenomenon, it is helpful to compare its dimensions with the old, and to capture the character, consistency and relevance of the historical trends involved.

The 'old' international division of labour imposed under colonialism was one where the production of manufactures was almost exclusively the preserve of a handful of advanced industrial countries. A League of Nations document published in 1945 estimated the percentage distribution of world manufacturing production in 1926–9 as follows: USA 42.9, Germany 11.6, UK. 9.4, France 6.6, Russia 4.3, Italy 3.3, Canada 2.4, Belgium 1.9, Sweden 1, Japan 2.5, Finland 0.9, India 1.2 and other countries 13.2.[1]

The countries which are today referred to as the 'developing countries' or the 'Third World' were the producers of so-called primary – that is, unprocessed – raw materials and agricultural products, and the exchange between the two groups – as a result – was unequal. The League of Nations document refers to Africa, Asia (excluding the USSR), Latin America and southeastern Europe as the 'economically young areas' and laments the fact that in 1926–9 these areas represented 69 per cent of the world's population, but only 10 per cent of its manufacturing industry.[2] This figure of 10 per cent included the manufacturing industry of Japan which accounted for a quarter of the total. So if we subtract this quarter and deduct a not unreasonable 0.5 per cent for southeastern Europe, we arrive at a figure of 7 per cent as the Third World's share of world manufacturing output. Fifty years later, at the time of the Second General Conference of UNIDO (United Nations Industrial Development Organization), held at Lima in 1975, this very same figure of 7 per cent again crops up as the Third World's share of world industrial output. The Third World, of course, today still has about two-thirds of the world's population, this time without the 100 million Japanese being included.

Emboldened by this drama of a seemingly unmoving history, the Lima Conference resolved to call for a change of this distribution to 75:25 by the year 2000 as the *minimum* needed to reduce world inequalities to more tolerable proportions. The 25 per cent became widely known as the LIMA Target and it was included as one of the six main Third World demands for a new international economic order (NIEO) adopted by the General Assembly of the United Nations.

The demands for a new international economic order – which revolve around more equitable economic exchange relationships between the old industrialized countries and the Third World – were coined at a time when awareness of a new international division of labour, and of newly industrializing countries (NIC's), invaded the consciousness of the people and the governments of the old industrialized countries. This awareness was the more painfully and negatively shaped by the circumstance that economic recession, deindustrialization and mass unemployment were accompanied by a significant import penetration of industrial products from the so-called newly industrialized countries. However, a major reason for the concern over manufactured exports from developing countries in general and the NICs in particular is that they are part of a general expansion of such exports from 'new sources' which include Japan, Eastern Europe, Spain, Portugal and Greece as well as some Third World NICs. By 1977 all these new sources together accounted for nearly half of US and EEC imports of non-chemical manufactures, while US–EEC trade itself accounted for just 20 per cent of each import market.[3]

In the public mind, the newly industrializing world was increasingly identified with the Third World, or at any rate a privileged part of it. Practically overnight, the objects of our charity, pity or guilt turned into rivals: competitors for our jobs and markets. Gone were the days when 'trade not aid' had featured so prominently on the agendas of progressive movements all over Britain. Instead, indiscriminate measures of protectionism became the stuff that our 'alternative strategies' were made of.[4]

Casual empiricism on the part of various national and international bodies, each of which recognizes a different list of NICs, has not helped in this confusion. The Organization for Economic Cooperation and Development (OECD), for example, has a top list of 10 NICs and a second list of another 13, selected on the basis of three criteria: rapid penetration of the world market of manufactures; a rising share of industrial employment and an increase in real gross domestic product (GDP) per capita relative to the more advanced countries. Its top list of 10 includes four countries in Southern Europe.[5] The World Bank, on the other hand, restricting itself to a characterization of countries where manufacturing accounts for 20 per cent of total GDP, comes up with a list of 16 'semi-industrialized' countries. In addition to the four Southern European countries, Israel and Turkey are also included – two countries which are difficult to classify at the best of times.[6] Britain's Foreign and Commonwealth Office has worked with an even wider list including Israel and Malta from the Mediterranean, and Poland, Romania and Hungary from Eastern Europe.[7]

The inconsistency of this classification is all the more unhelpful because throughout these official documents source data are presented which refer to the NICs as a group, often without reference to the original selection of countries. In secondary literature, the distortion becomes magnified when authors collate data canvassed from different international organizations, without realizing that they are talking about different countries. In this essay I shall restrict myself to a list of eight Third World NICs (see table 4.1). I have selected these eight because, of all Third World countries, they are the ones that originally appeared on the OECD's top list and on the World Bank's list. Note, however, that Taiwan, having been expelled from the International Monetary Fund and the World Bank in 1980 when the People's Republic of China decided to join has – for its sins – fallen off the record of all World Bank documentation. Because of Taiwan's previous recorded importance as an NIC, this has significantly distorted the year-on-year comparisons of NIC performance. In what follows I shall mainly use the World Bank's World Development Report 1983 as a data source, but I shall include data for Taiwan, obtained elsewhere.[8] Finally, it is worth mentioning that India is in the paradoxical situation of being at once one of the poorest countries in the world, but in terms of manufacturing output and exports, sometimes referred to as a newly industrializing country. In line with the World Bank's classification I have not here included India as an NIC.

The reader will now already be aware that there is little coincidence either of fact or of interest between the Third World's demands for a new international economic order (including a new division of world industrial production) and the emerging new international division of labour. In the next section this lack of coincidence will become still further clarified when we analyse the industrialization record of the Third World.

Industrialization in the Third World: the Record

We can assess the record of industrialization in the Third World on the basis of four criteria:

1 The degree of *structural* transformation of the national economies in terms of the relative contribution of *manufacturing output to GDP*;
2 The degree of structural transformation in terms of the relative absorption of *labour in the manufacturing* sector, for there is little point in having a rapidly advancing manufacturing sector if few people participate in this sector, and, as so often happens, the majority are marginalized from the productive process;
3 The changing *composition of exports*, for this is a measure of a potentially more equal economic relationship with the world market in general, and the advanced industrial countries in particular;

Table 4.1 The newly industrialising countries of the Third World[A]

	Population 1981 Millions	% share of industry in GDP 1981	% share of manufacturing industries in GDP 1981	% population employed in industry 1981	% of all developing economies' manufacturing exports 1981	% share of OECD countries' direct investment stock in all developing countries (1978)[C]	of which in the manufacturing sector[D]	% share of multinationals in all manufacturing exports[E]	% share of multinationals in all manufacturing industry[E]	Debt outstanding (1982)[F]
S. Korea	38.9	39	28	29	12.0	1.8	73.4	27 (1978)	11	$39 bn
Hong Kong	4.0	31	24	57	13.9	2.5	100.0	16 (1972)	–	–
Singapore	2.4	36	30	39	8.0	2.1	100.0	92 (1978)	83	–
Taiwan[B]	18.1	45	33	42	13.8	2.1	100.0	–	–	–
Brazil	120.5	37	27	24	5.9	15.1	77.1	43 (1969)	44	$89 bn
Mexico	71.2	37	22	26	2.6	6.7	76.9	34 (1974)	39	$85 bn
Argentina	28.2	38	25	28	1.4	3.7	–	30 (1969)	31	$38 bn
Philippines	49.6	37	25	17	1.6	2.0	54.3	5 (1970)	–	$16 bn

Source
A.   World Bank; World Development Report 1983; various tables (except where indicated).
B.   Figures for Taiwan are taken from Taiwan Statistical Data Book 1983.
C.   OECD, International Investments and Multinational Enterprises, 1981.
D.   J. M. Stopford and J. H. Dunning: Multinationals; company performance and Global trends.
(Note: the percentages for Singapore and Hong Kong are estimates, and according to correspondence which the writer has had with the authors, they are probably wild over-estimates. But even if these percentages are lowered, it would not alter the main thrust of the argument which is that in 1978 between one third and one half of FDI in the manufacturing sector in the Third World was absorbed by the group of 8 NIC countries.)
E.   UN Centre for Transnational Corporations, Transnational Corporations in World Development, Third Survey, 1983.
F.   *Guardian*, 16 December 1982.

4   the *qualitative pattern of the industrialization* process, because this will tell
us something about the extent to which industrialization will take root as a
self-propelling indigenous force, or to what extent it is a mere by-product
of industrial development going on elsewhere.

1

In respect of *structural* transformation there is little doubt that the Third World
– when viewed as a whole – has made significant advances over the past 30 years.
Whereas in 1950, the share of manufactures in the combined GDP of developing
countries was no more than 12 per cent, in 1980 it was 20 per cent.[9]

However, this structural transformation has been very uneven between the Third
World economies, and raises serious questions regarding the continued relevance
of the term 'Third World' as an adequate descriptive category. At one end of
the spectrum there are some 48 countries containing about one quarter of the Third
World population where industrialization has hardly begun, and is still below or
at the 12 per cent mark. At the other extreme we find the eight newly industrializing
countries of the Third World, where the contribution of the manufacturing sector
to GDP ranges between 25–35 per cent, entirely comparable to that of the 'old'
industrialized countries. As a matter of fact, the old industrial countries have over
the past 20 years experienced 'deindustrialization', an average decline in manufacturing output relative to GDP of 5 per cent since 1960 and an even greater
decline of labour employed in industry.

The unevenness of industrial progress between Third World countries was
succinctly put in the UNCTAD (United Nations Conference on Trade and Development) annual trade report of 1982: 'fewer than 10 newly industrialized developing
countries accounted in 1980 for nearly 30 per cent of developing countries' GDP
and nearly half of their manufacturing output, even though their share of the
population of the underdeveloped world was no more than 10 per cent.'[10] The
big gap between the two groups is largely filled with the near 50 per cent of the
developing countries' population who live in India, Pakistan and China. And
although industrialization is taking place in these countries as measured by relative
and absolute size of the manufacturing sector, as well as composition of exports,
the impact of this process of industrialization on the distribution of employment
as between agriculture and industry remains insignificant.

2

Unfortunately, when we examine the *labour absorption rate*, there are no data
series available in respect of international comparisons of persons employed in
manufacturing industry. What we do have (from the World Bank) is a measure
relating to the number of people employed in industry (which includes besides
manufacturing also construction and mining). It is interesting that, while for the
old industrial countries the percentage share of industrial employment in total
employment matches the contribution of industry to GDP (the weighted average
for the industrial market economies group being 36 per cent for the industry to
GDP ratio and 38 per cent for the industrial employment to total employment
ratio), for the newly industrializing countries there is a gap of 11 per cent with
only 28 per cent of people employed in industry as against a weighted average

of 39 per cent industrial output in GDP. This gap is even bigger for the World Bank's middle-income group, suggesting for all but the three notorious 'labour exporting' economies, (Singapore, Taiwan and Hong Kong) a pattern of industrialization unable to absorb labour, because of the capital-intensive nature of the industrialization process.

3

The tell tale signs of a new international division of labour relate to the *economic exchange* between the old industrial centres and the Third World: while for the Third World as a group the participation rate in world industrial *production* has remained quite static over a long period, as we have seen, its share in world manufacturing *exports* has grown from practically zero in the colonial period to 6 per cent in 1960 and an estimated 11 per cent in 1979. In fact in this latter period, exports of manufactures from the Third World as a group grew faster than either world manufacturing output, or world manufacturing exports. Excluding oil, the composition of merchandise exports from all developing countries as a group changed from one where in 1955 only 20 per cent of the value was contributed by manufactures as against 40 per cent in 1975.[11]

But here too, the distribution in export performance has been so uneven between Third World countries as to make a nonsense of the practice of speaking of the developing countries as a group. In 1980, the total value of all the world-market economies' manufacturing exports came to just over one trillion dollars. Of this total the old industrialized countries contributed 87.4 per cent, and all the 'developing' world 12.6 per cent. But of this 12.6 per cent, the eight Third World NICs took 7.3 per cent while the four southern European NICs took 2.7 per cent, leaving a pitiful 2.6 per cent for the rest of the Third World – including India.[12]

4

Finally in this empirical assessment of the international economic order, a word about the pattern of industrialization, both in the Third World in general and in the newly industrializing countries in particular.

A great deal has been written about the dependent nature of the process of industrialization embarked upon by most developing countries soon after their liberation from formal colonial rule. In the 1950s, the eloquent appraisal by various UN specialists, like Raoul Prebisch,[13] put paid to the ideologically conceived wisdom of the theory of comparative advantage, upon which the old international division of labour had rested. They exposed the inherently unequal nature of the exchange between, on the one hand, poor countries trading unprocessed primary commodities, and on the other rich countries trading manufactures. A strategy based on import-substitutive industrialization was – for a time – seen as the only path to development. In brief, this was a development strategy based on the *home* production of hitherto *imported* finished manufactures. Within a decade, however, the strategy of import substitution was itself widely criticized by both conventional and radical economists. While conventional economists debated the many domestic inefficiencies and costs associated with high levels of protection, the radical economists focused on the policy's propensity to generate new forms of external dependency and the associated widening international and domestic inequalities which together distorted the industrialization process. As countries lacking in technological and industrial infrastructure tried to increase their domestic production of finished manufactures, so they had to encourage foreign companies to set up the production facilities for them. The result was a pattern of industrialization subject to foreign ownership and control, frequently slotted into the multinational companies' global strategies of process and product specialization as well as marketing, dependent on foreign inputs of intermediate goods and know-how for which non-market prices had to be paid (so-called 'technological rents'), a return flow of profits (dividends, royalties) which over time exceeded the original value of the capital brought in, and, last but not least, a choice of production technology compatible with the advanced countries' organic composition of capital (i.e. very capital intensive) but unable to offer much employment for the masses of the population. And so, while – on paper and in national accounting terms – economic progress was being made, domestic inequalities widened and increasing sections of the poor were excluded from the development process. In 1964, the Brazilian President summed it up with the legendary words, 'Brazil is developing but the people are not'. Some radical writers saw the entire thrust of the ideology of developmentalism and modernization with its centre-piece of industrialization as nicely timed and construed to fit the changing needs of the leading branches and countries of world capitalism for new market outlets for producer goods.[14]

After a more or less promising initial start in the majority of the smaller developing countries, the widening social inequalities and the resulting narrowing of the domestic market put a break on the policy of import substitution. The need to contain popular discontent following this failure led in many countries – especially in Latin America – to the rise of military and bureaucratic authoritarian regimes.

By contrast the apparent industrial success of the newly industrializing countries was due mainly to two kinds of conditions, each facilitating a further physical expansion of industrial activity.

1.   There were a number of countries which had a sufficiently large potential domestic market to stimulate new forms of cooperation with transnational capital, which deepened the industrial structure and which took the import-substitutive strategy one step further into the basic-goods sector. Brazil, Mexico, Argentina, India, South Africa and Turkey are examples of this strategy. The consolidation of bureaucratic authoritarian regimes, however, occurred here too because the new dependency created by foreign penetration and control over the industrial producer-goods sector increasingly had to rely on the state as direct agent and ally in production. The counterpart of this process was the expulsion of sections of the national bourgeoisie as well as the working class from the productive process. This second stage of import substitution tended to suffer from the same externally induced distortions as the first stage; after a while it too ran up against the same bottleneck of a restricted domestic market. At this historical juncture which was reached in the larger Latin American economies in the late sixties and early seventies, there were real political options available, as Latin American *dependista* writers Cardoso and Faletto have pointed out.[15] The choice was between, on the one hand, a widening of the domestic market through some degree of social reform and a reorganization of production relations coupled with substantive democratization, or – on the other hand – a redirection of the industrialization process towards exports coupled with a tightening of the grip of the autocratic political machine. For a number of reasons – the new integration of world industrial production on a global scale by transnational capital, and the need to earn foreign exchange imposed by debt-peonage (both of which we shall discuss below) as well as the rigidity of the internal class structure, – the 'successful' NICs all opted for the export-orientation strategy. In this way, instead of seizing the opportunity to consolidate their by now relatively well-advanced industrial production structure by integrating it within the wider domestic economy and society, many became instead 'sub-imperialist states', 'relay stations' or 'staging-posts' for transnational capital, penetrating with their industrial products the markets of other less-developed countries. And so we find German Volkswagen kits made in Brazil and sold for assembly to Nigeria.[16]

2.   Export-oriented industrialization was adopted right from the start – in the early 1960s – by a small group of South-east Asian economies (Singapore, Hong Kong, Taiwan, the Philippines and Malaysia). Skipping the import-substitution phase, the strategy involved attracting foreign 'branch plant' investments by transnational enterprises. Productive activity in these branch plants consists of very specific, labour-intensive, usually assembly-type operations, which are wholly dependent on imported intermediate goods, equipment and raw materials, and whose output is entirely destined for re-export. The success of this latter group of countries in attracting such 'split-site' production is due almost entirely to the availability of a cheap and relatively docile labour force and the presence of autocratic governments willing to suppress it, as well as willing to offer favourable tax and other legislation to foreign investors, in especially designated areas called *free-trade*, or export-processing, zones. A free-trade zone is like a country within a country, fenced off by barbed wire or concrete walls from the rest of the territory and guarded in some cases by a 'zone police'. A survey for the Asian Productivity Organization (APO), defines the free-trade zone as 'an enclave in terms of customs – territorial aspects and possibly other aspects such as total or partial exemption from laws and decrees of the country concerned'.[17]

By 1980 there were 53 free-trade zones in developing countries (out of a total of some 80 the world over) employing just under one million people.[18] Because production in these zones is part of the multinational corporations' global product and distribution flows, they are largely irrelevant to the establishment of an integrated industrial complex in these countries, for there are few if any linkages with the host economy. There are two further reasons why this type of labour-export oriented industrialization is highly suspect. For one thing, competition between developing countries for such investments is at present so intense as to nullify any social advances that have been made in host-government bargaining with transnational capital over so-called 'performance requirements' (i.e. local value-added criteria, training of local personnel, ownership patterns and so on). The cheapness and the degree of oppression of labour are being used in an ever more ruthless struggle to attract foreign investment. Second, as a result of cut-throat competition now taking place amongst the leading branches of world capitalist industry (notably in the electronics and computer sectors), the competitive advantage of labour-exporting less developed countries is being eroded because of automation. Some key industries have already returned to the developed countries, including garment and textile industries, where computerization has eliminated many of the labour-intensive tasks, once the competitive preserve of cheap labour economies.[19] A major impetus for such 'relocation back north' will be the neo-protectionist measures now gradually and stealthily being reintroduced in all OECD countries and which effectively place import restrictions on imports from the developing world.

Industrial Relocation and the Transnationalization of Capital

Although the extent of multinational corporate involvement in the industrialization process of the Third World varies, there is little doubt that the multinational corporations have played a significant and dominant role in the relocation of industrial activity from the old industrial centres to the new. All newly industrializing countries, including those in the Third World, have in the past 20 years pursued aggressive 'open door' policies, encouraging private foreign investment in their industrial sector, and more especially in the export-oriented part of that sector. These policies have paid off in so far as they have succeeded in attracting a disproportionate share of all foreign direct investment in the manufacturing sector of the Third World. The degree of concentration is attested in table 4.1, column 6. In 1978, 65 per cent of all private foreign direct investment stock in the Third World was absorbed in manufacturing industry. From table 4.1 we can see that 36 per cent of all private foreign direct investment stock was located in the eight Third World NICs and the next column tells us that easily two-thirds of this again was concentrated in the manufacturing sector, suggesting that between one-third and one-half of all foreign direct investment in Third World industry is concentrated in those eight countries. Equally telling are the next two columns which give estimates of the share of industry and exports accounted for by the multinational corporations in the Third World NICs. About one-third of manufacturing exports from NICs takes place under the wings of the multinational corporation. And an EEC estimate for *all* developing countries' manufacturing exports puts the figure even higher at 45 per cent.[20]

So much for the data. The more interesting question is why, and why did multinational corporations decide to relocate certain forms of industrial activity to specific countries when they did?

The answer to these questions lies in a very complex set of interacting political, technological, financial and economic forces. Together they have combined to affect a profound transformation in the nature of the world capitalist system: the *forces* of production and the *relations* of production have become organized on a global scale, with far-reaching consequences both for capital–state relations and for capital–labour relations. In what follows, I shall describe the political, technological, financial and economic forces in turn, and their interrelationship.

*The internationalization of capital and the universalization of the
nation state in the post-war period.*

Whenever writers describe the enormous expansion of post-war multinational
corporate investments, three yardsticks are commonly used:

1 The faster growth of such investments as compared with the growth of world
   product;
2 The faster growth of the overseas or 'foreign' production by multinational
   corporations compared with the growth of world trade;
3 The expanding geographical spread of multinational companies as measured
   by the number of affiliates they control in different countries.

A favourite measure of number 3 is the fact that whereas in 1950, 80 per cent
of the world's largest 250 multinationals had affiliates in fewer than six countries,
and a mere 1 per cent controlled affiliates in over 20 countries, by 1976 this ratio
had reversed: with only 16 per cent of these largest multinationals having affiliates
in fewer than six countries and 20 per cent having affiliates in more than 20.[21]
Rarely mentioned in the use of such empirical indicators is that during the same
period, the number of nation states increased even faster: the number of nation
states has trebled from 50 to 150 since World War II. While not wishing to dispute
the fact that the growth and dominance of multinational corporations is the single
most important development of the post-war economy, we need to make the point
that this growth and development is, paradoxically, at least in part a function
of the universalization of the nation state itself.

Indeed, the internationalization of capital has been speeded up by the emergence
of many different nations. We mean this not merely in a literal and legalistic
sense of sovereignty having been accorded to a number of territories which were
previously administered as one colony: say one India having subsequently become
three: India, Pakistan and Bangladesh. We also mean it in a political and economic
sense: the concept of the nation state in the post-war period carried more than
a mere notion of sovereignty; it involved a *neo-mercantilist* conception of the
state as having responsibility for the administration and development of the national
economy. It is today the universally recognized task of the state to make the nation
'stronger', in every sense; politically, militarily and economically. This neo-
mercantilist conception applies equally to old and new states.

The corollary of the universalization of the neo-mercantilist state has been a
multiplication of customs, economic legislation and currency areas, which forced
multinational companies into a counter-offensive: 'internalizing' in rapid
succession commodity and final product markets, technology and intermediate
goods markets, and finally financial markets as well. The basic proposition of the
theory of internalization as an explanatory theory of the growth of firms *in general*,
is that market imperfections and failures, particularly in the buying and selling
of essential inputs and outputs, as well as diseconomies associated with the bringing
together of interdependent activities, lead to so-called 'transaction costs' which
the firm will want to eliminate by bringing these markets within its own organizational structure (thereby replacing market processes by administrative fiat), and

undertaking these transactions itself. At the same time, firms which have a specific advantage such as monopolistic ownership of a particular technology, will want to benefit from this advantage by internalizing that asset as opposed to selling it to another producer. While internalization theory was originally developed to apply to the multi-plant uni-national firm, it is even more relevant as a theory explaining the growth of the multinational firm. For, with the multiplication of nation states all eager to add their own myriad forms of government fiat to already-existing market imperfections, the incentive became all the greater for multi-nationals to effectively internalize the world market for commodities, finished products, technology and finance.

To give a simple example, tariff barriers erected to encourage domestic industry force the multinational to produce locally what had previously been the subject of cross-border trade. As we have seen in the previous section, this essentially 'defensive' strategy entirely matched the import-substitutive needs of the less-developed countries. But in the immediate post-war period it was also one of the driving forces behind the 'American invasion' of the European countries, who were struggling behind protective measures to reconstruct their war-damaged economies. Already by 1971, the value of 'international production' (that is the value of production by multinationals in countries other than where they originate) was greater than the value of international trade.[22]

This simple example reflects only a first stage in the post-war internationalization of production: one in which MNCs internalize activities so as to circumvent and counteract government fiat in order to protect the markets for their final products. A second stage comes when multinationals start taking full advantage of the diversity of host-country financial, fiscal and economic legislation, and start to *fragment* the production process itself on a global scale, farming out different parts of the production process to different affiliates in different national locations, and integrating this production process in one grand global synergy with each affiliate carrying out some part of the production process but not the whole. This global fragmentation allows multinationals to positively manipulate the '*transfer prices*' of those parts (intermediate goods, product parts, know-how, design, etc.) which are shunted between affiliates, taking due advantage of differences in customs and tax legislation; and all this, in order to maximize profits, not in any particular location but on a *global scale*. The existence of so-called tax-haven countries was a mere added bonus because it allowed the declaration of global profits to occur in locations where corporate taxation was non-existent or extremely low. Throughout the sixties and seventies tax havens such as the Bahamas and Bermudas were amongst the largest recipient countries of inter-national capital flows. Today there is a moderately successful and concerted attempt on the part of national governments to grapple both with the use of such tax havens for corporate profit maximization and with the manipulation of transfer prices. But neither of these attempts will significantly erode the corporate advantages of internalizing international trade flows. For, as long as international patent law prevails, companies will always be able to minutely detail the precise inputs, technology and know-how that go into the making of their patented products, and fix prices for these inputs by administrative fiat. And it is precisely the heavy trafficking in these intermediate inputs that has been the hallmark of corporate global accumulation in the past two decades. The growth of so-called intra-firm trade in intermediate goods and technology has exceeded by a wide margin the growth of world trade. It is estimated that as much as two-fifths of world trade today consists of such intra-firm trade.[23] As one Fiat manager in Nigeria cheerfully commented about the local 95 per cent indigenously owned Fiat assembly plant: the total value of all imported parts, services and components per car assembled in Nigeria adds up to a figure four times the value of a ready-made car from the parent plant in Turin!

It is no coincidence that the leading branches of world industry in the post-war period, namely consumer durables (the motor industry, electrical goods, etc.) pharmaceuticals, and today also the electronics industry, were not only amongst the fastest-growing multinationals but also the ones which developed along the lines of global product and process specialization that we have just described. For it is precisely those products which are a complex composition of many mechanically (and nowadays also electronically) integrated parts which lend themselves most easily to international specialization and global fragmentation. This is a timely reminder that interrelated with the political processes described in this section, technological forces too were responsible for the internationalization of production.

Technological developments

Apart from the advantage of increasing economies of scale associated with long production runs of each component or discrete activity of production, the global fragmentation of production was also stimulated by two other technological developments.

1 The *decomposition* of the production process into simple tasks suitable to be carried out by unskilled labour. This permitted the tapping of vast reservoirs of labour in underdeveloped areas and at a time, moreover, when organized labour in the advanced countries had succeeded in driving up wages (including the social wage) to the point where it had begun to erode the profitability of capital investments there.
2 Technical innovations in three sectors basic to transport and communications. Revolutionary strides in containerized shipping made dispersal of production facilities profitable; improved engineering techniques provided the complex communications network crucial to the speed of operations, and pervasive computer applications made possible the virtually instantaneous data processing vital for maximization of global profits and market shares.

For a while, the transfer of jobs, and of parts of the production process – while fragmented – did raise the possibility of the genuine transfer of technology to the underdeveloped areas. As long as the final product was integrated by way of mechanical engineering, the potential existed for a 'debundling' of the investment package. For instance, host governments eager to increase the local value added of a foreign managed or owned assembly plant, could bargain over the local sourcing of various inputs and components. With a mechanically engineered final product, the component could be disassembled, and local suppliers could be trained up to meet company specifications. In this way some genuine transfer of technology and local know-how, as well as local industrial linkages and multiplier effects, could be won from foreign involvement in the economy.

There is today, however, a reasoned concern that developments in information technology permitting the substitution of discrete components and activities with micro-electronic devices will in turn replace the *mechanically integrated* product with a computer-controlled *systems-integrated* product and production process. Furthermore, the emergence of new forms of global *tele-management* based on integrated systems of trans-border data flows internal to the multinational corporation, is bound to accelerate the hierarchization of international economic relations, and weaken the association between foreign direct investment and the effective transfer of technology still further. On the one hand, the computerization of control functions, of logistic coordination and of financial management will increase the degree of centralization of the multinational firm, reducing the autonomy of local affiliates. On the other hand, the fact that affiliates can access remote engineering and scientific know-how, will mean that they will not need to develop this know-how locally.[24]

Developments in international finance

Until recently analyses of the strategies of multinational corporations have rarely taken into account the internationalization of other types of organizations, in particular banks. From 1945 until the mid-sixties, the international growth of multinational corporations occurred largely through self-financing, that is: direct investment abroad by multinational companies in wholly-owned subsidiaries. From the mid-sixties, this pattern changed quite dramatically to one where external financing through overseas local borrowing became increasingly more important. There are three interrelated forces at work here which were responsible for this change:

1. The development of the Eurodollar (later Eurocurrency) markets vastly increased the store of international funds available for overseas investments, and encouraged an enormous growth of international banking. The Eurodollar market is a legacy of the Bretton Woods monetary system which had elevated the dollar to the status of the world's key reserve currency. Over time this led to an effective overvaluation of the dollar and a consequent accumulation of dollars in European banks. The practical impossibility of converting all these dollars back into so-called 'native' dollars, gave rise to a *novel* banking practice; namely the lending and investing of dollar deposits in Europe and in other parts of the world where chronic balance-of-payments deficits created a need for borrowing in dollar denominations. Between 1960 and 1970 the Eurodollar market grew from 5 billion to about 100 billion.[25] With the recycling of petrodollars after 1974, it grew still faster to about 1,000 billion in 1980. It gives food for thought to compare this 1,000 per cent increase with the near-stagnant world output and trade figures of 40 and 60 per cent respectively in the 1970–80 period.[26]

2. The internationalization of American banks has become a significant feature of the international economic order. In the mid-1960s, the US government initiated various forms of legislation designed to stem the outflow of capital by American multinational corporations. At the time, these American multinationals were responsible for about three-quarters of worldwide foreign direct investments. So as not to hinder their internationalization, most US multinationals chose to borrow from abroad. This in turn, stimulated US banks to set up branches overseas to continue to service their clients (as well as, one might add, participate in the booming Eurodollar business which thus far had been the sole preserve of the European banks). In this connection, there are two further developments in American banking worth mentioning: much of US banking legislation in the past had always been devised to separate banking activities from commercial activities, and to prevent banks from investing long-term finance in industry. In practice, banks could get around that legislation by means of the trust laws which permitted the trust departments of banks to hold and manage the securities of third parties. But it wasn't until 1968 that the 'dyke that separated the sea of commerce from the sea of banking' sprang the main leak. In that year the First National City Bank came up with the idea of creating a holding company structure allowing it to escape from the strict rules of American banking legislation. The novel idea was that the bank would itself become a subsidiary of its own creation: the holding company. Rapidly, the largest US banks adopted the 'one-bank holding company status'. These holding companies permit the banks to offer new types of financial services as well as non-banking services to the corporations in whom they have a financial interest. With one of these new types of financial services, leasing, a gradual transfer of ownership of production facilities from the corporations to the banks is now taking place. Moreover, internationalization proved an excellent means for US banks to increase their shareholdings in multinationals. By establishing so-called 'offshore funds', that is, investment trusts outside the US – usually in a tax haven – the bank, as custodian of the fund's securities, can manage these funds and control them, while it cannot establish an investment trust in the US.[27]

By 1975, American banks provided one-quarter of the long-term financing of US multinational corporations, and about 50 per cent of all their financial resources.[28] As a matter of fact, the growth of what are now referred to as transnational banks including Japanese and European, as well as American, in the past ten years has dwarfed the growth of the multinational corporations. In 1981, the combined assets of the top 100 banks were the equivalent of more than half of global gross domestic product and more than double the combined sales of the top 200 industrial corporations.[29] In their capacity as stockholders, creditors and counsellors, the transnational banks exert a major influence and control over the multinational corporations. Interlocking directorships further cement the close relations between the two; according to one research estimate, 75 per cent of US corporations share at least one director with a bank.[30]

The initiative for the merger between banking and commerce has not wholly come from the banks; another trend has also been noted in the past decade. This is the development of the *financial function* of industrial corporations, involving the setting up by the industrial corporation of finance subsidiaries, insurance companies and even banks. Finance subsidiaries are subsidiaries set up to manage the receivable portfolios of the firm. Paradoxically, the development and importance of finance subsidiaries (invariably the most *centralized* function today in all multinational corporations) owes much to a historical current which contrasts with the one that stimulated the banks into internationalization: the *collapse* of the Bretton Woods system in 1971, the inconvertibility of the dollar and the return of freely fluctuating exchange markets, forced the MNCs to internalize the world's foreign-exchange markets, and offered them the opportunity to make profits not just by producing commodities in different countries and by administering the trade flows between them, but also by manipulating the cross-border financial flows resulting from that trade.

3.   A final component of recent developments in international finance has been the economic nationalism of especially Third World governments which has led to a change in the *equity–debt* ratio of foreign operations inside these countries. In an effort to control foreign operations, host governments have tended to nationalize all or part of such activities and have sought alternative financial resources for them. These alternative financial resources have come from international banks eager to find outlets for accumulated Euro- and petrodollars. While in 1970 foreign direct investments to the Third World were slightly larger than the flows of such *in*direct investments to them, by 1980 the latter ran a clear lead with a ratio of 3:1.[31] The consequence of this changed equity–debt ratio has been the *debt explosion*, and the attendant vulnerability of the international financial community to potential sovereign defaulters.

New distortions

The changed equity–debt ratio of foreign-controlled ventures inside the Third World generates new distortions in the pattern of economic development and industrialization:

1.   The resulting 'debt-peonage' forces governments into ever more aggressive export-oriented patterns of economic development and industrialization. This export bias jeopardizes the chances for national economic integration and the development of local industries geared to meet the needs of the people. What is more, because the debts are denominated in the currencies of the dominant nations of the *capitalist* world, the export orientation will result in an even closer – dependent – relation with the capitalist world market. This excludes new and potentially more beneficial relations with the centrally planned economies of the world.

2.   The changed equity–debt composition can lead to quite grotesque inefficiencies because of the institutional separation of financial responsibility from operational control. It is important here to remember that interest on loan capital constitutes a contractual obligation that needs to be discharged irrespective of the profitability of the enterprise or project for which the obligation was contracted. At the same time, the reduced *equity* exposure of the foreign company which runs the enterprise under management contract and/or technical or service agreement, obviates the need for foreign management to worry about locally assessable profitability criteria, because dividends (i.e. return on equity) are no longer the *raison d'être* of the foreign involvement. Rather, from the parent company's point of view, the local affiliate or joint venture is quintessentially a *trading* partner, from whom it wishes to buy cheap and to whom it wishes to sell dear. The scandal of the Palau electricity generating project is an illustrative case in point.[32] Here, a British firm, International Power Systems Ltd, was reported to have sold the Palau government a power station twice the size needed by that small nation. The project is being financed with an unusual loan structure in which two London-based banks are putting up £32 million, underwritten by the British Government-backed Export Credit Guarantee Department and further guaranteed by a consortium of five international banks. Criticism of the project has centred on the fact that the projections of net profits from the proposed facilities prepared by International Power Systems were unreasonably high and could not be seriously considered as potential revenue to meet Palau's financial commitments under loans. Payment of these loan commitments from the country's general operating funds would virtually eliminate essential public services to the people of Palau.

As this example illustrates, in the case of state-owned ventures, it is extremely difficult to assess the economic viability of projects when government transfers to the state-owned enterprises can forever be called upon to balance the books. The World Bank reports that available data for state-owned enterprises in 24 developing countries in 1977 showed a small operating surplus before depreciation. However, the report continues, '*no account was taken* of interest payments, subsidized input prices, taxes or accumulated arrears. Proper provision for these items and depreciation would show state-owned enterprises in many of these countries to be in deficit.[33] The existence in many developing countries of centralized state financial institutions responsible for the raising of foreign credit and the channeling of this credit to individual state enterprises encourages the malpractice of prejudicing one project's future viability with another project's bad debts: foreign credit raised to finance one project all too easily finds its way into another project's arrears payments. The tightening of the screw of the international debt crisis has occasioned the International Monetary Fund (IMF) and the World Bank to elevate this malpractice to the status of a 'conditionality' norm: in all rescheduling negotiations it is now insisted that central governments of recipient countries accept full responsibility for debts of all public enterprises in their country, including local and regional ones, and irrespective of whether such existing loan agreements had been originally guaranteed by them.[34] In addition, the commercial banks are now insisting that debtor governments assume responsibility for *private*-sector debt too! In several cases – Chile, Argentina – the debtor governments have now done so.[35]

There is clearly very close collaboration between transnational banks, multinational corporations and host-governments, which forms the tripod structure of new international relations of production encasing the new international division of labour. But the second half of the 1980s will also witness a growing 'cooptation' of the states of the advanced countries within this structure (either bilaterally or through multilateral cooperative structures such as the World Bank, IMF, etc). The 'emergency rescue packages' put together to prevent large sovereign borrowers (Mexico, Brazil, Argentina) from defaulting, and involving direct financial intermediation on the part of governments of advanced countries, is a witness to this trend. It is no coincidence that the largest sovereign borrowers in international financial markets are also among the group of NICs described in this essay. Just four Third World NICs, namely Mexico, Brazil, Argentina and South Korea account for more than half of the total outstanding loans of private banks to non-OPEC developing countries, for some 85 per cent of the net floating interest debt and almost all of total net private banks 'exposure' (i.e. excluding guaranteed export credits) to non-OPEC developing countries.[36]

Conclusions

This essay has been very wide ranging, because of the need to give the reader a sense of the complex changes in the world capitalist system now under way. For the new international division of labour is not just about the relocation of industry from traditional sites to new ones. This is only one aspect of a reorganization of world production taking place both at the level of forces and relations of production. The essay has also been largely descriptive: it has not addressed the many theoretical controversies now raging in respect of the nature of imperialist expoitation inside the Third World, whether it is progressive in terms of some preconceived sense of historical development, or retrogressive – reducing the opportunities for national development and liberation.[37]

Nor has the essay attempted to survey the theoretical controversies regarding the character of the world imperialist system and its tendencies: within the Marxist tradition alone one can point to several different models of imperialist development. Depending, for example, on the writers' interpretation of state–capital relations within the advanced world, there are, on the one hand, those who speculate on a reassertion of American hegemony in the world (the so called '*super-imperialist*' scenario);[38] while on the other hand, for some writers, the *inter-imperialist rivalries* between the US and its competitors, Europe and Japan, are the key to the further unfolding historical drama of imperialism;[39] again others place much emphasis on the weakening of the link between international capital and its home base. These latter writers now speak of a *post-imperialist* stage in which increasingly international capitalist institutions such as the IMF and the World Bank will play a governing role, determining international economic exchanges and world hierarchies.[40]

Because of the shortage of space we cannot possibly do justice to these very interesting theoretical debates. Instead, we will concentrate in these concluding remarks on just a few themes which are pertinent to socialist practice both in Europe and in the Third World, and which logically follow from our analysis.

Capital–state and capital–labour relations

As we have seen, the internationalization of forces of production is coordinated by new international relations of production: a new collusion of interests between three or even four participants: the multinational corporations, the transnational banks, the governments of finance- and technology-importing countries, and perhaps even the governments of capital-exporting countries. In this new co-operative venture, the governments of the host countries (which increasingly will include advanced countries too, Britain in the recent Nissan deal being a case in point) act as 'sovereign brokers' making available resources (labour, land and capital) for international profit maximization on terms which mostly reflect highly competitive inter-nation world-market conditions, but which at the same time may negate and suppress domestic market forces. Few people realize that about 40 per cent of the costs of inward foreign investment in the UK is borne – through government subsidies and incentives – by the British taxpayer.[41] In some countries the subsidies and incentives are higher still.

The implication of this is that, while capitalism is now establishing itself as a transnationally integrated system, it restricts the spread of capitalist relations of production on a national scale, as *government fiat* rather than domestic market conditions determine the price of land, labour and capital to be offered to transnational capital. Adopting neo-classicists' terminology, we might say that today we have a world market for world-market imperfections! We therefore have to ask the question: what determines the price of these world-market imperfections; what is it that determines the inter-state competition for transnational capital; what determines the terms of transational involvement in economy and society, and most importantly how can we as socialists ensure that these terms make a progressive contribution to national development, liberation and socialist internationalism? The answer to these questions calls for a two-tier programme of action:

1. We need to fully support and foster the development of international codes of conduct for the behaviour of transnational enterprises, and international social legislative movements in the widest sense, e.g. international trade unionism as well as social codes developed by international organizations such as the International Labour Office. This task is all the more urgent as at present inter-nation competition for participation in global production has already led advanced countries such as Britain to set up free-trade zones offering transnational capital conditions for valorization of capital (e.g. work conditions, wages, tax incentives, etc.) competitive with those existing in less-developed parts of the world. This implies a globalization of conditions of production to the lowest denominator existing within the global system. Already, in Britain, the first 'no-strike' deals between the electricians' union, EPTU, and foreign inward investors (Toshiba and Sanyo) have been struck. Internationalization of production thus threatens to erode the standards of living and the status of labour attained through much struggle in the advanced countries. But the international definition of these terms and conditions needs to be fed by internationally organized grassroots involvement. It demands the internationalization of the class struggle.

2. We need to support national liberation struggles inside the newly industrializing countries themselves. The initial concern here should be focused on the appalling creation of misery occurring inside these countries as a result of their participation in global industrial production. It is particularly in evidence now that debt-peonage exacts the heaviest toll yet from the masses of peasants and workers. For example, the financial 'rehabilitation' of Mexico (i.e. the successful rescheduling of its debt) has involved an IMF imposed austerity programme which has cost the Mexican workers a 30 per cent cut in wages, increased the number of under- and unemployed to 50 per cent, reduced gross domestic product by 4.7 per cent in one year, and has increased food prices to the point where now 30 million Mexicans according to the government are seriously undernourished.[42] The social tensions engendered by this situation in all of the larger debt-ridden Latin American economies may force through a process of democratization that may yet succeed in redefining the relationship with international capital. In this redefinition the threat of debt-defaulting is a powerful weapon, provided it is applied by the Third World as a solid bloc. We should support such a Third World debtors' cartel, not only for the sake of the people of the Third World but also for the sake of our own labour movement. For it follows, that under the now-emerging international equalization of capital – labour relations, the social emancipation of labour and work conditions in the Third World can halt the decline of our own. The price for labour in Mexico and other Third World countries does have a bearing on the price for labour paid in this country.

A corrollary of this position is that a future Labour government in Britain should take a very hard look at the way in which the British state is at present being coopted into the quadrangle of international relations of production as financial mediator in debt-rescheduling packages.

The new international division of labour and the Third World

This essay has shown that the new international division of labour cannot be equated with the economic development of the Third World. On the contrary, the reconstruction of international capitalism on an integrated global basis has not only marginalized those areas of the Third World excluded from participation, but it has also dislocated the economies of those countries subjected to it. For the former, crude attempts by advanced countries to introduce indiscriminate protectionist measures necessarily affect unprocessed agricultural commodities as well as industrial products. This is a double blow, since the terms of trade for agricultural products have declined to their lowest level since World War II. The newly industrializing countries can in part escape the full force of this protectionism, because many imports originating in the transnationally integrated sector are exempted.[43]

A socialist government in any of the advanced countries would need to develop a planned programme of international trade, sensitive to the different ways in which Third World countries are differentially integrated into the world market. This would almost certainly require the formulation of some hard, radical alternatives to the Brandt proposals for international trade which the Labour movement in Britain and elsewhere seems to have adopted rather uncritically. For example, it might include *selective* import controls with the criteria of selection being the source of value added in production, thus penalizing those multinational industries whose exclusive objective is the re-export into Britain of products originating here but assembled in 'run-away' sweatshops in the Third World. It would also include a sensitive reassessment of international commodity agreements, keeping in focus the fact that many Fourth World countries now dependent on the export of 'obsolete' primary products, would be better advised to marshall their scarce agricultural resources for the benefit of local food production. And finally, it would involve recognition and support for genuine south–south trade, and not trade of the subimperialist kind described before.

The newly industrializing countries not only attract the bulk of foreign direct investments, but because of the close integration between, and mixing of, equity and debt flows they also attract a dominant part of available international bank lending as well. To make matters still worse, in their anxiety to protect their transnational banks' interests from potential sovereign defaulters, the governments of advanced countries (as well as international financial organizations) are now redirecting their aid flows to those very same countries. What this means is that the reconstitution of capitalism on a global scale and its concentration in a number of selected countries has absorbed practically all available international financial resources, leaving less development assistance for the poorer countries. A socialist programme should be concerned about the present mixing of commercial and public flows to the Third World and make sure that whatever public assistance is available is targeted on the poorer countries only.

While the category Third World as denoting a homogenous unit is no longer very useful, it still has uses as an ideological category: its use mobilizes Third World countries for example to take the so-called south–south trade seriously. Indeed, south–south trade has grown rapidly over the past decade. However, the debt peonage of the newly industrializing countries also pulls them in the other direction: an increasing orientation towards western markets in whose currencies their debts are denominated. Carrying every argument presented so far to its logical conclusion, it would seem in the best interest of the people in the Third World for the advanced countries to abandon the concept of the Third World as a guiding category in planning international trade and aid flows with the poorer countries. At the same time for the countries and the people of the Third World it makes sense to continue to unite under a single ideological banner so that they may extract more favourable economic concessions yet from the advanced world.[44]

Notes

1   League of Nations, *Industrialization and Foreign Trade* (Geneva, 1945), p. 13.
2   Ibid., p. 13.
3   Colin J. Bradford, 'The Rise of the NIC's as Exporters on a Global Scale', in Louis Turner and Neil McMullen, *The Newly Industrializing Countries, Trade and Adjustment*, (London, Allen and Unwin) p. 7.
4   Calls for import controls, whether general or selective, formed a key element in the so-called Alternative Economic Strategy debates of Labour's early years of opposition to the Thatcher government. Their centrality had been inspired by the link established by the Cambridge Economic Policy Group between import penetration of finished manufactures and deindustrialization in Britain. The Cambridge group had proposed a tariff on finished manufactured goods of 30 per cent rising to 70 per cent by 1990. See CSE, *The Alternative Economic Strategy*, (London, CSE Books and the Labour Co-ordinating Committee 1979); Francis Cripps *et al.*, *Manifesto, A radical strategy for Britain's Future*, (London, Pan Books, 1981); Andrew Glyn and John Harrison, *The British Economic Disaster*, (London, Pluto Press, 1980) (the discussion in chapter 5 on alternative economic strategies) and the Transport and General Workers' April 1980 pamphlet '*Control Imports Now*'.
5   OECD, *Report of the Secretary General* (Paris, OECD, 1979).
6   *World Development Report, 1979* (Washington, IBRD, 1979), p. 87.
7   Foreign and Commonwealth Office, *The Newly Industrialising Countries and the Adjustment Problem* (HMSO, 1979).
8   *Taiwan Statistical Data Book*, 1983.
9   UNCTAD, *Trade and Development Report*, (Geneva, 1981).
10 UNCTAD, *Trade and Development Report*, 1981, p. 102.
11 Brandt Report, *North-South, a Programme for Survival*, 1980.
12 Calculated on the basis of *World Development Report 1983*, (Washington, IBRD, 1983), column 'Value of manufactured Exports'.
13 R. Prebisch, *Towards a New Trade Policy of Development*, vol. II of *Proceedings of the United Nations Conference on Trade and Development* (Geneva, UNCTAD,

1964). A seminal version of this paper had appeared as an ECLA document in 1950 and was mainly concerned with Latin America: R. Prebisch, *The Economic Development of Latin America and its Principal Problems* (New York, Economic Commission for Latin America, 1950).

14   For a lengthier exposition of this argument, the reader is referred to chapter 1 in this volume; note particularly comments there on the Alliance for Progress. The social and political contentions which ISI engenders are discussed in chapter 5.

15   F. Cardoso and E. Faletto, *Dependency and Development in Latin America*, (Berkeley: University of California Press, 1979).

16   For more on 'sub-imperialism', see chapter 10.

17   *Survey of Duty-free Export Zones in APO Member Countries*, Asian productivity Center, SYP/11/75, July 1975, p. 86. Quoted in Tsuchiya Takeo, 'Free Trade Zones in South East Asia', in *Monthly Review*, February 1978, p. 29.

18   *Transnational Corporations in World Development*, Third Survey (UN Centre on Transnational Corporations, 1983), p. 155.

19   J. Rada, *The Impact of Microelectronics. A Tentative Appraisal of Information Technology*, (Geneva, ILO, 1980).

20   Quoted in OECD, *International Investments and Multinational Enterprises*, (Paris, OECD, 1981), p. 19.

21   R. Vernon, 'The Product Cycle Hypothesis in a New International Environment, *Oxford Bulletin of Economics and Statistics* 41, no. 3 (August 1979), pp. 255–67.

22   *Multinational Corporations in World Development* (UN, ECOSOC, 1973), p. 14.

23   Cf. *Transnational Corporations in World Development, Third Survey*, pp. 160–1.

24   Christiano Antonelli, *Transborder Data Flows and International Business – a pilot study*, prepared for the OECD working party on Information, Computer and Communications Policy, (Paris, OECD, 2 June 1981). Quoted in Dieter Ernst, *Restructuring World Industry in a Period of Crisis – the Role of Innovation*, UNIDO/IS.285 December 1981, p. 305.

25   Eugene Versluysen, *The Political Economy of International Finance*, (Farnborough, Gower, 1981), p. 39.

26   UNCTAD, *Trade and Development Report 1982*, p. 75.

27   Oliver Pastre, *Multinationals: Bank and Corporate Relationships*, (JAI Press, Greenwich, Conn., 1981) part II.

28   Ibid.

29   F. F. Clairmonte and John H. Cavanagh, 'Transnational Corporations and global markets: Changing power relations', in *Trade and Development, an UNCTAD Review*, no. 4, (1982), p. 154.

30   Cf. Pastre, *Multinationals*, p. 28.

31   *Development Cooperation*, Review of the OECD Development Assistance Committee, based on statistical tables in Annexes of the 1970 and 1982 reviews.

32   The *Guardian*, Monday 4 June 1984, p. 16.

33   The World Bank, *World Development Report*, 1983, p. 74, emphasis added.

34   Cf. Robert Wood, 'The Debt Crisis and North–South Relations', *Third World Quarterly*, July 1984, p. 709.

35   Ibid., p. 710.

36   *External Debt of Developing Countries, 1982 Survey* (Paris OECD, 1982), p. 8.

37   For one aspect of these controversies, the reader is referred to Bill Warren, *Imperialism, Pioneer of Capitalism* (London, New Left Books, 1980). A good up-to-date discussion of the 'Warren' controversy, and more generally the debate about the effects of the new international division of labour on Third World industrialization, may be found also in Rhys Jenkins, 'Divisions over the New International Division of Labour', in *Capital and Class*, no. 22 (Spring 1984), pp. 28–57. See also in the same volume

W. Andreff, 'The International centralisation of capital and the reordering of world capitalism', and A. Lipietz 'Imperialism or the beast of the apocalypse?'.

38   An example of the 'super-imperialist' scenario is presented by the French writers Yann Fitt, A. Faire and J. P. Vigier, in *The World Economic Crisis* (London, Zed Press, 1979). The American Marxist journal *Monthly Review* and especially its editor Paul Sweezy also stand firmly within this tradition. American hegemony also features prominently in the work of James Petras on dependency: *Critical Perspectives on Imperialism and Social Class in the Third World* (New York, Monthly Review Press, 1979).

39   A long-standing proponent of the 'inter-imperialist rivalry' variant is E. Mandel. See especially *Late Capitalism* (London, New Left Books, 1976). Mary Kaldor's *The Disintegrating West* (Harmondsworth, Penguin, 1981, has helped to popularize this view in Britain.

40   Cf. Richard L. Sklar, 'Post imperialism: a class analysis of multinational corporate expansion', in *Comparative Politics*, 9 (1) (1976), pp. 75–92. See also David B. Becker, 'Development, Democracy and Dependency in Latin America: a post-imperialist view', *Third World Quarterly*, April 1984, pp. 411–31.

41   See OECD, *International Investment and Multinational Enterprises* (Paris, OECD, 1983), annex pages 222–32 on incentive policies in the UK.

42   Peter Chapman, *The Guardian*, Friday 27 April 1984.

43   In particular the US tariff schedules 807.00 and 806.30 are thought to have contributed to the transfer abroad by multinationals of 'divisible processes'. For, under these schedules, import duty is paid only on the value added abroad of any imported product.

44   This chapter was submitted in October 1984.

5

The Crisis in the Third World

MORRIS SZEFTEL

'One has the feeling that everything is collapsing around us,' wrote the *Zambia Daily Mail*, surveying a deteriorating economy in 1978.[1] This sense of ruination has been widespread in much of the Third World[2] over the past decade – and for good reason. The crisis of accumulation which has beset the world capitalist order during that time has been particularly severe in its impact on the poorest and most peripheral societies of that order.[3] In Africa, Asia and Latin America the misery produced by recession has gone far beyond the industrial decline, intensified exploitation, unemployment and inflation experienced in the core countries of the capitalist system. For these regions, crisis has also frequently meant the disruption of industrial and agricultural production, the creation of a spiralling debt burden which will be a yoke on future generations, rising prices and falling incomes, hunger and even famine. The increasing social conflict which has followed in the wake of such crises has threatened the very survival of some states and societies. More commonly, it has produced increased social and political protest and increasing political repression, violence and war.

The process has not affected the Third World evenly or equally. A small number of countries have been able to manage the crisis with some measure of success and have even done quite well out of recession. This handful may even replace traditional industrial centres in particular production sectors such as steel or shipbuilding. But for the majority of countries, the crisis has been damaging – eliminating markets for export commodities, drying up sources of foreign exchange and so forcing cuts in imports which, in turn, undermine inputs into manufacturing and agriculture and so reduce local production levels. This has made it difficult to repay international debts incurred to finance economic growth programmes and has frequently forced further borrowing to maintain basic activities, to prevent the collapse of projects already started and even to repay existing debts on schedule. For some countries, especially in Africa, the effects of the crisis can accurately be described as catastrophic. But few societies anywhere in the Third World have not had some price to pay.

Nor has the crisis been even or equal in its impact on the peoples of the Third World. Different communities and different classes have paid different prices as capital accumulation is restructured on a world scale. For a tiny minority, even in the worst-affected countries, there have been opportunities for personal enrichment. In parts of South-east Asia a new class of industrial and finance capitalists would seem to be emerging.[4] Elsewhere, there have been, at least, opportunities for profiteering and speculation arising from shortages and ruin. The majority have had less to cheer about. Even in the enclaves of economic growth, success has generally been based on ruthless repression of the workforce in order to keep wages very low, and on the repression and expropriation of the peasantry to ensure low commodity prices and the conversion of land to plantation and capitalist agriculture. In the more seriously affected areas of the Third World, there has been rising unemployment, falling real wages and rising prices for basic consumer staples in the towns, growing poverty, landlessness and marginalization in the countryside. A process of expropriation of the peasantry from the land, underway for more than a century in some places, has been accelerated by the crisis.[5] For many peasants, the capacity to produce a subsistence has been crucially, even permanently, undermined: the process is most starkly visible in Africa, but it occurs in Asia and Latin America as well. And with this crisis has come an increasing incidence of brutality, violence and political repression in attempts to check resistance to immiseration, to force the poorest communities and classes to carry the main burden of attempts to restore international and local profit margins, and to prop up state systems rapidly running out of popular legitimacy.

A chapter such as this one cannot hope to present any kind of comprehensive analysis of how the crisis affects the multiplicity of complex and varied social formations of the Third World. Yet the very fact that crisis is ubiquitous, that it affects so much of the earth, indicates the existence of common features and general forces which can be pointed out – however briefly and sketchily. The first section of the paper seeks to identify a few key features of the crisis which are widespread throughout the Third World. In the second section, an attempt is made to account for the origins and perpetuation of the crisis. It is suggested that, for all their seriousness, present events are only symptomatic of a deeper, more enduring crisis arising from the way in which the Third World was incorporated into the international division of labour. It is this deeper crisis that structures the nature of poverty, the problems of creating any kind of viable strategy of development and the difficulties of ever escaping the effects of the present recession. The third section turns to the political systems which derive from the specific position of the Third World in the international capitalist order. This permits some insight into the increasing levels of political instability and repression produced by the present crisis. Finally, a fourth section considers the response of the dominant agencies and states of the international order and the ways in which they have sought to influence the Third World during the last decade to their own advantage. By way of conclusion, some enduring consequences of the current situation are suggested.

The Present Crisis in the Third World

The international crisis of capital affected the Third World with especial severity from the mid-seventies. It ended a period in which, despite major problems, there had been a degree of growth in a number of countries. This growth had, in turn, encouraged optimism that rational and coherent policies could be devised by individuals, states and international organizations acting together to promote 'development'. Thus the United Nations, for instance, declared the sixties to be the decade of development. Such a perspective was in keeping with the times after 1945. The political independence of numerous former colonies made nationalism an economic as well as a political goal. The alleviation of poverty became a central element of international political discourse: there was much talk of the need to 'catch up' with the industrial west. For the first time, development became a self-conscious end, the subject of purposive political action and economic strategy. Growth was no longer simply the by-product of market forces or even of a class-determined process of accumulation. Instead, it was the subject of a national political will and effort, the interplay of democratic decision-making and economic expertise.

The independence of India in 1947 was particularly important in shaping this view. Of course, the Russian revolution of 1917 had made public policy and planning a real alternative to market forces as a mechanism of accumulation and thus offered a model of self-reliant industrialization as a substitute for hoping that the market and private capital would provide. This model was strengthened with the victory of the Chinese communists in 1949. But it was India which offered a non-revolutionary path, one in which reform rather than revolution might permit a process of industrialization within the structures of the existing world order. The 'Indian model' appealed to European social democracy as well as to many non-Marxist socialists in the Third World: it offered parliamentary democracy rather than bureaucratic determination, indicative planning instead of the command economy, a major state role in economic affairs without state ownership, an admixture of planning and market forces, of private and public capital.[6] As in the west, the 'mixed economy' created hopes for progress without the pain of revolutionary change, of social justice without class struggle. It suited the 'national' aspirations of Third World leaderships; and it offered a cooperative (rather than confrontational) adjustment of economic and political relations between post-colonial states and former colonial powers. The western powers, and related international agencies, supported and sponsored a variety of general and specific strategies for development in non-communist states: bilateral and multilateral aid tied to particular projects, import substitution industrialization and agrarian green revolution among them.[7]

Such strategies brought some significant statistical gains to some Third World countries in the sixties and early seventies – especially in manufacturing, but also in the production of food grains. Such cases were not the norm and often the figures owed as much to the low material base from which growth was measured as to any real change brought to the lives of the mass of the population. Nevertheless, the successes were sufficient to generate a degree of optimism about the prospects for industrial and agrarian transformation. They were also used to advocate the necessary elements of a successful growth model, in particular the proper role which the state should play in the process. Where growth had not occurred, it was frequently suggested that the fundamental problem lay with excessive or misdirected state intervention.

Arguments abound about the proper attitudes of Third World governments towards local capital, multinational corporations, western governments, aid agencies, peasant producers and so on.[8] In the case of Brazil, for example, it was possible to argue that 'the Brazilian miracle' derived from the dynamism of multinational industrial development directed and protected by a powerful, authoritarian state which also sponsored local capital accumulation and ensured unhindered access to labour supplies.[9] In the Far East the combination of authoritarian regimes sponsoring indigenous capital accumulation while providing an open-door policy for multinational investment in certain industrial sectors and ensuring a quiescent labour force seemed to succeed through much of the present crisis. In general, right-wing repressive regimes which were highly interventionist against labour and for capital were seen as progressive, market-oriented and successful. The less they interfered with 'the world market' (i.e. western capital) and the more fiercely they regulated and structured the local market on behalf of capital accumulation and against redistribution, the more successful they seemed to be and the more favourably they were regarded in western circles. Where development strategies did not succeed – and Africa was to prove their least fertile ground – the failure of the state to promote investment and entrepreneurship was frequently seen to be the problem and policies which discouraged capital invest-ment were identified.[10]

For the vast majority of Third World countries, growth did not occur in any significant way. But the successes produced an international development ideology which explained to the laggards where they had gone wrong: inefficiency, corruption, grandiose projects, bureaucracy and, generally, 'too much socialism, not enough free enterprise' which had frightened investors away. The success stories yielded specific policy models which were advocated by western govern-ment and international aid agencies and adopted with varying degrees of enthusiasm by local elites and ruling groups in the Third World – often because the policy or programme was written into the grant of aid. In some cases policies were urged on Third World countries when they had already failed somewhere else: thus import substitution enjoyed a new currency in Africa in the sixties after its failure was already evident in Latin America where it was subject to a ferocious critique.[11] Nevertheless, while Third World exports grew faster than imports between 1965 and 1973, (as shown in table 5.1) and while primary commodity prices continued to rise, the general optimism of this development consensus could be sustained – despite the errors, problems and the warnings of underdevelopment theorists.[12] By the mid-seventies, however, the development utopia looked more threadbare.

The crisis of overproduction[13] in the industrial capitalist centres followed a period in which many Third World producers had enjoyed rising commodity prices for their primary products. This brought increased foreign exchange earnings which were, in turn, used to undertake relatively ambitious industrial development policies and also to finance essential social investment programmes in housing, health, education and infrastructure. Such policies were themselves expressions of the internationally encouraged development ideology of the sixties. Unfortunately, falling profit rates in the west produced falling levels of demand for primary commodities as industrial retrenchment proceeded. Such demand fell in terms of price and, often, in terms of physical volume too. Its consequence was sharply reduced export earnings. In addition, the mid-seventies also saw a sharp increase in the price of oil and petroleum prices. Energy costs rocketed precisely at the moment when many Third World countries, particularly in Africa, had become increasingly oil-dependent because of expanded transport structures, industrialization policies,

Table 5.1 Growth of merchandise trade and changing terms of trade

World Bank Category[1]	Average Annual Growth Rate (per cent)				Terms of Trade (1980=100)	
	Exports		Imports			
	1965–73	1973–83	1965–73	1973–83	1979[2]	1983
Lower-income economies	1.5	0.9	−2.0	1.4	108	96
of which: Sub-Saharan Africa[3]	2.4	−4.0	2.3	−2.2	88[3]	94
Lower middle-income economies	4.8	0.1	4.5	1.4	98	94
of which: Sub-Saharan Africa[3]	6.9	−5.8	6.5	8.2	95[3]	99
Upper middle-income economies	5.7	0.5	9.7	4.0	100	97
High-income oil exporters	11.4	−5.8	10.1	18.7	68	105
Industrial market economies	9.4	4.2	10.0	3.0	106	100

Notes:

1 World Bank categorization of economies is as follows: (i) lower-income economies are those with a per capita GNP not exceeding US$400 in 1983 – 35 countries. (ii) lower middle-income economies have a per capita GNP between $400 and $1,500 in 1983 – 37 countries. (iii) The upper middle-income category seems less clearly defined. It includes 'richer' Third World countries (Chile, Brazil, Mexico), some 'poorer' oil producers (Algeria, Venezuela), some Third World countries with per capita GNP above $1,600 (Jordan, Syria, Malaysia), some Third World enclave growth points (Hong Kong, South Korea, Singapore) and some poorer European countries (Portugal, Greece). In general, countries range from per capita GNP of $1,640 to per capita GNP of $6,850 (Jordan and Trinidad respectively). (iv) High-income oil exporters are Oman, Libya, Saudi Arabia, Kuwait and the United Arab Emirates. Oman's 1983 per capita GNP was lower than that of the oil-producing Trinidad listed in the previous category! (v) The 19 'industrial market economies' are all western European except for the United States, Canada, Japan, Australia and New Zealand.

2 1979 indices for terms of trade are taken from the *World Development Report 1984*, pp. 234–5.

3 All figures for Sub-Saharan Africa are taken from the Report of 1985. Terms of trade indices are for 1981, not 1979, and 1983.

Source:
The World Bank, *World Development Report 1985* (Oxford, Oxford University Press, 1985), pp. 190–1, except as noted above.

and the adoption of green-revolution technology in the agrarian sector which were based on petro-chemical fertilisers. The oil crisis meant a need for massive increases in import bills precisely as export earnings fell. The consequences were enormously disruptive after 1973: new development projects in agriculture, industry and transport were put in jeopardy, capital was unavailable to complete projects in hand, large numbers of workers (often newly incorporated into the labour market from the land) were laid off. In many cases in Africa, capital was no longer available to meet recurrent expenditures necessary to sustain social programmes. Table 5.1 shows the deterioration in export and import growth rates and the deteriorating terms of trade after 1980. Such figures probably mask the enormity of the problem to a substantial degree because they do not reflect the crucial imports that have been forgone in order to try to balance international payments.

It is important at this stage to stress that the crisis was not evenly distributed throughout the world economy. Different countries and different sectors within countries have experienced the crisis differently. Some enclaves of multinational capital in East and South-east Asia, for instance, have exhibited remarkable resilience and have even experienced growth. By ruthlessly suppressing wages, they have even managed to attract capital – often at the expense of declining industries in the capitalist core economies. Even here, the crisis has not been absent, however: South Korea, for example, experienced a 6 per cent decline in gross national product (GNP) and a $27 billion debt by 1981 rising to $37 billion in 1982. This led to a temporary freeze in foreign investment which was only resumed after 'stabilization' measures including severe cutbacks in consumption were implemented.[14]

Where regimes have managed to impose the burden of paying for the crisis on their workforces, they have often been able to attract investment and so participate in a process of international capital restructuring. For Third World oil exporters, in contrast, the oil price rise produced initial affluence and an increase in consumption (particularly on the part of ruling classes); but as tables 5.1 and 5.2 indicate, this proved transitory. The depression had, by 1982, squeezed oil prices and revenues and even these countries faced deteriorating terms of trade and declining output. For most Third World countries, the impact has been generally negative and in many cases, in Africa especially, even catastrophic. Not only has there been a deterioration in terms of trade and output, but also a collapse in production in some sectors of some economies. As table 5.2 indicates, average annual growth rates of per capita GNP fell from 4.1 per cent in the 1965–73 period to negative rates in 1982. The poorest African countries experienced a fall from 1.3 per cent to negative growth by 1981.

Throughout the whole process, it is the poorest who have paid most for the crisis of capital: in the industrial core economies, it is the working class which has borne the brunt of capital restructuring; throughout the Third World, it is the working class and peasantry which have paid through rising prices, falling wages and commodity prices, and reduced agricultural opportunities; and on a world scale, the crisis has had the most devastating effect on the 35 poorest countries – to whom most of this paper refers – where there has been a collapse in production in certain sectors. For many of these countries, it is difficult to envisage the means by which they can escape their present decline.

Table 5.2 Average annual growth rates of per capita GNP in the Third World

Country group	Percentage annual growth of GNP per capita					
	1965–73	1973–80	1981	1982	1983	1984
All developing countries	4.1	3.3	0.8	−0.7	−0.1	2.1
Low-income Asia	3.2	3.5	2.5	3.4	6.0	5.3
Low-income Africa	1.3	0	−1.7	−2.6	−2.6	−1.5
Middle-income oil importers	4.6	3.1	−0.8	−2.0	−1.6	1.1
of which:						
East Asia and Pacific	5.6	5.7	3.7	1.9	4.5	3.4
Middle East and North Africa	3.5	4.3	−2.5	2.6	0.5	−1.3
Sub-Saharan Africa	2.0	0.5	4.1	−4.8	−5.4	−5.4
Latin America and Caribbean	4.5	2.9	−4.1	−4.8	−4.5	1.1
Middle income oil exporters	4.6	3.1	1.5	−2.3	−3.6	0.1

Source:
The World Bank, *World Development Report 1985*, (Oxford, Oxford University Press, 1985) p. 148.

The unevenness of the crisis has been sectoral as well as spatial. Even in many parts of the Third World where the crisis has been severe, there has still been a growth in manufacturing, for example, and some restructuring in favour of the industrial sector.[15] Countries such as India and Brazil, among others, have managed to sustain investment, albeit by heavy international borrowing. And while industry has suffered severely in other parts of the Third world, especially in low income countries, no sector has been more seriously affected than agriculture in Africa.

Here more than a decade of investment (albeit always inadequate) in new, more capital-intensive techniques, has culminated in the eighties in a famine which is one of the great tragedies of the century. There is little hard evidence of how many people have died of famine, of how many have been permanently brain-damaged by it, or of the extent of the ecological collapse of vast areas and populations. Reports indicate the inadequacy of aid efforts, the inefficiency and incompetence of international relief and government agencies, and the sheer violence which the famine has imposed on millions of peasants and refugees. While it is clear that the famine has been particularly severe where it has coincided with, or been exacerbated by civil war (Ethiopia, Somalia, Sudan, Mozambique) or the influx of refugees, it has otherwise shown little discrimination between countries which were previously considered successful exponents of development and those which were not. The statist orientation of left-wing regimes such as Mozambique was criticized for inefficiency in the agricultural policies pursued even before the famine,[16] but the famine has also visited Sudan where multi-national investment in schemes designed to make the country the 'breadbasket' of the Middle East have proved disastrous.[17]

Peasants have starved where war has displaced them or destroyed their crops; they have starved where resettlement and collectivization schemes have failed disastrously. But they have also starved where marginalized to make room for large-scale commercial agriculture or where scarce resources have been committed to imported agrarian technology which the crisis has then disrupted or terminated. This has interfered with the capacity of people to grow food for themselves and the capacity of the agrarian sector to produce food rather than export crops. The crisis has also ensured that many countries could not buy grain (plentiful on international markets) so that the decline of production as a result of drought and disruption turned to hunger and then famine. Again, it is the poorest economies which have suffered the most, the poorest people within them who have starved to death (essentially the rural peasantry) and the most powerless among them who have starved first (women and children). And even where famine has not occurred, it is important to stress that hunger has increased: almost all sub-Saharan African states experienced declining agricultural production during the crisis and all faced a diminishing capacity to pay for food imports.[18] In this sector, in particular, the gains of the sixties have essentially been negated and now appear to be illusory.

The Debt Crisis

More general than the decline of production in certain sectors and the fall in output in many countries has been the increasing indebtedness of the Third World to the governments and banks of the main capitalist countries. This debt has been directly the result of the world crisis and the deteriorating conditions in which the production of commodities for export occurred. As Third World countries experienced ever worsening terms of trade and consequent problems of preserving the economic and political structures they had developed, so they became increasingly dependent on borrowing. Initially, borrowing preserved investment plans, but as the crisis deepened it became necessary in order to offset balance-of-payments deficits; in some countries it even became necessary in order to meet certain recurrent costs in order to keep key programmes going.[19] At the same time, the severity of the crisis ensured that there was a diminishing capacity and willingness to lend on the part of western governments: although such governments remained the main creditors until 1982, they were faced by debtors who found it increasingly difficult to meet their debt obligations from 1979. The traditional sources of bilateral lending and aid were thus contracting as demand rose.

The crisis of overproduction nevertheless meant that increasing quantities of capital could not find avenues for investment at attractive rates of profit within the capitalist core economies. Large liquid oil revenues further increased the capital held in private banks for investment. The merchant bankers were thus happy to lend to desperate Third World borrowers prepared to pay higher rates of interest on loans – particularly where such borrowers had already achieved high growth rates or where state policies seemed to guarantee high returns and political stability.

While bankers found countries such as Brazil and Mexico attractive investment outlets, the financial markets also extended lending throughout the Third World with only the very poorest economies or the most politically unattractive being excluded. If the bulk went to the high-growth economies of the Third World, capital also flowed to territories where mineral wealth, stability or simply the willingness to pay high interest rates existed: if South Africa, Taiwan and South Korea were especially attractive, capital nevertheless also went to Zambia, where 90 per cent of exports were represented by copper which could no longer be mined profitably, to Zaire where the regime was involved in a notorious level of graft.[20] It is important to stress that the merchant bankers had not suddenly changed their age-old opinion about the attractiveness of lending to Third World countries; they did so now because of falling rates of profit in the industrial economies and because they could demand higher interest rates from borrowers who were in no position to argue. The borrowers, in turn, had access to private western capital on a previously undreamt of scale, but they were borrowing at rates far greater than those prevailing in the bilateral and multilateral aid packages previously negotiated.[21] And they were often dependent on prevailing market rates in the determination of the cost of particular loans, so that the high interest rates characteristic of monetarist restructuring policies in the west hit them particularly hard.

The situation was further aggravated by the fact that Third World countries were borrowing in a crisis which reduced their capacity to generate production capable of servicing (let alone repaying) these debts. And much of their borrowing was less to generate new productive capacity than to meet the contingencies of the crisis. By the late seventies 'the debt crisis' had already been identified as a characteristic of the crisis. So prevalent has international indebtedness become, and so intractable the problem of debt servicing, that the debt is increasingly seen by some as a structural feature of the world economy. Wood for instance, argues that

> problems of international debt have assumed such centrality in the affairs of third-world countries that it no longer makes sense to treat the debt crisis as a discrete series of events. The debt crisis defines an era. . .[22]

Figures abound, and vary greatly, of the extent of the debt and its burden, They vary depending on the source and on what is being counted. The World Bank (the primary source used here), for instance, measures medium and long-term public indebtedness, but estimates that for some major borrowers the short-term debt would increase the size of their external debt by some 30 per cent. In a few cases short-term obligations are more important than the others: South Africa, for one, was suddenly confronted by merchant bankers calling in short-term loans in the wake of popular resistance to the regime; the result was a short-lived threat to the survival of the apartheid state itself. Perhaps the best way of illustrating the impact of medium and long-term indebtedness is through the World Bank's 'debt ladder', illustrated in figure 5.1. This measures debt as a proportion of gross national product and of exports and debt servicing as a proportion of exports. It shows how the situation has changed from 1970–2 (on the eve of the crisis) to 1980–2 (when the crisis was possibly at its worst so far). For virtually every country depicted on each dimension, the ladder indicates a deteriorating situation. The burden of debt servicing is indicated again in a different form in table 5.3 where interest on debt as a proportion of exports is given for 1983. In that year, 23 countries – compared with 18 for the previous year – had to spend more than a fifth of export earnings to pay interest on external debts. As with most other dimensions of crisis, the external debt is a particularly serious threat to Africa. Table 5.4 demonstrates that per capita indebtedness for most countries in that continent is very close to the level of per capita GNP for 1983. In some cases (Gambia, Guinea-Bissau, Ivory Coast, Liberia, Mali, Mauritania, Somalia, Sudan, Togo, Zaire and Zambia) the per capita debt exceeds per capita output.

It is important to stress that the debt crisis affects both the capitalist centre and the Third World periphery but it does not do so in the same way or to the same extent. For the merchant bankers awaiting repayment of loans and interest, 'the global economy is sitting on a debt bomb.'[23] To them, the crisis is potential rather than actual: having made loans far in excess of their equity, the problem is that they will not obtain repayment or interest; that is, that debtors will default on their loans. For the banks and the governments that represent them, the danger is that widespread defaulting will undermine the very foundations of finance capital itself. This is not an impossibility. Many observers have doubted the capacity of debtors ever to repay their debts. Tanzania's President Nyerere stated in 1985 during a visit to Britain that 'Africa's debt burden is now intolerable. We cannot pay. You know it and all our other creditors know it.'[24] Lord Lever has called for parts of the debt to be written off over a period to permit Third World countries the possibility of recovery.[25] Even more frightening for the moneylenders is the prospect that a group of major debtors will unilaterally renounce their debts. For this reason, there has been a preparedness to reschedule debts when they become due and when new conditions can be negotiated. But there has been much concern about the visible hostility of the governments of Brazil and Mexico to their

Table 5.3 Servicing of external public debt as a proportion of total exports (percentages debt servicing/exports for 1983 unless otherwise noted)

Countries where debt service is more than 20% of exports

Costa Rica 50.6	Turkey 28.9	Uganda 22.3 (1981)
Morocco 38.2	Brazil 28.7	Guinea 22.2
Mexico 35.9	Pakistan 28.1	Burma 22 (1981)
Algeria 33.1	Egypt 27.5	Colombia 21.3
Ecuador 32.5	Yemen PDR 25.1	Kenya 20.6
Zimbabwe 31.6	Argentina 24	Congo 20.5
Ivory Coast 31.0	Dominican Republic 22.7	Malawi 20.3
Bolivia 30.5	Tunisia 22.3	

Countries where debt service is more than 15% of exports

Uruguay 19.8	Nicaragua 18.3	Philippines 15.4
Peru 19.6	Togo 16.8	
Nigeria 18.6	Afghanistan 16.2 (1980)	
Chile 18.3	Jamaica 15.4	

Countries where debt service is more than 10% of exports

Venezuela 15.0	Somalia 13.1	Syria 11.3
Honduras 14.9	Indonesia 12.8	Thailand 11.3
Paraguay 14.9	Zambia 12.6	Jordan 11.2
Bangladesh 14.7	South Korea 12.3	Papua New Guinea 11.2
Ghana 14.2	Sri Lanka 11.9	Sudan 11.2
Cameroon 13.9	Guatemala 11.7	Zaire 10.9 (1982)
Yemen Arab Republic 13.9	Ethiopia 11.5	India 10.3
Senegal 13.7 (1982)	Central African Republic 11.3	Mauritania 10.1

Countries where debt service is more than 5% of exports

Madagascar 7.4 (1980)	El Salvador 6.4 (1982)	Haiti 5.0
Sierra Leone 7.2	Mali 6.1	
Panama 6.8	Malaysia 5.9	
Liberia 6.6	Tanzania 5.1	

Note:
The debt service level would appear to fluctuate significantly in a large number of countries from year to year (Costa Rica's rising from 12.5% of exports to 50.6% from 1982 to 1983 to note the most extreme case). In general, fluctuations arise because debts are rescheduled, or because new loans are made, or because more accurate counting becomes possible. In general, the trend would seem to be for the debt service burden to be rising over time: countries paying more than 20% of exports in this way increased from 18 in 1982 to 23 in 1983, for instance; those paying more than 15% declined from 12 to 9 as countries moved into the higher debt category; those paying over 10% of exports rose from 12 in 1982 to 24 in 1983; and the number paying 5% to 10% fell from 16 to 9. Overall, the number of countries burdened by debt servicing of 5% or more of total export earnings rose from 58 in 1982 to 65 in 1983 – although this might have represented the ability of the World Bank to obtain data as much as a widening of the debt burden. Compared with figures for the early seventies, the debt service burden in the eighties seems even more dramatic.
Source:
The World Bank, *World Development Report 1985* pp. 204–5, and *World Development Report 1984*, pp. 248–9.

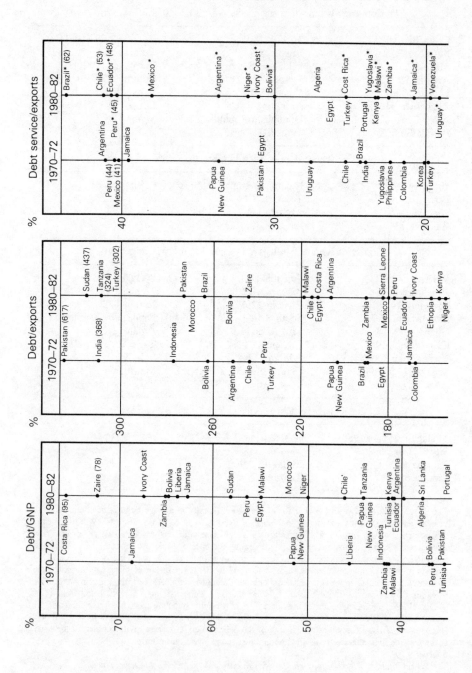

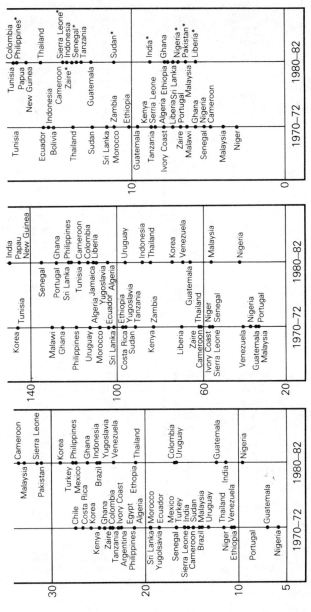

Note:
Debt is defined as a medium- and long-term public and publicly guaranteed plus private no-guaranteed debt outstanding and disbursed. Short-term debt is not included. For the major borrowers, the inclusion of short-term debt would raise the external debt registered during 1980–2 by about 30 per cent. The debt service figures used are those for actual (not contractual) debt service paid during the period. Exports cover goods and total services. An asterisk indicates that the country rescheduled its debt between 1975 and 1984.

Source:
Reproduced from the World Bank, *World development report 1985*.

Figure 5.1 The World Bank's Debt Ladder

Table 5.4 Africa's debt burden 1983/4

Country	Total Debt (US$million) 1983	IMF share (US$million) 1984	Debt per capita (US$)	GNP per capita (US$) 1983
Benin	932.2	11.4	250	290
Botswana	530.3	—	589	920
Burkina Faso	697.6	11.4	107	180
Burundi	581.6	16.4	135	240
Cameroon	3,320.5	30.7	357	820
Central African Republic	379.7	35.8	158	280
Chad	243.8	8.5	53	—
Congo	2,092.3	11.1	1,230	1,230
Equatorial Guinea	152.3	13.2	380	—
Ethiopia	2,036.8	100.3	62	120
Gabon	1,402.4	—	2,003	3,950
Gambia	291.0	33.7	415	290
Ghana	1,708.2	525.1	140	310
Guinea	1,627.7	32.3	286	300
Guinea-Bissau	206.2	3.7	258	180
Ivory Coast	7,107.6	648.8	799	710
Kenya	4,169.0	428.3	230	340
Lesotho	244.1	4.3	175	460
Liberia	1,148.6	237.3	574	480
Madagascar	2,339.5	173.9	254	310
Malawi	1,073.0	127.0	165	210
Mali	1,392.3	84.3	196	160
Mauritania	1,872.3	41.4	1,170	480
Mauritius	755.0	160.7	839	1,160
Niger	1,053.3	56.8	179	240
Nigeria	20,884.5	—	230	770
Rwanda	436.7	10.7	79	270
Senegal	2,540.2	234.7	423	440
Sierra Leone	610.0	97.6	190	330
Somalia	1,644.2	114.3	365	250
Sudan	11,000.0	677.7	545	400
Swaziland	260.4	13.5	372	870
Tanzania	3,356.1	60.2	170	240
Togo	1,076.1	63.5	384	280
Uganda	1,488.8	343.9	110	220
Zaire	5,497.2	688.4	179	170
Zambia	4,361.7	753.8	727	580
Zimbabwe	2,967.9	259.3	396	740

Note:
Total debts include short and long-term debts (disbursed and undisbursed) in 1983. IMF loans are for end of 1984. They include credit tranches, as well as drawings. Debt per capita is total divided by 1982 population figures. GNP per capita is based on United Nations population estimates as at mid-1983. Published debt data are considered to underestimate real debt levels by substantial margins.
Sources:
South, no. 57, July 1985, p. 31. Derived from IMF, World Bank and Bank for International Settlements. Fourth column (per capita GNP 1983) is from The World Bank, *World Development Report 1985*, pp. 174, 232.

creditors during rescheduling negotiations. In June 1984 seven Latin American debtor countries met in Columbia to discuss their economic problems. The present government of Peru was elected on a platform of radical change in the management of the debt burden. All this has produced clear signs of anxiety among creditors and the American administration, but there are few signs that anyone will unilaterally repudiate their debts – not least because they would be cut off from any further credit.

For the Third World, in contrast, the debt crisis is not a potential but an actual one; it has already occurred. Many countries have seen the all-too-limited social, industrial and urban gains of the previous decade wiped out during the last ten years. In Latin America per capita income has been falling since 1981. The Inter-American Development Bank has calculated that a full decade of rising incomes had been wiped out by 1982 in several Latin American countries where per capita gross domestic product (GDP) fell to 1972 levels or lower. In the region as a whole, GDP levels in 1983 were lower than in 1977 and in a few cases lower than in the sixties. It estimated that 30% of the labour force in the region was unemployed in 1983 and that inflation stood at 85% for 1982/3 (in Argentina it reached a high of 568% in 1983/4).[26]

In Africa, the debt is small in absolute terms when compared with Latin America or Asia. But its debt-service burden is far higher and its capacity to repay is far lower. For all the anxieties of the bankers about the enormity of the debt owed by Brazil, Mexico and Argentina, the problems these countries confront are smaller than those of Africa. Their relative levels of industrialization hold out the prospect that they will be able to generate the surpluses necessary for repayment and servicing. What is a small problem for merchant bankers is a seemingly intractable one for the African debtor countries. For many of them (and for the less indust-rialized states of the rest of the Third World) repayment of the debt has ceased to be a realistic project for the foreseeable future and servicing the debt has become a central concern of economic activity. The prospect of a perpetual 'debt peonage' has become part of their political agenda.

This degree of pessimism is not fanciful, as the World Bank projections for the rest of the eighties shown in table 5.5 indicate. In projecting the course of the crisis into 1990, The World Bank computes an optimistic (high) and a pessimistic (low) scenario. In the high scenario, Third World indebtedness will generally be higher in 1990 than at present but should be 'levelling off' in absolute terms and falling as a proportion of GNP and of exports. But even this optimism has little to comfort the low-income countries of Asia and Africa. For them the projection indicates a rising aggregate indebtedness constituting a greater burden on output and exports than at present. In the pessimistic projection, debt servicing for all developing countries would rise from 19.7% of exports in 1984 to 28% in 1990. In the case of low-income African economies, this increase would be from 19.9% to 37.5%.

The prospect that conditions will be roughly as at present going into the next decade if all goes well and that circumstances will deteriorate sharply if they do not, is a grim one. Nor can it be much comfort to anyone in Africa and Asia that the fraternity of economists has tended to be rather too optimistic in its predictions throughout the crisis. There is ample reason to take the pessimistic rather than optimistic prediction as more likely.

Table 5.5 Third World debt in 1984 and as projected for 1990 by the World Bank

(figures for Third World, low-income Asia and low-income Africa; in US$ billions or percentages, as appropriate)

	All developing countries			Low-income Asia			Low-income Africa		
	1984	High 1990	Low 1990	1984	High 1990	Low 1990	1984	High 1990	Low 1990
Debt outstanding and disbursed ($billion)	702.5	716.2	741.4	54.1	93.2	78.8	27.2	27.1	29.6
Interest on medium- and long-term debt ($billion)	−59.3	−44.9	−76.3	−1.9	−3.5	−4.2	−1.0	−1.0	−1.5
Debt as percentage of GNP	33.8	24.7	27.8	9.7	11.9	10.3	54.6	44.6	51.5
Debt as percentage of exports	135.4	98.2	133.1	100.0	131.0	148.4	278.1	250.3	328.1
Debt service as percentage of exports	19.7	16.0	28.0	8.4	10.6	15.6	19.9	25.2	37.5

Note:
The table is based on data on 90 third-world countries. Under low-income economies, the report groups 35 countries, only one of which, Haiti, is not in Asia or Africa. The two low-income categories here would therefore refer to these 34 poorest countries in the world.
Source:
From The World Bank, *World Development Report 1985*, table 10.5, p. 142.

Immediate Consequences of Indebtedness

The primary consequence of the debt crisis has been to make the International Monetary Fund even more central to policing international trade and balance of payments. This has been the traditional regime of the IMF and one under which Third World borrowers, always short of investment capital, had traditionally chafed.[27] Indeed, lending by merchant bankers was much easier to obtain than access to IMF loans and drawing rights and was seen by many borrowers as a welcome alternative to the policy constraints imposed by the IMF on governments seeking its assistance. But as the crisis became more sharply defined and the volume of debt escalated, credit from private financial sources became tighter and interest rates rose. As table 5.6 indicates, bank lending became increasingly expensive during the seventies. Faced with growing balance of payments problems and escalating debt burdens, many governments were forced to call in the IMF for further credits. The special drawing rights available to members thus assumed a strategic importance greater than during the earlier decade of expansion. In turn, the merchant bankers insisted on IMF approval of economic and fiscal policies before they would agree to reschedule debts or advance new credits. The IMF thus became crucial as a source of support for governments in trouble and as an arbiter of policy whose imprimatur alone would guarantee commercial loans. By the end of 1983, 21 Third World countries had renegotiated their debts to other governments and 26 had rescheduled debts to commercial banks – almost as many as in the previous 25 years.[28] Other governments had avoided such an exercise by the use of IMF drawing rights. Table 5.4 indicates the small but significant status of the IMF itself as a creditor in Africa; it is particularly important in Ghana, Kenya, Ivory Coast, Sudan, Zaire and Zambia.

Table 5.6   Terms of public borrowing

Category	Average rate of interest (%)		% Increase
	1970	1982	
Low-income economies	2.8	4.9	75.0
Middle-income economies	6.0	11.7	95.0
Lower middle-income economies	4.5	9.8	117.8

Source:
World Bank, *World Development Report 1984*, p. 250.

In consequence, the IMF has become the central regulating institution in debt management, economic adjustment and international banking policy. It has imposed stringent economic conditions on governments seeking its lending facilities or requiring its approval for new commercial credits or renegotiation of debts. In return for access to special drawing rights and other credit facilities, the IMF has typically imposed a package of 'stabilization' policies. It has thus become the main agency for ensuring that the 'debt bomb' does not go off under the commercial banks. Its stabilization measures are an expression of monetarist banking orthodoxy applied to the international level. The measures enforce the openness of

Third World economies to international trade; they remove tariffs and other obstacles to international price equalization to ensure competition and flexible prices responsive to the international market. Limits are generally imposed on the size and scope of the public sector which is required to eliminate deficit budgeting and to balance revenue and expenditure. The encouragement of private capital is emphasized and foreign investment is regarded as essential to compensate for the lack of local investment capital – provided that it does not produce new balance of payments problems.

This package has generally been accompanied by three additional requirements. Firstly, currency devaluation to promote flexible prices and encourage exports (Zambia, for instance, underwent 40 per cent currency devaluation by early 1985 and has subsequently had to accept a further 70 per cent by early 1986) has been a general feature of IMF conditions. Secondly, deflation by drastic cuts in public spending is advocated. And thirdly, 'export-led growth' is the key element which is seen as earning the revenues to repay debts and ensuring balance-of-payments stability. Public-sector growth and public spending are seen as undermining this stabilization programme, producing rigid prices skewed by subsidies, uncompetitive real wage rates and the protection of inefficient local industries.[29]

The IMF policies thus typically impinge on Third World economies at three levels: at the level of monetary policy, requiring a credit squeeze and increased interest rates; at the level of exchange policy requiring devaluation; and at the level of budgetary policies requiring the contraction of the public sector and thus a reduction in the available level of income. Such policies, it is argued, will make Third World countries embark on more realistic development plans and will open their economies to the more dynamic forces of private initiative and capital competing on the international market.

The long-term prospects for this monetarist strategy are the subject of much argument – not least in Britain where the experiment has produced little for even its devotees to cheer about.[30] What is not arguable is the short-term impact on Third World economies which have experienced the package. There it has produced more unemployment, drastic cuts in social programmes and the collapse of many projects essential for future development but not producing an immediate surplus. The effect on inflation has been minimal save in the sense that accelerated recession produced by the package has had the time-honoured effect of wiping out demand and also of closing down public sector production units. Devaluation has not boosted exports since the demand for them is not available in a deindustrializing west; indeed it has often simply resulted in exports earning less foreign exchange and thus making debt servicing even harder.[31] It has also meant a further fall in the level of physical imports and the further decline of output in consequence. In the longer term, the insistence on export promotion, on foreign investment and the lack of protection for local industry, and on the destruction of the handful of social programmes which previously sought to improve the stock of human resources, is even more questionable. It is a reassertion of precisely the circumstances which the original post-war development project sought to overcome.

Given the effect of IMF control over Third World debtors, it is not surprising that governments of all political complexions have been highly critical of the IMF. If repudiation has not seemed a viable response to date, there have been a number of critiques of present policies. The most interesting intervention so far has come from Cuba's Fidel Castro. He called for a period of grace to give debtors in Latin America and Africa a breathing space and for agreements to scale down the burden of interest.[32] The proposals earned Castro support among Latin American regimes normally hostile to Cuba. The government of Peru, too, has insisted that debt-servicing should not constitute a burden on the poorest members of that society, and similar comments have come from Brazil.

Such government responses to the IMF are hardly surprising. Quite apart from its impact on the public sector and hence on state interests, the IMF policy has extracted an enormous price from the peasantry and working class through unemployment, falling real and even money wages, declining product markets, increasing costs of agricultural inputs and basic foodstuffs; all have been at the heart of the IMF strategy.

As in Europe, monetarist strategies have reduced wage levels while making wage goods more expensive. In consequence, the period has been characterized by social tension and increasing political conflict. Strikes, food riots, rural protests and mass agitation have all placed pressure on governments charged with implementing stabilization policies. Military coups and political repression have been the response in many countries; a record of political repression in the Third World has been greatly exacerbated by the debt crisis. Reports of torture are widespread. There is barely a country in Africa, Asia and Latin America which has not experienced an increase in political turmoil.

Crisis has sharpened communal conflicts and often made them more violent. Class conflict has also intensified, with trade unionists often leading increasingly politicized organizations in countries like Brazil, Chile, Zambia and the Philippines. Peasant protest, rural violence or guerilla activities occur across a wide spectrum of countries – the Philippines, India, El Salvador and Brazil, for instance. In Sudan in 1985 even the petty bourgeoisie and elements of the professional classes took to the streets in the protests that toppled the Numeiri regime.[33] Universities have been closed and students jailed in such profusion that these events no longer merit much comment.

Such crises and struggles ensure that, despite the scarcity of capital, spending on weapons and the technology of repression continues to increase in the Third World.[34] If the present crisis ensures a desperate shortage of ploughshares, there is nevertheless an abundance of swords. The military coup has become the typical state form. A number of bloody regimes, armed to the teeth, perpetrate a succession of tortures and atrocities against their citizens. The death squad and the systematic murder of political opponents, working-class activists and peasant organizers somehow has become less surprising in El Salvador than it was in Chile or Argentina. The Indonesian regime's bloody annexation of East Timor occasioned less comment that its initial liquidation of communists. The cycle of repression grows directly out of the present crisis and the burdens imposed by debt stabilization policies. But it also has deeper roots in the nature of the development process in the Third World over a long period. It is to these deeper roots that we must now turn attention.

The Permanent Crisis in the Third World

Thus far we have considered Third World crisis in terms of the impact of the global economic crisis on attempts to promote development and ensure the basic conditions of survival and economic reproduction. Such an approach does not explain why the crisis should manifest itself in such a different form from that taken in the industrial core countries. Indeed, the crisis often takes the *opposite* form in one compared to the other: capitalist bankers worry about being repaid while Third World debtors try to find the means to service their debts; over-production in the centre closes off profitable investment and piles up unsold commodities while in the periphery the means to produce scarce and essential goods does not exist; and food mountains pile up while millions do not receive minimal nutritional needs even where there is no famine. These contradictions indicate that an explanation must go beyond the present situation to an under-standing of the peculiarities of the development process in the Third World and to the nature of its relationship to the central capitalist economies.

Certainly, it is not possible to take refuge in simple explanations about 'greedy bankers' abandoning commercial prudence in their lust for interest, or in 'irres-ponsible Third World governments' indulging in grandiose projects and borrowing without heed to prospects for repayment.[35] We have already seen that each was responding either to the falling rate of profit or to increasing balance-of-payments deficits. Nor does a similar formula about government inefficiency, corruption and waste carry matters further; even the grossest racist would struggle to assert that these have been causes in *all* countries in crisis or that those regimes fortunate enough to have escaped the worst effects of the crisis have been entirely free from such problems. If such factors play a part in some cases, they do not do so in all. And in general they are a symptom of a more fundamental process rather than variables with an independent force of their own.

Two other explanations need to be taken a little more seriously. The first is that excessive state intervention, misconceived policies of protecting local industries at the expense of high costs and inefficiency, burgeoning bureaucracy and general welfare policies which poor countries cannot afford have combined to weaken Third World economies and leave them defenceless against recession. This is certainly the thrust of IMF prescriptions and is popular with elements of the extreme right now in power in many parts of the west. The criticism is often directed at 'socialist' programmes in the Third World (which covers a wide spectrum of opinion) but can also be directed at state interventionism in right-wing authoritarian regimes such as Brazil or Nigeria.[36] Unfortunately for this line of argument, the debt crisis shows no such ideological or policy discrimination: indeed, the ability to run up huge debts has been most easily available precisely to those countries considered most agreeable to merchant bankers. Nor do the monetarist orthodoxies visited on the people of Chile and Argentina appear to have produced any greater degree of economic health and resilience than inter-vention in Brazil; quite the contrary. And the famine in Africa has affected states of all ideological and programmatic hues; indeed the coincidence of war (often externally induced) appears to have had a far greater disruptive effect than policy.[37] Nor does this line of argument attempt to explain how particular states have embarked on particular choices of development strategy, namely how history and international circumstances have helped to shape the form of state and the nature of policy.

The second line of reasoning locates the crisis in the Third World in the sudden explosion of oil prices prompted by the OPEC cartel after 1973. This is a more complex problem and can certainly be considered an important catalyst of subsequent events. Wood, for instance, has indicated that the oil price increases may have cost the oil importers of the Third World some $260 billion more than had oil prices simply risen in keeping with the US wholesale price index and that this sum represents more than half the increased external indebtedness of these countries.[38] OPEC revenues also created a lake of petrodollars in merchant banks all looking for investment outlets and thus available to fund the lending to Third World countries. But one should take care not to make this event a sufficient explanation of present problems, nor to argue that the Third World predicament was brought upon itself by greedy oil sheiks:

1 The dollar market was far greater than its petrodollar component.
2 Debts incurred were almost double that of the oil price rise in costs and much of that was attributable to vast increases in oil-company profit margins rather than to OPEC revenues.
3 Balance of payments difficulties were at least as much attributable to cuts in imports by capitalist countries of Third World primary production as to increased oil bills.
4 It would be well to note that the cost of food imports from the main capitalist countries during this period increased even more sharply than did oil costs. As Wood notes, bank lending to the Third World was rising even before the oil price rise and was exacerbated rather than caused by it.

What the oil price increases do indicate is the tremendous vulnerability of the Third World economies to fluctuations and forces external to them and their inability to manage outside pressure or make alternative arrangements. When the major industrial economies are buoyant, they tend to benefit from high demand and price levels. When capital must restructure to restore profit rates, they are quickly disrupted. They are *dependent* for their growth, stability and survival (in their present form at least) on external economic forces. Dos Santos described this condition of dependence as

> a situation in which the economy of certain countries is conditioned by the development and expansion of another economy to which the former is subjected. The relation of interdependence between two or more economies . . . assumes the form of dependence when some countries (the dominant ones) can expand and be self-sustaining, while other countries (the dependent ones) can do this only as a reflection of that expansion . . . The concept of dependence permits us to see the internal situation of these countries as part of the world economy.[39]

The severity of the present crisis is rooted in the nature of Third World relations to the world capitalist economy. These relations impose different conditions on different countries within the international division of labour. In one place, the world crisis produces falling rates of profit and capital exports while elsewhere it manifests itself in the decline of production and the emergence of debt peonage.

Any explanation of the current crisis must thus look beyond contingent and immediate events, such as the oil price rise, to historically determined, structural characteristics of the Third World. The dramatic character of the debt crisis and famine makes it easy to forget that crisis is not new to these countries. Indeed, long before the crisis of overproduction became fully apparent in the mid-seventies, the majority of Third World countries experienced persistent poverty, hunger, indebtedness, shortage of productive capital, lack of growth, great social inequality, political instability and repression. The crisis in the Third World has been a permanent one. Famine was frequent in India in the nineteenth and early twentieth centuries. It occurred on a large scale in China in the early decades of this century and has been frequent in Brazil since the war. The military regime has been a common feature of Latin America and Africa whether or not there has been a world recession. Hunger and poverty have been part of the normal life experience of the majority of people of the world whether or not 'the dynamic forces of the marketplace' were in full force. India, for example, the country which generally seemed to encapsulate all the crises of underdevelopment, has been conspicuously absent from the major horror stories of the world's press during the present crisis. In a work which redefined the terms of all subsequent discussion of development and underdevelopment, Paul Baran noted that the 67% of the world's population living in the poorest countries accounted for 15% of world income in 1949.[40] In contrast, in the richest countries, 18% of the world population enjoyed 67% of its income. Little would seem to have changed in this stark dichotomy. In 1969, 25.4% of the world population had access to 79.1% of world income in the richest countries while the 67.3% living in the poorest states accounted for 13% of the world's income[41] – even setting aside the question of great income inequalities within the Third World. The present crisis is likely to have increased such disparities rather than to have modified them.

Such disparities signify a relationship and not merely a statistical coincidence. The unequal and uneven distribution of international resources reflects a process involving more than three centuries of interaction with the west. This process predates the rise of industrial capitalism itself and helped to shape that rise as part of a prior accumulation.[42] Nor is the need for capital exports to offset falling rates of profit any more a new feature of global crisis than hunger and indebtedness. It was a major element of the expansion of industrial capital from the nineteenth century and has been described in various theories of imperialism.[43] The present situation is itself an expression of that history of capitalist imperialism as it continues; it is that historic process which has ensured that the present crisis is a global one to an extent unknown previously. What has characterized the development of capitalism within the Third World has been its *unevenness*. Uneven development has been a consequence of particular Third World territories being subsumed within the capitalist mode of production at different times according to different dynamics. Each territory has been incorporated in its own way – a product of the pre-existing non-capitalist modes of production, of the peculiar role which history and nature required it to fill in the global division of labour, of the resistance and response of the local inhabitants, and of the particular shifts and changes periodically produced by capital restructuring in the industrial core countries. In the process, Third World states have themselves come to exhibit internal unevenness in the development of capitalism. Thus, internationally and nationally, there is a process of uneven development spatially or regionally, sectorally, and culturally, as parts of the globe are differentially incorporated into the capitalist mode of production. Social formations have emerged in which elements of different modes of production are articulated, in which social relations characteristic of different modes coexist within and between groups, regions, communities, and, indeed, individuals. Such a combination or articulation of modes and relations within specific social formations, and between them and the imperialist system, is necessarily characterized by a high degree of contradiction in social relations.[44] They are societies experiencing transformation and upheaval as classes and individuals located within particular sets of social relations are moved into relations characteristic of different production regimes. Such territories are more complex and exhibit higher potentials for political conflict than states where the social formation more simply approximates a full-fledged capitalist mode of production.

Merchant capital and uneven development

The uneven development of the capitalist mode of production in the Third World reflects an ongoing process rather than a one-off articulation between capitalist and non-capitalist modes of production. European expansion into the rest of the world begins with the 'pre-history' of capitalism. Plunder formed an important mechanism for the transfer of wealth to Europe which provided a form of accumulation important to later economic transformation.[45] The slave trade was a crucial element in the organization of economic relations between Africa, Europe and the Americas. And Laclau has noted that settlement by Europeans in Latin America produced the feudal organization of the *hacienda* and *latifundo*.[46] Thereafter capitalism inserted itself in various territories in various waves and phases, first in the form of merchant capital and later as industrial capital. These phases differed in terms of time and sectoral activity as well as in terms of the nature of the territory subordinated within the global system. As capitalism is restructured and transformed in the central countries, so its character is constantly reshaped and restructured in the Third World to meet new requirements (not least at the behest of the IMF). Production relations not typical of capitalist production relations are thus also continually restructured in the same way, so that it is not really possible any longer to refer to them as 'pre-capitalist' or 'traditional' social relations.

The most profound influence in the various phases and forms by which capital has impinged upon the Third World has been that of merchant capital. Its influence has continued into the present, even where it has ceased to be the dominant form. Merchants invaded the Third World for plunder and with goods for trade. They were essentially pragmatic, acting towards a desired end and no further. They were certainly not interested in social engineering or 'civilizing missions'. Where their interests were served by simple trade relations, permitting them to buy cheap and sell dear, they were content to confine their activities in this way. Far more often, however, they found themselves required to intervene in broader economic and political issues in order to organize and safeguard markets in which they controlled profits and from which they excluded competition. Thus it became necessary to reorient many territories from their own, previously developed market structures towards commodity relations with them and Europe. From here it was a natural progression for them to organize production by the indigenous populations to guarantee supplies of required commodities. And this in turn frequently necessitated the creation of new political regimes which would ensure the redirection of local labour power to commodity production for the international market.

Where they could utilize family and village units for commodity production of export goods, they did so.[47] Where larger scale production was needed or where the local organization of labour could not be converted to the new trade economies, they employed coerced labour – including slavery, from which they also benefited as traders. The plantation economy was an important form of production regime during the merchant capitalist period, using slave or coerced migrant labour to produce agrarian commodities on a large scale at low costs. It was a form that made possible the profitable supply to western consumers of sugar, tobacco, jute, cotton and vegetable oils; for a time it was even used to produce opium for the Chinese market.[48] Where necessary, merchant capital even went into the business of government (though seldom profitably) setting up colonial regimes to repress dissent, organize markets, provide supplies of labour necessary to produce the required commodities, and protect their control over trade. The most famous case was the East India Company's rule over India until 1857 where a vast administrative and military apparatus was set up to promote and defend the company's interests.[49] But there were many others.

Marx considered merchant capital to be a powerful force in dissolving pre-capitalist production relations and introducing commodity relations.[50] This was certainly the case in the Third World. The creation of a new pattern of trade destroyed old markets and the production processes on which they rested. Where production interfered with merchant interests, production was reorganized to remove the obstruction and to destroy competition. Thus the East India Company destroyed much of the Indian handicraft industry[51] and disrupted the independence of the local artisanry. But Marx also considered that the dynamism of merchant capital as an agency for commercializing production relations did not extend to a capacity to transform the forces of production or to inaugurate a process of accumulation capable of sustaining itself – something that only industrial capital proper could achieve. Again, the evidence of the Third World would tend to confirm this proposition. Far from transforming social relations to facilitate productive capital, merchant capital tended to exclude European industry from any unmediated access to Third World markets, taking on the role of middleman for itself. Where production needed restructuring to provide it with the commodities for trade, it employed extra-economic, rather than market, forms of labour regulation and exploitation – slavery, the plantation, the *hacienda* or feudal landlord, and family-based petty commodity production. It frequently bolstered reactionary local classes and institutions to facilitate its ability to control production and trade, thereby entrenching them for generations.[52]

The process of transformation inaugurated by this phase was to shape the character and problems of the Third World today. The restructuring of markets destroyed previous trade patterns and production processes, a factor made worse by the conscious destruction of some indigenous production processes in order to eliminate competition or to cut off alternative opportunities for labour. In place of this was put a new orientation to European export markets which required the conversion of large quantities of labour power to commodity production and away from internal needs. The economies of such territories frequently became internally 'disarticulated', depending on the production of one or two export commodities to purchase other goods they had previously produced themselves. Such economies typically became dependent, primary producing, mono-economies, forced to import large quantities of commodities from the revenues of a single-export product. In the process, there was no revolutionary transformation of the productive forces or establishment of the pre-conditions for a 'transition to capitalism' along the lines of the European or American experience.

The production regimes established relied on extra-economic coercion of labour, on exploitation through absolute rather than relative surplus value, or through ground rents levied by 'feudal' or 'semi-feudal' landlords, or through state taxes and levies which creamed off agricultural surpluses and forced peasants into wage labour, or through unequal exchange, the characteristic form of surplus appropriation by merchant capital. Pre-capitalist forms of production and trade were thus undermined, indigenous populations converted to commodity production for the world market, territories made dependent on export earnings in foreign markets where they did not influence price, and work processes based on regulated supplies of labour instituted. Far from being a dynamic force capable of transforming productive forces, merchant capital proved to be the agent of uneven development, at one and the same time acting to dissolve some pre-capitalist production relations and to conserve others, producing new social relations underscored by profound contradictions and conflicts, not least manifest in the absence of any internal dynamic of reproduction.

In human terms, this process of change acted to transform some class relations while preserving others in a form compatible with the needs of merchant capital. Peasants were converted into petty commodity producers in some cases; although the organization of family labour altered little, they now produced for the international market rather than for themselves or for local exchange. Given that the forces of production in their hands remained essentially the same, this change ensured that they now frequently did not produce an adequate subsistence for themselves. In other cases, they were converted to wage labour, but not as a new proletariat separated from the means of production and forced to sell labour power to industrial capital. Instead, they were frequently converted into migrant workers moving between town and country, between peasant work and unskilled or semi-skilled labour. In this form, their wages could be squeezed to a bare subsistence while their families sought to produce their own subsistence on the land. Again, the failure to revolutionize the productive forces ensured that wage labour remained poorly compensated and based on absolute surplus value forms of exploitation while the families of migrants tried to continue peasant production in circumstances where the family division of labour had been disrupted. Still others found themselves as the tenants of landlords who extracted surplus from them in the form of ground rents or of obligatory labour. In many parts of the Third World – but South Asia in particular – the burden of such rents undermined the capacity of peasants to realize a subsistence.

In effect, what was inaugurated was a process, now more than two centuries old in some countries, of undermining the capacity of the mass of rural people to produce a subsistence, let alone a surplus. In this way, the separation of rural producers from the means of production was started. It was exacerbated by the entrenchment of landlord interests whose control over the peasantry was greatly increased under merchant capital. In India, for instance, the *zamindar* (tax collector in the Moghul Empire) was given perpetual rights to his office and the area he administered in order to coopt him into the East India Company state. Since his tax target was low, he now could concentrate on rack-renting the peasantry in his own interest. Thus, in one measure, was created a class of 'parasitic landlords' according to Moore.[53] As the peasant ceased to be able to meet rent obligations and produce a subsistence, so increasing debt and landlessness became apparent. Elsewhere, the colonial state acted as the agent of extraction – in the form of taxes and levies on peasants and also through monopoly marketing boards which creamed off part of the market price for state purposes.[54] Here too, the self-sufficiency of the peasantry was undermined and a process of separation initiated.

All the problems of debt, poverty and hunger which we discussed earlier are rooted in the character of this transformation and the legacy of merchant capital. The Third World is in debt because it is dependent on the sale of primary commodities to the industrial centres of capital in order to generate the revenues needed to purchase scarce manufactures and food. Rural populations experience hunger because relatively large quantities of labour power are expended on the production of export commodities rather than food. Although some 70 per cent of Third World populations live on the land, many such countries are food importers and exporters of agricultural produce. Hunger is also generated by agricultural decline, or rather the decline in the capacity of peasants to feed themselves, which results from the expropriation of peasant production through ground rents, state taxes and levies, and from the breakdown of the family labour unit through labour migration. Famine has been closely correlated to rural indebtedness (as in nineteenth century India),[55] to production of export crops (as in Brazil's north-east)[56] and to the collapse of production in labour reserves (as in southern Africa)[57] as well as to drought and war. The overall economic dependence on primary exports also contributes to hunger when falling commodity prices result in balance-of-payments problems and cutbacks in food imports. A dependent export economy lacks the productive capacity and resources to adjust to the crisis and borrowing and 'aid' become its only alternatives. Debt is thus a function of the character of uneven development and the distortions produced by the form of capitalist development.

It is important to stress that the structures introduced through merchant capital were not simply transitory problems to be taken care of by an enlightened industrial capitalism rushing to the rescue. The organization of production introduced by commercial capital has proved more resilient than its sponsors and it influences the pattern of industrialization. It is also worth noting that merchant capital remained the dominant form of capitalist intervention for a considerable period in many parts of the Third World. Kay, for instance, argues that it is only in the thirties that industrial capital can be said to have started to enter most of sub-Saharan Africa.[58] Even in India, where company rule ended in 1857, merchant capital remained influential, and even in the 1920s, Indian merchants were exercised by the extent to which they remained excluded from markets and credit. Nor has the international division of labour established under merchant capital altered substantially. As table 5.7 indicates, the trade profiles of selected Third World countries continue to indicate the nature of specialization within the global production process: Third World countries remain primary exporters and depend for manufactures and food on the industrial centre.

Industrial capital in the Third World was initially concentrated in extractive processes such as mining. It generally involved the advance of far greater quantities of capital than had ever been contemplated by merchant capital, and introduced new, sometimes relatively advanced, levels of productivity. But in other respects it reinforced rather than undermined the process of change already discussed. It was generally confined to small enclaves with its ancillary industries and provided only limited forms of involvement for the local population. It continued, and in fact extended, the export orientation of the Third World economy with hardly any of its production being utilized in the local environment. It increased dependence on the international economy for a large variety of production inputs. It seldom promoted the development of an industrial proletariat, preferring to utilize migrant labour in unskilled and semi-skilled work at low wage levels. In southern Africa, among a number of cases, it divided skilled and other work along racial lines, thus dividing the working-class politically. The labour reserve economy in that region, with men migrating to the towns and women surviving on the land, was essentially a feature of mining-company rather than merchant-capitalist policy. Mining thus produced rural decline and urban squalor and poverty rather than any dynamic process of transformation. Once again, the peculiarities of uneven development resulted in capital investment taking a different form in the Third World compared with the European model.

Rise of the multinational corporation

After 1945, western industrial investment increased rapidly and enormously in the periphery and began to revolutionize productive forces and relations on a scale previously unknown. The process of surplus extraction through merchant capital and early industrial forms was complemented and superseded by the vast expansion of multinational capital investment throughout the world. This was particularly the case with US capital. In 1901 only 23 American companies had operated a foreign subsidiary (only three of which were in the Third World) compared with 186 in 1967 (182 were in Latin America and 158 in Asia and Africa). In the case of manufacturing subsidiaries, the total rose from 18 to 185 between 1901 and 1967 (only three had Latin American subsidiaries and none were in Asia and Africa in 1901 compared with 171 and 134 respectively in 1967).[59] In 1929 US direct investment abroad was $3.7 billion in industrial countries and $3.5 billion in the Third World. By 1973, the values were $74.1 billion and $27.9 billion.[60] The bulk of this international expansion was therefore in Europe, but the Third World component was strategically important to the United States (in 1970, for instance, it showed almost twice the return on capital of investments in other industrial countries despite far lower investment levels and half the reinvestment rate).[61]

Investment by multinational corporations has been even more important to the Third World. The massive technological and financial resources at their disposal makes such corporations the dominant organizational expression of the global economy. The increase in investment thus encouraged hopes that Third World countries might redefine their position within the international division of labour. Even if production processes imported in this way were parts of larger circuits of capital, even if investment essentially shifted redundant technologies to the Third World to take advantage of lower wage levels, the prospect of escaping from the primary-producer level of dependence to this higher form was attractive to many. Even for some socialists, the prospect that international capital might

Table 5.7 Trade profiles of selected Third World countries

Country	Main exports	Main imports
Africa		
Angola	crude oil, coffee, diamonds	transport equipment, iron, steel, textiles, beverages, medicines
Benin	cotton, cocoa, ground nuts	food, machinery, textiles
Botswana	diamonds, meat, minerals	machinery, food, fuel
Burkina Faso	cotton, nuts, livestock	textiles, food, machinery, consumer goods
Cameroon	cocoa, coffee, timber	machinery, fuels
Congo	oil, timber	machinery, food, equipment
Ethiopia	coffee, hides, skins	machinery, manufactures, fuels, cotton, chemicals
Ghana	cocoa, wood, minerals	manufactures, food, fuels, equipment
Ivory Coast	cocoa, coffee, timber	manufactures, fuels, industrial inputs
Kenya	coffee, oils, tea, fruit, vegetables	machinery, oil, paper products, metal products, textiles
Lesotho	wool, mohair, diamonds	maize, building materials, clothing, machinery, equipment
Liberia	iron ore, rubber, coffee, diamonds	food
Malawi	tobacco, tea, sugar	manufactures, machinery, fuels, fertilizers, building materials
Mozambique	cashew nuts, textiles, tea, cotton, sugar	machinery, equipment, textiles, oil products
Nigeria	crude oil	machinery, manufactures, chemicals, intermediate industrial inputs
Sudan	cotton, peanuts, sesame seed, gum arabic	textiles, oil products, food, transport equipment
Tanzania	coffee, cotton, sisal, diamonds	petroleum, manufactures, machinery, fuels, food
Zaire	copper, coffee, zinc, diamonds	food, consumer goods, mining and transport equipment, fuels
Zambia	copper	machinery, transport equipment, food, fuels, manufactures
Zimbabwe	tobacco, food, asbestos chrome, copper	machinery, transport equipment, petroleum, wheat, maize
Asia		
Bangladesh	jute, jute products, hides, skins, tea	grains, fuels, cotton, fertilizers manufactures
India	stones, clothing, iron, steel	machinery, fuels, food, fertilizers
Indonesia	oil, timber, food, rubber, natural gas	rice, wheat, chemicals, iron, steel, machinery, consumer durables
Malaysia	rubber, timber, crude oil, tin, palm oil	industrial inputs, manufactures, machinery

Table 5.7 continued

Country	Main exports	Main imports
Pakistan	rice, cotton fabrics, carpets, cotton, yarn, leather	food, edible oils, fuels, machinery
Thailand	rice, tapioca, rubber, tin, maize, sugar	machinery, fuels, metals, chemicals, fertilizers
Latin America		
Argentina	maize, wheat, meat, wool, hides, oilseed, manufactures	machinery, fuels, iron, steel, manufactures
Bolivia	tin, minerals, gas, oil, coffee, cotton, sugar	food, chemicals, capital goods, pharmaceuticals
Brazil	coffee, soya, iron, manufactures	minerals, fuels, capital goods, fuels
Chile	copper, minerals	machinery, industrial inputs, foods, consumer goods
Columbia	coffee, textiles	machinery, chemicals, industrial inputs
Cuba	sugar, nickel, copper ores	machinery, manufactures, fuels
Ecuador	oil, coffee, bananas	machinery, food, chemicals, fuels
Mexico	crude oil, coffee, metals	machinery, industrial inputs
Nicaragua	bananas, coffee, cotton, meat, chemicals	agricultural products, chemicals, oil, machinery
Peru	copper, fishmeal, silver, lead, zinc, coffee	food, machinery, iron, steel, chemicals, intermediate manufacturers
Venezuela	crude oil, oil products	machinery, chemicals, manufactures, wheat
Middle East/North Africa		
Algeria	crude oil, oil products wine, fruit, vegetables	capital goods, food, semi-finished goods
Egypt	oil, cotton, yarns, fabrics, foods, aluminium	manufactures, consumer goods
Kuwait	oil, oil products	food, consumer goods, capital goods
Libya	crude oil	everything else
Caribbean		
Barbados	sugar, molasses, rum	food, machinery, fuels
Dominican Republic	sugar, coffee, cocoa, gold, chemicals	food, oil, raw materials
Guyana	bauxite, sugar, rice	manufactures, machinery, food, fuels
Jamaica	alumina, bauxite, sugar	fuels, machinery, food, fertilizers
Trinidad and Tobago	oil, oil products	crude oil, machinery, metal products, manufactures, food

Source:
Extracted from *South*, no. 59 (September 1985), special socio-economic survey of the Third World.
Commodities are listed in descending order of importance to balance of payments in the early eighties.

play a progressive role in the Third World and so finally create the basis for a sustained accumulation process seemed at least a welcome relief from autarchic prescriptions about the problems of building capitalism in one country.[62] Here the East Asian economies with rapid growth rates and the Brazilian model of a partnership between foreign and local capital and the state seemed instructive.

Unfortunately, the general performance of industrial multinationals has not lent itself to this optimism. Such problems have been exhaustively debated and so only need a brief mention. Multinationals are regarded by many observers as creating as many problems as they solve and even as being essentially harmful in their effects. It is argued that they increase dependency on foreign imports and markets; that they introduce inappropriate technologies which create enormous costs in imports and dependence on foreign skills; that they bring very little capital with their investments since they tend to raise much of their venture capital from scarce local sources, that they do not pass on their technical skills so that when they leave there is no new body of skills in the Third World country; that they reinvest little and export large surpluses through dividends and transfer pricing techniques; that they generate little employment through their capital-intensive methods; that they generate few exports because of an unwillingness to compete with other subsidiaries of the same conglomerate; that they produce demonstration effects and taste transfer through their marketing techniques which in turn undermine local industries and push up imports; and that they undermine national sovereignty by their influence over economic policy and even by direct political challenge to the state. In many cases, multinationals have not produced a momentum towards self-sustained growth but instead have contributed to a worsening balance of payments and debt crisis because of low levels of capital imported from abroad, poor export performance and increased import burdens to meet their many specialized requirements (themselves often inflated by transfer pricing between units of the same corporation).

Furthermore, rather than transforming the production process as hoped by their advocates, much direct industrial investment and many multinationals seem content to continue in the traditions of Third World exploitation already laid down: the use of absolute surplus value, extra-economic labour coercion and migrant labour. Thus their investment does not always make any difference to the nature of the accumulation process. *International Business Week*, [64] for example has expressed concern about the emergence of 'hollow corporations' – multinationals that no longer bother with production but simply contract out to independent operators in the Third World, a new variant of the putting-out system. In agribusiness, multinationals have frequently shown little desire to transform the forces of production, preferring to use plantation regimes or peasant labour contracted to crop targets. In the case of the 'banana republics' of Central America, the whole apparatus of the state has been constructed around the need to reproduce and manage such labour regimes. And one multinational, Del Monte, even builds its advertising around the strong, silent *gringo* appearing before an anxious set of *peons* who wait for his approval: 'the man from Del Monte, he say yes'. Far from revolutionizing the agrarian sector in the Third World, multinationals often seek to perpetuate non-capitalist production relations without which certain agrarian commodities could not profitably be marketed in the west. Nor do they solve the problem of hunger; indeed, they often exacerbate it by structuring production around luxuries for consumption by the affluent or by westerners. Little of the food they produce anywhere in the world feeds the people of the Third World except as famine relief. Their technology has long been criticized for its ecological effects – high chemical inputs which have been described as a process that mines the soil rather than farms it.[65] Perhaps the most glaring instance is found in Brazil where a previous history of industrial multinationals polluting the cities is now being paralleled by vast deforestation which will make room for beef production to supply hamburger meat to the United States.

Whatever the arguments about whether or not the multinationals are capable of resolving the crises of development in the Third World (and it is not, in any case, possible for *all* Third World countries to assemble transistors, package printed circuits, etc.) the dominance of industrial capital in the Third World has been short-lived. The debt crisis has produced a new phase in the subordination of the underdeveloped countries to capital before industrial capital had the ability to transform production relations, for the debtors are now in thrall to finance capital. It is now the banks and the international financial agencies which directly regulate the development of capitalism in the periphery. Just as finance capital in the west involved the amalgamation of industrial and bank capital under the control of the latter, so too has the process now arrived in the Third World. It is now the banks and the IMF that manage the system of debt peonage. The IMF's 'medicine' subordinates internal accumulation – the one hope for an end to indebtedness – to the organization of production for export, essentially of primary products. Bank capital, too, it would seem, has no use for a Third World in which the capitalist forces of production develop freely. Instead it forces many countries back into their 'colonial' role within the division of labour. They must export to service their debts in order to borrow further to service the next debt deadline. Attempts at industrialization, the focus of the development process since 1947, have once more been shelved.

The Politics of the Crisis

The contemporary crisis has induced enormous strains and tensions in the Third World states it has affected. Numerous upheavals can be directly attributed to the decline of production, debt, hunger and famine or can be seen to have been intensified by them. The crisis in the Third World is thus political as well as economic. But it is no mere reflection, or end-product of economic forces and contradictions: it has its own logic and its own level of determination as well. Indeed, in one sense, it is the political domain which defines the special character of the current crisis of international capital. The period after 1945 was characterized by the greatest expression of nationalism in human history. More than three-quarters of the world's population was affected by demands for self-determination. It is precisely this national self-assertion that focused attention on the problems of development, precisely this that made the need to promote economic growth an international priority. In a sense, such 'problems of development' did not 'exist' under colonial rule or imperial domination – cycles of capital accumulation were understood in terms of metropolitan considerations. The struggles for political independence expressed a contradiction between the international development of capitalism on a world scale, on the one hand, and the struggle of Third World peoples to 'recapture their own history', on the other.[66] It is precisely changed political ends and structures which confronted the needs of Third World people against the profitability of international capital, which makes questions about whether development is best served by greater self-reliance or increasing integration into the international economic order of central concern.

Because development and nationalism are closely related, the state in the Third World occupies a central and strategic role. It is the state to which nationalist aspirations were directed, the state which thus became the locus of struggles to redefine the relationship of particular societies with international capitalism, and the state to which various groups and interests looked for redress after centuries of imperial exploitation and oppression.

Imperialism has systematically excluded the indigenous population from power and property within Third World societies. This had been part of the formal institutional structure of colonial states but it was also true where the state had long passed out of colonial control but where foreign capital completely dominated the production relations – as in Latin America. Although indigenous classes owning private property had developed under these regimes, they remained extremely weak in relation to metropolitan capital. The institutions of the state were seen by people from all classes as essential to any attempt to weaken imperial interests and undertake some level of social transformation. Third World nationalism varied greatly from one territory to another in its intensity and in its commitment to change and social justice, but virtually all focused on the state as the mechanism for promoting their interests.

Yet enormous contradictions attend this central role of the state, arising from its relationship to the international capitalist system, from its form and relation to civil society, from its class character and from the historical moment of its formation. Nationalist movements awakened and played on popular dreams of transformation and justice. They mobilized people in the name of democracy and parliamentarism (the heart of their justification of anti-colonial ideologies) and committed their future programmes to economic growth and development. Yet political independence did not produce, nor was it the product of, economic independence. And dependency was – as we have seen – a reflection of a structure of production and labour process which had not revolutionized the productive relations in such a way as to sustain a self-reproducing process of accumulation. At independence (and far beyond it in places like Latin America) economic power remained with metropolitan capital which continued to dominate individual Third World economies – generally in the form of bank, industrial and plantation capital – and hence to determine the parameters of economic policy and the nature of the accumulation process. Foreign capital, very often in alliance with a subordinate landed and local bourgeois interest, perpetuated the 'colonial' character of economic activity and influenced political policy – a process often described as 'neo-colonialism'.[67] In many cases this power remained so strong that independence came to be regarded as 'mere flag independence'.

So dominant has been the continuity of foreign capitalist control that many observers have all too quickly concluded that nothing changed at independence and that decolonization, except where socialist experiments were attempted, counted for little or nothing. In many cases national movements had been shaped,

influenced or even selected by their colonial predecessors and continued to exhibit
a marked deference to the metropolis after independence.[68] Even where not, the
institutional arrangements governing independence stressed continuity rather than
change. Post-colonial states inherited the bureaucratic structures, rules and even
personnel of the colonial state apparatuses.[69] They took over colonial military
forces. Independence constitutions invariably enshrined the rights of private
property, requiring that compensation be paid at full market rates for expropriated
property and thereby protecting the interests of the local and foreign bourgeoisies
alike. (In the Kenyan case, for instance, the British government itself paid settlers
to permit Kenyans to purchase their land, while in the case of Zimbabwe, the
constitutional provision which most irked the national leadership – but which they
were finally forced to accept – was the guarantee that all land redistribution would
be by consent and proper compensation of the owners.)

Yet to dismiss decolonization in this way is to ignore the enormous contradictions
with which it invested the development process – and to ignore the relevance
of a great deal of recent history and popular action. Put simply, the state apparatuses charged with ensuring this degree of continuity no longer simply represented
the interests attached to the project. While foreign capital continued to dominate
and determine, decolonization meant, by definition, that it no longer exercised
hegemony over the indigenous population – it had lost its legitimacy in a struggle
which had been precisely about taking control from foreign interests and ending
foreign domination. The post-colonial state had excited mass hopes that an
internally directed process of accumulation could be inaugurated. This had been
achieved, in most cases, by movements which themselves threw up no new,
alternative hegemonic classes. National movements were typically collections of
many interests, alliances of social classes united by a common, foreign enemy
led by a motley group of intellectuals, members of the intelligentsia, individuals
from the functionary strata of the colonial state and fragments of the petty
bourgeoisie and even, occasionally, of the landed classes. After independence,
the local class alliances began to dissolve as competition between contradictory
class projects could not be reconciled (the Sandinistas of Nicaragua being one
of the most recent cases). As Clive Thomas notes, 'in the periphery, where both
the traditional classes of the capitalist social formation (workers and capitalists)
are underdeveloped, and where both of these classes are small in numbers and
qualitatively weak, there is no clearly hegemonic ruling class.'[70]

Nowhere are the contradictions produced by uneven development starker than
at the level of the state and politics in the Third World. The state itself is the
product of struggle between national forces and imperialism.[71] In the colonial
situation, it was the clear expression of the interests of metropolitan capital and
ruled on its behalf. In the post-colonial situation, however, metropolitan capital
continues its domination but loses control over the state. The new state is run
by a variety of petty bourgeois elements together with functionaries of the old order
who generally occupy the coercive state apparatuses. The post-colonial state also
has a very different relationship with civil society. In the colonial context the
indigenous population was excluded from the state; now it is incorporated through
the franchise – a voice achieved as a direct consequence of demands for independence. This franchise precedes the achievement of the vote in many industrial
countries (it came to many Africans before it was given to Afro-Americans in the

US south or to the women of Switzerland, for instance).[72] More importantly, it gives to the peasants and workers of the Third World the potential to demand policies of social justice and economic redistribution before any major revolution in the productive forces and any autonomous process of accumulation has begun; in contrast, this capacity to make legitimate demands on the system came to European workers long after such a process was underway. Not only is there a 'vacuum' in terms of class hegemony, therefore, but the rules whereby class domination must be legitimated are essentially different in the Third World.[73]

The state in the Third World has little control over the accumulation process – partly because foreign capital continues to determine its social relations and also because the laws of its reproduction are determined in the international political economy. But the state is the focus of interventionist imperatives directed towards development and social justice, themselves legitimized by the demands for independence. It must inaugurate a process of accumulation which somehow reconciles (or chooses between) the demands of peasants and workers who constitute the new electorate (but who are often not completely integrated into the dominant political organizations in control of the state) on the one hand, and the 'realities' of foreign capital domination and world economic forces.

These factors make the stability of the state precarious. The need for the embryonic indigenous propertied classes to develop and assume a hegemonic position in civil society is obstructed by imperialism and underdevelopment, as well as by pressures for resources coming from below. And the prospect of incorporating the masses into a legitimate state order (and thereby negating their ultimate revolutionary potential) is rendered impossible by the lack of development, the strength of imperialism and the difficulties of implementing even the most basic social reforms, let alone some real measure of social justice. In addition, as observed in the previous section, the forces of capitalism do not halt the process of incorporating the Third World into the international division of labour. Multinational investment in agribusiness expropriates and impoverishes the peasantry rather than converting it to any new prosperity – landlessness increases and so does proletarianization, women have their land confiscated to make way for prestige projects, the family labour unit is broken up and its access to means of production diminished, food production is displaced by export production. Inflation attacks the wages of urban workers before any other class or group. Debt ends food imports and imposes austerity on the poor. IMF 'stabilization' destroys efforts to invest in education, health and equality. Whatever the inclinations of the petty bourgeois elements in government, the world economy and the nature of underdevelopment ensure that mass expectations of the state are unlikely to be even remotely met. In consequence, the revolutionary potential of political contradictions in such states is high – despite the lack of organization from which peasants and workers typically suffer in the Third World.

The class character of such contradictions is amplified by the fact that, given the weakness of the local propertied class, 'the state is frequently used as an instrument to promote the formation of such a class.'[74] The apparatuses of the state have an instrumental value – they are a crucial source of income and status for individuals and perhaps the single most important resource for entry into the local bourgeoisie.[75] State loans, contracts and policies all serve the needs of a developing bourgeoisie and petty bourgeoisie. These are augmented by a system of plunder in which the resources of the state are looted by corruption and patronage.[76] For all the concern of the IMF and capital about 'unrealistic' schemes to provide for the poor, it is the bourgeoisie whose welfare is mainly served by the Third World state. In addition to the backing it provides, the state is also the primary organizer of labour, regulator of the labour process, controller of worker and peasant organizations and general factotum for capital. Being heavily dependent on revenues provided by capital – especially foreign companies earning hard currencies in the export sector – governments generally act to protect their sources. The nature of the colonial state as the force subordinating local interests to capital is elaborated in the post-colonial situation through a variety of controls affecting the working day, the right to organize, the wage, and the right to strike. The difference is that now the interests of local capital come to be mediated alongside – and sometimes at the expense of – foreign capital.

The state is thus confronted by the simultaneous need to promote accumulation, sponsor a ruling class and legitimize class rule. Such a project would tax the capacities of the state in advanced capitalist economies where a degree of control over the accumulation process exists and where it is possible to disperse some part of the surplus through 'the welfare state'.[77] It is extremely problematic in the Third World. The most obvious source of legitimation for this project is 'development'; this was, after all, the basic appeal to the masses during the demands for independence. Unfortunately, for all the reasons we have seen, it is neither possible to plan for growth nor, during the last decade, to experience it in most cases. This produces the need for alternative legitimation strategies. One alternative is the reintroduction of nationalism as a developmental ideology, promoting self-reliance and accumulation and articulating a strong anti-imperialist rhetoric. Such a strategy runs the risk of alienating foreign capital entirely while failing to build a mass base to sustain the regime through its quarrels with imperial interests. It is popular with the local bourgeoisie but this class is unlikely to be able to promote growth to an extent which can offset pressures from below and from outside. The strategy has been tried in countries like Peru and Zambia with only limited success. Another approach is through a series of strategies claiming a socialist basis. One form is 'socialism', a rhetorical position in which private capital is promoted while constant appeals to popular desires for greater equality are put forward. In some moments, Zambia has played this card but the classic instance is that of India. There the Congress Party has promoted the growth of a national bourgeoisie while increasing the size of the state sector (referred to as 'socialist') and seeking to dissolve pre-capitalist bonds in the agrarian sector. It is a strategy in which economic nationalism and private property parades as socialism. India has been able to pursue it with a large injection of capital from the USSR and USA but it has been difficult to sustain as a believable ideology since 1967.[78]

'Socialism' can take other forms, however. In Jamaica, for instance, the Manley government sought to implement a number of far-reaching reforms and to limit the influence of foreign capital. There was never any suggestion of a Marxist orientation, but the programme went beyond the promotion of a local bourgeoisie (a class strongly opposed to the Manley government) to proposals for greater mass participation in economic growth. The weakness of the strategy proved to be the unwillingness of local or international capital to tolerate its diminished influence and power; the regime was destabilized and economic crisis became the method of its electoral overthrow.[79] Alternatively, socialism can be a strategy of revolution in which worker and peasant class interests become the basis of state policy and private property is either abolished or, as in the case of Nicaragua, subjected to stringent controls. In this case the problem of legitimizing state power among the broad mass of the population is undertaken at the expense of private property. But experience in Angola, Mozambique and Nicaragua would indicate that it is difficult to sustain against violent aggression which inevitably follows unless the protection of an external power is sought. Thus one form of dependence can be exchanged for another, or a constant struggle in a war of attrition must be endured.[80]

The difficulties of legitimizing state power and class rule in the Third World, allied to the weakness of development programmes and capital accumulation, further influences the expansion of state intervention in the economy. Attempts to control the accumulation process and solve the political contradictions besetting them encourage many states to increase state control over property. Various governments 'nationalize' foreign capital in strategic sectors (often retaining the foreign interest as a minority shareholder) or enter into new joint ventures with overseas firms (this latter is often popular with multinationals who see the state as guaranteeing their interests). Although such undertakings are generally represented as socialist, they are not confined to such regimes; indeed, there are few non-communist states in the Third World with state sectors as large (relative to total production) as those of India and Zambia.[81] The strategies are representative of an attempt to reconcile popular demands with the imperatives of capital accumulation rather than any programme of socialization of the productive forces. As Thomas observes:

> the expansion of the role of the state in these economies is not a 'voluntary' development, but it is structurally and organically linked to the requirements of internal accumulation in these countries. . .*all* regimes in the periphery are impelled to do so by structural necessities of their internal social situations and the historically formed links between their economies and those of the centre. . .while in the capitalist centre countries. . .state intervention grows out of the cyclical crises that accompany the growth of output, in peripheral societies it is the *absence* of growth, the *scarcity* of capital, frequent *crises* in world commodity markets, and so on that foster state intervention in the system of economic reproduction.[82]

Foremost among the 'and so on' factors, we would identify the problems of resolving class contradictions and legitimating the emergence of a new ruling class.

The weakness of ruling class hegemony and the problems of incorporating peasant and working-class interests in the political order cannot be overstated. The peasantry and working class of the Third World do not have a stake in the post-colonial state. They have not been incorporated into a settled political process or an established order of economic rewards. No one is offering them a video recorder or cheap Central American fruit juice for breakfast or low cost Korean-made shirts in return for obedience. The independence struggle mobilizes their expectations without the petty bourgeois state personnel having the capacity or class interest to meet them. This was appreciated early in the classic work of the right-wing American political scientist, Samuel Huntington[83] – a work more often criticized than read. He argues that in the Third World, political mobilization has imposed pressures on political institutions which cannot be managed by the apparatuses or the elites that run them. Huntington's solution, writing from the perspective of the existing structures, is to build institutions and to 'demobilize' demands made on them. Democracy is made secondary to stability. Whether state personnel and political leadership groups have or have not read Huntington, their response to crises of class conflict and accumulation have been along similar lines.

State *forms* in the Third World have undergone frequent changes as crises of accumulation and political turmoil have racked them. In many cases, particularly in Asia and Africa, the initial attempt to incorporate the masses into the state order took the form of manipulation. In the rural areas, political groups employed non-capitalist lines of cleavage and solidarity to manipulate support. The nature of uneven development and the failure of capitalism to transform social relations in the Third World has meant that many pre-capitalist social relations not only survive but have been reinforced by a particular, even peculiar, experience of capitalist development. Different groups and different areas have been differentially incorporated into the international division of labour. This ensures that communal ties, such as religion, caste, race, ethnic group and region often have a material basis or interest within the international system. They are thus capable of being politically activated and used for the gathering of support or the mobilization of competition.[84] And they are singularly appealing to petty bourgeois and bourgeois elements who cannot legitimately seek political support in terms of class loyalty. In peasant societies such non-capitalist lines of cleavage are typically activated in the form of factions and patronage – in clientelist systems. Clientelism is typically the politics of class domination where one class controls another through non-class links.[85]

The problem with this kind of politics is that such ties are easily dissolved by social transformation – the increasing landlessness and class polarization in the Indian countryside, for instance, has eroded the clientelist base of the Congress Party[86] – and by disappointment over the gap between aspirations and performance. The state has thus increasingly undertaken exercises in narrowing the range of demands which can legitimately be made on it or of excluding mass demands altogether. As class contradictions become more difficult to contain, therefore, there has been an increase in coercion and a decrease in democracy. This has often been achieved by *ad hoc* measures – such as abolishing the right to strike or organize or publish on the part of workers – or by changes in the form of state itself. One such change, characteristic of Africa, has been the one-party state, a form which frequently opens up many opportunities for local level political participation but which generally narrows the arena of national political debate and reduces the capacity of different classes to organize politically. It can also provide the avenue for a more direct access by the bourgeoisie to the apparatus of the state and to its resources.[87] Fanon's claim that the one-party state was 'the dictatorship of the national bourgeoisie' is not without foundation.[88]

The military regime has been a more important and characteristic means of reducing access to the state in the Third World – indeed, the failure of African one-party states to contain political protest has resulted in many of them giving way to the army. Although there are isolated instances of military regimes broadening the popular base of politics – the Nasser coup in Egypt being perhaps the most important – in general their intervention has furthered the interests of foreign capital (often honouring debts which civilian governments were tardy in repaying) and of local property (whether landlord or bourgeoisie). In Latin America, military regimes tended to defend the interests of foreign investment and of the landlord class – often to the displeasure of the local bourgeoisie. More recently, especially since the Cuban revolution, they have tended to encourage landlord interests to commercialize their agricultural holdings and to promote the local capitalist class in partnership with multinational companies. A similar role has been played by the army in Pakistan.[89]

In Africa, coups have followed economic crises in which widespread opposition to government policies had developed. Their officer leaders have been much less successful either in revolutionizing agriculture or in promoting the local bourgeoisie (although important steps in this direction have been taken, for instance, in Nigeria) but have tended to defend foreign creditors' interests – perhaps an expression of the colonial army origins of many such leaders. Whatever the inclination, they have been merciless in suppressing working-class rights, attacking peasant landholdings in the interests of agribusiness, suppressing all political dissent and imposing economic austerity programmes. The military can be most accurately understood as the regime of last resort of private property.

In some cases (Latin America especially) mass protest has developed beyond spontaneous outbursts of anger or occupational interest-group activities. Where mass protest has become organized and exhibits a capability for political action to promote class power, some regimes have not stopped at a simple military takeover. It has become a feature of all too many Third World regimes that they seek to destroy the organizations representing workers and peasants and to liquidate their members. The *bestial regime* has become a feature of the political terrain. Such regimes characteristically seek to murder their opponents and the social groups from which they are drawn. They spawn murder squads, kill civilians on a mass scale, torture and maim: in essence they seek to resolve class conflict at the political level by murdering their class opponents. In countries such as Argentina, Chile, Guatemala and El Salvador there have been periods when people have 'disappeared' forever or been tortured and mutilated on a mass scale or simply been killed; Herman and Petras have referred to 'death-squad democracies' to describe some of these regimes.[90] Eventually, peace established, such regimes may begin to liberalize their rule but it is a liberalization built on the grave not on consent.

Not all states have had to adopt repressive forms. India, for instance, has preserved the parliamentary form while promoting the development of an industrial and financial bourgeoisie and, more recently, a commercial agrarian class. It has done so through a succession of Congress party governments which have used clientelist politics to maintain sufficient support among workers, peasants, the rural poor, religious and ethnic minorities as well as the national bourgeoisie. The preservation of the anti-colonial coalition, through a strategy of nationalism and state intervention in the economy mitigated by some degree of concessions to the mass, has allowed for the legitimation of bourgeois rule. The bourgeoisie, in turn, has accepted a slower rate of accumulation as the price of state protection. Yet even here, this formula has rested on landlord control over much of the peasantry and on growing violence and repression against peasants and workers in the rural areas. The emergency of 1975 crystallized such class conflicts and, while this has subsequently abated, recent moves by the new Rajiv Gandhi administration to accelerate bourgeois accumulation may well give a new edge to class struggles in India.[91]

More typical are cases such as Pakistan, where the local bourgeoisie was far less developed than in India and where rural pre-capitalist interests dominated the countryside. Here the influence of foreign capital dominates, the state depends on receipts from migrant labourers working in the Middle East (their remittances equal the balance of payments deficit of Pakistan) and the defence of reactionary landlordism and foreign capital has required a procession of military regimes, each more brutal than the one before.[92] In Latin America, an array of bestial military regimes has defended property against the working class and peasantry and sought to advance the interests of foreign capital and of the national bourgeoisie. During the eighties, a number of armies have returned to the barracks and handed over to civilian governments. But they also have handed over massive debts, IMF austerity programmes, an attack on the interests of the poor which has provoked protest which not even the might of military repression has been able to still. Herman and Petras suggest, in fact, that the return to civilian rule is a strategic retreat only:

> Is it possible that the new civilian rulers are 'fall guys' whose allotted task is to take primary responsibility for assured economic failure? The military regimes and their US partners have built up an unmanageable foreign debt and allowed social and economic sores to fester while they 'developed' their own bank accounts, have now moved to the wings to wait. The civilian governments imposing IMF – banker conditions on their long-suffering populations will not be able to meet any popular needs and demands. On the contrary, they find themselves in the position of enforcing further cut-backs on basic needs. Can democracy survive in such an environment?[93]

Whether civilians attempting to reintroduce democracy or military personnel enforcing class dictatorship, the oppressive character of many Third World regimes and the problems they face in controlling class conflict and mass protest has been exacerbated by the present crisis. More than ever, many of them depend on support, weapons and the technology of repression from abroad. The structure of international inequality, the stability of the international capitalist system – particularly in time of crisis – rests increasingly on local repression supported and supplied from abroad. It is to this imperial interest that we must now turn.

Evil Empires

This paper has treated imperialism in terms of structures and process, as the institutional arena which defines crises of underdevelopment and in which they play themselves out. But these structures are embodied in concrete states, organizations and factions which pursue policy priorities and react to immediate problems and events. If structure and process are the most crucial influences, it is nevertheless true that actors making short-term contingent decisions, especially in times of crisis, help to shape them. In the context of debt and famine, the policies of the major international economic agencies and of the western powers at present are extremely important. These policies have tended to compound the political instability of Third World regimes and to make them increasingly dependent on coercion to survive. They have, in consequence, become increasingly dependent for the means of coercion on those states and organizations on which they are economically dependent. Most of all, the role played by the United States during the present crisis has been crucial. As the major capitalist power, the US accounted for 55.6% of direct foreign investment throughout the world in 1970 (out of an estimated book value of $250 billion expanding by 10% to 20% per annum before the world crisis).[94] Its contributions to the IMF ensured that it holds an effective veto over any international adjustment policies of which it did not approve. While it does not and did not always dictate policy to such organizations, it had a major influence on the nature of the international agenda with regard to debt and also, as the main exporter of food grains, on hunger and famine. The increasing dependence of its main allies on US investment and military capability made the other western powers far less an independent source of international policy during the crisis. To a large extent the course of the crisis in the Third World has followed the course derived from IMF and United States policy.

Much has already been written about the role of the IMF in this paper. The consequences of its monetarist and export-oriented 'stabilization' measures has been seen to exacerbate problems of debt and of production rather than to resolve them. Here it is sufficient to note simply that such policies have clear political consequences: they attack working class and peasant interests more severely than those of the local bourgeoisies or bureaucracy; they actively promote the interests of multinational corporations in Third World societies, they consciously 'roll back' the Third World state and in the process dismantle political programmes aimed at some measure of autonomous economic development. Their political effects are fundamental and contradictory. On the one hand, they reduce the capacity of Third World debtors to formulate economic policy for themselves (the IMF has been conspicuous in overseeing even the budgets of some African states). On the other, they reduce the capacity for local accumulation and attack the living standards of the poor, thus ensuring increased political upheaval and the need for the state to spend on its repressive apparatus. This is a clear political pro-gramme (it is only the economic content of the IMF package that is unclear and incoherent) and its outcome is the subordination of Third World peoples to the international market under repressive state apparatuses guaranteeing export commodities before local consumption.

Where Third World states have fallen into the clutches of IMF adjustors after pursuing policies aimed at social reform, the effect has been not only to dismantle their programmes of change but also to destabilize their regimes. The role of the IMF in restoring dependent development is illustrated in figure 5.2. This shows the experience of Jamaica where the Manley government finally had to go into an election in the midst of massive consumer shortages produced by austerity budgets and during a rising tide of political violence. It was replaced by the pro-American, pro-capital administration of Edward Seaga proclaiming a new prosperity to be funded by American generosity. Seaga's utopia has been less than overwhelming. Jamaica has experienced little growth, has sacked thousands of public-sector workers, devalued the currency and cut subsidies on consumer items in line with IMF policies, without attracting new investment. In 1984 and 1985 two major bauxite multinationals closed down their refining operations at a massive cost to earnings and foreign-exchange revenues. In 1985 riots followed a 20 per cent rise in petrol prices. All polls indicate that the Seaga regime would be swept from office but no election is due until 1988.[95] Meanwhile his government remains to impose the IMF doctrine on Jamaicans.

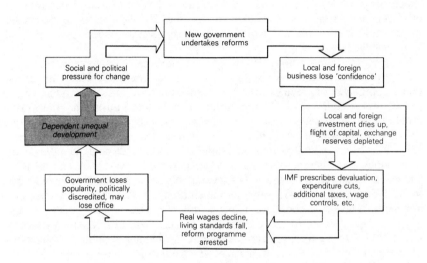

Figure 5.2 Role of the International Monetary Fund in restoring dependent development

Source: Norman Girvan, Richard Bernal and Wesley Hughes, 'The IMF and the Third World: the case of Jamaica', *Development Dialogue*, no. 2 (1980).

It is important to stress that the IMF strategy is not 'inevitable', that it does not represent the sole logic of imperialism. There is more than one way to run capitalism. One alternative, for instance, was proposed by the Brandt Commission.[96] This offered a plan for a more enlightened system of international capitalism in which multinationals would use their capital and technology as a dynamic agent of development of the Third World. The Brandt Report does not envisage a future for the nationalist economic strategies favoured by the Third World previously; its whole purpose is to advocate a greater integration of the international economic order. In this it hopes to achieve a reduction in the levels of inequality which might be derived from capital playing a more progressive, less extractive role. There have been many criticisms of this approach – and there is much to criticize. But it set out to find a method of breaking the cycle of immiserisation and crisis while preserving the international capitalist system – a sort of global Keynesianism.[97] The problem for Brandt and his colleagues is that multinational capital has little desire to play such a progressive role when it can make super-profits through the present structures or to invest in Third World countries when it can expatriate its profits through transfer pricing and dividends. Nor did this set of proposals find favour among western governments, despite the list of distinguished former leaders on the commission. One of the consequences of the crisis in the industrial countries has been the rise to power of extreme right-wing governments committed to reducing the share of output accruing to labour and increasing that enjoyed by capital. Given this view of their own societies, it was never likely that they would treat the Third World any more benignly. Instead, the policy pursued has been compulsion to open markets to capital, a cheapening of primary commodities through a reduction of returns to the direct producers and through massive currency devaluations, and a widespread increase in coercion. It is a policy in which the IMF stabilization measures have fitted comfortably.

The Reagan administration in Washington has been the central force in 'adjusting' the Third World to 'the new realities'. In this it has continued with many of the policy approaches of previous American administrations since 1945. It has sought to use American power to maintain influence and control throughout the world, protecting its investments, its access to strategic and valuable primary commodities and its relations with various Third World regimes. This is what one would expect any great power to do. The Reagan administration has also continued the policy of previous administrations of trying to contain the Soviet Union and its allies strategically and economically and of seeking to prevent it extending its influence in the Third World. As with other administrations, this has been undertaken on a number of levels – economic, political, military. To an extent greater than in the past, it has used its influence in the IMF and the World Bank to impose policy directions on Third World governments and has tied aid to political obligations imposed on recipients. Little of this is new; what it different is the aggressiveness and brutality with which policy objectives have been formulated and implemented.

American foreign policy has, certainly in this century, been very directly bound up with the interests of American capital. And capital in America is not an ideologically incoherent force dependent on some state to act as 'collective capitalist' on its behalf. From an early date it has concerned itself both with shaping popular consent to its hegemony (its advertising, not least, sells patriotism as well as products) and with handling key levers in the formulation and execution of state policy.[98] In particular, capital has evolved a plethora of think tanks, talk shops and public servants concerned with foreign policy and America's global power. For many years this process was dominated by the Rockefeller funded Council on Foreign Relations[99] which combined a liberal world view with an insistence on the use of American military power where necessary to protect client regimes and US corporate interests. Its policies were the dominant wisdom of the establishment until the Vietnam War where the domino theory produced by its thinkers carried the United States into one the great crimes of this century in an area of little strategic or economic value to America. This crisis brought in its wake also the liberation of the Portuguese empire in Africa, despite CIA efforts to take control of the process and install friendly clients there.[100]

In consequence, American foreign policy thinkers shifted their focus to include European and Japanese allies to formulate a global strategy for western capitalism in general rather than for America alone. The Council on Foreign Relations sponsored the Trilateral Commission which also included a wide-range of trans-Atlantic opinion.[101] In America, a Trilateral member, Jimmy Carter, with a government packed with trilateralists, gained the presidency in 1976. The Carter administration sought, in the wake of the Vietnam War, to accommodate Third World aspirations to some extent and not to reduce them always to global world power conflicts. Carter made a number of speeches about how America needed to shed its 'inordinate fear of communism' and how it could not be the policeman of the world. He outlined a strategy for American policy based on moral ('human rights') and economic competition with the Soviet bloc and on incorporation of Third World regimes by meeting their hostility from the right. The transfer of the Panama Canal to Panamanian sovereignty was denounced within months of Carter taking office and the stress on human rights was considered, by Henry Kissinger, to be a greater threat to US clients in Latin America than to socialist regimes around the world. Ultimately, the 'loss of Iran' discredited Carter domestically. If his policies had been popular in many parts of the Third World, those who sold it abroad (such as Andrew Young) were anathema to the right. By 1979 even the Council on Foreign Relations luminaries had abandoned Carter and he was replaced by Reagan.

Part of the electoral appeal of Reagan was his promise to reassert national power after the 'humiliations' of the Carter years. The foreign policy outlook packaged as part of the Reagan campaign promised the full use of economic and military power in prosecuting perceived American interests. 'Human rights' was replaced by the determination to support pro-western dictatorships and to undermine 'communist' regimes in the Third World. Reagan generated enthusiasm with his dismissal of the Carter strategy, proclaiming that America did not care whether or not the rest of the world loved her, only that it 'respected' her. The Council of Foreign Relations was superseded by two extreme right-wing lobbies: the Heritage Foundation and the Committee on the Present Danger.[102] In the years since 1981, personnel from these groups linked to the Reagan administration have participated in the evolution of what is now called the Reagan Doctrine, which extends the rights America reserved for itself under the Monroe Doctrine in its own hemisphere to the rest of the world. Essentially, Reaganism has reasserted the linkage between Third World nationalism and the spread of Soviet communism which informed US policy before Carter. In economic affairs, it has promoted the market philosophy and monetarist prescriptions of the IMF, but has also used economic sanctions against regimes of which it does not approve – including the use of food aid to influence Third World policy (aid was not readily available to Ethiopia and Mozambique until famine became an internationally popular issue, for instance).[103]

In addition, it has committed political and military resources to changing the political map in the Third World. It has given military assistance to unpopular right-wing regimes confronted by popular uprisings. There is a host of generals throughout the Third World armed to the teeth by the United States against their own populations. In addition, regimes without a popular base of support which depend mainly on repression to survive have been assisted in holding off popular revolutions and developing more legitimate political institutions. The most notorious example has been the support given for El Salvador's death squads through military aid and the sponsorship of narrowly based 'elections' there and in Guatemala.[104] A second form of intervention has been to assist anti-communist and pro-western movements in parts of the Third World. A number of these are in fact largely artefacts of US aid, having virtually no popular base or being compromised by association with previous despotisms; few would survive for long without external sponsorship. Thus a variety of *contra* organizations in Nicaragua are funded and trained to commit atrocities against a civilian population which does not support them, while the Reagan administration proclaims them 'the moral equivalent of our Founding Fathers'.[105] Nicaragua's Sandinista regime, legitimized by electoral support greater than that given to Reagan in his own elections, is decried as a dictatorship installed by an electoral facade, while regimes elected in El Salvador, Uruguay and Guatemala, when their opponents were not permitted to contest the elections, are held to be a positive step towards full democracy.

A third element in the Reagan Doctrine in the Third World is American support for clients who act to subvert or destroy target regimes. Thus the policy of 'constructive engagement' has given the South African government a blank cheque to sponsor movements and even to support them militarily against the governments of Angola and Mozambique. A similar commitment to removing apartheid has not been evidenced.[106] A blank cheque has also been given to Israel as was instanced by the Begin regime's savage invasion of the Lebanon. A fourth element of the policy has surfaced more recently. This involves client Third World regimes which have become so corrupt and so unpopular that they are threatened with overthrow by popular forces. Where such movements cannot be confronted, efforts have been made to contain and coopt them. Thus the Duvalier regime in Haiti was removed (the Americans actually announced the event before it happened!) and a client military-led clique installed in its place; it has not halted the mass protest in the least. In the Philippines, too, a rigged election, mass protest (involving even the mass of the local bourgeoisie alienated by debt and economic decay) and the growing strength of guerilla struggles among rural workers, led to the replacement of Marcos by a coalition headed by Aquino. The coalition was helped to power by right-wing military leaders (interestingly after a visit by US envoy Philip Habib) and struggles to capture this revolution before it proceeds too far along the road of reform, or before it is entirely taken over by US interest, are underway.

In 1986 a fifth dimension of this policy has emerged. This is referred to as 'anti-terrorism' and permits the use of military attacks on targets believed to represent terrorist movements or to harbour terrorism. It is, of course, a necessary tactic for states to brand all groups they oppose as terrorists and to blur the difficult distinctions to be made between armed struggle (aimed against state power and institutions) waged against foreign occupation or unjust tyrannies, on the one hand, and terrorism (violence against civilians and non-participants) on the other. But it is breathtaking to watch a state which has become the main exporter of violence against the Third World, the main sponsor of brutality against civilian populations by states or by guerillas, assume the right to dispose of all other terrorists.[107] In the meantime, acts of terror, often obscene in their victimization of the innocent, help to fuel this cycle of violence and repression on which the Reagan regime seems to thrive. The costs to the west are likely to be heavy in the long term: throughout the Third World a generation is growing up which regards the United States as the main enemy of humanity. In Pakistan, anti-government demonstrations quickly become anti-American as well. The same is true throughout the Middle East and Latin America. At present, recession and force maintain a degree of cowed obedience – but then the same could have been said of Iran after the

CIA backed overthrow of Mossadeq in 1953. It is increasingly unlikely that people in Europe or the Third World will accept that this strategy can be justified by a propaganda claiming that Soviet behaviour is even worse. For the Third World, certainly, those who declaim about evil empires describe also themselves.

Conclusion

The crisis in the Third World is an expression of the international crisis of capital. But it takes a singular form and has more destructive consequences in the Third World because of the historical experience of uneven capitalist development. This produced characteristic problems of poverty and stagnation which have proved resistant to efforts since 1945 to generate a sustained process of growth and development. The crisis of the last decade has sharpened the contradictions and suffering produced by underdevelopment. In turn, it has itself been exacerbated by the policies pursued by international capital through the IMF and the core states of the world economy. These policies have sought to terminate the political and economic gains made by the Third World during the sixties and early seventies: namely, to restore political control and access to cheap primary products undermined in the aftermath of the Vietnam War.

It remains to be seen which effects of the current crisis will be long-lasting or permanent. But a number will have a profound impact on the future needs and struggles of the Third World long after the international recession is past. The crisis has reduced the quantity and value of industrial output, often wiping out a decade of growth in the process. It has been particularly destructive of agricultural output which had been oriented towards cash production using petrochemical-based technology and which had hastened the destruction of subsistence production and the expropriation of the peasantry. In its place has come increased production for world markets rather than for local food supplies and increased reliance on agribusiness at the expense of family farming. The structural factors attending this process carry with them the implication of new, long-term constraints on Third World development.

The crisis and the international responses to it have dismissed the objective of independent development and self-reliance which informed the national aspirations of the post-war world. In its place has come control by foreign capital and international financial institutions. To some extent this process reasserts the bonds of neo-colonialism and dependency, albeit in a much altered form. With the collapse of self-reliant development has come a resurrection of export enclave structures as IMF adjustments have required that exports be given primacy. In some cases, this restoration has simply given additional emphasis to the old mono-economy of the colonial inheritance. Elsewhere, this original base is no longer available or is rapidly wasting away. Here exports may be generated in new sectors but it may also be, in poorer countries, that no new source of debt-servicing will be easily created.

The crisis has also produced important political and social costs. Stabilization policies have savaged efforts to provide basic welfare services and to ensure a little social justice. In the process they have also undermined efforts to produce a future generation with the skills and infrastructure to promote growth. The crisis has, in short either reduced political independence on the part of the Third World or subjected national sovereignty to serious attack, either through economic management or through the use of force. As economic and political consequences of crisis have mounted, so political instability and conflict have increased. Democracy in the Third World has not been a particularly healthy animal, but the crisis has worsened the situation considerably. Repression has become one of the few public growth industries. The crisis has considerably sharpened class contradictions and struggles in the Third World, but this has been at a terrible cost in hunger, poverty, violence and brutality imposed on its most wretched citizens.

Such a bleak prospect will haunt at least the next generation of the Third World – and probably several more besides. What strategies and struggles will be needed to turn things round must exercise the minds of those committed to social justice and democracy. Clearly, for Third World countries simply to commit themselves to more of the same once the present cycle begins its upturn would be to condemn the future to further calamities. Unless there is a restructuring of the social relations presently being reinforced by international policy, nothing fundamental will be solved. It is held that there is a 'privilege of historic backwardness' in that such social formations are not required to replicate the costs of history. If this is so, it would be as well to question whether the traditional cycle of industrialization and exploitation needs to be repeated in the Third World – particularly in the distorted and obscene form it has taken. There is no guarantee that alternatives based on democracy and equality can be devised – but if they are not there is every likelihood that the grim experiences of the last half-century (during which millions have died from war and hunger) will be repeated several times more.

Notes

1 Quoted in Nigel Harris, *Of Bread and Guns: The World Economy in Crisis* (Harmondsworth, Penguin, 1983), p. 159.
2 The term 'Third World' is used somewhat apologetically – in the absence of anything better. There is a vast array of alternatives available but none of them is any more accurate and some are simply misleading. 'Third World' has the advantage of widespread current usage and agreement about the areas described by the term. But it must not be forgotten that it tends to lump together a vast range of societies, economies and cultures in a manner worthy of the great traditions of western ethnocentrism. Here it is used in a restricted way, to refer to territories which have the historical experience of being subordinated to the international expansion of capitalism and which continues to have the pattern of their economic development predominantly influenced by the process of international accumulation.
3 Third World territories are frequently described as peripheral capitalist economies in contrast to central or metropolitan capitalist economies in the industrial west. Peripheral status is one of the measures used to define the Third World by, for instance, Ben Crow, Alan Thomas *et al.*, *Third World Atlas* (Milton Keynes, The Open University, 1983), p. 8.
4 The 'newly industrializing' economies of Taiwan, South Korea, Singapore and Hong Kong have experienced high growth rates as enclaves for western capital investment but have also begun to spawn an indigenous Asian class of finance capitalists and industrialists. Much less success has come the way of the Philippines, Malaysia or Indonesia. This essay, on the assumption that not all countries can become capital

enclaves – indeed that for one to become so precludes the possibility for others – does not focus on such 'success stories' and is unapologetic about not doing so.

5   The process is represented in the literature as the failure to increase agrarian output and to transform production relations on the land. But it involves everywhere the collapse of peasant indebtedness and dependence on landlords (especially in South Asia) and increasing out-migration. More recently it is compounded by agribusiness and international aid agencies (in alliance with Third World governments) kicking peasants out to set up large-scale, prestige projects.

6   See, among many sources: Francine R. Frankel, *India's Political Economy, 1947–1977: The Gradual Revolution* (Princeton, Princeton University Press, 1978); Anupam Sen, *The State, Industrialization and Class Formations in India* (London, Routledge, 1982); Pranab Bardhan, *The Political Economy of Development in India* (Oxford, Basil Blackwell, 1984).

7   Introductions to these issues are widely available, including: Ian Roxborough, *Theories of Underdevelopment* (London, Macmillan, 1979); Charles K. Wilber (ed.), *The Political Economy of Development and Underdevelopment* (New York, Random House, 1st edn 1973, 2nd edn 1979,); Teresa Hayter and Catherine Watson, *Aid: Rhetoric and Reality* (London, Pluto, 1985); and Hamza Alavi and Teodor Shanin (eds), *Introduction to the Sociology of 'Developing Societies'* (London, Macmillan, 1982).

8   In addition to titles listed in note 7, see also Tamas Szentes, *The Political Economy of Underdevelopment* (Budapest, Akademiai Kiado, 1973); James Petras, *Critical Perspectives on Imperialism and Social Class in the Third World* (New York, Monthly Review Press, 1978); Robert B. Cohen et al. (eds), *The Multinational Corporation: A Radical Approach – Papers by Stephen Herbert Hymer* (Cambridge, Cambridge University Press, 1979); Ronaldo Munck, *Politics and Dependency in the Third World* (London, Zed Press, 1984); Martin Fransman (ed.) *Industry and Accumulation in Africa* (London, Heinemann, 1982); Richard J. Barnet and Ronald E. Muller, *Global Reach: The Power of the Multinational Corporations* (New York, Simon and Schuster, 1974).

9   See Peter Evans, *Dependent Development: The Alliance of Multinational, State and Local Capital in Brazil* (Princeton, Princeton University Press, 1979); Celso Furtado, 'The Brazilian "Model" of Development', in Wilber, *The Political Economy of Development and Underdevelopment*; Philippe Faucher, 'Industrial policy in a dependent state: the case of Brazil', *Latin American Perspectives* VII (1) (Winter 1980).

10 This view is frequently expressed by western public officials, particularly in the Reagan administration, and is at the heart of IMF policies towards the Third World during the last decade.

11 Roxborough, *Theories of Underdevelopment;* Fernando Henrique Cardoso and Enzo Faletto, *Dependency and Development in Latin America* (Bentley, University of California Press, 1979); André Gundar Frank, *Latin America: Underdevelopment or Revolution* (New York, Monthly Review Press, 1969).

12 For underdevelopment theory, see Frank, 'Latin America' Wilber, *The Political Economy of Development and Underdevelopment*; Roxborough, *Theories of Underdevelopment*; Szentes, *The Political Economy of Underdevelopment*; Robert I. Rhodes (ed.), *Imperialism and Underdevelopment: A Reader* (New York, Monthly Review Press, 1970). Among many critiques, see John Taylor, *From Modernization to Modes of Production* (London, Macmillan, 1979) and I. Oxaal, T. Barnett and T. Booth (eds), *Beyond the Sociology of Development* (London, Routledge, 1975).

13 Ernest Mandel, *The Second Slump* (London, Macmillan, 1978).

14 Harris, *Of Bread and Guns*, p. 158–9.

15 World Bank, *World Development Report 1984*, tables 2 and 3, pp. 220–3.

16 Phillip Raikes, 'Food policy and production in Mozambique since independence', *Review of African Political Economy* 29 (July 1984).

17 Jay O'Brien, 'Sowing the seeds of famine: the political economy of food deficits in Sudan', *Review of African Political Economy* 33 (August 1985).

18 On food and hunger, see *Review of African Political Economy* 33 (August 1985), Special Issue on War and Famine in Africa; and Special Task Force, 'Food and Agriculture Situation in African Countries Affected by Calamities in 1983–85', Report no. 6, Food and Agriculture Organization, United nations, UN/FAO World Food Programme, Rome, 30 September 1984 (mimeograph). On problems of imports, see below.

19 Third World countries had needed to borrow capital long before the present crisis because investment policies of even modest proportions could not be funded from domestic savings, even where already low levels of consumption were squeezed. The imbalance between saving and investment is particularly dramatic in Africa: in 1973, investment was 16.8% of GNP while savings were 14.3%. But in 1983, investment was 14.7% and savings 5.4% of GNP. If one considers that aggregate levels had also fallen considerably, as had aggregate consumption levels, the enormity of the crisis becomes clearer. See The World Bank, *World Development Report 1984*, p. 24, and *1985*, p. 151).

20 'Mobutu's empire of graft', *Africa Now*, March 1982. See also Jacques Depelchin, 'The transformation of the petty bourgeoisie and the state in post-colonial Zaire', *Review of African Political Economy*, 22 (October–December 1981).

21 See table 5.6.

22 Robert E. Wood, 'Making sense of the Debt Crisis: a primer for socialists', *Socialist Review* 81 (1985), p. 9.

23 Ibid., p. 10, and also Harold Lever, 'The Debt Won't be Paid', *The New York Review of Books* XXXI (11) (28 June 1984).

24 *South*, July 1985, p. 35.

25 Lever, 'The Debt Won't be Paid'. See also Harold Lever and Christopher Huhne, *Debt and Danger: The World Financial Crisis* (Harmondsworth, Penguin, 1985).

26 Wood, 'Making Sense of the Debt Crisis', pp. 10–11.

27 See, for instance: Cheryl Payer, *The Debt Trap: The IMF and the Third World* (Harmondsworth, Penguin, 1974); Hayter and Watson, *Aid*, chapter 3; Latin American Bureau, *The Poverty Brokers: The IMF and Latin America* (London, Latin America Bureau, 1983); and especially *Development Dialogue*, 1980 (2), special issue on the IMF.

28 The World Bank, *World Development Report 1983*, p. 34.

29 Albert Fishlow, 'The state of Latin American economics', in Inter-American Development ment Bank, 1985 Report: *Economic and Social Progress in Latin America – External Debt: Crisis and Adjustment*. See also Hassanali Mehran, *External Debt Management* (Washington, International Monetary Fund, 1985).

30 See D. Coates and G. Johnston (eds), *Socialist Arguments* (Oxford, Martin Robertson, 1983); *idem, Socialist Strategies* (Oxford, Martin Robertson, 1983).

31 Tanzania's foreign exchange earnings from coffee fell from $393 million in 1983/4 to $224 million in 1984/5 despite constant levels of physical output. Zambian officials, after a 40% devaluation imposed by the IMF, noted that this simply reduced the capacity to buy imports. 'Our balance of payments crisis does not arise out of a lack of competitiveness of exports – we sell copper twelve months before it comes out of the ground,' one local banker commented. Devaluation has damaged local production levels by making it more difficult for Zambia to fund the purchase of overseas inputs. Meanwhile copper reserves are wasting and copper output will fall by about a third over the next 20 years. Instead of being able to fund alternative production activities, the Zambians have had to contend with a 60% fall in copper prices over the last decade and an escalating debt: *South*, July 1985, pp. 35–6. In 1986, another IMF dose of stabilization forced a further 70% devaluation of the Zambian Kwacha! See *Financial Times*, 18 April 1986.

32 *South*, July 1985, pp. 21–2.
33 Abbas Abdelkarim, Abdalla El Hassan and David Seddon, 'From Popular Protest to Military Takeover: an analytic chronology of recent events in Sudan', *Review of African Political Economy* 33 (August 1985). See also *Review of African Political Economy* 26 (July 1983), special issue on the Sudan.
34 Eiichi Shindo, 'Hunger and Weapons: the Entropy of Militarisation', Review of African Political Economy 33 (1985); Saadet Deger, *Military Expenditure in Third World Countries* (London, Routledge, 1986); Robin Luckham and Dawit Bekele, 'Foreign Powers and Militarism in the Horn of Africa', and James F. Petras and Morris H. Morley, 'The Ethiopian Military State and Soviet–US Involvment in the Horn of Africa', both in *Review of African Political Economy* 30 (1984).
35 Wood, 'Making Sense of the Debt Crisis', notes that these are two favourites among current scapegoats. Here we suggest that, far from being derelict, both bankers and governments acted rationally within the logic of international capital.
36 Indeed, many figures within the Reagan administration clearly favoured Argentina over Brazil when negotiations about debt-servicing began, on the grounds that Argentina was a free market system while Brazil featured large-scale state intervention in the economy.
37 The socialist states of Ethiopia, Mozambique and Angola would seem to have done worst in terms of food production. But all have been stricken by long-running civil war and all have been victims of western policies of witholding food aid. Where war has hit non-socialist economies (as in Uganda and southern Sudan) the record is little better. And the products of multinational agribusiness or of state-sponsored large-scale projects do not bear too close examination.
38 Wood, 'Making Sense of the Debt Crisis', p. 12.
39 Theotonio dos Santos, 'The structure of dependence', in Wilber, *The Political Economy of Development and Underdevelopment*, 1st edn, p. 109. See also Cardoso and Faletto, *Dependency and Development*, and R. Chilcote (ed.) 'Dependency and Marxism', a special issue of *Latin American Perspectives* VIII (3 & 4) (1981).
40 Paul Baran, *The Political Economy of Growth* (New York, Monthly Review Press, 1957).
41 Ibid., Penguin edn, 1973, pp. 267 and 75 respectively, the second set of figures from the Introduction by R. B. Sutcliffe.
42 See Karl Marx, *Capital*, vol. I, part 8: 'The So-Called Primitive Accumulation' (Harmondsworth, Penguin, 1976).
43 These are well documented elsewhere and will not be repeated here. But the outstanding single introduction to them is in A. A. Brewer, *Marxist Theories of Imperialism: a Critical Survey* (London, Routledge, 1980).
44 The idea of uneven development is present in the work of Lenin and Bukharin, but has its clearest expression as 'the law of uneven and combined development' in Trotsky's *History of the Russian Revolution* (London, Sphere, 1967) vol. 1, chapter 1. See also the elaboration in George Novack, *Uneven and Combined Development in History* (New York, Merit, 1966) and in M. Lowy, *The Politics of Combined and Uneven Development: the Theory of the Permanent Revolution* (London, Verso, 1981), part One. The idea of the articulation of modes of production is rather narrower but focuses on the fundamental process by which capitalist production relations become enmeshed (articulate) with non-capitalist production relations to form complex and historically peculiar modes. See the discussion in Brewer, *Marxist Theories of Imperialism*, and in Harold Wolpe (ed.), *The Articulation of Modes of Production* (London, Routledge, 1980). Both methods are concerned therefore to explore the contradictions and conflicts produced in transitional societies. They are blended impressively in Ken Post, *Arise Ye Starvelings: the Jamaican Labour Rebellion of 1938 and its Aftermath* (Holland Martinus Nijhoff, 1978).

45   Baran, *The Political Economy of Growth*, pp. 277–85, describes the plunder of India
     between the battles of Plassey and Waterloo, a period crucial to industrialization in
     Britain.
46   Ernesto Laclau, 'Feudalism and capitalism in Latin America', *New Left Review* 67
     (1971) and in Laclau, *Politics and Ideology in Marxist Theory* (London, Verso, 1977).
47   In West Africa, where family labour was converted to the production of commodity
     production yielding export crops, Samir Amin speaks of 'the Africa of the colonial
     trade economy'. See Samir Amin, 'Underdevelopment and Dependence in Black
     Africa: Origins and Contemporary Forms', *Journal of Modern African Studies* 10
     (4) (1972).
48   See G. L. Beckford, *Persistent Poverty: Underdevelopment in Plantation Economies*
     (Oxford, Oxford University Press, 1972).
49   Ramakrishna Mukherjee, *The Rise and Fall of the East India Company* (New York,
     Monthly Review Press, 1974).
50   'The transition from the feudal mode of production takes place in two different ways.
     The producer may become a merchant and capitalist. . . This is the really revolutionary
     way. Alternatively, however, the merchant may take direct control of production
     himself. But, however frequently this occurs as a historical transition. . . it cannot bring
     about the overthrow of the old mode of production itself, but rather preserves and
     retains it as its own precondition.' Marx, *Capital*, vol. III, chapter 20, p. 452. Marx
     notes that trading capital is far older than the capitalist mode of production and that
     it has an historically independent existence mediating commodity exchanges between
     different modes of production. Here I am suggesting something more than this, namely
     that when merchant capital loses its domination to metropolitan industrial capital, it
     nevertheless is frequently profitable for industrial capital to preserve certain pre-
     capitalist production relations on which it can base its extraction of surplus value.
     Gold mining constructed on the backs of impoverished African women scratching
     out a (sub-) subsistence, permitted the exploitation of their men at wage levels below
     the cost of subsistence and reproduction of the working class.
51   Mukherjee, *The Rise and Fall of the East India Company*, and Baran, *The Political
     Economy of Growth*. Also Barrington Moore Jr., *The Social Origins of Dictatorship and
     Democracy: Lord and Peasant in the Making of the Modern World* (Harmondsworth,
     Penguin 1969).
52   Thus, for instance, the East India Company confirmed the *zamindars* in office in
     perpetuity and gave them rights in land – neither of which they had enjoyed before.
53   Moore, *The Social Origins of Dictatorship and Democracy*, chapter 6.
54   The use of marketing boards to extract surplus from the peasantry continues into the
     post-colonial period. See, for instance, Gavin Williams, 'Marketing without and with
     Marketing Boards: the Origins of State Marketing Boards in Nigeria', *Review of African
     Political Economy* 34 (1985). From here it is a short step to using loans and credits
     to cream off further surpluses through graft by public officials: Morris Szetfel,
     'Corruption and the Spoils System' in M. Clarke (ed.), *Corruption Causes, Con-
     sequences and Control* (London, Frances Pinter, 1983).
55   In India, a Famine Commission in 1880 found two-thirds of the peasantry in debt,
     half of them with little prospect of redeeming the debt. In 1901 another Famine
     Commission found that a quarter of the peasantry in Bombay had lost their land to
     moneylenders. Between 1929 and 1939 the estimated rural debt doubled. See Sen,
     The State, Industrial and Class Formations, chapter 7.
56   In the sixteenth and seventeenth centuries, north-eastern Brazil became a sugar-
     plantation economy, displacing parts of the peasantry from food production. Later
     mineral extraction superseded the emphasis on sugar, though plantation production
     continued. Famine became a frequent occurrence in the region in the sixties and
     seventies. See A. G. Frank, *Capitalism and Underdevelopment in Latin America*

(New York, Monthly Review Press 1967); T. Dos Santos, 'Brazil: The Origins of a Crisis' in R. H. Chilcote and J. C. Edelstein (eds), *Latin America: The Struggle with Dependency and Beyond* (Wiley, 1974); E. Feder, *The Rape of the Peasantry* (New York, Anchor, 1971); J. De Castro, *Death in the Northeast* (New York, Vintage, 1969), F. Juliao, *Cambao – the Yoke* (Harmondsworth, Penguin, 1972), P. Gallet, *Freedom to Starve* (Harmondsworth, Penguin, 1972).

57 In what Amin calls 'the Africa of the labour reserve economy' (Amin, 'Under-development and Dependence in Black Africa'),state-regulated systems of migrant labour remove from the land large parts of the family production unit but also force part of that unit to remain behind to grow as near to a subsistence as can be managed. The breakdown of the division of labour on the land, without any development of the productive relations, produces a regime of malnutrition and slow starvation. In bad years it is expressed as localized famines. See H. Wolpe, 'Capitalism and cheap labour power in South Africa', *Economy and Society* 1 (4) (1972); M. Legassick, 'Forced Labour, industrialization and racial differentiation' in R. Harris (ed.), *The Political Economy of Africa* (London, Wiley, 1975); R. Palmer and N. Parsons (eds), *The Roots of Rural Poverty in Central and Southern Africa* (London, Heinemann, 1977); Colin Murray, *Families Divided: The Impact of Migrant Labour in Lesotho* (Cambridge, Cambridge University Press, 1981).

58 Geoffrey Kay, *Development and Underdevelopment: a Marxist Analysis* (London, Macmillan, 1975).

59 Stephen H. Hymer, 'United States Investment Abroad', in Cohen *et al. The Multinational Corporation*, pp. 208–38.

60 David H. Blake and Robert S. Walters, *The Politics of Global Economic Relations* (New Jersey, Prentice-Hall, 1976), p. 79 and chapter 4.

61 US Department of Commerce, *The Multinational Corporation: Studies of US Foreign Investment*, vol. 1 (Washington DC, US Department of Commerce, 1972), Appendix I.

62 See especially, Bill Warren, *Imperialism: Pioneer of Capitalism* (London, Verso, 1980) and G. Kitching, *Development and Underdevelopment in Historical Perspective: Populism, Nationalism and Industrialization* (London, Methuen, 1982).

63 The literature on multinationals is vast. A valuable introductory article is by Ronald Muller, 'The multinational corporation and the underdevelopment of the third world', in Wilber, *The Political Economy of Development*, 2nd edn. See also H. Radice (ed.), *International Firms and Modern Imperialism* (Harmondsworth, Penguin, 1975); Barnet and Muller, *Global Reach*; Cohen *et al. The Multinational Corporation*; Sanjaya Lall, *The Multinational Corporation* (Macmillan, 1980); G. Lanning with M. Mueller, *Africa Undermined* (Harmondsworth, Penguin, 1979); N. Girvan, *Corporate Imperialism: Conflict and Expropriation* (New York, Monthly Review Press, 1976).

64 3 March 1986, p. 52.

65 Michael Perelman, *Farming for Profit in a Hungry World: Capital and the Crisis in Agriculture* (New York, Allenheld, Osmun, 1977).

66 An expression used by the late Amilcar Cabral in a speech in the Free Trade Hall in Manchester in 1972. In the foreword to Basil Davidson, *The Liberation of Guinea: Aspects of an African Revolution* (Harmondsworth, Penguin, 1969) he also writes of 'the return of Africans to history'.

67 See for instance Colin Leys, *Underdevelopment in Kenya: the Political Economy of Neo-Colonialism* (London, Heinemann, 1975).

68 Aristide Zolberg, *Creating Political Order* (New York, Rand MacNally, 1966) argues that colonial regimes frequently legitimized particular movements by their readiness to negotiate with them and not with others.

69 For instance, Ruth First, *The Barrel of a Gun: Political Power in Africa and the Coup D'État* (Harmondsworth, Penguin, 1970); Dilip Hiro, *Inside India Today* (London,

Routledge, 1977) especially chapters 16, 18; W. H. Morris-Jones, *The Government and Politics of India* (London, Hutchinson, 1971, 3rd edn); and Asok Chanda, *Indian Administration* (London, Allen and Unwin, 1967).

70 Clive Y. Thomas, *The Rise of the Authoritarian State in Peripheral Societies* (London, Heinemann, 1984) p. 65.

71 See, for instance, Anil Seal, 'Imperialism and Nationalism in India', *Modern Asian Studies* VII (3) (1973); and, in a different vein, W. Ziemann and M. Lanzendorfer, 'The State in Peripheral Societies', *Socialist Register*, 1977.

72 On 'timetables of democracy', see Goran Therborn, 'The Rule of capital and the rise of democracy', *New Left Review* 103 (1977).

73 On problems of the class character of post-colonial states, see Carolyn L. Baylies, 'State and class in post-colonial Africa', in M. Zeitlin (ed.), *Political Power and Social Theory*, vol. 5, 1985, (Greenwich, Conn., JAI Press, 1985).

74 Thomas, *The Rise of the Authoritarian State*, p. 70.

75 See Carolyn L. Baylies, 'Zambia's economic reforms and their aftermath: the state and the growth of indigenous capital', *Journal of Commonwealth and Comparative Politics* XX (3) (1982); Carolyn L. Baylies and Morris Szeftel, 'The rise of a Zambian capitalist class in the 1970s', *Journal of Southern African Studies* 8 (2) (1982); N. Swainson, 'The rise of a national bourgeoisie in Kenya', *Review of African Political Economy* 8 (1977); Colin Leys, 'Capital accumulation, class formation and dependency – the significance of the Kenyan case', *Socialist Register*, 1978.

76 See note 75 and Morris Szeftel, 'Political graft and the spoils system in Zambia – the state as a resource in itself', *Review of African Political Economy* 24 (1982).

77 Claus Offe, *Contradictions of the Welfare State* (London, Hutchinson, 1983) has focused attention on the contradictions confronting the contemporary state. A variety of perspectives on the issues raised is found in the important collection of readings, David Held *et al.* (eds), *States and Societies* (Oxford, Martin Robertson/Open University, 1983) especially in parts 3, 4, 5.

78 The increasing differences between rhetoric and reality produce much anger as in David Selbourne, *An Eye to India: The Unmasking of a Tyranny* (Harmondsworth, Penguin 1977); and Selbourne, *Through the Indian Looking-Glass* (London, Zed Press, 1982).

79 Norman Girvan, Richard Bernal, and Wesley Hughes, 'The IMF and the Third World; the case of Jamaica', *Development Dialogue*, 1980 (2); Latin America Bureau, *The Poverty Brokers* pp. 85–108.

80 M. Wolfers and J. Bergerol, *Angola in the Front Line* (London, Zed Press, 1983); R. Ruben (ed.), *The Transition Strategy of Nicaragua* (London, Free University, 1982).

81 Sen, *The State, Industrialization and Class Formations*, chapter 6; and Bardhan, *The Political Economy of Development in India*, especially chapters 4, 5, 8; M. L. O. Faber and J. G. Potter, *Towards Economic Independence – Papers on the Nationalization of the Copper Industry in Zambia* (Cambridge, Cambridge University Press, 1971); Anthony Martin, *Minding Their Own Business: Zambia's Struggle Against Western Control* (London, Hutchinson, 1972).

82 Thomas, *The Rise of the Authoritarian State*, pp. 53, 85.

83 Samuel Huntington, *Political Order in Changing Societies* (New Haven, Yale University Press, 1968).

84 Morris Szeftel, 'The political process in post-colonial Zambia: the structural bases of factional conflict', in *The Evolving Structure of Zambian Society*, Proceedings of a Conference at the Centre for African Studies, University of Edinburgh, May 1980.

85 Peter Flynn, 'Class, Clientelism and Coercion: some mechanisms of internal control', *Journal of Commonwealth and Comparative Politics* 12 (2) (1974); Hamza Alavi, 'Peasant classes and primordial loyalties', *Journal of Peasant Studies* 1 (1) (1973).

86 And in the process made rural India a far more brutal place, one where violence against peasants and/or 'untouchables' has become commonplace. The use of the police as an instrument of landlord class power is not unknown. The Naxalite rebellion of the seventies shows clearly that peasant anger is often close to the surface. Even in the cities, the patronage system would seem to be breaking down as privileged elements protest against affirmative-action measures.

87 See Cherry Gertzel, Carolyn Baylies and Morris Szeftel, *The Dynamics of The One-Party State in Zambia (Manchester, Manchester University Press, 1984).*

88 *Frantz Fanon, The Wretched of the Earth* (Harmondsworth, Penguin, 1967) chapter 3.

89 Hassan Gardezi and Jamil Rashid (eds), *Pakistan – the Roots of Dictatorship: the Political Economy of a Praetorian State* (London, Zed Press, 1983) is an interesting collection of papers describing the nature of state power, the role of the military within it and its relationship to international imperialism and debt crisis. See also Tariq Ali, *Can Pakistan Survive?* (Harmondsworth, Penguin, 1983).

90 Edward S. Herman and James Petras, '"Resurgent Democracy": Rhetoric and Reality', *New Left Review* 154 (1985).

91 See, for instance, 'Rajiv Gandhi's New India', Interview with the Indian Prime Minister in *South*, October 1985, pp. 17–20; and Achin Vanaik, 'The Rajiv Congress in Search of Stability', *New Left Review* 154 (1985).

92 Tariq Ali, *Can Pakistan Survive?*, and Gardezi and Rashid, *Pakistan*.

93 Herman and Petras, '"Resurgent Democracy"', p. 91.

94 Blake and Walters, *The Politics of Global Economic Relations*, p. 77.

95 *The Times*, 27 March 1985.

96 *North–South: a Programme for Survival*, Report of an Independent Commission on International Development Issues, under the chairmanship of Willy Brandt (London, Pan Books, 1980).

97 For critiques see, inter alia, Gavin Williams, 'The Brandt Report: a critical introduction', *Review of African Political Economy* 19 (1980), and Hayter and Watson, AID. See also, on a related theme, T. W. Parfitt, 'The Lome Convention and the New International Order', *Review of African Political Economy* 22 (1981).

98 See, for instance, Gabriel Kolko, *The Triumph of Conservatism* (Glencoe, Free Press, 1963), and James Weinstein, *The Corporate Ideal in the Liberal State 1900–1916* (Boston, Beacon, 1968).

99 L. H. Shoup and W. Minter, *Imperial Brain Trust: the Council on Foreign Relations and United States Foreign Policy* (New York, Monthly Review Press, 1977). See also Kees Van Der Pijl, *The Making of an Atlantic Ruling Class* (London, Verso, 1984).

100 John Stockwell, *In Search of Enemies*, (New York, Norton, 1978).

101 Holly Sklar, (ed.), Trilateralism (Boston, Mass., South End Press, 1982) L. H. Shoup, *The Carter Presidency and Beyond* (Berkeley, Ramparts Press, 1980); and see too Fred Halliday, *The Making of the Second Cold War* (London, Verso, 1983) pp. 18, 214–33.

102 Jerry Sanders, *The Peddlars of Crisis* (London, Pluto, 1983); and Halliday, *The Making of the Second Cold War*, especially chapter 5.

103 The use of food as a weapon in the Third World is not new (at least in its contemplation). Ray Bush, 'Unnatural Disaster – the politics of famine', *Marxism Today* 29 (12) (December 1985) notes a 1974 CIA report on the 'virtual life-and-death power' over 'the needy' which food surpluses would give the United States. It has been a common complaint among field personnel of relief agencies that food needs were not met in some countries even though there was a long period of time in which future famines were apparent and that this lack of action was correlated with the political complexion of particular Third World Regimes.

104 Herman and Petras, '"Resurgent Democracy"'. The 'disappearance' of people in these countries continues apace – it is only the international concern about such state terrorism that has declined.

105   The clear implication of this claim, namely that Franklin, Jefferson, Adams *et al.* were torturers, mutilators, murderers, rapists and thieves should be regarded with some scepticism. The bestiality of the contra operations should not be underestimated: lacking any political support, and thus being unable to wage an armed struggle, they seek to destroy social and economic life instead by terrorizing the polulation. Civilian targets are favoured over military ones, those with scarce skills employed in education or agrarian development are especially singled out for murder. Mutilation is employed systematically to terrify the people in the hope of breaking their will to resist.

106   In southern Africa, US involvement is less direct than in Central America. But the model still applies. Supplies are channelled through client states and 'voluntary organizations', terror is employed against civilian targets, food supplies are destroyed in order to induce hunger and chaos. In Mozambique, for instance, South Africa, Portugal and some Middle East clients of the US support a collection of desperadoes called the MNR. Lacking not only political credibility but even a programme, it acts simply to terrorize and destabilize – indulging in acts as gross as those employed by the contras: disembowelment and mutilation. Angola is confronted by a slightly more credible opposition in Savimbi's UNITA but it is still no more than a US–South African client working to deny independence to Namibia as well as to fight the Angolan government. In early 1986 the US Congress decided to permit the Reagan administration to arm Savimbi openly (as opposed to having to do it through client regimes). In 1985, the US began to host get-togethers of the leaders of its motley employees, presumably to encourage an exchange of ideas which might produce better political results than thus far achieved.

107   In 1985, a senior State Department official commented that 'we debated whether we had the right to dictate the form of another country's government. The bottom line was "yes", that some rights are more fundamental than the right of nations to non-intervention, like the rights of individual people' (*South*, October 1985, p. 37). The consequence of this Reagan doctrine is therefore that the United States has the right to export terror, to arm and pay people to murder and mutilate in order to further 'the rights of individual people'. More people who die because of acts of terror do so at the hands of American clients than from any other source today. In this context, the brandishing of expressions like 'democracy' and 'civilized world' in the propoganda battles at present being waged between different groups of terrorism, is a gross violation of truth and language to justify criminal behaviour.

6

The Arms Race and the Cold War

DAN SMITH

The Appeal for European Nuclear Disarmament, launched in Spring 1980, begins with these sentences:

> We are entering the most dangerous decade in human history. A third World War is not merely possible, but increasingly likely. Economic and social difficulties in advanced industrial countries, crisis, militarism and war in the Third World compound the political tensions that fuel a demented arms race.[1]

As the 1980s have progressed, events have only confirmed that judgement which is shared by more and more people. Mass disarmament movements are major political forces in several countries, especially in Western Europe, not only capable of mobilizing large demonstrations, but spearheading a generalized anxiety about the state of international politics and the risk of war.

The dangers of the 1980s result from a combination of the new Cold War and an intensified arms race. In the sense in which we will use the terms in this essay, such a combination has not been experienced before. The first Cold War was not accompanied by an arms race; the current arms race began in the absence of Cold War. It is the unprecedented co-occurrence of these two processes which so imperils us today.

Both the arms race and the Cold War are complex processes, with deep roots in the USA and USSR, the main protagonists, as well as in other countries – not least in Western Europe – which are also bound up in them. In understanding the detail of what happens in these processes, attention must be focused on the main institutions involved – on the military, the political leaderships and their calculations, on the arms industries. To explain their driving forces, these aspects need to be set in a more general theoretical context. A number of theories have been advanced to explain the arms race and the Cold War, and they are briefly scanned in a later section. Many of them fail by focusing only on one of the multiple dimensions of these complex processes. The theoretical explanation advanced below, after a consideration of the details of arms race and the Cold War, attempts to embrace all their dimensions within an understanding of the general political requirement for military forces, military spending and nuclear confrontation. This political requirement relates directly to the economic and social demands of two different socio-economic systems, but how it is determined is largely left out of the discussion, since it requires a further level of analysis which is beyond the scope of this essay.

One result of both the way in which this essay is structured and the approach which informs it is that, from time to time, aspects of the arms race or the Cold War are explained in terms of but one of the interlocking elements that together comprise the general theoretical explanation. These can be regarded as building blocks in the argument and should not be mistaken for its conclusion.

One other comment is necessary by way of introduction. Because this essay is about the arms race and the Cold War, it is naturally very largely concerned with the USA and the USSR. However, the view of the world which informs the essay is not bi-polar. That is, the power of the USA and the USSR, though great, is limited. There are other sources of power in the world than these two states. For example, the USSR is economically inferior to some capitalist countries to which it is militarily superior. More importantly, the USA and the USSR neither control nor initiate every major development in world politics, not even those in which they are intimately involved. Indeed, in many respects the current Cold War can be explained as a reaction by the USA to the threat to its power and interests which emerged from its advanced capitalist allies and from the Third World in the 1960s and 1970s. The importance of the weak links in the Cold War chain is stressed in the final section.

The Arms Race

In 1945 the USA detonated the world's first three nuclear weapons: one for practice, one on Hiroshima in Japan on 6 August, the third on Nagasaki three days later. In 1949 the USSR detonated its first nuclear explosive. By that point, the USA had about 200 nuclear bombs and 121 Strategic Air Command bombers capable of carrying and delivering them.[2] With those aircraft based in allied countries the USA would be in a position to make a nuclear attack against the USSR – devastating by the standards of the day, puny by the standards of the 1980s. A decade later, the USA had many thousands of nuclear weapons of an incredible variety of types, with a strategic arsenal consisting of around 1,500 strategic bombers. The first intercontinental missiles were being developed and deployed, and the development of submarine-launched ballistic missiles was well under way. At the same point, the USSR had begun deploying nuclear missiles targeted on Western Europe, and had a bomber force much smaller than the USA's capable of attacking the USA with nuclear weapons. That was also the period when, under Khrushchev, the USSR's Strategic Rocket Forces were established as a separate wing of the armed forces and the development of long-range ballistic missiles, already begun, was given major priority under the direct management of men like Brezhnev and Ustinov.[3]

It is in the late 1950s that the arms race can be said to have begun. Before then, to the extent that there was an arms race, it had only one competitor: the USA had an effective nuclear monopoly till the mid-1950s and a strategic nuclear monopoly till the end of the decade. Britain, the only other nuclear-weapon state, had a strategic nuclear force comparable in size to the USSR's and able to make nuclear strikes on Soviet territory but, in developing a new generation of nuclear weapons, was beginning to face the problems of cost which would eventually force it out of the front ranks of the arms race.

The term 'arms race' is best understood as a metaphor embracing the processes of acquiring arms in the US and the Soviet blocs. It usually focuses particularly on nuclear weapons, and often also on US and Soviet weapons to the exclusion of those of their allies. While the term catches the edge of competition and confrontation, it cannot be treated too literally. Not only does the 'race' lack a clearly marked finishing line, it is also clear that the pressure of competition with the antagonist is far from the only spur on either side to acquiring arms.

The metaphor is also complicated by the nuclear status and aspirations of other states. Following the USA and USSR in 1945 and 1949, Britain 'went nuclear' in 1952, France in 1960 and China in 1964. In 1974, India detonated a nuclear explosive, but is not believed to have a nuclear arsenal at present. In 1979, strong evidence came to light that a nuclear test had been conducted by South Africa, which does not permit international inspection of its most sensitive nuclear facilities. Israel has been reported, by the CIA among others, as having a small nuclear arsenal but, like South Africa, with which Israel appears to have cooperated in nuclear technology, it has neither confirmed not denied its nuclear status. As a result of the diffusion of nuclear-energy technology, more than 20 other states have the technical capacity to develop nuclear weapons within a relatively short period. Whether or not they would do so depends on political choice in their given circumstances in the light of their political and strategic ambitions. In recent years, most concern about further nuclear weapons proliferation has focused on a relatively small number of states: Argentina, Brazil, Iran, Iraq, Libya, Pakistan, South Korea and Taiwan. Thanks to the trade in non-nuclear military equipment and technology, they all have relatively sophisticated means of delivering nuclear explosives to targets.

The conventional arms trade and the risk of nuclear weapons proliferation are related to the central nuclear and conventional arms race in a variety of ways.

1.   In most cases the technological basis for further states to develop nuclear weapons is the technology they have imported ostensibly or genuinely for purposes of nuclear energy. From that, nuclear infrastructures – including scientists and technologists as well as plant and equipment – have been developed to a degree which provides some independent technological capacity. Despite multilateral and bilateral agreements meant to control the use of imported nuclear materials, the possibility exists of clandestine diversion of ostensibly civil technology to military ends.

2.   The development of nuclear energy in the Northern Hemisphere was largely a by-product of the requirements of military programmes. The nuclear trade then represented a means of utilizing capacity for indirectly funding domestic nuclear programmes in the supplying countries. Indeed, the distinction between civil and military nuclear industries is largely academic and propagandistic. Correctly viewed, there is but a single nuclear industry, with military origins and both civil and military uses.[4]

3.   The conventional arms trade is (like the nuclear trade) used in part as a means of utilizing capacity to sustain domestic military industry in the supplying countries. Large military establishments and largely or wholly self-sufficient arms industries – not just in the USA and USSR, but also in countries such as Britain, France, the Federal Republic of Germany and Italy – are judged to be essential to the permanent confrontation between the US and Soviet blocs. They are only viable, however, with the aid of exports of equipment and technology in an increasingly competitive international arms market. The reasons for the expansion of the arms trade since the early 1970s are to be found as much in these pressures to export as in the ambitions of the importing states.

4.   Efforts to stem the tide of nuclear proliferation are stymied because of the linkage made by many non-nuclear states, especially in the Third World, between stopping proliferation and getting reductions in existing nuclear stockpiles, especially those of the superpowers. An example of power based on military and especially nuclear capability has been set. Its strength is linked to the strength of the model of military power established by the USA in the era since 1945, and followed virtually without exception by every other state with the wealth to waste.[5] The risk of any specific state developing nuclear weapons depends on its own reading of its interests, ambitions, circumstances and capabilities. The chances of that risk being reduced by getting tighter international controls on the nuclear trade and nuclear activities in general are diminished by the refusal of the existing nuclear-weapon states to jettison what they see as the advantages and privileges of nuclear status. By flouting Article VI of the Non-Proliferation Treaty, this refusal jeopardizes the entire 'non-proliferation regime' which includes not just the Treaty but also a series of other agreements and controls.[6] Removing the threat of nuclear proliferation requires ending the nuclear arms race.

Nuclear Weapons

Estimates of the total number of nuclear warheads in the world are vague and contradictory. Estimation is complicated by secrecy, by the use of the figures for propaganda and the consequent temptation to lie about them, and by the genuine difficulties of calculation. The usual approximation for the world total of nuclear weapons is 50,000 or more. About 26,000 are owned by the USA, between 18,000 and 26,000 by the USSR, and in the region of 1,000 each by Britain, China and France. Rather more precise (though not necessarily more accurate) figures are available for specific categories of weaponry. At the end of 1983, the USA was estimated by one major source to have 9,665 strategic warheads and the USSR to have 8,880.[7] The Reagan administration plans to add about 12,000 warheads to the US strategic arsenal by 1994.[8] Whether all these warheads will survive a decade of Congressional wrangling is, of course, currently unknowable. Soviet production plans are not known, but can be assumed to be somewhere in the same region as the USA's. In any case, the figures are now so vast and the degree of overkill so great that precise numbers matter less and less.

Many observers stress that the real danger of this accumulation of destructive power lies not in the quantity of new weapons, but in their quality. The increasing accuracy of nuclear weapons has been highlighted, for it is this above all which provides the possibility of a 'first strike' aimed at crippling the other side's retaliatory nuclear forces. While the accuracy of weapons has improved on both sides, the USA has made the greater strides in other requirements for a first strike. It has done this not only in the associated infrastructure of satellites and communications, but also in its current development of a naval capability for attacking the USSR's missile-launching submarines. These, hiding in Arctic waters, provide the hitherto invulnerable capacity for nuclear retaliation on which the theory of deterrence depends.[9] While most experts agree that neither super-power has yet achieved a genuine first-strike capability, these developments are a recipe for panic in future superpower crises; they provide the potential link between a limited US–Soviet confrontation at any point around the globe and a nuclear war.

Nuclear Strategy

These developments in weaponry increase the risk of nuclear war only because they are linked to developments in strategy – in the management and ideology of armed forces. Military strategy is not simply a technical instrument. The choices made within it – for these or those weapons, for doctrines for deploying or employing them, for priorities in the use of finite resources, for organizing people in military systems – may be codified in manuals and sets of rules, but they do not thereby become objective or scientific. Rather, they result from subjective preferences of the institutions involved – military, industrial and political.

The key development since the late 1960s has been the continuing elaboration of doctrines stressing the possibility of limiting and, therefore, of surviving and winning a nuclear war. Official US nuclear strategy now calls for the ability to 'prevail' in war; at the same time, Soviet military strategy is directed towards winning a nuclear war should one occur.

It is, however, necessary to distinguish briefly between the US and Soviet approaches. Western propagandists consistently argue that the USSR has a nuclear war-fighting doctrine and that the west's own planning for nuclear war reflects only a prudent response to this, not a readiness to launch nuclear conflagration. Aside from the fact that NATO's strategy is predicated on willingness to use nuclear weapons whether or not the USSR has already done so, this *apologia* for western war-fighting doctrines obliterates a crucial distinction between Soviet and American strategic theory. In US thinking, nuclear deterrence of aggression by the USSR is posited as the prime means of preventing war between the superpowers from occurring. From this starting point, it is intellectually quite respectable to argue that nuclear deterrence must involve a number of options for when and how to use nuclear weapons, and that these options can include willingness to start a nuclear war, readiness to limit it, and the capacity to win it – even though the resulting doctrine is both very different from what most people think of as deterrence and extremely dangerous. In Soviet thinking, what prevents war from occurring is more complex. It is related to the concept of a 'balance of world forces' which restrains imperialism's basic aggressiveness. Fear of the consequences may help dissuade aggressive imperialists from unleashing nuclear war, but essentially the prevention of war is seen as a political business. On the other hand, the conduct of war is military business, and it is above all the military's business to win. Thus, if politics fails to keep the peace, the military must win the war and, beforehand, must have planned accordingly. Soviet military strategists have therefore not followed their American counterparts' example of elaborating increasingly sophisticated versions of the concept of nuclear deterrence; rather, they have concentrated on operational military doctrine. It is on these that western propagandists focus when pointing to Soviet war-fighting strategy; they ignore the political concepts within which that strategy is situated. These concepts were first developed in the debate on nuclear strategy which followed Stalin's death. There are some signs that in the past 20 years they have become more a set of rules learned by rote than a living theory which actually guides Soviet force deployments. But in principle, at least, the USSR has a more political concept of war avoidance, whereas the USA's is on the level of a technical fix.

On the face of it, strategies which stress the possibility of starting and winning nuclear war seem more likely to lead to such a war than to prevent it. The problem US policy-makers have attempted to address is that preventing nuclear war may be only one goal in a crisis between the superpowers. In 1970, Richard Nixon asked whether it was right for the US President to have only the choice between annihilation and surrender.[10] Under his administration, the search for strategic options between annihilation and surrender was intensified. The point was to find a way in which the use of nuclear weapons could be a realistic option. In the process, nuclear war becomes more thinkable, for the President, if not for ordinary people, and therefore more likely.

The standard defence against these criticisms is that having options for the limited use of nuclear weapons makes the threat of their use that much more credible, thus strengthening nuclear deterrence. Paradoxically, the theory is that making nuclear war more likely makes it less likely.

The key problem for strategic policy-makers concerns the unusability of nuclear weapons. Continuing studies of the effects of nuclear weapons have produced the concept of the 'nuclear winter'. This holds that the smoke and dust from multiple nuclear explosions will be so thick worldwide that they will absorb the sun's rays and temperatures will be sharply reduced. Consequently, people anywhere who survive the immediate effects of blast and fire, and the following radioactive fall-out, will die from hypothermia, even in summer, or from starvation in the famine which will follow massive failure of the crops.[11] But even before this theory gained credence and publicity in late 1983, the problem of unusability existed. Not only does it apply in the case of war with a nuclear-armed opponent, but even in the case of attack on a non-nuclear state.

Let us consider the case of the US war in Vietnam. The USA did not use nuclear weapons against the Democratic Republic of Vietnam. According to the theory of deterrence, by which US decision-makers operated, this restraint could not have been due to fear of Soviet retaliation: the USSR should have been deterred from that by the USA's own massive nuclear arsenal. Consequently, it must be concluded that using nuclear weapons was rejected because it would not have served a useful purpose. There are three main reasons why this was so:

1 It was not clear that the USA's problems in the ground war in South Vietnam would be solved.
2 There would have been a strong and probably violent reaction from the anti-war movement in the USA and elsewhere around the world. A heavy political price would have been paid because of predictable popular revulsion.

3   One effect might have been to increase the pace of nuclear-weapons proliferation which, at that time, the USA was committed to preventing.

It was not, therefore, goodwill that prevented the USA from using nuclear weapons against North Vietnam, which it was already pounding with non-nuclear bombing, but a pragmatic consideration of the price that would be paid for doing it. In many ways, nuclear weapons are (or were) unusable.[12]

It is worth noting in passing that US interest in strategic options for limited nuclear war grew with the debacle in Vietnam and the realization that US conventional forces could not easily be employed in large-scale actions abroad. The 'Nixon doctrine' of equipping states such as the Shah's Iran to do the conventional dirty work themselves was complemented by an effort to make nuclear weapons more usable by identifying options for limited use. The key to understanding this pairing is that no American 'boys' would then be involved in non-nuclear regional wars, and only a few highly trained and carefully selected 'boys' are involved in using nuclear weapons.

As one would expect, the problems of using nuclear weapons are even sharper in the case of a nuclear-armed opponent. Starting a nuclear war if it cannot be limited is an act of suicide. But the NATO and US strategy of readiness to start a nuclear war if necessary was already in existence by the late 1960s. Thus the search for options for limited use of nuclear weapons was always directly concerned with the central deterrence equation with the USSR, as well as with the problems of US power in the Third World.

Sadly for the theorists of limited nuclear war, there can be no certainty of keeping a nuclear war limited, not even a strong possibility. This results from technical problems of command and control – because communications would be hampered by the side-effects of nuclear explosions – as well as from weaknesses in the command hierarchies and the tendancy, once committed, to follow through even as disaster looms.[13] It is possible, it must be said, that a nuclear war started at a very low level could be limited, but, firstly, it would need to be such a low level that it is far from clear that any strategic goal could be achieved and, secondly, even starting at such a low level, the probability is that it could not be limited. Accordingly, starting a nuclear war even with the intention of keeping it strictly limited, remains an act of suicide.

The combination of highly accurate nuclear weapons and strategies for initiating and winning nuclear war is extremely threatening. Their mere existence could exacerbate a superpower crisis and bring on a nuclear strike by one side in the effort to pre-empt the other's anticipated attack. Thus, many commentators have concluded that nuclear weapons should be reserved for the task of deterring nuclear attack and should only ever be used in retaliation to a nuclear strike.[14] Although this is probably the popular vision of deterrence, it would be a major step away from the strategy of the USA and NATO. However, the logic of using nuclear weapons is flawed even at this level. If the initial attack was massive, then deterrence has clearly failed; there is no rational purpose in the post-humous vengeance exacted by retaliation. Moreover, radiation and 'nuclear winter' will ensure that retaliation would worsen the already-desperate situation in the country which was attacked first. On the other hand, if the initial attack was limited, then even similarly limited retaliation will most probably merely propel the conflict up the escalation ladder with the same ultimate outcome.

Under any circumstances, then, whether as first strike or as retaliation, in a massive blow or a limited dose, the threat to use nuclear weapons against a nuclear opponent is a threat to commit actions which are pointless, self-destructive or both.

There remain two important issues to consider. First, even if the theory of deterrence is so seriously flawed this does not mean that nuclear weapons have no deterrent effect. Anybody who is criminal enough to be willing in principle to commit mass murder with nuclear weapons might yet reconsider, on thinking about the consequences of retaliation. On the other hand, the fact that nuclear weapons could reasonably be expected to have this effect does not mean that deterrence has 'worked' – that is, it does not show that there has really been something to deter. Second, even if one accepts the first point and also assumes that there has been something to deter, one cannot therefore assume that the use of nuclear weapons is forever ruled out because it would be pointless and/or self-destructive. To begin with, one cannot assume that this recognition is universal. Indeed, it is quite clearly not: it is notable by its absence in NATO and US nuclear strategy. Moreover, because the reality of strategic planning is different from the model of retaliation-only, the potential exists for either superpower in a crisis to fear that the other's strategy and weapons mean it will make the first strike unless pre-empted. The result is a nuclear hair-trigger.

The logical *impasse* of strategic nuclear theory and the dangers of the current situation are not likely to encourage the leaders of either the USA or the USSR to attempt to break out of the nuclear confrontation. They are more likely to remain as a continuing source of niggling disquiet, impelling a search not for radical political solutions but for yet further technical fixes to irresolvable dilemmas. This will most likely be expressed through the development of new weapons, the elaboration of new strategic refinements and possibly a revived interest in achieving measures of arms control by bilateral agreement. President Reagan's interest in star wars – anti-missile defences based in outer space can partly be understood in the light of these problems: if a defence against nuclear weapons is possible (and the 'if' is very big), then the side which possessed it would have greater freedom to use nuclear weapons. Of course, if one side can construct such a defence, the other side can probably match it sooner or later, and what can be constructed can probably be circumvented.

This unwillingness to make a decisive break out of nuclear confrontation is not simply a result of the lack of sense or vision of the superpower's leaders. In the west, nuclear deterrence has from the outset been the travelling companion of confrontation with the USSR and the Cold War. As such, it has been a crucial component of US hegemony. The USSR's nuclear arsenal is a factor in its emergence as a genuine global superpower. For all the idiocies and risks of nuclear weapons and strategy, the fact remains that they are central features of a global system of power which will not be unravelled simply as a result of elegant arguments.

Cold War

There are two ways in which the term 'Cold War' is commonly used: by one group of writers and commentators, to characterize relations between the US and

Soviet blocs since 1945; by another group, to characterize specific phases of particularly intense antagonism between the two blocs.[15] The choice between the two is partly a matter of convenience and even mere semantics. But there is also a point of substance: the first usage sometimes risks implying a more or less even fabric to US–Soviet relations between the blocs since 1945, thus denying very important fluctuations and suggesting that the whole fabric is immutable.

Four major periods in relations between the blocs can be identified, though the dating is not always crisp and the phases melt into one another. The first Cold War lasted from 1946 until the mid-1950s. It was succeeded by a period lasting to the late 1960s which has been characterized as one of 'oscillatory antagonisms' – a phrase whose clumsiness masks its conciseness.[16] This was followed by 'détente' – a relative relaxation of tensions in which some major bones of contention (most notably in Europe) were settled, and the superpowers expressed and acted on a joint interest in arms control while continuing their nuclear build-ups. The major distinction between détente and the preceding phase was the greater consistency of less hostile relations. The second Cold War began in 1979 and remains with us: it is associated with a renewed US military build-up, a more threatening rhetoric, a renewed willingness to use military power directly and indirectly, the failure of arms control and a generally perceived increase in the risk of nuclear war.

The term 'Cold War' not only characterizes a process and a period, but also a specific policy. In the first Cold War, before the term took on the pejorative connotations it now has, the policy was so-named in the USA – for example, in a major National Security Council report in 1950: 'Every consideration of devotion to our fundamental values and to our national security demands that we seek to achieve them by the strategy of cold war.'[17] At the same time, the USSR under Stalin had its own interest in the first Cold War and its own Cold War policy, though it did not call it by that name. With the second Cold War, the issue is rather different: while it can be convincingly understood as an American policy, corresponding to a particular reading of US state interests, it is not possible to make the same claim of Soviet policy, except in the very subsidiary sense of the policies the USSR has adopted in response to the US shift into Cold War.

Intensified antagonisms and confrontation in both Cold Wars are, of course, expressed at the level of *inter*-bloc issues. But, although it is realistic for the leaders of each superpower to find the policy and actions of the other a threat to its interests and power, the reasons for the periodic intensification of confrontation are to be found also at the level of domestic and *intra*-bloc considerations.[18]

The First Cold War

One aspect of the periodization outlined above is related to the perception of the Cold Wars as deliberate and largely US policies. The first Cold War began in 1946 – not immediately with the ending of World War II as is often supposed. A major debate occurred in elite circles in the USA, mostly out of public view, during 1945 and 1946. At stake was how to understand the USSR, its nature as a state and its political aims. One view, eventually vanquished, saw the USSR as one state pretty much like any other, ready to act in its own self-interest but pragmatic, amenable to reason and international law. This view had prevailed during the World War. A second view saw the USSR as the old, expansionist and imperialist Tsarism dangerously combined with the revolutionary credo of Marxism-Leninism. This view was victorious within the US administration. The loyalists of the first view either changed their minds or were shifted out of office in the latter part of 1946, their places taken by the apostles of a global mission against 'World Communism'.[19]

The immediate result was the launching in early 1947 of the 'Truman doctrine' of 'containment' of the USSR and its allies, the expulsion of Western European Communist Parties from coalition governments, the launching of the Marshall Plan for economic reconstruction in Western Europe, along with the decisive steps towards assimilating the Western zones of Occupied Germany into the Western economy. It was not until the Autumn of 1947 that Stalin changed his own policy, in the name of which Communist Parties had cooperated in the early stages of economic and political reconstruction in Western Europe, to one of outright hostility and confrontation with the USA and its European Allies.[20] In 1948, one of the peak moments of the first Cold War occurred, as Stalin unsuccessfully attempted to elbow the Western allies (Britain, France and the USA) out of Berlin by means of a prolonged blockade.

On the American side, the first Cold War did not simply happen. It was not the product of a chance combination of circumstances, nor a mere defensive reaction to Soviet expansionism (which is how the official ideology posed it then, as now) – though this is not to deny the obvious fact that Soviet power did expand in Eastern Europe in the years immediately after World War II. Though all its consequences were not foreseen, it was a deliberate and conscious policy, arrived at after an intense debate, with specific aims, and it was remarkably successful. It was, effectively, the policy by which the collapsing European empires were replaced by a new American world power. This was not an Empire in the old European sense, but it was nonetheless a system of hegemony and domination, of global military presence, of subjugated and allied states, of economic domination and exploitation.

Perhaps most importantly, the first Cold War acted as a means of ideological and political mobilization. The post-1945 period was far from the first stage of international expansion of US power; the Caribbean, Central America and the Pacific had long since received its attentions. But the US public was assumed after 1945 to retain its traditional reluctance to finance an expansive foreign policy. The Cold War, combining the sense of an American mission to modernize the world with the sense of growing threat from the USSR, mobilized US public opinion to support aid to Europe, an international network of military bases and a more ambitiously activist role. This was conducted both through the glorification of the American 'mission' (variations on British and French themes – the 'white man's burden' and the *mission civiliatrice*), and through the hounding, purging and destruction of dissident opinion in the USA itself. At the same time, since this broke the power of the most militant trade unions, the Cold War mobilization permitted an intensified exploitation of labour within the US domestic economy. Similarly, the ideology of the Cold War acted to *de*mobilize opinion in Western Europe, to accept US leadership. What matters here is not just the breaking of the government coalitions with communist parties in 1947 (in Belgium,

France and Italy), but the winning of the major Western European political parties apart from the communists to Atlanticism – to the view that security, stability and prosperity depended on US leadership. Europe's impoverishment after 1945 created the economic weakness which opened the door not just to economic aid from the USA, but to its politics and ideology as well.[21] At the same time, the USA was securing its position in Third World countries by creating national security states run by pro-American local elites based on the ideology of anti-communism and Cold War. The first Cold War thus regulated inter-state relations under US leadership in a large part of the world, and simultaneously established the basis for popular consent, where necessary, to the new patterns of world power.

For the USSR, the functions of the first Cold War bear some resemblances, though on a smaller scale, and even though there are some indications that, in the form it took, it was forced upon Stalin rather than sought. It provided a means of sealing against Western pressure and influence the newly forming Soviet bloc, which was intended both to provide a protective western belt of states and to divide Germany so as to prevent its re-emergence as a powerful state.

A number of factors made Soviet hegemony in Eastern Europe more brutal than US hegemony in Western Europe. Although the confrontation of the Cold War provided a necessary legitimation within and among the communist parties for Soviet leadership, the ingrained habits of Stalinism understood show trials and repression better than the orchestration of consensus. Despite their many ambiguities and weaknesses, the political traditions of Western Europe were stronger and maturer. In negotiations which led to NATO's formation, the USA sought a virtually unfettered right to intervene in Western European politics, but the allies refused.[22] Other US 'allies' and their citizens in the coming years were less fortunate.

Perhaps more importantly, the USSR had few alternatives once it was set upon dominating Eastern Europe. It emerged from the war in a terribly debilitated state – enormous losses of human life, large-scale destruction of urban centres and of the most productive agricultural zones, destruction and disarrangement of industry. If only because of its great size and population, the USSR was in gross terms wealthier than the countries of Western Europe, but it is not at all clear that it was any better off. Compared to the USA, it was impoverished. Large-scale economic aid was not as available for manipulating Eastern European states – also impoverished – into subordination and dependency. Only in the case of Czechoslovakia was economic aid used to real political advantage, and then only because the US administration had decided in 1947 to withhold aid in an attempt to force the communists out of the coalition government. This gross tactical error left the door open for Soviet aid with no political strings attached to strengthen the hand of an already strong and popular Czechoslovakian Communist Party. Further tactical errors by the non-communist politicians in early 1948, together with the communists' better organization, street mobilizations and control of the police permitted the formation of a wholly communist government.[23] In the other countries of Eastern Europe, it was not economic aid but the presence of the Soviet army which was the main instrument in establishing hegemony; in Czechoslovakia, as elsewhere, the secret police, the show trials and the purges followed to cement hegemony in place.

All this was done in the name of advancing both socialism and Soviet security. Since then, the questions of ideology and insecurity have been indivisible in Eastern Europe. A political challenge is automatically seen as a security threat. Whether or not US policy-makers actually did conceive of attacking the USSR or the Eastern European states and rolling back Soviet power by military means, the rhetoric and the antagonisms provided surface evidence of the need for cohesion in the Soviet bloc, while the military and political manoeuvres of the USA provided a more concrete demonstration of the threat. Similarly, of course, Soviet military occupation of vast tracts of Eastern Europe together with the rhetoric of Stalin and his local cohorts from late 1947 provided the evidence required to confirm Western European acceptance of the need for unity under US leadership.

Thus, the first Cold War was primarily about the organization of power blocs. For the USSR this ended its isolation and provided a framework for security against invasion from the west which had eluded the rulers of Russia for centuries. For the USA, the gain was a stable political basis for economic growth. The liberal world economy which the USA sought and dominated *required* the Cold War. The predictable necessity of military actions to prevent exploited states and people breaking from the US economic orbit could be explained in terms of the Cold War, in terms of an unremitting struggle between the two blocs or, more propagandistically, between the forces of freedom and the Soviet tyranny. The success this system brought to capitalism was unprecedented.

Détente

Maintaining the military strength needed in its role of underwriting the world economy was not cheap for the USA. The war in Vietnam especially brought this home. At the same time, US and Soviet accumulation of thousands of nuclear warheads was both costly and beset with risk. To the extent that the superpowers operated from shared perspectives in the period of détente, it was to limit the costs and risks of permanent confrontation.

Other factors, however, were at least as important in taking relations between the two blocs out of the ice of the first Cold War, through the varying temperatures of the 1950s and 1960s, into the relative warmth of détente by the late 1960s. The different actors in the process of détente each had their own motives besides preventing nuclear holocaust.

The USA's massive military investment – trimmed by the Eisenhower administration in the 1950s, enormously augmented under Kennedy at the start of the 1960s – could not prevent the USSR's rise and rise as a military power. By the late 1960s, the US strategic monopoly was long past. Moreover, the USSR was well into a major change in its naval deployments. While the number of ships did not increase, their types and their roles changed: following the example set by other great powers, the Soviet navy became capable of maintaining a global presence, even if at a rather lower level than the USA could manage because the USSR lacked a worldwide network of support bases. From the mid-1960s, in the wake of Khrushchev's fall, the USSR also strengthened other elements of long-range military capabilities. Perhaps most significantly in American eyes, it stepped up its support for the Democratic Republic of Vietnam, helping bog down the USA in a war which was becoming increasingly hopeless and debilitating.

There was pressure for détente in Western Europe. The economic prosperity of the Federal Republic of Germany by the 1960s and its increasing military contribution to NATO was not matched by a commensurate political status. It was not a member of the United Nations; it had no peace treaties with Eastern European states. The development of *Ostpolitik* under the guidance of Willy Brandt, first as Foreign Secretary in the 'Grand Coalition' government of Christian Democrats and Social Democrats, then as Chancellor (i.e. equivalent to Prime Minister), was a response to this anomaly. *Ostpolitik* was based on the recognition that for the Federal Republic to be accepted as a state with equal rights to all others, an accommodation was necessary in Europe with the Soviet bloc. At the same time, France under de Gaulle's leadership had withdrawn from NATO's integrated military command and developed an independent nuclear force. As part of the more independent and greater international role which these developments signalled, de Gaulle also sought a new relationship with the USSR, one which was different from the USA's and therefore less confrontational.

From the US perspective by the time of President Nixon's inauguration in 1969, a policy of détente with the USSR provided a way of meeting these various challenges. It could be something akin to a superpower 'code of conduct'. This entailed a recognition that the supposedly backward USSR had become a genuine global superpower, in military terms at least. It was hoped it could act as an alternative means of constraining Soviet actions, especially in relation to revolution in the Third World, where the US world system was facing its most serious challenge, without inhibiting US policy in a similar way. This is why the USA consistently sought to link progress in nuclear arms control during the 1970s to restraint by the USSR (in Angola, for example) and why, as détente ended in 1979, the first US reaction to the Soviet invasion of Afghanistan was to suspend the process for ratifying the arms-control treaty agreed with the USSR that summer. Opportunities for the USSR and its Eastern European allies to import capital investment and goods from the west on favourable terms were supposed to act as a further inducement to 'reasonable' behaviour in the Third World. Détente also offered a way of accommodating pressures in Western Europe for a changed relationship with the USSR by absorbing them, thus limiting the damage that might have been done to Atlantic relations if policies had begun to diverge sharply. Détente, therefore, was a policy which coalesced out of the need to respond to several different problems emerging simultaneously.

From the Soviet perspective, détente was never supposed to limit its own freedom of action. Rather, the reverse: it was supposed to limit the USA's freedom of action. Or, more accurately and also more subtly, it was thought to reflect the US leaders' own recognition that their freedom of action was more limited than hitherto, that they could not settle major international issues without Soviet involvement, that the USSR was a great power on equal footing and deserved to be treated with the appropriate respect.[24] This was the 'changed balance of world forces' to which Soviet politicians constantly referred. At the same time, Soviet leaders saw détente as a means of enhancing their security in Europe by gaining an acknowledgement of the post-1945 status quo.

In Western Europe, and especially in the Federal Republic of Germany, this was a small price to pay for solving problems created by the business left unfinished at the end of World War II. The confirmation of West Berlin's odd status as a western enclave in the German Democratic Republic and the recognition of the Federal Republic were important not only in themselves, but also as signs that major bones of contention had been removed, that the division of Europe could remain in place without serious risk of war. At the same time, the benefits of trade with and investment in the Eastern bloc countries were widely touted. This fitted with the dire need of some of the Eastern states for western investment as a way of fuelling economic growth and increasing prosperity without requiring structural political or economic change. But while the Eastern European leaders saw economic interchange with the west as a way of staving off political change, some western leaders hoped that it would lead to a liberalization in the Eastern bloc.

Détente reflected a real change in relations between the blocs and responded to developments within each bloc. However, it did not reflect a change in the basic condition of confrontation. The military build-up continued on both sides throughout détente. The very fact that motives for détente were not wholly shared and often conflicted not only reveals the continuing theme of confrontation but also was itself a factor in bringing détente to an end in the late 1970s. Important as détente was, especially in briefly establishing a safer framework for confrontation with less risk of nuclear war and some hope that nuclear arms could be reduced, it remained essentially superficial. For both superpowers, it was a tactic in their confrontation rather than an end to it.

This weakness of détente was complicated by the fact that the major inhibition on US policy in the Third World was not détente. It was the so-called 'Vietnam syndrome' – the unwillingness to consider more foreign military adventures after the political and military trauma of Vietnam. Throughout the 1970s, there were politicians trying to find ways to put the Vietnam syndrome to rest; as their pulling power increased near the end of the decade, détente was an inevitable victim.

The supporters and opponents of détente in the USA worked from similar assumptions. Neither sought an end to confrontation – simply, one group sought to pursue it differently. Both saw the US–Soviet axis as the deciding axis in world politics. This is a critical assumption of the whole ideology of the Cold War: at its crudest, Soviet policy is identified as the cause or at least as a major irritant in every problem the USA faces in international politics – not just in Third World revolution, but in disputes with allies and the increase in costs of oil and other raw materials. The fact is, of course, the world is not like that. With the exception of increasing Soviet military strength, the main challenges to US world power in the 1960s and 1970s had a limited connection with the USSR or none at all. The USSR did not instigate the Vietnam War – what was at issue was an independence struggle which had been going for decades before large-scale Soviet aid in the 1960s and the climax in the 1970s. No more did it instigate the other Third World revolutionary movements of those years, though to some it gave varying degrees of direct and indirect assistance. Economic competition from Japan and Western Europe and the rise of the newly industrializing countries had nothing to do with the USSR, which was also not responsible for the rise in oil prices, the 1970s slump in world trade, inflation or unemployment.

Resting on a false premise, détente held out false hopes. It could not create a swift liberalization of Eastern Europe; it could not restrain the USSR or its allies in the Third World; it certainly could not restrain challenges from the Third

World; which were nothing to do with Soviet actions. And détente could not even stop the arms race which was widely seen as its most important function. As a result, public support for détente in the West fell away. False premises led to false promises, then to disillusion and a feeling of betrayal. The failure of détente to deliver the goods encouraged the reaction of renewed militarization.

The Second Cold War

There are two basic reasons why détente was replaced by a new Cold War at the end of the 1970s. One derives from the continuing conditions of confrontation between the US and Soviet blocs. The other stems from the American response to the problems it faced in exerting international power. We shall examine them in that order, without arguing that either one is more important than the other.

In assessing the continuity of the underlying confrontation, the general attitudes, culture and ideology of the Cold War are all important factors. At no point in the period of détente was there a fundamental reassessment in either power bloc of the nature of the other. There was no basic change in the way each thought about the other, and that is not really surprising, for the material conditions of confrontation had not changed. On the one hand, the socio-economic basis in each bloc remained the same as it had been; on the other, armed forces were neither removed nor reduced and the strategic nuclear stockpiles of both the USA and USSR grew rapidly.

Indeed, the continuing momentum of military technology was itself a major factor in eroding détente. But it is important not to reify this momentum: it is not a natural force, but the product of human decisions in political affairs and in powerful institutions in both the USA and the USSR – the armed forces and their supporting bureaucracies, the great military–industrial corporations in the USA and the design bureaux and production centres in the USSR, the associated centres of scientific and technological research and development. These were mobilized in the name of east–west confrontation, security and power. They are major elements of US and Soviet economic life. Although their importance is hard to quantify, some indicators can be given. In the USA, 70% of government spending on research and development, and one-third of all research and development spending, goes to the military.[25] In excess of 6 million people in the USA and 15 million in the USSR owe their livelihoods directly to military spending.[26] About 7% of US national wealth is spent annually on the military, and western estimates for the Soviet figure range from 10% to 20%.[27] The continued existence of these institutions requires constant activity, expansion, new projects to work on. New projects are justified because they provide 'improvements' over their predecessors. The need for these improvements is explained in terms of the strategic environment, understood in heavily ideological terms to which the political leaderships also subscribe. The issue is not only that these institutions now have a major interest in continuing their own operations whether they are profit-based or not, though that is obviously a major factor in the USA. The issue is that although it is in principle possible to dismantle all or parts of them, to do so would require a momentous decision against strong internal opposition, and this is not possible in the absence of basic change in the conditions of confrontation. Much easier than taking such a big decision is to continue to take the smaller ones which accrue over time and cumulate into the appearance of yet another new sophisticated weapon system. Yet, and here is the viciousness of this particular circle, the institutions involved in developing and producing arms are themselves now a part of the conditions of confrontation. They thrive on the ambience of insecurity they help create.

It is when one focuses on the basic conditions of confrontation as they have developed over 40 years that it is possible to agree with E. P. Thompson when he says, 'What is the Cold War now about? It is about itself.'[28] There is an element of self-reproduction which was by itself a major factor in the death of détente and onset of a new Cold War. No political strategy seeking to remove the threat of nuclear war can have much claim on our attention if it does not tackle the inertial momentum of the ideology, institutions and politics of the Cold War. One can add that it is when focusing on this element of continuity in the causes of the new Cold War that one can attribute blame more or less evenly on the USA and USSR. Although the USA initiated the arms race, by the 1970s the USSR was undeniably a roughly equal contestant.

But that is only part of the explanation for the onset of the second Cold War and the dangers which accompany it. For the USA, the first Cold War can be understood as an instrument of policy in the construction of a new world order; equally, to the extent that it is not the product of inertia, the second Cold War can be understood as the American response when the international order went into crisis.

The major symptoms of crisis are the well-known economic ones: the definitive breaking of the long wave of boom and prosperity from the early 1950s to 1974, the ensuing cycle of recession and inadequate recovery, the combination of inflation and mass unemployment, the huge accumulation of debt in the Third World. Short-term responses to the crisis have included the rejection of several key assumptions of the liberal world economy, most notably in the reappearance of closed trading blocs and a growth in serious economic disputes between capitalist states. Crucially, this period of crises has revealed that the USA lacks, in the 1970s and 1980s, the power it had in the 1940s and 1950s to act as the major organizer of the world economy. To understand the onset of the second Cold War it is necessary to understand what happened to this power.

As the pre-eminent superpower, the USA incurred enormous costs. High military spending held back development of non-military industry in the USA, producing lower productivity growth and slower economic growth than its major competitors. With the exception of Britain, which insisted for most of the period on retaining the appurtenances of Empire, they profited from the political framework established by the USA with its global military presence, network of bases and system of alliances. For the USA the costs of providing this framework included a major outflux of dollars, which led to a prolonged period of dollar weakness that in the end meant the dollar-based international monetary system had to be abandoned. The USA's world role also led to the trial of strength in Vietnam, eventually lost by the USA at an enormous cost in political confidence and economic strength. The ending of the Vietnam debacle coincided with the beginning of greatly increased oil prices in 1973–4.

In a sense, we could say that the system established by US power worked so well for the other advanced capitalist states that it began to undermine US power. In addition, by the mid-1970s the poorer parts of the Third World were proving harder to control and the resource-rich countries were beginning to exert some power. Yet, despite a deep resentment of an exaggerated image of the power of the Arab oil-exporters, US public opinion was clearly and firmly set against further military adventures overseas. Moreover, the USSR's military strength and global power appeared to be increasing at precisely the time when the USA's appeared to be declining.

US world power was thus challenged in four arenas: in relations with allies (which are also economic and commercial competitors); in relations with the Third World, even with ostensibly 'pro-western' regimes; in the confrontation with the USSR; and in relation to the US population and its unwillingness to sanction the international exercise of US military power.

The strategy of a new Cold War as a response to this accumulation of problems is essentially – though not in so many words – set out in an influential 1979 article in *Business Week* which, diagnosing a 'crisis of the decay of power', proposed a programme of military revitalization as the key to re-establishing US power.[29] This article is interesting because of the close correspondence between its proposals and the programme followed by the Reagan administration since 1981, having been more hesitantly initiated by Carter from 1979. The key to the strategy was the reconstruction of western unity, primarily by stressing the unity of western interest against the Soviet threat. Western unity itself is seen as requiring a new cohesion behind (or under) US leadership. This itself requires a reassertion of US leadership, something which can only be achieved in the military sphere where, despite its other weaknesses, the USA remained a long way ahead of all its allies. From this follows the primacy of the Soviet threat (in its fullest, most global sense) as the ideological glue for new-found unity.

The construction of a political constituency for a new Cold War was already well under way by the time the *Business Week* article was published. A new political coalition was forged between the 'new right', the neo-conservatives and mainstream Republicanism. A major offensive on public consciousness was combined with highly organized lobbying within the various corridors of power.[30] The Carter administration attempted to ride out the storm by absorbing many of the policies of military build-up itself: its final military budget contained a huge increase in spending. But Carter was associated with the years of détente and weakness, and crippled by his inability to get the hostages out of the US Embassy in Iran. He was replaced by the 'great communicator', offering renewed strength, prosperity and confidence – and a major military build-up.

The success of the second Cold War as an instrument for reasserting US power cannot yet be fully assessed. Despite the 1983 intervention in Granada, reluctance to commit combat forces in Central America remained strong even in 1985 as the preparations were being stepped up. US Congress and public opinion seemed ready to support pressure being put on the Sandinista government in Nicaragua, but unready to support the mining of the harbours. The 1986 bombing of Libya was highly popular. In a context of deep political alienation in the USA, reflected in very low voter turn-out for the 1984 Presidential election, Reagan's re-election confirmed his own political standing and the acceptability of the general thrust of the new Cold War, but did not yet reflect readiness completely to slough off the Vietnam syndrome. His re-election owed much to the inadequacy of his opposition and to the general confidence engendered by the economic 'recovery' of 1984 financed by massive Federal budget deficits. If the recovery turns out to be short-term only, Reagan's authority and appeal may be sharply reduced as the end of his second term approaches.

The record is similarly mixed in other respects. While the NATO allies have been prepared, in the face of unprecedentedly large public opposition, to push through the first stages of deploying new cruise and Pershing II missiles in Western Europe, unity in other matters has not noticeably improved. There have been constant disputes over interest rates, energy, steel, trade policies, the Siberian gas pipeline, the Middle East and Central America. Part of the *Business Week* strategy was to get the allies to increase military spending – partly to prevent them from taking unfair advantage of the USA's own military build-up by continuing to steal US markets, partly as a concrete pledge of allegiance. With the exception of Thatcher's Britain, this has not happened – and by mid-decade the Thatcher increase in military spending seemed set to come to an end. The rhetoric has been firmed up almost everywhere, especially and perhaps most surprisingly in France since the election of President Mitterand in 1981, and there are strong signs that the Japanese government would like to increase its military strength. On the other hand, the end of détente and the military build-up have helped prompt a massive reconsideration of nuclear weapons and nuclear strategy, of the reliability and even rationality of the USA as protector of Western Europe. The strength of the mass disarmament movements in Western Europe is a serious problem for US and NATO decision-makers: in terms of public opinion the alliance is more split than at any time – by 1985 the governments had fallen in line with the new Cold War, with the exception of Holland and Greece, but the people had not. This is not merely the result of distrusting Reagan: it reflects the disparate interests on the two sides of the Atlantic and the Western European trajectory over the years towards a greater independence on most matters except strategic policy. However, not only does Reagan occasionally exacerbate the problem (as when he jokingly announced the imminent nuclear bombardment of the USSR in August 1984 during a sound test before a radio broadcast), it also seems so far that the problem of Western European public opinion cannot be solved through the strategy of Cold War.

On the other hand, the USA's choices under any administration are limited. Essentially, the alternative to the attempt to reassert US power is to accept relative decline as gracefully as possible. Most observers of American society would agree that being 'number one' is enormously important in all kinds of ways. Cultural resistance to acknowledging and accepting decline in US power is very powerful: a candidate for the US Presidency campaigning on a slogan of being 'number two', is not likely to get far.

What, then, of the USSR? There is no evidence in the late 1970s and early 1980s of the kind of major shift in Soviet policy that we have just mapped out in US policy. Indeed, the last few years of Brezhnev's rule and the period of transition through Andropov and Chernenko have been marked by inertia. This is evident in the difficulty of achieving economic reforms and in foreign policy. Long after the USA had unilaterally buried détente, the USSR continued to go on about it (although the invasion of Afghanistan may have marked a relatively early assessment that détente was neither so durable nor so important that it should act as a major constraint in other crucial policy decisions). As the truth of détente's demise sunk in, this rigidity equipped the USSR badly in the propaganda battle over arms control, and has thus helped strengthen the grip of the Cold War lobby in the USA, until Gorbachev's new leadership began to practise a more flexible and appealing diplomacy.

However, the second Cold War has proved useful in the Soviet bloc for social and political discipline in the face of the gathering consequences of the system's economic and ideological weaknesses. While the independent trade union, *Solidarnosc*, was allowed to run for longer than the independence of the 'Prague Spring' in 1968, and while it was fairly clear that, for fear of the consequences within Poland, the Soviet leadership did not want to intervene with its own armed forces as it had in Czechoslovakia in 1968, and more bloodily in Hungary in 1956, it did not in the end prove hard to sacrifice *Solidarnosc* on the altar of the new Cold War. The pressure of western rearmament was enough to cohere a group within the Polish leadership with the resolve to suppress the union. Yet the suppression of *Solidarnosc* has done nothing to solve the problems in Poland or Eastern Europe as a whole.

Functions and Dysfunctions

The combined costs of the arms race and Cold War are clear. The resources, both human and inanimate, used in building up huge arsenals are thereby unavailable for other uses. In advanced capitalism, the evidence is clear that states which spend relatively high proportions of national wealth on the military experience relatively slow rates of economic growth.[31] The employment of scientists and technologists in this field renders them unavailable for other tasks, whether in civil industry or in helping meet the urgent needs of the poorest people of the world. The arms race, and the permanent confrontation and current Cold War which provide its political setting, add up to a gruesome misdirection of resources.

Militarism spawns militarism. We see the effects of this in the growing military spending of states outside the central confrontation of the two blocs, in the burgeoning arms trade, in the development of domestic arms industries in Third World countries. Militarism also spawns militarism in the core countries of the bloc confrontation. We see this in culture, in language, in education, in the games children play. We see it in the militarization of the policing function. We see it, and not only in Britain, in the steady disintegration of the services of the welfare state while the warfare state grows apace.

Finally, there is the risk of nuclear war. Fear of its consequences can provide no reliable safeguard against its occurrence. A hostile confrontation can never be stable. As long as it is unstable, the propaganda claim that 'deterrence is working', even if true (which is inherently unprovable either way), can provide no real comfort for tomorrow. Many western strategic commentators appear to believe that nuclear deterrence can impose stability (essentially defined as a retention of the status quo and the avoidance of nuclear war) on the shifting sands of world politics. Not only is that a gross delusion, once again over-rating the political power of both superpowers, it is also the opposite of the truth: nuclear deterrence is itself one of the conditions of confrontation, and therefore of instability. Nuclear strategies which stress the utility of nuclear weapons could raise the stakes in a future superpower crisis to the point where war seemed inevitable to one side or the other, at which point a pre-emptive strike might seem the rational option. The prospect is nightmarish: it is not inconceivable.

One can readily understand that the leaders of the main protagonists have little concern for two of the costs of the arms race and Cold War. Neither the unavailability of resources for alleviating problems in the poorest regions of the world nor the militarization of culture can be expected to bother them much. Yet the other economic costs of high military spending and the awesome risks of nuclear war would seem to fall, to some degree at least, within their framework of calculation. Why, then, are these costs accepted? A price is paid: what are the goods provided or services rendered?

Here we enter an area of major controversy. Venturing into it in the confines of this essay, it is virtually impossible to do justice to the many theories which have been offered, but a brief scan of some of the main points is useful.

Crude economic determinism does not explain why these costs are incurred, though can sometimes explain how they are absorbed. In particular the once fashionable underconsumptionist theory of military spending – according to which the function of high military spending is to absorb unproductive surpluses and stabilize the system – has fallen on hard times as the capitalist system has gone into crisis despite high military spending (indeed, partly because of it).[32]

A number of other theories have also competed for our attention. Perhaps the classic one, not only in academic studies but also in newspaper editorials and everyday conversation, is the action–reaction theory. According to this account, the state is a rational strategic actor which responds to (and even makes) threats in what it perceives to be its own interests. It is, of course, possible for the state, to 'get it wrong', to calculate imperfectly, and hence be not perfectly rational, but that does not damage the theory. Rather, it stresses the role of rational discourse in challenging and changing the policy where necessary. But the weakness of this theory is in its assumption that a state can act with a single will, when close study of how state policy is actually implemented reveals that to be a pipe-dream.

Challenging that account are theories according to which the arms race is domestically determined – i.e. without reference to the supposed international competitor or the state's international ambitions. Indeed, in many such accounts the state's international ambitions are entirely the product of, for example, the power of the military–industrial complex, especially large, profit-motivated corporations which carve everything up between them. Some approaches concentrate on the particular role of the scientists and technologists 'who have succeeded in creating a world with an irrational foundation, on which a new set of political realities has in turn had to be built'.[33] Other approaches direct attention at the role of politics and rivalries within the permanent military bureaucracies in producing high military spending.[34]

Each of these theories catches some elements of the process of armament, but each is incomplete. E. P. Thompson has proposed the concept of 'exterminism', suggesting that over the years the states involved in the arms race have developed an 'exterminist' drive. He warns against the temptation in rational discourse to assume that the object of analysis must possess its own rationality.[35] This concept or metaphor neatly catches the risks of the process and much of the tone and, crucially, does much to explain the *dysfunctions* of the arms race and the Cold War. But what it does not really do is explain their functions.

The general theoretical explanation of the functions of the arms race and Cold War which has informed this essay should be clear from the discussions of the two Cold Wars. The emphasis falls upon a *political* requirement in advanced capitalism for high military spending and permanent confrontation with the USSR. This requirement is to be understood in terms of the organization of the international order since 1945. Periodic needs for more intense confrontation – the Cold Wars – have influenced policy at the moments when the new order was created and when it went into crisis. The requirement for military spending is met through a series of institutional transmission mechanisms – the military, the arms industries and the bureaucracies – which, once established, develop their own interests and, within the framework of the state's general requirements, a relatively autonomous momentum. Consequently, these institutions can meet the state's requirements in an apparently irrational manner. But it is irrational only in the light of the state's general requirements, not in the light of the specific requirements of these institutions (e.g. for profits, new work, a bigger share of the budget). In analysing how these institutions meet their requirements, much of the work done by theorists of the military–industrial complex and the military bureaucracies is very useful – illuminating in explaining what goes on, though weak in attributing too much power to the objects of their study. The role of these institutions has grown, however, particularly because they are the sole repositories of expert knowledge on their own field of operations. As a result of this privileged status, they can protect themselves against the consequences of what may seem irrationality in terms of the state's general requirement, and even become parts of the process by which the state's general requirements are set.

The USSR's requirement for high military spending can be viewed in much the same light. Again, the emphasis is on a political requirement as part of the continuing organization of its own system of power and international influence. But while the first Cold War can be seen to have corresponded to particular Soviet interests at the time, the second Cold War cannot – thus the Soviet emphasis on détente long after it was dead. This approach absorbs many aspects of the partial theories discussed above into a more embracing account.[36]

The requirement for permanent confrontation and high military spending is, to a limited but definite extent, rational. That is, they provide a way, given the interests, goals and standpoints of the leaderships, of meeting certain requirements on both sides. As instruments of power, armed forces are and always have been fundamental. Moreover, although the Soviet threat is exaggerated and its basis distorted by western propaganda, and although something similar happens in the USSR about the western threat, it is not irrational for the leaders of each superpower to see the other as a threat to their own power and influence.

However, it is necessary to make several points to qualify that argument. Assessing what is rational fundamentally depends on standpoint. To say it is rational for them does not mean it is rational for the rest of us. Different actors in the process have different rationalities: what makes sense to bureaucrats does not always make sense to arms manufacturers, generals or political leaders. Even to the extent that it is rational at any level, that does not guarantee a safe outcome, neither for state leaders nor for their citizens, for neither the USA nor the USSR has total control of everything that goes on in the world. It is quite possible for two perfectly rational courses of action to run head-on into each other with disastrous consequences. Here, much also depends on the time-scale over which the assessment of rationality is made: what solves today's problem may bring on tomorrow's disaster. Finally, to say that it is rational does not mean it is acceptable morally or in any other sense.

The importance of this argument is that it compensates for some of the arguments associated with the disarmament movements which have stressed the irrationality of the drive to nuclear war and the regular disjuncture between what would seem to be in states' interest and what they actually do. Those arguments are not to be rejected: they are not only right in principle as well as detail, they have also been enormously important in mobilizing massive opposition to the arms race and Cold War. But, to identify a political strategy which can overcome the threat of nuclear war, we need also to identify who has what kind of stake in the system which creates the threat in the first place. And that we cannot do merely by focusing on the horror and the idiocy of the system. A strategy for disarmament depends on identifying both the functions and the dysfunctions of the arms race and Cold War, in equal measure.

Nuclear Disarmament

While there is some objective basis for the US strategy of Cold War as a means of reasserting hegemony, there is much that militates against it. Recession and crisis simultaneously emphasize the need for unity among the USA's major allies, and make it harder to achieve. Should unity win over rivalry, one effect will be to strengthen the US hand for further military intervention in Third World countries, possibly with participation from pliant allies. Yet should the attempt to reassert the USA's hegemony over its major allies be unsuccessful, the other option of gracefully accepting relative decline is unlikely to be taken, and even more unlikely to be durable if it were taken. The result of this refusal could be increasing instability and temptation into a series of reckless adventures, in turn increasing the danger of nuclear war.

The USSR's leadership of its own bloc remains unchallengeable, but it is facing its own problems – both domestically and in Eastern Europe, both economic and political. It is engaged in a costly and difficult as well as brutal war in Afghanistan, though so far its economic and political costs have been less than the USA incurred in Vietnam. Its influence in the Third World is not as wide or as deep as that of the USA and its allies, and the Soviet record of retaining its positions of advantage is not strong. It is also currently emerging from the political transition out of the Brezhnev era. It is not clear that the Gorbachev leadership will have the cohesion, the confidence, the domestic strength or the subtlety either to resist US provocations or desist from provocations of its own.

The dangers of the new Cold War are extreme. They have called out a massive popular reaction. The challenge to these dangers can only go so far (and not far enough) if the appeal for change is based solely on an assertion of common humanity and common peril. This appeal is fundamental – the absolutely necessary condition of political movements opposing nuclear weapons, nuclear strategy and nuclear confrontation. But beyond that, the political structures from which these dangers derive must also be challenged.

As an abstract exercise, it is quite possible to imagine east–west confrontation without nuclear weapons. Indeed, some proposals for nuclear disarmament must be assessed carefully in the light of the possibility that a nuclear arms race could merely be replaced by a conventional one. Nuclear weapons themselves are technical artefacts, not political processes. But nuclear weapons and strategy are inextricably tangled up with the basic politics of confrontation and world power. Western European states continue to predicate their security policies on US military capabilities, especially the nuclear 'umbrella': this is the one surviving, largely unchallenged dimension of US leadership of its allies. The USSR's nuclear arsenal is a key element of its claim to be a global superpower and, while it does not have the same role in ensuring its control of the states in Eastern Europe that the US arsenal has in relation to Western Europe, it must be regarded by the Soviet leadership as a means of protecting its sphere of influence against external challenges. We could assume that rational leaders of the USA and USSR would wish to avoid a nuclear war, but in responding to their other interests they have also embarked on a course which could lead them still to such a war. It certainly cannot be assumed, on the basis of all the experience of the era since 1945, that either superpower left to its own devices would recognize an interest in achieving nuclear disarmament. To seek to remove or even merely reduce the danger of nuclear war, whether the proposition is to do this by unilateral or multilateral actions, is necessarily to seek a major change in some of the key terms of international politics in the late twentieth century.

It does not need to be stressed that this necessary task is enormously ambitious. Without mapping out a utopian design for the future, which might attract us in its rational simplicity but could paralyse us through its practical inaccessibility, the task is to identify those points at which a political challenge must be directed in order to set up a process leading away from nuclear war and towards disarmament. The targets for this challenge are US interventionism, the Atlantic alliance, the division of Europe into opposing armed camps, and Soviet control of Eastern Europe.

US interventionism means not merely armed intervention, but the entire paraphernalia of global military presence. In challenging it, we also challenge the right and the capability of the advanced industrial states to impose their will by any means on other parts of the world. In the Atlantic alliance, the particular target is the now vulnerable Western European assumption that security is necessarily based on a dependent partnership with the USA in order to resist an inherently threatening USSR. As we challenge that assumption and attempt to shift the strategic consensus, so we shall automatically challenge the division of Europe achieved at the end of the World War II, not in the sense of attempting to change national boundaries, but in attempting to erode the hermetic sealing of two spheres of influence against each other. And if those related challenges are mounted with any degree of success, we would be lifting the pressure of western militarism against Eastern Europe which provides one of the key legitimations of Soviet dominance. The effect should not be over-estimated, yet it might provide some greater room for manoeuvre for more autonomous forces in Eastern Europe and change the international environment sufficiently to encourage some change in Soviet policy.

The challenge of disarmament is not only a matter of international politics. Both the institutions and the culture of the permanent arms race must be included in a political strategy seeking to end confrontation and remove the danger of nuclear war. At one level, this can be addressed through proposals for converting military industry to other uses. At another, it demands a more profound rejection of the fears and the values which underlies militarism and confrontation, of the assumptions and culture of national chauvinism and sexism that help keep us in thrall.

All of this demands a willingness to face up to the character and interests of the ruling classes both in the west and in the USSR.[37] There is a clear willingness among some sectors and members of western ruling classes to face up to the dangers of nuclear confrontation and its costs, and they have produced many proposals for alleviating them. Yet, in the end, they founder on their inability to drop their allegiance to specific class assumptions about power and a refusal to relate the nuclear danger to the system of international power. They have opened doors, challenged consensus and spurred new thinking. They have helped dispel some of the power of the nuclear myth. Many of their contributions to the debate are extremely valuable, but they are unreliable allies.

There remains an unaccountable temptation among some socialists to see the USSR as an inherently more reliable ally. It is reasonable to argue that the USSR's current foreign policy, despite its military involvement in Afghanistan and its continuing military build-up, is less provocative and dangerous than the USA's under Reagan. But this assessment reflects only short-term considerations: primarily, it derives from the inertia of Soviet policy in Brezhnev's last years and since. It is also reasonable and, indeed, essential to counter the western propaganda accounts of the Soviet threat – the menacing bear, ever poised to strike westwards, held back only by increasing western military expenditure. A more convincing account can argue that the USSR has no inherent interest in either the military conquest or the nuclear incineration of Western Europe, though the circumstances in which an offensive or incineration might be launched are all too easily imaginable.[38] Along with this it is necessary to counter the exaggerated accounts of Soviet military power which we are daily fed by our governments and communications media. It is also true that many (though not all) of the USSR's negotiating positions in arms control talks in the 1980s have been 'fairer', given the rules of the arms control game, than the USA's. In particular, the Soviet desire to include British and French forces in talks on long-range nuclear weapons in Europe is quite just, and the suspicion of US plans to develop space-based defences against nuclear missiles is not only just but also widely shared in the west.

However, to add all these valid points together into an assertion that the USSR is inherently more peaceful than the USA, and that this can guide a political strategy for disarmament, ignores the role of Soviet armed force in repressing freedom in Eastern Europe. It ignores the Soviet war in Afghanistan. It ignores the fact that a self-described socialist state has a so-called defence policy based on the threat of wiping out the working classes of advanced capitalist countries. It ignores the promotion of militaristic values in Soviet schools. And it ignores a lot else besides.

The counter-argument used by some, that the USSR has been forced into these postures and policies, has several flaws.[39] It accepts the basic logic of nuclear deterrence, and therefore of continued military confrontation and the permanent risk of nuclear war. It fails to think of alternative courses of action that a different Soviet leadership could have followed. It puts no pressure on the USSR to take any major initiatives towards ending the arms race, and thereby seems to accept that that goal must remain dependent on the policies of the USA. It accepts as axiomatic that the Soviet response had to be a response in kind – both in types and numbers of weapons; when western propagandists accuse the USSR of having more weaponry than it needs for defence, they are being hypocritical because the same can be said of the USA, but the point is valid for all that. The fact that the USSR has largely reacted in the arms race rather than initiated its various rounds may make it less culpable than it might have been – though it might also merely reflect its relative technological backwardness – but does not exonerate it from the responsibility to seek and initiate solutions to these pressing problems. If the USSR were a reliable ally for disarmament, if it were inherently more peaceful than the USA, there is much that it could have done to enlarge détente and much that it could be doing now.

The reaction in kind by the USSR reveals its own acceptance of the logic of power and military strength followed by all great powers. Its control of its Eastern European neighbours and its role in world politics depend heavily on its military strength – and are thus necessarily linked to confrontation with the west. The ruling group in the USSR is not about to surrender that advantage and compete for influence and power, for example, on the basis of economic penetration of other countries, something for which it is poorly equipped. Nor is it about to surrender those basic conceptions of power and politics. And it is those conceptions, in both east and west, which could hurl us into nuclear war.

If one faces the investment on both sides of the Cold War in continued confrontation, several things become clear:

1 A strategy for disarmament must identify the weak links in the chain of the Cold War.
2 Achieving disarmament measures cannot be left to the standard operations of secret diplomacy, bilateral and multilateral negotiations. To do that would be to put the solution in the hands of those who got us into this mess in the first place.
3 Accordingly, the demand for unilateral measures of disarmament is the only one which makes political sense, although it is certainly reasonable to expect that a process of disarmament would also involve multilateral agreements.
4 The source for a challenge to the logic and politics of Cold War and nuclear confrontation can only be found in mass movements which reject the entire gamut of both western and Soviet orthodoxy on these questions.

The strength of those movements in the early 1980s is one of the few optimistic signs in international politics. Strangely, the disarmament movements are more political than much of their polemics, which have tended to remain at the level of the humanistic appeal. Their experience since their upsurge in 1980 in Western Europe has shown that, willy-nilly, a challenge to nuclear weapons, strategy and confrontation is a challenge to the underlying political structures. As a result, there is no need for socialists to attempt to inject politics into the movements. Not only is that process distastefully arrogant and dangerously sectarian whenever it is tried, it is also superfluous. It is not necessary to be uncritical about the movements to understand that their mobilization of popular feeling and their willingness to take non-violent direct action against the arms race – the peace camps, the blockades – have mounted a challenge to the military establishments and strategic consensus which is unprecedented and powerful.

In Western Europe, the disarmament movements have moved into the political mainstream. Their initial challenge to the new cruise and Pershing II missiles immediately became a challenge to the NATO strategy which justified the new weapons, and led automatically to a challenge to US strategic leadership. That fits well with the Western European trajectory away from accepting US economic and political leadership. Since the USA's effort is directed at using its strategic primacy to reassert economic and political leadership, the disarmament movements are striking at the heart of the problem.

To a much greater extent than has happened in Eastern Europe (because of the Soviet grip), or in the Third World (where external aid is often an absolute necessity, but one which brings political problems whatever its source), or with the aversion of US public opinion to engaging US combat forces in action overseas (because it is both limited and unreliable), Western Europe has become a weak link in the Cold War chain. The intensified danger of nuclear war has coincided with a crisis in the US-led international system – a coinciding which is not coincidental. The result has been a wider understanding of the oppositions between the American superpower and its European allies. This understanding, to be sure, is fragmented and unclear, but the seeds have been sown and the roots are beginning to take. In Western Europe, the priority is to wean public political consciousness away from its dependence on two myths – the myth of nuclear deterrence, and the myth of the unity of US and European interests. Breaking this dual dependence will require also a challenge to the other dimensions of Cold War politics, not only those we experience in Europe but throughout the world. It is the strength of the mass movements, and that alone, which offers us the chance to do it.

Notes

1 The Appeal is reprinted in E. P. Thompson and D. Smith (eds), *Protest and Survive* (Harmondsworth, Penguin, 1980).
2 D. R. Rosenberg, 'US nuclear stockpile, 1945–1950', *Bulletin of the Atomic Scientists*, May 1982.
3 See D. Holloway, *The Soviet Union and the Arms Race* (New Haven, Yale University Press, 1983). Brezhnev, of course, became Party leader and President, Ustinov became Defence Minister and apparent kingmaker for the Andropov succession.
4 S. Durie and R. Edwards, *Fuelling the Nuclear Arms Race* (London, Pluto Press, 1982).
5 M. Kaldor, *The Baroque Arsenal* (London, André Deutsch, 1982), especially chapter 5.
6 The Stockholm International Peace Research Institute (SIPRI) is the best monitor of the state of the non-proliferation regime. See *World Armaments & Disarmament: SIPRI Yearbook* (London, Taylor & Francis, annual). Article VI of the Non-Proliferation

Treaty obliges the Parties to negotiate in good faith for an end to the arms race, for nuclear disarmament and for general and complete disarmament. The Treaty entered force in 1970.

7 *SIPRI Yearbook 1984*, pp. 24, 27.

8 P. Rogers, *Guide to Nuclear Weapons 1984–5* (Bradford, Bradford School of Peace Studies, 1984), p. 6. Rogers gives a slightly higher figure than SIPRI (see note 7), for US strategic nuclear warheads, of above 10,000.

9 *END: Journal of European Nuclear Disarmament*, no. 11, August-September, 1984.

10 *U.S. Foreign Policy for the 1970s: A New Strategy for Peace*, report to US Congress by Richard Nixon, President of the United States, 18 February 1970, p. 22.

11 The fullest statement of nuclear winter theory to date is P. R. Erlich, C. Sagan, D. Kennedy and W. Orr Roberts, *The Cold and the Dark* (London, Sidgwick & Jackson, 1984). A briefer presentation of the main points which the non-scientist will find more readable is C. Meredith, O. Greene and M. Pentz, *Nuclear Winter* (London, Scientists Against Nuclear Arms, 1984).

12 The failure to think this issue through has led one contributor to this volume to declare elsewhere his support for the 'balance of terror' in the name of Third World liberation. See E. Mandel, 'The Threat of Nuclear War and the Struggle for Socialism', *New Left Review*, no. 141, September–October 1983.

13 The major study is D. Ball, *Can Nuclear War Be Controlled?*, Adelphi paper no. 169 (London, International Institute for Strategic Studies, 1981). Among prominent and powerful adherents to the view that nuclear war *cannot* be controlled was Harold Brown, Secretary for Defense under Jimmy Carter, even at the time he was administering US nuclear doctines on the basis that it can be controlled: *US Defense Department Annual Report: Fiscal Year 1982* (Washington DC, US Department of Defense, 19 January 1981).

14 E.g. Lord Carver, *A Policy for Peace* (London, Faber & Faber, 1982) and Lord Zuckerman, *Nuclear Illusions and Reality* (London, Collins, 1982). Carver is former Chief of the Defence Staff, Zuckerman former Chief Scientific Advisor at the Ministry of Defence and to successive Prime Ministers. Americans with experience of high office have formulated similar arguments: M. Bundy, G. Kennan, R. S. McNamara and G. Smith, 'Nuclear Weapons and the Atlantic Alliance', *Foreign Affairs*, Spring 1982. For a more radical setting to a somewhat similar proposal on nuclear strategy, see J. W. Sanders, Security and Choice', *World Policy Journal*, vol. 1, no. 4, Fall 1984.

15 E. P. Thompson might have taken to exemplify the first group of writers, Fred Halliday the second: Thompson, 'Beyond the Cold War', in *Zero Option* (London, Merlin Press, 1982); Halliday, *The Making of the Second Cold War* (London, Verso, 1983).

16 Halliday, The Making of the Second Cold War, p. 3.

17 *United States Objectives and Programs for National Security*, a report to the National Security Council by the Executive Secretary, NSC-68, 14 April 1950, reprinted in *Naval War College Review*, May-June 1975.

18 A useful study of the US political context of alarmism is A. Wolfe, *The Rise and Fall of the Soviet Threat* (Washington DC, Institute for Policy Studies, 1979). The analysis is updated in *idem*, 'Domestic Sources of the "Soviet Threat"; in P. Joseph and S. Rosenblum (eds.), *Search for Sanity* (Boston, South End Press, 1984).

19 D. Yergin, *Shattered Peace* (Boston, Houghton Miflin, 1978).

20 F. Claudin, *The Communist Movement: From Comintern to Cominform* (Harmondsworth, Penguin, 1975), pp. 455–79.

21 A. Grosser, *The Western Alliance* (London, Macmillan, 1980).

22 C. Wiebes and B. Zeeman, 'The Pentagon Negotiations, March 1948: The Launching of the North Atlantic Treaty', *International Affairs*, vol. 59, no. 3, Summer 1983.

23 Yergin, *Shattered Peace*, pp. 343–50. For further discussion of the establishment of Soviet control of Eastern Europe after World War II, see chapter 2 in this volume.

24 J. Steele, *The Limits of Soviet Power* (Harmondsworth, Penguin, 1985).

25 *World Armaments & Disarmament: SIPRI Yearbook 1984* (London, Taylor & Francis, 1984), p. 170.

26 Estimates on a basis described in M. Kidron and D. Smith, *The War Atlas* (London, Pan, 1983), in note to map 27.

27 *SIPRI Yearbook 1984*, p. 127 and *The Military Balance 1984–1985* (London, International Institute for Strategic Studies, 1984). There are numerous problems in estimating the proportion of national wealth spent on the military, especially in the case of the USSR which uses a different measure (Net Material Product rather than Gross Domestic or National Product) and whose figures are trusted by no informed commentator in the west. The problems are discussed in D. Smith and R. Smith, *The Economics of Militarism* (London, Pluto Press, 1983), chapter 1.

28 Thompson, 'Beyond the Cold War', p. 168.

29 'The Decline of US Power', *Business Week*, 12 March 1979.

30 J. W. Sanders, *Peddlers of Crisis* (London, Pluto Press, 1983). On the rise of the new right in the USA see chapter 1 in this volume.

31 R. P. Smith, 'Military Expenditure and Capitalism', *Cambridge Journal of Economics*, March 1977, and *idem*, 'Military Expenditure and Investment in OECD Countries', *Journal of Comparative Economics*, March 1980.

32 Probably the best-known exposition of this approach is P. Baran and P. Sweezy, *Monopoly Capital* (New York, Monthly Review Press, 1966). For a later variation, see E. Mandel, *Late Capitalism* (London, New Left Books, 1975), pp. 274–309.

33 Zuckerman, *Nuclear Illusions and Reality*, p. 106.

34 See G. T. Allison, *Essence of Decision* (Boston, Little Brown, 1971) for the classic statement of this paradigm.

35 E. P. Thompson, 'Notes on Exterminism, the Last Stage of Civilization', in New Left Review (ed.), *Exterminism and Cold War* (London, Verso, 1982).

36 The approach is set out more fully in D. Smith and R. Smith, *The Economics of Militarism* (London, Pluto Press, 1983).

37 The mere mention of a ruling class in the USSR, of course, immediately lands one in the thick of a raging controversy. However, my use of the term is not merely polemical: it rests on the view that the *nomenklatura* (initially, those judged capable of holding responsible positions) in the USSR form a ruling class within which there are gradations of power. A concise analysis of the rise of the *nomenklatura* and the aptness of regarding them as a class is in L. Kochan and R. Abraham, *The Making of Modern Russia* (Harmondsworth, Penguin, 1983, 2nd edn), especially pp. 344–6, 434–6, 475–8, 508–9. For a contrasting characterization of the ruling bloc in the Soviet Union see chapter 2 in this volume.

38 See *Defence Without the Bomb*, the report of the Alternative Defence Commission (London, Taylor & Francis, 1983), chapter 2.

39 Examples of this approach are to be found in Mandel, 'The Threat of Nuclear War and the Struggle for Socialism', and R. Medvedev and Z. Medvedev, 'The USSR and the Arms Race', in New Left Review (ed.), *Exterminism and Cold War*.

Part Two

Conflict and Change in the World Order

7

The Third Great Revolution
The Experience of Revolutionary Socialism in China

GORDON WHITE

The Chinese revolution, which came to power in 1949, was the third great revolution (after France and Russia) and arguably the greatest, given the length and scale of struggle and the sheer numbers of people involved. Like its Russian precursor, China was another case of revolutionary socialism succeeding in a relatively backward and peripheral country, thereby 'turning Marx on his head'. In this century up to 1949, China was a desperately poor country which, while never formally colonized, fell victim to the depredations of the major imperialist powers, both western and eastern (Japan). As such, China was the first example of a succesful socialist revolution in those economically undeveloped and politically oppressed countries which later came to be known as the 'Third World'. Moreover, it provided a revolutionary recipe, a political map of the path to power, which was to serve as a model for revolutionary movements in Asia, Africa and Latin America.

The Chinese revolution was directed against internal economic backwardness, social injustice and political impotence. It was also directed against international subordination. Despite efforts at modernization, first by the Imperial government which collapsed in 1911 and, second, by the Nationalist (Kuomintang) regime in the 1930s, on the eve of revolutionary success in 1949 China exhibited the classic symptoms of economic backwardness, social debility and injustice. It had an overwhelmingly agricultural economy characterized by stagnant productivity and negligible technical change, heavy demographic pressures, low levels of gross investment and 'modern' commercialization, and static income levels. Agriculture was based on peasant households and there was substantial rural tenantry and inequality in land tenure, squandering of the rural surplus on unproductive expenditure and a high level of rural indebtedness. Though modern forms of economic enterprise had taken root, they grew in narrow enclaves (largely in a few big coastal cities or along the Yangtse River), were dominated by foreigners and employed only 2.4 per cent of the non-agricultural work force.

Foreign commercial privilege and political influence over Chinese domestic affairs had built up through decades of intervention, spearheaded by British traders and officials. The first dramatic clash between Britain and China was the Opium War of 1839–42, a historical watershed which began the 'modern' era of Chinese history. It started a century of conflicts between China and various imperialist powers. In the latter half of the nineteenth century, each Chinese defeat was formalized in a treaty which legitimized and extended the range of foreign economic and political influence. Sections of Chinese territory were directly appropriated as colonies: Britain had taken Hong Kong after the Opium War and Japan colonized the island province of Taiwan after the Sino-Japanese war of 1894–5. Rivalry between the powers intensified in the last decade of the century, sparking off a 'struggle for concessions' as each power sought to consolidate its foothold in China by establishing a territorial sphere of influence which fell short of formal colonization: the Germans in the north, the British in the centre, the French in the south, and the Japanese and Russians competing for control over Manchuria in the northeast.

Successive treaties opened more and more Chinese 'treaty ports' to foreign trade. Many of them established 'concessions', areas under direct foreign administration – the most famous of these were in Shanghai and Tientsin – operating on the principle of 'extra-territoriality'. China was deprived of the right to adjust her tariff rates, administer her customs and appropriate her customs revenues. Foreign factories established in the treaty ports after the Sino-Japanese war enjoyed special tax privileges for their products. This accumulation of foreign pressure and privilege accelerated a decline in the authority of the Chinese imperial government and growing popular resistance which toppled the dynasty in the national revolution of 1911.

After a phase of political anarchy under the warlords following the collapse of the 1911 revolution, a strong nationalist movement arose in the major cities and coastal provinces which led to the establishment of the Kuomintang government in 1928. The new nationalist government, under Chiang Kai-shek, sought to claw back national sovereignty from the imperialist powers and organize a programme of autonomous national development. During the 1920s and early 1930s, however, the shadow of Japan lengthened over China: the northeast provinces were detached and a Japanese puppet-state, Manchukuo, was established in 1932. Over the next few years, the Japanese penetrated further south and in 1937 swept into the interior. This ended the nationalist party's attempt to consolidate its rule and began an eight-year war against Japanese occupation.

The Chinese Revolution

Marxist socialism, the Leninist model of the vanguard party and the practical example of the Russian revolution exerted a powerful attraction as an effective cure for China's ills. Though China absorbed much of the ideology and organizational forms of Soviet socialism, the period of struggle between the founding of the Chinese Communist Party (CCP) in 1921 and nationwide liberation in 1949 saw the gradual adaptation of Marxism-Leninism to the Chinese context and the emergence of certain distinctively Chinese features of revolutionary theory and practice. The figure who exerted a predominant influence over this 'sinification' of Marxism was Mao Zedong (Mao Tse-tung), a founder member of the CCP and its effective leader from the mid-1930s onwards.

Unlike the Russian revolution, the Chinese revolution was born out of a prolonged military struggle: a civil war against the Kuomintang regime from 1927 to 1937 and 1945–9, and an anti-imperialist war against the Japanese between 1937 and 1945. Until its last stages, this conflict was a guerrilla war which gave the Chinese Communist Party part of its distinctive identity: a 'military' style of political action which spilled over into non-military matters; an emphasis on close, face-to-face relations between revolutionary organizations and the general population on whom the army depended for food and recruits; an ambiguous kind of military egalitarianism which sought equalization of condition (for example, through removal of rank insignia, similar living arrangements for officers and men) while retaining the hierarchy of command; and a sensitivity to the importance of 'self-reliance' for units and localities, deriving from the scattered nature of guerrilla warfare.

The main thrust of this long struggle was nationalist, whether the CCP was cooperating with the Kuomintang between 1921–7 to liberate China from the war-lords and unite her against the imperialist powers, or in the fierce struggle to drive out Japan during World War II. The CCP was able to present itself as a more effective instrument of national liberation than the self-proclaimed Nationalist Party which dithered in its opposition to the Japanese in the mid-1930s and appeared overly dependent on the United States in the late 1940s. At the same time, after a disastrous period of over-reliance on Soviet advice in the 1920s, the CCP steered a course which was independent of, indeed at times conflicting with, Moscow. These nationalist credentials not only helped it to strengthen its appeal among the labouring classes, but also to attract support from a wide range of other social strata, particularly the intelligentsia. When the CCP came to power in 1949, it claimed to represent a national coalition composed of peasants, workers, petty bourgeoisie (intellectuals, professionals, small business people) and national capitalists (who opposed foreign capital and Chinese 'comprador' interests who served it).

Though the CCP was a radical nationalist party, it was also a *revolutionary* party in class terms. In the first stage of communist activities between 1921 and 1927, under Soviet tutelage, the party formed an alliance with the Kuomintang and adopted an urban-oriented strategy which concentrated on organizing China's miniscule industrial working class. This strategy proved ineffective since the right wing of the Kuomintang, under Chiang Kai-shek, broke the coalition and turned against its radical elements and because communist organizations in the cities were very vulnerable to the resulting repression. In the bloody putsch in Shanghai in 1927, many of their members were arrested and summarily executed. This debacle began a process whereby the party, under the leadership of Mao, turned to the countryside as its base of operations and to the peasantry as its base of support. The new strategy relied on two core elements: first, to recognize the peasantry as a radical social force and lead them in an 'anti-feudal' revolution against landlordism which culminated in redistributive land reforms; second, to establish, consolidate and expand revolutionary 'base areas' which could be protected militarily and within which the beginnings of a new society could be created. The most influential of these was Yenan, in northern Shaanxi (Shensi) province, which was the communist headquarters during the anti-Japanese war.

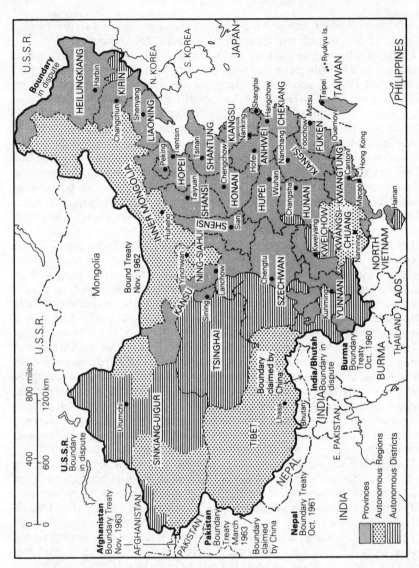

Map 7.1 The People's Republic of China

The experience in Yenan, where the communists retained undisputed control for a decade, was to have a crucial impact on the evolution of Chinese communism. It served as a matrix for alternative social, economic and political institutions. From this experience, Mao drew a conception of socio-economic development which stressed the capacity of organized human initiative to triumph over material backwardness; the developmental potential of widespread popular mobilization under the leadership of a revolutionary party; the economic value of grassroots, collective initiative in creating small-scale enterprises using 'intermediate' technology in a context of local self-reliance; and the virtues of indigenous Chinese ways of doing things, as opposed to foreign (either communist or capitalist).

Politically, the 'Yenan experience' was important because it developed the 'mass line' style of leadership which to some extent adapted Soviet-style Marxist–Leninist conceptions of the relationship between the vanguard party and its mass following along more egalitarian and participatory lines. The mass line represented an attempt to break down hierarchical barriers between officials and population, leaders and followers (for example, by minimizing visible signs of rank), to stifle incipient tendencies towards bureaucratization of the Party and government institutions (for example, by having officials do manual work) and to involve the general population in processes of social, economic and political transformation (for example, through mass movements, mass organizations such as peasant associations and economic institutions such as industrial and agricultural cooperatives).

To a considerable extent, the experience in Yenan and other base areas prepared the CCP for the tasks ahead after the success of the revolution and shaped the way it went about them. Yet the legacy of revolutionary struggle was ambiguous. The authoritarian impact of ideology and organizational methods imported from Soviet (i.e. Stalinist) Marxism–Leninism was deep-going. Moreover, the Yenan experience was only one part of the national revolutionary struggle. The protected base areas provided some scope for democratic experimentation; such methods would have been impossible, indeed suicidal, for party members working in the 'white areas' controlled by the Kuomintang or Japanese. The Party in the 'white areas' seems to have developed a political style much closer to that of Lenin's conspirational elite, forced by brutal repression to be secretive, hierarchical, strictly disciplined and organizationally separate from their following.

The Yenan experience did, though, contain many contradictions. The model of political organization and action established there was both participatory and authoritarian. The egalitarian and democratic components of the 'mass line' and the 'guerrilla style' operated within strict limits. Though we can agree with Mark Selden that the CCP's revolutionary struggle was 'built on foundations of participation and community action' and that 'for the first time the peasantry as a group was integrated into the political process,' the mass line was premised on a clear difference in power between cadres and masses, Party and non-Party, leaders and followers. Party and government officials may have made progress in democratizing their work-style and eradicating traditional barriers of status and deference, but basic inequalities of power remained between them and the population – thus egalitarianism coexisted with hierarchy. A massive upsurge of peasant involvement was the vital element of the revolutionary movement, yet mass participation had to be channelled to be effective and mass organizations had to be subordinated to Party control to serve the interests of the wider struggle.

Mass organizations were not allowed to develop into autonomous political forces capable of checking or supervising the institutions of state power. In short, communist leaders in both the guerrilla base-areas and the 'white areas' were true to Leninism, which they regarded as a political methodology attuned to the needs of revolutionary struggle. They carried this conviction with them into the era of post-revolutionary socialist construction.

The Chinese experience offered a model appropriate to the social and political conditions of the colonized territories fighting for national liberation and social revolution in the post-war era. It combined nationalism with class mobilization; it was rooted in the dominant class, the peasantry, yet sought to forge a national alliance of strata opposed to imperialism; it relied on large-scale mass-mobilization and guerrilla warfare, its ultimate success depending on the ability to defeat the enemy militarily. The Vietnamese revolution followed a similar path, as did the Mozambican, Algerian and Angolan revolutions later. The Nicaraguan revolution shares some of its features and several current guerrilla struggles – in the Philippines, Peru and El Salvador – are operating along similar lines.

As a plan for revolution which can be generalized to other Third World countries, however, its success depends on certain favourable conditions:

1.   The armed and repressive presence of the imperialist powers strengthens the capacity of the revolutionaries to build a strong political coalition and isolate domestic adversaries. In the Chinese case, the Japanese invasion provided a much-needed breathing space for a battered communist movement and stimulated a massive expansion of CCP power and prestige as the main bulwark against an external oppressor. If the imperial presence is less direct (i.e. not as a colonial or occupying power) or the colonial power hands over authority to a local elite, the nationalist component of the revolutionary coalition may be weakened.
2.   The coherence, stability and political appeal of the indigenous state is a crucial determinant of revolutionary success. In China, the Kuomintang state was divided, corrupt, administratively ineffectual, perched on a narrow class base and, in its later days, increasingly dependent on the United States. However, where the domestic state is able to extend its political base through nationalist appeals or domestic reforms and maintains a degree of political coherence and administrative effectiveness, the political task of the revolutionary movement becomes that much harder.
3.   Where geographical conditions do not favour guerrilla warfare, or where the military technology available to the counter-revolutionary state is relatively sophisticated, the 'people's war' strategy may prove very difficult, the guerrillas either being defeated militarily or contained in marginal areas. Thus there may be only a few countries where the Chinese revolutionary model may prove both applicable and successful.

The Chinese Experience in Socialist Development

At the point of nationwide liberation in 1949, the Chinese communist leadership, like their Russian precursors and Third World successors, faced the task of building socialism in a poor country. In these conditions, revolutionary socialism faces certain basic dilemmas. Rather than basing its political strength on the child of modern industry – the proletariat – it must depend on classes originally defined as secondary to the classic socialist project, notably the peasantry and petty bourgeoisie. Rather than a force for international working-class solidarity among advanced capitalist nations, revolutionary socialism has become the means by which poor nations 'catch up' in a world dominated economically by powerful capitalist nations. Rather than being founded on solid economic and cultural foundations built by capitalism, as Marx had envisaged, it has in effect become an historical substitute for capitalism: as the destroyer of 'traditional' socio-economic institutions and as an engine for rapid economic growth and social transformation. In this context, the process of socialist development is not a question of growing new socialist institutions in fertile ground already prepared by capitalism; it involves a dual process whereby the essential pre-conditions for socialist institutions must be established along with those institutions themselves.

Certain basic questions arise here:

1. To what extent do economic scarcity and social backwardness impose limits on the possibilities for establishing socialist institutions? For example, can socialist relations of production be established in a context of technically backward, household-based peasant agriculture, and, if so, what specific institutions will emerge and what is the timing of the transformation involved?

2. Since socialism is taking on the developmental role occupied elsewhere by capitalism, does not the logic of this 'developmental socialism' require policies and institutions which may be incompatible with socialist ideals? For example, to the extent that individual material incentives are necessary to stimulate increases in labour productivity, what implications does this have for the solidarity of the working class? If development implies an ability to raise investment levels sharply and restrain consumption, to change the relative balance between different socio-economic sectors, indeed to change the basic ways in which people feel and behave, does this not imply a high degree of centralized control, at least for the short and medium term? If so, then how does this hamper the development of effective socialist democracy?

3. Since 'developmental socialism' has historically been rooted in the process of backward, oppressed nations 'catching up' with the industrialized metropoles, an inherently nationalist process, does this not pose a serious impediment to the development of international solidarity? To the extent that capitalism retains its power at the global level, moreover, what kind of economic and political relationship should a socialist China adopt with it?

The Chinese experience emphasizes the tensions and conflicts which these dilemmas bring to the process of socialist development. The CCP leadership set out to achieve three basic goals: to strengthen China's power after a century of international humiliation and internal political decay; to raise the material and cultural standards of the Chinese population on the basis of a more productive economy; and to construct a socialist form of society which delivered the material gains of capitalism without its exploitation and inequalities. The achievement of these aims was seen to require a strategy of managed capital accumulation which would generate substantially higher levels of savings, channel these into productive investment, and raise levels of productivity throughout the economy through improvements in infrastructure, technology and human capacities. This would gradually restructure the economy away from backward agriculture towards technically sophisticated and highly productive forms of modern industry. The methods used would be radically different from capitalism: planning would be substituted for market, collective for individual incentives. In 1949 and consistently thereafter, these ambitious goals have been sought in a context of formidable constraints: pervasive poverty, low levels of technology, a declining availability of arable land, heavy population pressures, conservative social values, sclerotic social institutions and international hostility.

1949–57: Socialist transformation and the Soviet model

The initial phase of Chinese development, from 1949–57, consciously emulated the Soviet Union. There was a '*socialist transformation*' of ownership in industry and agriculture, involving a transition from 'lower' forms of ownership (private capitalist industry or household agriculture) to 'higher' (through cooperatives and collectives to 'whole people' or state ownership). Simultaneously came the beginning of '*socialist construction*' involving the establishment of a comprehensive planning system which would pilot a long-term programme of economic growth and structural change.

By 1956, all modern industry and commerce previously under private ownership had been brought under state management and a new state industrial sector was being constructed under Soviet tutelage. Agrarian transformation went through several phases, starting with a radical land reform after 1949 which dispossessed the landlord class and redistributed land and other agricultural means of production to peasant households. Immediately afterwards, the Party began a process of step-by-step collectivization of agriculture. This was seen as economically important to reap economies of scale, lay a basis for local capital investment and tie agriculture into the new industrialization programme; socially important to serve as a matrix for local welfare provision; and politically important to prevent class polarization in the countryside and consolidate post-revolutionary local institutions. The first stage was the organization of 'mutual aid teams' composed of five to 20 peasant families which pooled their labour, draught animals and tools, worked cooperatively but retained ownership of their land. The next step, during 1953 and 1954, was the organization of 'lower-level agricultural producers' cooperatives' (APCs), 'semi-socialist' institutions which pooled land in addition to equipment and labour. Land was farmed as a cooperative unit but each constituent household still retained ownership of its plot. Income was based partly on labour inputs and partly on the size of each household's contribution of land and other means of production. These lower-level cooperatives were relatively small, usually between 20 and 30 households. In 1955 began the transition to 'fully socialist' APCs, a producer cooperative comparable to the Soviet collective farm, composed of 130 to 200 households. Private ownership of land was in the main abolished (though households retained small private plots for domestic use) and income was based mainly on the quantity and quality of individual labour.

The phase of 'socialist construction' began in earnest with the first five year plan (1953–57) which followed the Soviet model in its strategic priorities and planning methods. It aimed to achieve rapid industrialization by sharply raising the level of investment and rechannelling it into productive activity: 52.4 per cent of state investment went into industry and only 7–8 per cent into agriculture where, it was hoped, the transformation of relations of production through collectivization would raise productivity without major technical change. Agricultural surplus was a major source of finance for the industrialization programme, captured by taxation and unfavourable price ratios between agricultural and industrial products.

During the plan period, the modern industrial, commercial and financial sectors were gradually incorporated into a system of centralized planning along traditional Soviet lines. Central planning agencies set strategic priorities and produced long-term (usually five-year) and short-term (annual) plans calculated on the basis of overall material balances (using input–output matrices). Government agencies at different levels transmitted orders on the output and distribution of goods to subordinate firms down a hierarchical chain of administrative command. These orders reached enterprises in the form of obligatory targets, leaving little autonomy for the enterprises themselves. While economic transactions within the state sector were subject to direct planning, relations between the state and other sectors had a market dimension (notably purchases from rural collectives, sale of industrial consumer goods and foreign trade). Agriculture was brought within the sphere of planning by the establishment of procurement quotas for produce which rural collectives were obliged to deliver at set (usually low) prices.

The results of this initial period of Sovietization were ambiguous. Socialist transformation had eliminated the former owning classes and laid the basis for a more egalitarian mode of development; an industrial working class was emerging in the cities. Economic achievements were substantial, with annual GNP growth at about 7–8 per cent during the plan period and an industrial growth rate at about 15 per cent. By 1956–7, however, serious economic problems had appeared and there was growing discontent with certain features of the Soviet model, both among the Party leadership and in society at large. The one-sided emphasis on heavy industry starved agriculture of resources; agricultural growth (at about 3 per cent per annum) was sluggish, as was the rise in rural per-capita incomes, and output of food-grains scarcely kept pace with population growth. The collectivization programme, while far more successful than its Soviet precursor, still brought many problems, (notably lack of producer incentives and managerial diseconomies in the larger collectives) and failed to achieve the hoped-for breakthrough in output. The tendency to favour capital-intensive forms of industry, also meant low rates of employment generation, very worrying with a population growth rate estimated at over 2 per cent per annum by the mid-1950s and a steadily increasing person–land ratio in agriculture. The introduction of a Soviet-style planning system brought an overcentralized rigidity to economic planning and a general bureaucratization of society. These issues provided the raw material for disagreements within the CCP leadership which were to intensify and provide much of the impetus for the political fluctuations of the next two decades.

1957–76: The rise and fall of Maoism

1957 to 1976 could be called the 'Maoist period' since it saw the rise of a distinctive approach to socialist development sponsored by the then chairman of the Chinese

Communist Party, Mao Tse-tung (in the official Chinese Romanisation, Mao Zedong) and his supporters. During the Cultural Revolution decade (1966–76), 'Mao Zedong Thought' (along with Marxism–Leninism) became the ruling orthodoxy of Chinese communism. Although Mao's thinking stayed within the general paradigm of Soviet Marxism–Leninism there were certain new elements which originated in his experience during the revolutionary war, especially in Yenan.

The impact of the Soviet-style strategy of the 1950s ran counter to Mao's beliefs in many ways and caused him much disquiet. While he did not wish to abandon the drive towards modern industry, he advocated the method of 'walking on two legs' towards industrialization, using intermediate and 'native' as well as advanced foreign technology, small-scale as well as large-scale enterprises, the collective as well as the state sector. Grassroots mobilization of resources through collectives could both maintain the momentum of growth and expand employment by substituting plentiful labour for scarce capital. The principle of local 'self-reliance' in industrialization reflected a broader commitment to decentralization: within the state machine from central to local governments, from the state to collectives, and from officials and experts to the 'masses'.

These ideas found dramatic expression in the *Great Leap Forward* launched in 1958. The Leap was an attempt to correct the imbalanced growth of the mid-1950s by attempting to drive ahead simultaneously in both agriculture and industry, heavy and light industry, using the strategy of 'walking on two legs'. The economy was divided into two sectors: on one side, the modern, relatively large-scale and technically sophisticated state sector; on the other side, the smaller-scale, more labour-intensive sectors (in both industry and agriculture) organized by local governments or collectives. While modern industry would still receive the lion's share of state investment, the other sector would rely heavily on local finances, labour-intensive small plants and a strategy of 'labour accumulation'. The latter involved the substitution of labour for capital through mass mobilization for infrastructural projects designed to increase agricultural productivity (notably irrigation, flood control and roads). The mass project was one of the lasting images of the Great Leap Forward – seas of human beings heaving stones, carrying bricks, tamping down earth and building walls and dams, armed with only the most basic of implements. The scale of mobilization was unprecedented, in China or elsewhere. Another lasting image of the Chinese countryside during the Leap was the proliferation of small workshops, notably one million 'backyard' iron and steel furnaces which involved 60 million people.

The *'rural people's communes'* which emerged during the Great Leap were an embodiment of Mao's vision and a matrix for the new strategy of local development and mass mobilization. They were designed to cope with the vastly enlarged scale of labour mobilization and to provide the social services necessary to allow greater female participation in work outside the home. They were formed by amalgamating existing collectives and were initially very large (over 30 times the size of the higher-level collectives, with an average membership of 4,614 households). They also increased the degree of collectivization of economic and social life: private household plots were appropriated, social provisions for child-care were expanded, food was distributed on a virtual rationing basis and partly consumed in public mess-halls. There was also a swing towards egalitarian payment systems.

But to Mao Zedong, communes were more than just 'higher' forms of economic organization. They were microcosms of society, 'the basic unit of the social structure of our country, combining industry, agriculture, trade, education and the military'. They also represented a fusion of the formal public power of the state with the local community. As such, they were the building blocks of a new socialist rural society, a matrix for the transition to communism.

Rural transformation was accompanied by changes in national planning. In September 1958, the principle of local decentralization was introduced, creating a 'dual track' system which combined vertical 'branch' control by central ministries with horizontal regional control by local governments. A large share (87 per cent) of industry formerly run by Peking was transferred to local governments. Henceforth, the planning process was to be more 'bottom up', the building blocks being seven large regions, each composed of several provinces and with its own plan. Within each locality (as within the new communes), the role of the Communist Party as the key agent of economic coordination increased, bringing a pervasive politicization of economic life under the slogan of 'politics in command'.

Within state enterprises, there was a serious attempt to change the hierarchical division of labour and authority established under Soviet tutelage. The managerial role of the Party committee increased at the expense of the factory director and greater use was made of 'non-material' incentives to motivate the workforce. Workers were given greater control over their conditions of work through small 'production groups' within the workshops (with elected leaders). Attempts were made to break down divisions between mental and manual labour: managers and technicians were required to spend more time on the shop floor, talking with manual workers or doing their jobs; workers were included in 'triple combination' groups (with managers and technicians) to solve work problems and come up with technical innovations. Though the impact of these changes was very uneven, they did change the climate of ideas and, in some enterprises (particularly the larger, more technically advanced) did make some difference to the social relations of production by increasing workers' initiative in determining their work conditions and making managers more responsive to worker interests.

Though the initial economic results of the Leap seemed positive, its frenetic atmosphere tended to inflate both production targets and reported results. In state enterprises, the reforms often led to a decline in work discipline and efficiency: partly because of opposition or apathy on the part of managers and technicians; partly because more active workers found it difficult to exercise their new powers due to lack of basic skills, while less active workers took advantage of relaxed disciplinary regulations to slack off; partly because the intense fervour generated by the Leap tended to polarize political debate and generate unnecessarily bitter hostilities. As for the new small-scale enterprises, much of their output was of such poor quality as to be useless (notably the products of backyard steel furnaces) and costs of production were often unreasonably high due to lack of requisite technical skills and poor labour organization. Most important was the Leap's disastrous impact on agricultural production. The local industrialization movement drained labour from agriculture; exaggerated optimism about agricultural output based on the fantastic yields of 1958 led to ill-conceived and economically damaging campaigns for technical transformation; the increased scale of labour organization disrupted established work routines and made management more difficult; the trend towards egalitarianism in distribution and abolition of the residual household economy reduced work motivation, rewarded slackness and created a mentality of 'everyone eating out of the same pot', with bad effects on labour productivity. Moreover, many of the local capital projects proved to be ill-planned and ineffective in raising agricultural output. Agricultural output and stocks of livestock and draft animals dropped alarmingly and the trend was exacerbated by poor weather. By 1960 there was famine in certain areas and later estimates indicate that as many as ten million people may have died in consequence.

1960 to 1965 was a period of economic recovery and growing political crisis, an interregnum between the two main upsurges of Maoism, the Great Leap and the Cultural Revolution. The economic crisis of 1959–61, which was further worsened by the abrupt withdrawal of Soviet technical assistance, prompted yet another reappraisal and change of course in development strategy. In an attempt to move towards a more balanced growth strategy, the principle 'Agriculture as the Foundation and Industry as the Decisive Factor' was introduced in 1960. This did not reverse the priorities of state investment. It meant, first, that plans for industrial development were in future to be based on a more realistic analysis of agriculture's capacity to sustain them and, second, in industrial investment greater emphasis was to be placed on those branches supplying agriculture with productive inputs such as chemicals and machinery.

Since local decentralization of the planning system had led to wasteful duplication and weakened overall economic coordination, there was a partial recentralization of planning power to Peking. Within state enterprises, the authority of the enterprise director was strengthened at the expense of the Party committee and the workforce; part of the power devolved to production groups was taken back by managers and technicians. The division of labour between managers and technical staff on the one hand, and routine and manual workers on the other, was reasserted; and though the practice of 'cadre participation in manual labour' was retained, in most plants it lost any real significance. Regulations on work discipline and production responsibility were also strengthened. Though 'workers' representative congresses' exerted some influence on welfare issues, they had no power over the major managerial decisions. Even if they had, however, their power would have been very restricted given the enterprise's lack of autonomy.

In the countryside, the basic unit of accounting and production organization was scaled down: first, to the 'production brigade', equivalent to the former higher-level collective and then to the 'production team', equivalent to a former lower-level collective. The result was a 'three-level ownership system'. The agricultural role of communes was reduced accordingly, but they retained governmental functions and ownership of large means of production, and still played a major role in organizing 'labour accumulation' projects, sponsoring local industry and technical change, and providing welfare services. This three-level system, based on the team, was to remain basically in place for the next two decades. Within communes, the degree of collectivisation of everyday life was drastically reduced: household economic activity was revived by the restoration of local free markets and private plots (about 5–7 per cent of a team's cultivated land); public mess-halls were abolished and egalitarian rationing systems dismantled in favour of more differentiated payment based on quantity and quality of labour performed.

As the economic crisis receded, a political crisis developed. A section of the CCP leadership were shocked by the impact of the Great Leap and resolved to avoid a repetition. For their part, Mao Zedong and his followers emphasized the positive elements, attributing negative results to haste, poor leadership by local cadres and uncontrollable factors such as weather. In their view, the central achievement, the commune system, was basically sound and should be retained, as should the emphasis on local self-reliance and labour accumulation. It was in the aftermath of the Great Leap that these alternatives began to crystallize, growing into a bitter conflict known to its Maoist participants as 'the struggle between the two lines'.

The Maoist position which emerged in the early 1960s provided a new view of the 'transition to socialism', that historical period of indeterminate length which leads from the initial period of 'socialist transformation' to the ultimate phase of 'full communist society'. According to Mao the new 'socialist society' contains attitudes and material conditions which obstruct a transition to genuine socialism and threaten a 'reversion to capitalism'. The 'transition to socialism' is not a smooth process based on gradual socio-economic improvement but is riven by deep conflicts. Institutions and people must continually be transformed alongside economic growth and technical modernization; otherwise, 'while the satellite goes up to the sky, the red flag falls to the ground'. The future of socialism – particularly the goals of classlessness, altruism, collectivism, egalitarianism and mass participation – must be secured in the present through political struggle. This struggle is to be conducted under the banner of 'the continuation of class struggle in socialist society' in a process of 'continuing revolution'. Its primary targets are 'new bourgeois elements' emerging throughout society and their 'revisionist' political representatives, 'those in authority taking a capitalist road' in the Party–state machine. In the cities, the key elements of class formation are the elites created by the new 'socialist' political economy: politico-administrative cadres and technical–professional intelligentsia. In the countryside, if collective institutions were to be weakened, a new process of 'polarization' would take place, leading to an emergence of a new rural bourgeoisie, the 'rich peasants'. The social mechanisms by which these actual or potential elites consolidated and extended their privileges had to be attacked and an effective counterweight created by mobilizing the 'masses' under the banner of the 'mass line'. Radical Maoism called for struggle against all manifestations of market economics, such as profits as the index of enterprise efficiency, prices as signals for economic behaviour, the use of highly differentiated wage scales and individual material incentives as spurs to productivity, and expanded interaction with capitalist economies abroad.

In the early 1960s other leaders such as then-president Liu Shaoqi and Deng Xiaoping, began to sponsor an alternative model which provided a different conception of socialist transition. They argued that the fundamental underpinning of socialist development was a rising level of economic productivity; to secure this, there was a need for market disciplines and material incentives, and for the separation of economics from politics. We shall call this the 'socialist market', 'market reform' or simply 'reform' position. Under the leadership of Deng Xiaoping, it was to become the dominant model of Chinese political economy after the death of Mao in 1976; I shall discuss it later. Elements of this programme were introduced in the early 1960s although Mao Zedong used his indisputable personal prestige to stifle these reforms and launch a counter-attack in 1966, the 'Great Proletarian Cultural Revolution'.

Though the mass movement stage of the *Cultural Revolution* only lasted about two years (1966–8) before being reined in by Mao Zedong with the aid of the army under Lin Biao, Maoist leaders managed to hold on to power throughout much of the Cultural Revolution decade (1966–76) until Mao's death. The period had major effects on development policy. Elements of the Great Leap were revived and strengthened. The principle of decentralization was continued by a transfer of planning power to local governments in 1970. The principle of local 'self-reliance' was also used to encourage rural collectives to expand their small-scale industry. The rural commune system was consolidated, retaining the 'three-tiered system of ownership' which had emerged after the Great Leap. Household economy was circumscribed but not abolished: peasant families could retain their private plots but local free markets were frowned upon. The main processes of rural economy were under collective management, usually by the smallest unit, the production team. Throughout the economy, individual material incentives and market indicators were castigated as 'bourgeois' and there was egalitarian pressure against high payment differentials.

The Maoists also launched an assault on the existing social division of labour, viewing it as a basis of special privilege and class formation and an obstacle to the development of truly socialist social relations. A number of policies were aimed at reducing the 'three great differences': between industry and agriculture, workers and peasants, mental and manual labour (the latter including differences between rulers and ruled, managers and managed, expert and non-expert):

1. There was an attempt to correct the bureaucratic tendencies of officials and managers by 'sending them down' to the grassroots or workshops to do manual labour.
2. There was an effort to raise the level of mass control over the management of factories and farms. During the initial radical stage of the Cultural Revolution (1966–8), many factories were taken over by workers' councils and the original management totally displaced. The principle of worker control was later diluted by the establishment of 'revolutionary committees' to manage enterprises, containing army representatives and former managers as well as workers.
3. There was an attempt to redistribute access to schools and colleges in favour of workers and peasants and to change the role of the educational system as a ladder to elite positions. School curricula were made less academic, exams were abolished and middle-school graduates were not allowed to proceed straight to university. They had to work in factories and farms for several years and were allowed into university on mainly political criteria. Unemployed urban graduates were mobilized to 'go down to the countryside' leaving their city homes to settle down for life in rural production teams (about 16 million were 'sent down' in this decade).

The 'Chinese model' of the Cultural Revolution decade seemed to many at the time to open an optimistic page in the depressing annals of Third World poverty, injustice and dependence on the one hand, and bureaucratic calcification in the 'socialist countries' on the other. Why was much of it rejected after the death of Mao in 1976?

Let us turn first to the social and economic aspects of the Maoist project; we shall discuss the political aspects later. There were some positive effects. Socially, Maoism pinpointed problems in the structure of post-revolutionary society (notably the danger of 'new class' formation) and left a valuable legacy of egalitarianism and popular defiance of established authority. Economically, it identified some of the defects in Soviet-style central planning; succeeded to some extent in restraining economic inequalities; consolidated the rural commune system and used it as a reasonably effective mechanism for local investment and technical change; developed small-scale, labour-intensive local industry as a valuable complement to state-led industrialization; and introduced a broader network of basic social services to the rural areas.

As a strategy of socialist economic development, however, radical Maoism was deficient not only in terms of the changes it sought to make, but also those it failed to make. Maoist policies did not pay adequate attention to questions of economic efficiency, expertise and productivity – these tended to be tarred with a 'bourgeois' brush. Under the banner of 'politics in command', economic decisions tended to become political decisions and the economy became a battle-ground for warring political factions. Excessively egalitarian payments systems in factories and farms reduced work incentives and hindered gains in labour productivity. Nor did the democratization of enterprises have a demonstrably beneficial effect on productivity and incomes. The effort to reshape the educational system had a serious effect on academic standards in the basic disciplines and weakened China's capacity for advanced research.

Maoism also embodied much more Soviet-style economics than was realized at the time. Maoist development strategy did not in fact favour agriculture in deciding priorities for state investment. The previous strategy of stressing industry over agriculture and heavy over light industry continued, as did the obsession with very high rates of investment at the cost of raising popular living standards. The Soviet-derived system of central planning established in the 1950s was still basically in place and Maoist reforms to promote local decentralization seemed to make matters worse by maintaining the bureaucratic essence of the previous system while losing the advantages of centralization. On the eve of Mao's death in 1976, the Chinese economy, formally presented as an example of 'central planning', was neither very centralized nor very planned. In the countryside, moreover, the restrictions on household agriculture and the insistence on moving to larger-scale collectives created many economic problems which Maoist leaders chose to ignore or blame on 'class enemies' or 'revisionism'. While overall economic performance during the Cultural Revolution decade was respectable, it was not outstanding (especially in agri-culture); it was being purchased at increasing cost and, even where relatively impressive (in the growth of heavy industry), did not sufficiently feed through into rising living standards. Stagnation or slow growth of incomes created a backlog of popular frustration which paved the way for alternative policies after Mao's death.

1976–85: The demise of Maoism and the rise of socialist market economics

The late 1970s saw the rise of an alternative 'reform' leadership under Deng Xiaoping. Mao's supporters in the CCP Central Committee were gradually weakened and isolated, eventually to be dismissed or forced to resign. These years also witnessed the rise of new 'socialist market' policies. The Third Plenum of the CCP Central Committee ratified an economic reform programme announcing a shift in the Party's main task towards 'socialist modernization'. The reformers criticized both ideas and institutions of Maoism and the central planning system inherited from the Soviet Union. They called for a sweeping redefinition of strategic economic priorities and thoroughgoing institutional reforms in the planning system. We shall concentrate here on the central issue of *the relationship between planning and markets* in a socialist economy, the nub of the reform position. Their programme had several key elements:

1. They attempted to separate the spheres of politics and economics, arguing that economics operates according to 'objective laws' which resist political intervention. They thus rejected the Maoist conception of economic development as a process of political mobilization. Motivationally, this gives a greater role for material incentives; institutionally it means that the Party and state should play less of a role in economic life. The previous planning system, argued the reformers, was in effect a complex bureaucratic hierarchy; economic management requires economic methods, therefore administrative agencies and controls should be reduced and state planning agencies should make more use of 'economic levers' such as price, credit, taxation, interest rates, subsidies and so on. In other words, the nature of planning should change from directive to indicative. State agencies would still be responsible for macro-economic planning but, in implementing the plan, they were to set fewer obligatory targets and more flexible guidelines, working through economic inducement rather than bureaucratic fiat.
2. This redefinition of the role of the state set the context for *decentralization* of economic decision-making power to enterprises and a *revival of market-type relations* between enterprises. The industrial enterprise was to gain greater power over investment, product mix, payment methods, pricing, material procurement and sales and was to behave more directly in pursuit of its 'independent financial interests'. Reformers argued that this would enliven industry by correcting the previous situation whereby enterprises had very little independent economic initiative.

The expansion of enterprise powers is an essential element of the reintroduction of markets; 'horizontal' links between enterprises were gradually to replace 'vertical' links between each enterprise and its bureaucratic superiors. Market exchanges of this kind would make enterprises more sensitive to their customers and would generate healthy competitive pressures. The performance of an enterprise would henceforth be reflected in its profitability. As the market sphere of the economy expanded, there would be lessons to be learned from the capitalist West and Japan. Capitalist management had two aspects, the exploitative and the scientific; the former should he shunned but the latter should be studied and used.

The principle of economic decentralization was also applied to agriculture. Through the new 'responsibility system', the economic role of rural collectives was reduced and most agricultural activities were sub-contracted by the production team to its constituent households.

The scope of market reform *proposals* has been very sweeping, while the actual *impact* of reforms over the past eight years has been uneven. From the vantage point of the mid-1980s, we can see that the overall degree of change in Chinese society and economy has been impressive. More state investment has gone into light industry to meet rising consumer demand and into social infrastructure such as schools, hospitals and housing. Reform policies have been particularly effective in raising output and incomes in the countryside where, by 1984, over 90 per cent of China's farm families had adopted the new 'responsibility' or 'contract system', reviving a *de facto* system of household agriculture. In the urban areas, the pace of change was much slower. Institutions were more entrenched and resistance more stubborn. Certainly there was no decisive shift towards a 'socialist market' economy.

By international standards, Chinese economic achievements since 1949 have been impressive, with an average annual growth rate of national income officially estimated at about 7 per cent between 1949 and 1983 (4.2 per cent in per capita terms). China has succeeded in enlarging and diversifying her industrial base while avoiding political or economic dependence on foreign countries. In 1983, China was the fourth largest producer of steel in the world, third in coal, sixth in electricity and seventh in crude oil. Technically, China now has the capacity to make and deliver nuclear weapons, put satellites in orbit, make super-computers and breakthroughs in certain areas of 'frontier' scientific research (such as synthesizing insulin). Agricultural growth performance is less impressive, but it is still respectable in comparative terms. By historical standards, the degree of structural change (measured by shares of industry and agriculture in GNP) is greater than comparable periods in the earlier experience of advanced capitalist countries; industry rose from 25 per cent to 55 per cent of GNP between 1949 and 1983. Yet China has hardly been transformed into an industrial society. In 1982, 84.4 per cent of the total labour force in industry and agriculture still worked in the latter. China could perhaps best be described as a 'semi-industrialized' country.

This economic progress has occurred in the context of a development strategy and institutional system which have brought substantial benefits to the bulk of the population. Incomes have risen substantially, particularly in the post-Mao era, and inflation, which was the scourge of the late Nationalist era, has been largely avoided. Rising average incomes partly reflect increasing levels of employment in the urban areas, the dependency ratio (the number of people supported by a wage-earner, including him/herself) has dropped from 3.3 in 1957 to 1.7 in 1983. This partly reflects greater female participation in the labour force which is one basic condition underlying the substantial increases in women's social and economic welfare (other factors include legal measures, child-care facilities and an official ideology of gender equality). In the countryside, although a substantial amount of 'surplus labour' exists in theory, employment opportunities have been provided either within the collectives or the households. Income differentials have been contained within reasonable limits, one consequence of the changes in ownership introduced in the early 1950s, thereby avoiding the extremities of wealth and poverty characteristic of most capitalist forms of development. Development policy has laid great stress on providing a basic level of welfare for the mass of the population; in the countryside the collectives provided the institutional underpinnings for this. Levels of popular access to education and medical care have risen markedly; by 1983 one in five people was a student and about one-quarter of the population had a junior high-school education or above. The number of hospital beds per 10,000 people increased from 1.5 in 1949 to 20.7 in 1983; the number of doctors from 6.7 to 13.3. Massive preventative health campaigns have eliminated or alleviated previously endemic diseases and standards of sanitation have improved enormously. In consequence, average life expectancy has almost doubled, from about 35 before 1949 to 68 years in 1981.

Whether one compares this performance to other Third World countries (the obvious case being India) or to some hypothetical capitalist alternative in China itself, Chinese socialism has brought developmental success. But there have been serious policy errors and there are defects in the basic institutions of socialist economy which have come to the fore over recent years. The reformers' criticisms of pre-1978 economic strategy and planning are well-founded and changes were overdue. Indeed the economic results of the reforms so far have been largely positive. Growth in national income accelerated after 1978, agriculture expanding particularly rapidly. Average per capita incomes increased at a rate far higher than earlier, with rural incomes outpacing urban.

But certain questions must be raised about the social and political as well as economic impact of the reforms. How viable is the reform project as a vehicle for long-term socialist development? It rests on two theses: first, that planning and markets can be made compatible in a socialist economy and, second, that *control* over means of production can be transferred (to households and enterprises) while retaining state or collective *ownership*. Considering first the relationship between plan and market, experience in China and Eastern Europe suggests that the productive complementarity claimed by reform economists is difficult to establish in practice. Plan and market are not only potentially contradictory principles of economic organization, but they also generate conflicting patterns of social relations and political power. Therefore any attempt to change the relationship between them will be fraught with social tension and political conflict. As the Hungarian economist Janos Kornai warns, instead of gaining the best of both worlds, reformers may end up with the worst, cancelling out the separate advantages of planning and markets. If traditional central planning introduced elements incompatible with socialist ideals, moreover, so may markets; they may lead to macro-economic instability, unemployment, growing inequalities and a weakening of collectivist morality.

Turning to the divorce between ownership and control, the transfer of power over factors of production, including labour, may lead to processes of private accumulation outside the state sector, which may not only generate social relations similar to capitalism but also begin a process of class differentiation in which dominant groups are able to exert powerful pressures on state policy to further their interests. Most reformers do not discuss these social dimensions of economic change and tend to assume that the 'state' and the 'planners' will be able to handle any such problems which arise. But this raises the central question of the nature of the socialist state, and its links with society and economy.

China and the World

It is important to put China's developmental experience in the context of her relations with the external world, since domestic and foreign policy have been so closely interconnected. The changes of the past two decades have been dramatic. From the pariah state of the 1960s, during the 1970s and 1980s China has increasingly become accepted as a responsible and influential member of the conventional system of inter-state relations. The political influence accorded to China on the international stage partly reflects current realities – her size, military establishment and strategic significance both geographically and as a balance between the two superpowers. It partly reflects a perception of her enormous *potential*, both economic and military. While some overseas observers may see this process as a kind of 'domestication' of a previously wild international animal, to China it is evidence of a growing recognition of her role in world affairs and willingness to admit her into previously closed international council-chambers.

The changes in China's international posture over the past 15 years have been dramatic but we must be clear about their character and content:

1. Some changes do not so much reflect new directions on China's part as mere adaptations to changing external realities over which China has little or no control (for example, the decline of the US threat in the late 1960s, or changing US–Soviet relations in the early 1980s).
2. Important changes, such as the *rapprochement* with the United States or the decision to expand economic relations with capitalist countries, began in the early 1970s during the Cultural Revolution decade and were clearly undertaken at Mao's initiative or with his approval. They cannot be seen merely as fruits of post-Mao liberalization.

Beneath the changes of the past 15 years, there are also fundamental continuities. Despite important changes in the international environment, foreign policy has continued to be shaped primarily in response to relations between the two super-powers and their specific encroachments on Chinese sovereignty and interests. Moreover, the basic goals of Chinese foreign policy have not changed. We can discuss these under three headings:

1. These is a desire to attain national integrity and maintain independent national freedom of manoeuvre. These aspirations are rooted in the Chinese experience of humiliation at the hands of the imperialist powers before 1949 and no doubt the experience of the somewhat stifling bearhugs of their Russian comrades during the period of Sino-Soviet collaboration in the 1950s. Most basic is the desire to re-establish what China sees as its own territorial integrity, reflected in the border conflicts with the Soviet Union over Siberia and with Vietnam over the islands of the South China Sea, the drive to reintegrate Hong Kong into the mainland through the agreement with Britain negotiated in 1984–5 and the clash with the

United States over the latter's continued support for an entity, the Republic of China in Taiwan, which China regards as a defeated and discredited competitive regime occupying one of its provinces. But the desire for sovereignty and independence extends beyond mere territorial considerations: it is reflected in China's commitment to protecting its own distinct social, cultural and political identity, including its own definition of socialism, and to avoid excessive dependence on or alliance with any major foreign power, whether this be the Soviet Union in the 1950s or the United States in the 1980s. Moreover, China's own past experience as an exploited and dominated poor nation continues to find expression in support for other countries in the Third World which face similar problems.
2.   The desire to create a rich and powerful nation is one which Chinese communist leaders share with their Imperial and Nationalist predecessors. This means a powerful drive to catch up with the advanced industrial nations (by current reckoning, this will be achieved by 2050) and to create a nation which has the economic and military power necessary to underpin global political influence. Relations with the external world are a crucial element of this strategy since they can provide an impetus for rapid modernization through commercial, financial and technological flows. This 'modernization imperative' contains certain policy dilemmas and gives Chinese foreign relations a deep ambivalence: as a poor country which claims to be part of the Third World, China participates to some degree in the struggle of the poor nations of the south against the north; as an incipient great power with pressing and comprehensive needs for advanced economic and military knowledge and equipment, there is pressure to draw closer to the industrialized capitalist powers, particularly the United States and Japan.
3.   There is a desire to project Chinese interests and influence abroad, both at the regional and global levels. This involves a slow transition from a position of weakness whereby foreign policy is dominated by the need to act defensively against powerful external pressures, notably 'competitive containment' by the Soviet Union and United States, to a position of strength from which the Chinese government can take the initiative in pressing its interests and exerting its influence internationally. Their ability to do this depends partly on the country's growing economic and military might, partly on the diplomatic ability to build international coalitions on key issues.

While these objectives have remained unchanged, China's capacity to achieve them has increased and the post-Mao era has brought new ways of pursuing them. To the extent that the Dengist economic reforms have improved economic efficiency and accelerated real rates of economic growth and technical change, they have strengthened China's relative economic weight, particularly since this has occurred in a context of international recession. Defence policy has changed to favour rapid modernization of the armed forces (to fight a 'people's war under modern conditions') and it is likely that recent years have seen an increase in China's ability to deter hypothetical Soviet or US threats in both nuclear and conventional arenas (these policies were accelerated after China took a mauling in the punitive attack on Vietnam in 1979). The ability to mount a nuclear retaliatory attack against both the USSR and the US has been increased by developments in ICBM technology and there are signs of plans to develop a long-range 'blue-water' naval capacity to project Chinese influence into the oceans.

The sweeping domestic changes in ideology and policy introduced by China's post-Mao leaders have important implications for foreign relations. We shall discuss these changes under two broad headings: strategic, geopolitical issues, on the one hand, and economic relations on the other. China's strategic view of the world and thus its general foreign-policy stance has become less militantly 'ideological' in several senses. Though the world is still seen as riven with conflict (notably the potentially cataclysmic rivalry between the superpowers), earlier views of an international coalition against both superpowers (imperialist and social-imperialist) or against Soviet 'hegemonism' in the 1970s have been replaced by a less antagonistic view of international relations which sees a multipolar world (including six basic elements: China, the United States, the Soviet Union, Europe, Japan and the Third World) with China involved in a complex mesh of accommodation and conflict in a complex world. The earlier 1970s attempt to incite the United States against the Soviet Union has gradually been replaced by a willingness to view both superpowers in more similar terms and to settle into a classic balance of power triangle between them. Gradual détente with the Soviet Union has been accompanied, at the ideological level, by a disappearance of erstwhile Maoist attacks on 'revisionism' which extends beyond acceptance of the Soviet Union as 'socialist' to a recognition of the legitimacy of Eurocommunism.

In relations with the Third World, the clarity and vehemence of earlier Chinese championing of poor and dominated nations has waned, though not disappeared. The complexity and divergent interests of Third World countries have prompted more cautious, differentiated policies. Aid programmes have been cut, and the 'Third Worldist' themes so central to Maoist ideology have lost much of their force. This said, China continues to support the south on north–south issues and champion the rights of individual countries which are seen as victims of superpower molestation (such as Nicaragua or Afghanistan).

The 'socialist' aspect of Chinese foreign policy, moreover, is more difficult to discern. Certainly there is no commitment to exporting a revolutionary Chinese version of socialism to compete, say, with a Soviet alternative; this is hardly surprising since no clear-cut alternative exists at present except a rather vague attachment to economic reform. Nor is there a commitment to support revolutionary movements within countries except where they embarrass a hostile government (as in Kampuchea) or assist some broader strategic objective (as in Afghanistan). China's anti-imperialism is directed against not only the 'capitalist' United States but also the 'socialist' Soviet Union. The only external military engagement of recent years was with a formerly fraternal socialist power. In general, in its international relations China has come to play an increasingly conventional game by recognizing and dealing with governments in power with relatively marginal attention to the views or aspirations of socialist movements within those countries. Indeed some of the arch-enemies of contemporary socialist movements, such as Nixon, Reagan, Thatcher or Pol Pot, have been prime beneficiaries of Chinese praise or support.

A trend exists in foreign policy which mirrors changes in Chinese society itself, namely the transition from a revolutionary to a stabilized, development-oriented state, from an exploited and dominated peripheral Third World country to an increasingly credible contender for the title of 'great power'. The complexity and ambiguities of current Chinese foreign policy reflect these unfinished transitions.

The transition to great power status should not be interpreted to mean that Chinese foreign policy will necessarily become more 'pragmatic' or cynical. Indeed, the opposite may be the case; weakness is a root cause of the 'pragmatic' need to compromise with one's opponents while strength provides the resources to pursue one's ideological predilections, as the other two superpowers show clearly. Each attempts to impose its own version of the good society on its weaker neighbours and clients. However, not only is Chinese power not yet finally established as a world force, but the Chinese conception of the nature and direction of its own society is in flux. Chinese theorists talk of a new third era in the history of socialism, one of structural reform and rapid economic growth. If this vision solidifies into a creed, it could form the ideological basis for a new era of Chinese foreign policy which projects a revised Chinese image of the good society on the world stage.

Nowhere are the current contradictions and uncertainties in China's foreign relations more apparent than in the changes in China's economic relations with the advanced capitalist countries during the post-Mao era. The desire to create a rich and technically advanced society which underpins the rise to great-power status has led China to adopt an 'open-door' policy towards those countries which not only have capitalist social systems putatively anathema to the goals of the Chinese Communist Party but also constitute the major targets of China's remaining 'Third Worldist' commitments. Moreover, while increased contacts with capitalist industrial countries may well bring economic and technological benefits, they pose a threat to the Chinese leadership's desire to maintain distinctive forms of cultural, social and political development within China's borders.

The logic of the open door, which has been elaborated since the cardinal Third Plenum of 1978, is rooted in the post-Mao vision of 'socialist modernization' and in the thesis that backward countries which seek to catch up with advanced countries must utilize the advantages offered by the latter. The economic case is a strong one. Trade can be beneficial in that it can stimulate domestic economic activity and incomes through access to expanded markets overseas and enables the import of basic capital goods essential to industrialization. Absorption of foreign capital, in the form of loans and direct investment, can supplement scarce domestic capital supplies, introduce advanced technology and expertise and provide employment. Additional foreign exchange, can also be generated by 'exporting' part of China's surplus labour power.

The period since the death of Mao has seen a gradual opening of the door to the outside world, beginning with expanded trade and then extending to other forms of economic interaction, notably loans, wholly owned or joint-enterprise foreign investment and the opening of 'special economic zones' to attract foreign capital. Trade growth exceeded overall economic growth, increasing by 150 per cent between 1978 and 1984 and the ratio of exports to GNP rose from 6.8 to 9.4 per cent. The tourist industry also expanded rapidly; in 1984, nearly 13 million tourists visited China, bringing in a foreign exchange to the tune of US$11.3 billion. Between 1979 and 1985, China also introduced US$17.3 billion in foreign finance, of which US$5.4 billion was direct investment. Joint ventures involving Chinese and foreign capital have proliferated (over 700 were established in 1984 alone). They include luxury tourist hotels, Coca Cola plants and cooperation with Hitachi to produce colour television sets and with Volkswagen to assemble cars and engines. By early 1985 there were 74 wholly-owned foreign firms in operation. By 1985, over 47,000 Chinese workers were working abroad on contracts (usually construction) and contracts for this 'labour service' signed in 1984 were worth over US$1.6 billion. In 1980, four 'special economic zones' were established, the most important of which was Shenzhen on the borders of Hong Kong. These provided incentives to foreign investors, such as low taxes or tax holidays, a cheap and disciplined workforce, favourable tariffs and profit repatriation terms and burgeoning infrastructure. By the end of 1984, these zones had signed over 4,700 agreements with foreign companies and had attracted about US$2 billion of foreign investment. In 1984, 14 coastal cities were opened to foreign investment and the island of Hainan in the south was declared an open 'development region'. Systematic attempts have also been made to introduce foreign business expertise, notably through the establishment of management training centres by the United States, Japan, Canada, the EEC and other western countries.

Experience up to the mid-1980s suggests that the net economic benefits of the open-door policy have been substantial in terms of generating foreign exchange for essential imports, raising incomes, generating employment and absorbing foreign technology and expertise. Moreover, many of the potential costs of such policies which have been identified in other Third World contexts have been avoided by China's large size (which means a low foreign trade ratio) and the relative strength of the Chinese state in managing foreign economic relations. But China has not avoided some of the potentially serious economic problems characteristic of such open-door policies elsewhere in the Third World. A good deal of the technology imported from OECD countries has not been absorbed productively. In 1984, there was a binge of imports of small computers, the utilization rate of which in certain areas was estimated to be between 5 and 15 per cent. Some of the large imported turnkey projects, such as the Baoshan Iron and Steel Complex near Shanghai, have been poorly conceived and implemented and encountered large cost over-runs. Rapidly escalating demand for hi-tech imports, some of it without adequate economic rationale but more as status goods, a 'keeping up with the Wangs' for both consumer and capital goods, has exerted pressures to increase China's foreign debt. So far the government has kept this to a manageable level.

The economic results of the special economic zones have also been somewhat disappointing. Though the figures on gross output value look pretty impressive, they conceal important problems. First, the state has pumped large amounts of investment capital (one Chinese expert sardonically called them 'blood trans-fusions') to make the zones more attractive to foreign business. Second, since the economic calculus of overseas capital is very different from that of the Chinese government, development of the zones has been pushed in several predictable directions: while the government wishes new industries to be export-oriented, foreign business has sought to use the zones as an entry into the Chinese domestic market; while the government has hoped to attract advanced technology industries, most of the new enterprises are labour-intensive, often merely involving assembly or simple processing of imported goods and components; while the government has sought to develop industry, much new investment has gone into real estate and commerce where returns are quicker and greater.

Chinese officials and economists recognize these problems and see them as an inevitable aspect of the first stages of development of the zones, to be solved by better policies and more effective administration. Throughout this approach to the problems runs the assumption, sometimes optimistic to the point of naivety, that the government will be able to retain effective managerial control both within the special economic zones and the other 'open' areas of the country. The dilemma here is comparable to that in the 'post-reform' economy generally, i.e. the need to replace the previous system of politico-bureaucratic controls with a new system of 'indirect' regulation. Clearly the open-door policy has led to multifarious economic activities which the state has extreme difficulty in controlling, such as black marketing in foreign currency and imported commodities, or diversions of foreign exchange allocations to unsanctioned purposes. The increased power granted to enterprises gives them greater ability to evade official regulations and cover their traces through 'creative accounting'. Joint and foreign-owned enterprises in the special economic zones have made extensive use of the means of evasion familiar elsewhere in the Third World, such as transfer pricing. More worrying from the government's point of view is the extent to which its own officials, including Party cadres, have become involved in various kinds of corrupt or illegal dealing, for the benefit of themselves, their friends and relatives or their units. In 1985, for example, it was revealed that officials in the new 'development region' of Hainan Island had been involved in a widespread operation to sell imported goods illegally at high profits – the head of the local government was dismissed with some of his colleagues. This is not a mere question of corrupt individuals. One would expect the stratum of officials, who are losing privileges, power and prestige because of the reforms, to attempt to recoup some of their loss by cashing in their residual power for material gain, particularly in such a lucrative area as foreign trade.

This kind of event casts doubt on the reliability and effectiveness of state institutions in coping with the economic problems arising from the open door; they also raise the issue of its general *social* and *political* impact. Clearly increased foreign contacts have brought some beneficial effects, notably greater exposure to democratic ideas and practices which counter the narrow ideological dogmatism and political authoritarianism of the previous system. However, many of the ideas and institutions which have flooded into China since 1977 have been, implicitly or explicitly, anti-socialist (whatever definition of 'socialism' one uses). Moreover, the 'demonstration effect' of high standards of living in the industrialized countries, notably the United States, have generated unrealistic consumer demands which are linked to idealized views of capitalist economics and liberal democratic politics. The spread of western business ideology has been sanctioned and encouraged by the Chinese government, for example, through management training centres established by major OECD countries. The spread of foreign-linked 'unhealthy tendencies' such as corruption, 'speculation', 'profiteering', smuggling, prostitution and the like has undermined standards of public morality generally as well as any attachment to socialist ideals. These problems are of course more severe in the special economic zones where the officially recognized system is one of 'state capitalism' – a capitalist economic system with a socialist state administration – but they have spread throughout Chinese society.

CCP leaders have condemned this as 'spiritual pollution' and launched intermittent campaigns in an attempt to build a 'socialist spiritual civilization'. But it is too easy to blame these problems on 'subversion' by baleful foreign influences; to a large degree they reflect the political and ideological vacuum within China. CCP leaders face a basic dilemma: they have been successful in undermining the ideological legitimacy and popular appeal of two forms of 'socialism', viz. Soviet-style centralism and its Maoist alternative, but have yet to develop a credible alternative themselves. Small wonder then that external influences flood in to fill the vacuum and 'socialist' cadres seek to line their pockets from the opportunities offered by the open door. If Chinese 'self-reliance' is to have any distinct social, moral or political content, a new form of 'Chinese socialism' needs to be developed. This will require some fundamental rethinking about the nature of the socialist state and socialist democracy − it is to these issues that we turn in the last section.

Revolutionary Socialism and Democratization

The Chinese state which emerged in 1949 embodied the basic features of the Marxist–Leninist model. It is a complex set of interlocking institutions in which the CCP occupies the dominant position. In theory, the Party is society's political agent within the state, charged with the task of controlling the government bureaucracy and armed forces. In reality, the Party is itself the focal component of the state and exercises power over society at large. Though other parties have been allowed to exist and though there is a formal representative system of people's congresses (i.e. legislatures), the Party controls all significant levers of power and brooks no organized opposition.

Within the Party, the flow of power is governed by the Leninist principle of 'democratic centralism' which, in practice, is far more centralist than democratic. The Party exerts control over society through a political nervous sytem of Party branches in all major social institutions. The population is also grouped into 'mass organizations' such as trade unions, youth associations and womens' federations which are likewise subject to the CCP's 'centralized leadership' and lack any significant autonomy. The government apparatus, which is parallel to and penetrated by the Party, is a vast administrative network engaged in the organization of economic and social life.

This ensemble constitutes a formidable apparatus of authoritarian power. Though the flow of power is largely downwards, however, one should not adopt a totally one-dimensional view. Central power has been limited by regional power; a certain degree of influence does flow up from the bottom, whether within the Party or the economic planning system. Nor should we underestimate the degree of semi-formal or informal consultation between cadres and their subordinates which serves as a channel for popular influence to filter upwards. Rural collectives were often highly participatory, moreover, even though their autonomy was restricted by Party control and government exactions.

Nor should the degree of state power over society be overestimated in line with the model of 'totalitarianism'. State controls have been loosened or broken in certain periods (notably during the Hundred Flowers Movements in 1956–7 and the Cultural Revolution in 1966–8). During 'normal' periods, moreover, large sectors of society, notably the rural population, have resisted state control and all social sectors have devised strategies to defend their autonomy. State managers are clearly able to exert far less power than they would like and in many areas of policy they are weak or virtually impotent.

To the extent that this authoritarian form of regime constitutes an unavoidable response to pressing problems, the grossly unequal distribution of power can lay some claim to be rational and legitimate. The Chinese state has been largely successful in restoring China's unity after the anarchy of the early twentieth century; in protecting and projecting national power against external forces; and in guiding China through the first stages of rapid industrialization. But as the scale of internal and external pressures decreases and the weight of socio-economic achievements mounts, the rationale for authoritarianism wanes. There are considerable differences between the conditions of the 1950s and those of the 1970s–80s. In the former, China faced the armed hostility of the United States, was struggling through the bootstrap stages of 'primitive accumulation' and still attempting to establish new socialist institutions; in the latter period, the external threat has declined, the pressures of scarcity have begun to ease and the new institutional system is already obsolescent.

Conversely, the lack of democracy becomes increasingly objectionable because democratization is not only an intrinsic part of *socialist* development, but also an essential pre-condition for higher levels of socio-economic progress. It is hard to conceive of a socially creative, economically flexible and technically dynamic society with a sclerotic, authoritarian political system. From this point of view, the Leninist state becomes increasingly like a chrysalis which plays a crucial transitional role in the evolution of a butterfly but will not open to allow it to fly away.

The Chinese political system is undemocratic: power is highly centralized and hierarchically organized, the mechanisms of public accountability are weak or non-existent and, despite some progress towards the protection of individual rights in the post-Mao era, citizens are still vulnerable to state action. Thoroughgoing democratization will require progress in at least four areas:

1. The democratic rights of *individuals* vis à vis the group, organization, collective or state need to be protected and strengthened by an autonomous legal system and by institutionalized checks on bureaucratic or political injustice (for example, through special appeal and arbitration procedures, or ombudsmen). The language here is liberal, but individual rights are human rights which cannot be dismissed as 'bourgeois' but must be incorporated into genuine socialist politics.

2. The democratic rights of the population as *citizens* should be increased; i.e. their ability to influence the direction of society as a whole through electoral processes, representative institutions and sectoral associations.

3. Individuals have a democratic right to form relatively autonomous *corporate groups* (such as trade unions, chambers of commerce, community associations, policy pressure groups, occupational associations) which have some scope to represent and press for the interests of their members.

4. The democratic rights of individuals or collectives as *producers* or 'citizens of the workplace' should be extended. The principle of self-management, already realized to a limited extent in Yugoslavia, is crucially important here.

A sceptic might reply that this democratic shopping list is utopian, arguing that the room for political manoeuvre in China is very small, that such fundamental democratization is incompatible with the basic institutions and aspirations of revolutionary socialism, and that recent experiences of democratization, such as the Cultural Revolution (1966–8) and the Democracy Movement (1978–80) were not very successful.

The Maoist project was indeed fundamentally flawed. Though the Cultural Revolution did witness a massive upsurge of genuine democratic politics, it was still a form of sponsored democracy, set in motion by and ultimately under the control of a group of top CCP leaders. Moreover, the unfettered mass movement of 1966–8 led to organizational conflict and factional rivalry, which made it vulnerable to suppression by the armed forces on the grounds of restoring 'unity and stability'. For all their stress on 'proletarian politics' and mass participation, the political behaviour of radical leaders, including Mao himself, was often dogmatic and authoritarian and constrasted with their egalitarian message. Most important, despite the revolutionary rhetoric of the Cultural Revolution, the Maoists failed to break the Leninist mould by offering an alternative model of participatory socialism which would have transferred real, not symbolic, power to the population. Maoist leaders used hierarchical methods to foster egalitarian-ism, authoritarian methods to foster democracy and attempted to mobilize mass initiative by invoking a neo-traditional obedience to the infallible figure of Mao Zedong. This said, the Cultural Revolution did generate a new spirit of popular defiance of authority and criticism of established institutions which found later expression in the Democracy Movement.

The Democracy Movement itself was similar to the Cultural Revolution in the sense that it released pent-up, previously repressed frustrations, involved a good deal of spontaneous mass political action yet at the same time depended on sponsorship from top CCP leaders (this time, Deng Xiaoping). The movement's activists boldly and bravely launched a sweeping critique of the existing distribu-tion of power, raised the fundamental issue of the need for democratization and proposed a wide range of structural reforms. But the impact of the movement was superficial and short-lived for a number of reasons. First, like the Cultural Revolution it depended on political patronage and flourished during a period of leadership conflict in the CCP; when high-level conflicts were resolved and the Party line redefined, the Movement was an early casualty. It had served its purpose in discrediting the previous Maoist leaders and their policies; when it turned its critical attention to Deng and his followers, repression was sure to follow. Moreover, though most of the Movement's activists could be loosely defined as 'workers' (many of them with a history of activism during the Cultural Revolu-tion), they were relatively marginal to the working class as a whole, and the broad scope of the systemic issues they raised tended to distance them from the more mundane concerns of the general population. They also disagreed among them-selves on political issues, allowing the resurgent Party to brand them as 'anarchic'; their interest in western democracies and contacts with foreigners also made them vulnerable to charges of 'anti-socialism' and 'national betrayal'. Their political appeals were also undercut by Deng's promises of material progress and early successes in delivering on these promises after 1978, which led to rapid rises in urban and rural incomes.

Though the Democracy Movement was silenced by 1980, the period of Dengist reforms did bring some limited improvements in Chinese political life. The range of economic, intellectual and cultural freedom expanded considerably, and the intrusion of the state into the private sphere declined. Within the Party, there is greater scope for debate and disagreement; outside the Party there have been limited steps towards democratization. In 1979, for example, the principle of direct elections was extended to county-level People's Congresses; in enterprises, the role of 'workers representative congresses' has been increased to give workers a limited say in management decisions. But these have a marginal impact on the overall distribution of power which is still set in the Leninist mould; nor do they go very far in increasing the accountability of public officials.

The case for further democratization is clear. Apart from the self-evident proposition that a distinctively *socialist* transition is unthinkable without it, it is also developmentally essential. China has passed that phase when the argument that democracy must be subordinated to the priorities of industrialization still carried weight and has already entered a new stage when democratization must be seen as a *pre-condition* for further social and economic advance. The obstacles to democratization are still severe. China is still a poor country where the struggle for everyday life limits the capacity of citizens to devote significant time and energy to political activity. The dead hand of traditional authoritarian political culture still grips hard; and conservative vested interests in the Party–state apparatus are still powerful.

But will democratization make or break Chinese socialism? Two broad scenarios are possible: in the first, the regime attempts to ignore or suppress intensifying contradictions; this exacerbates the situation, and drives an aroused population into abortive and short-lived political upsurges which provoke renewed waves of repression. The Cultural Revolution and the Democracy Movement share certain elements of this scenario, and the Polish case is also comparable. A second scenario provides the possibility for a more incremental process of progressive change relatively free of antagonistic conflict, violence and repression. A coalition is forged between a progressive section of the Party–state elite and democratic forces in society to sustain the momentum of change and push through a series of gradual but cumulatively radical reforms.

While the Chinese experience so far has been more like the former, the post-Mao context gives more grounds for hoping that the second scenario may gain momentum: the limited movement towards liberalization of economic and cultural life, the redistribution of economic power through the reforms, greater freedom for the intelligentsia and higher incomes for workers and peasants, limitations on the administrative sphere of the state and the political sphere of the Party. The stage seems set for a process of democratization that will be a protracted war of attrition. In the short and medium term, this will increase the power of ordinary citizens to determine the decisions which affect their lives at all levels and to render public officials accountable for their actions. In the long term, this will be nothing less than the realization of Marx's idea of the population 'repossessing' the state institutions which stand over them.

The struggle for democracy will also be multi-faceted, operating in many different arenas and taking many forms. Since the notion of 'politics' is so sensitive in Leninist systems, some 'political' battles will have to be fought on different terrains, notably economic efficiency. To the extent, for example, that the economic reforms bring about a thoroughgoing decentralization of economic power, the potential for political democratization increases. In terms of political arenas, though, action in the national arena is essential, raising critically the 'big issues' of political system, ideology and distribution of power, its potential for the near future is likely to be limited since it poses a direct challenge to party hegemony. It will probably be confined to *zamizdat* activity and perhaps, in a more subdued form, campus politics. The 'gadfly' function of this type of 'dissident' politics can be considerable and it may predispose the Party leadership to accept more 'moderate' reforms. At the national level, these would include two major areas: first, the attempt to realize constitutionally proffered political rights through codified legislation; second, the extension of the principle of direct elections for office, for both Party and government officials.

However, a long-term strategy of 'non-reformist reforms' will probably be more feasible if it works up from the base of society, starting with the grassroots politics of everyday life and gradually moving up to capture the citadels of national power. The *locality* is an important area of democratization. The example of Taiwan suggests that lively (even though circumscribed) local politics are feasible even under a one-party, authoritarian system. In the countryside, the nature of local politics has become more important since the abolition of the commune system and the *de facto* revival of household agriculture. Here it is the new 'village committees' and revived township governments which provide the insitutional context for local politics; in the cities, it is the 'street' or 'neighbourhood committees'. The most basic level of democratization is that of the *enterprise*. The economic reforms have opened the way towards enterprise self-managemnent along Yugoslav lines, but progress so far has been disappointing. To take it further would seem to require a coalition of Party reformers and organized workers which is not in evidence. The situation may change if the economic reforms increase the power of enterprise managers, thus stimulating workers to demand self-management as a way to protect their interests.

It is difficult to assess the prospects of this gradualist strategy of democratization. For instance, the example of Yugoslavia suggests that basic level democratization through self-management and a radical decentralization of economic decision-making power from state to enterprises does not lead to a significant democratization of national level politics. Conservative party leaders may tear up even small sprouts of democracy as a threat to their institutionalized power. Such responses will not remove problems, however, but intensify them, creating the kind of build-up of political steam which exploded in the Cultural Revolution and the Democracy Movement. The Party faces some difficult choices. Even if it retains its monopoly position, it must accept a considerable diminution of its ability to control events. Moreover, to the extent that diverse social interests begin to assert themselves politically in organized form, the Party faces the choice of how to incorporate these into the political system: either directly by transforming the Party itself away from the traditional model of the elite vanguard to a 'pluralist' institution which represents the conflicting interests of society; or indirectly by setting up some form of 'corporatist' arrangements whereby the Party 'licences' certain representative interest groups and bargains with them.

It is clear that genuine democratization will require a major change in the role of the Party. Historical experience suggests that, whereas in the earliest phases of socialist transition, the Party is seen as the solution, in later stages, it becomes the problem. This problem reflects deep contradictions at the root of the politics of revolutionary socialism which still await solution.

8

The Middle East in International Perspective
Problems of Analysis

FRED HALLIDAY

Introduction: Wars of the 1980s

In the post-war period the Middle East has been the most consistently unstable and strategically alarming of any region of the whole Third World. It was there, in the crisis over northern Iran in 1946, that the first Cold War began. It was in the Suez crisis of 1956 that European–US contradictions reached their highest point, and that the Soviet Union, for the only occasion yet recorded, threatened a direct missile assault upon the advanced capitalist world. In 1967 and 1973 Arab-Israeli wars occasioned crises between the USA and the USSR more dangerous than any that arose over Indo-China or Europe, less dangerous only than that which erupted in 1962 over Cuba. The 1970s and early 1980s have provided event after event that placed the Middle East at the forefront of international concern: the OPEC price rises of 1971–3, the Iranian revolution, the protracted agonies of the Lebanese civil war and the Israeli invasion of that country, the Iran-Iraq war. Events in what President's Carter's security adviser Brzezinski termed the 'Arc of Crisis', encompassing Afghanistan, Iran, South Yemen and Ethiopia, played an important part in the onset of the second Cold War. Whether their intensity is assessed in terms of the impact upon east–west relations, the challenge to the workings of the international market, or the apparent threat to regimes in place in the region, the events of the past few decades are clearly of major sustained importance, both for the Middle East itself, and for the outside world.

To look for a common pattern or cause in the conflicts that have ravaged the Middle East in the 1970s and 1980s is futile.[1] The societies themselves are too different, their distinct political characters and state formations already too diverse, to permit of any unified *endogenous* explanation. To replace such an explanation from within by invoking one common *external* factor would also be misleading. Cold War writers have tried to blame all the problems of the Middle East on Islam or Soviet influence. It would be equally simplistic for socialists to ascribe these events solely to the workings of imperialism. Imperialism certainly has played a part – whether it be understood as the historic legacy of colonial rule and capitalist penetration, with all its disruptive impact, or as the contemporary workings of western powers, and particularly the USA, in the region, both directly and through local allies, Israeli and Arab. The external factors must remain in the picture;

but the recent conflicts arise equally from forces located *within* these diverse societies themselves. This can be seen by examining two of these conflicts, the war in Lebanon, and the Iran-Iraq war.

The war in Lebanon arose from the long and unresolved crisis within that country that had been developing ever since independence from France in 1943.[2] The initial political arrangements reached at independence, the National Pact, had established a form of power-sharing between representatives of the Christian and Muslim bourgeoisies: positions in the state, from the president down, were to be allocated by religious affiliation; the two confessional elites and their allies were to run the state's policies together. Lebanon was to occupy a correspondingly cautious place within the Arab world, part of the Arab world but to a considerable degree insulated from its politics.

The main problem with this 1943 system was that it took inadequate account of change, internal or external. Internally, the demographic balance shifted in favour of the Muslims, while within each community new social forces emerged that did not accept the dominance of their respective elites. The most striking case of the latter process was the rise of a Shi'ite Muslim community that rejected the Sunni Muslim leadership, and which constituted much of the poorer population of Beirut. An initial attempt to challenge the Lebanese system of forces favourable to Arab nationalism developed in the 1950s: but this ended abruptly in 1958 with the intervention of US marines, at the request of the Christian leader and President Camille Chamoun. The US intervention was, in the short run, successful. Internal change at the political level, and the appeals of Arab nationalism to the Muslim population, were contained. But social change did not stop and the class and confessional conflicts within Lebanese society only festered the more as they failed to find expression at the political level. The result was that by the mid-1970s Lebanon faced an explosive domestic situation, born of the inability of the political system to adjust to changes within the society.

External factors then compounded the internal and played a significant role in generating the explosion. Lebanon's Christians did not feel themselves to be part of the Arab nationalism that swept the region in the 1950s and Lebanon stayed out of the Arab-Israeli wars. But it was not possible to insulate Lebanon completely from the turmoil of the Arab world. Its economy was a satellite of the oil-producing states, in that monies from the oil-producers were invested and spent on services in Lebanon. So it was sensitive to developments in the Gulf. The Muslim community was increasingly drawn to Arab nationalism, and the Syrians themselves never accepted that Lebanon was entirely a separate state: after 1943 Damascus continued to regard Lebanon as within its sphere of influence. Most important, however, was the presence within Lebanon of a Palestinian exile community which from the early 1970s became politically and militarily mobilized against the Israeli state to the south. This Palestinian community established a loose alliance with the political representatives of the Muslim community; it increasingly became an autonomous and unassimilable factor within Lebanese politics.

The civil war that broke out in 1975 had, therefore, several dimensions. It was a war between confessional groups – Christians and Muslims – and between social forces within each group. The Palestinians sought to ally with the Muslims, but found no stable alliance either with the Sunni leaders, or with the representatives of the Shi'ites. At the same time, Syria became increasingly involved, first on one side, then on the other, trying to re-establish some coalition of confessional groups that could govern the country under its direction. In 1978 and, more importantly, in 1982, an added force intervened directly, namely Israel. The Israelis hoped to assist the Christians to re-establish domination, and to crush the Palestinian forces in Lebanon. But the Israelis failed and were forced in the end to withdraw from Lebanon. A decade of civil war, and of intervention by Syria and Israel, had not produced a new coalition to replace that which had been swept away by the explosion of 1975. If a complete disintegration of Lebanon was improbable, the fragmentation, destruction and bitterness occasioned by the war certainly made any new stable political system the harder to achieve. Confessional hatred, social tension and the dynamics of warlordism in each camp made restabilization remote.

A different combination of confessional, social, national and international factors contributed to the other major war of the early 1980s, that between Iran and Iraq that began in September 1980.[3] The immediate cause of this war was the Iranian revolution of the previous year. Like virtually all revolutionaries, Khomeini sought to spread his revolution: he advocated a set of universal revolutionary ideals and believed that the security of his new regime could best be ensured by the establishment of similar regimes elsewhere. His call for a generalized Islamic revolution led his new regime within months into conflict with neighbouring Iraq, and into support for dissident Islamic groups within that country. Ethnic factors also played a part: antagonism between Arabs and Persians was fanned by both sides, and each sought to encourage ethnic dissidents within each other's state – the Iraqis encouraging Kurds and Arabs in Iran, the Iranians assisting Kurdish rebels in Iraq.

The deeper causes of the conflict lay in the rivalry of Iran and Iraq within the Persian Gulf region that had been evident for more than a decade, and which had led Iran, then under the Shah, to wage a long, destabilizing, covert war against Iraq in the early 1970s. Temporarily halted by an agreement between the two states in 1975, this regional rivalry was reopened by the Iranian revolution of 1979. The Iraqis, faced with what appeared to be a determined new challenge from Iran, decided to hit first and to press their cause in the regional contest. So they attacked in September 1980. They expected a rapid victory over Iran, but instead became embroiled in a massive land and air war that they could scarcely sustain. Both sides had played their part in the outbreak of the war, and both suffered terribly in the killing and destruction that followed.

After five years of war, neither side was able to achieve its combat goals. Iraq had failed to defeat Iran in its initial attack: by the summer of 1982 Iraq had withdrawn its forces from enemy territory and was calling for peace on the basis of a return to the status quo. Iran, while unable on its part to defeat Iraq, was occupying some Iraqi territory and proclaimed itself determined to continue the war until its goals were met. These included the removal and 'punishment', presumably execution, of Iraqi President Saddam Hussein, the payment of war damages of $150 billions or more by Iraq and the condemnation of Iraq as the aggressor by an international tribunal. On some occasions, Iranian leaders implied that they would continue the war until an Islamic Republic like their own had been established in Iraq. Whether Iran would persist in these demands despite its inability to prosecute the war successfully remained to be seen.

Both sides could not have fought the war that they did without external supports.

Both needed money and this they obtained from selling their oil and, in the case of Iraq, from sympathetic Arab states. Both also needed arms, since they had little or no domestic arms-production capacity. Iraq experienced no difficulty in obtaining arms, since most Arab states, the Soviet Union, France and the USA supported its cause. Iran did face much greater difficulties and no states, apart from Libya and Syria, were willing openly to support it. But Iran was able to obtain substantial supplies of arms for cash payment on the world market, from capitalist sources and from North Korea, and thus acquired at least part of the external inputs it needed to sustain its war effort.

Yet despite these external inputs, neither state could be said to be acting at the behest of or under the control of other states. Despite many suggestions to this effect, it was impossible to see any outside power actively encouraging or prolonging the war for its own interest. The outbreak of the Iran-Iraq war, and its long extent, underlined the considerable autonomy of the states involved and of the tensions within them that led to the outbreak of war.

The example of these two conflicts – the Lebanese civil war, and the Iran-Iraq war – underline two of the most salient features of the contemporary Middle East, and of its place in the overall pattern of world conflict. One is the apparent explosiveness of this region and of the political systems within it: this is why the Middle East has been more consistently a source of international concern than any other region of the world, including Indo-China, since the end of World War II. The second salient characteristic is the considerable independence of these conflicts from the broader skein of international politics. The contemporary Middle East cannot be understood apart from the historical experience it underwent in the colonial era, the character of its economic links to the advanced capitalist countries, and the impact upon it of the Soviet-American rivalry. But while these international factors provide a context and often a catalyst, it is equally important to locate the conflicts of the region in their specific, local origins and to develop judgements and political assessments that take these particular factors into account. It is, indeed, in the tension between these two characteristics that the specific difficulty of analysing the Middle East lies: of inescapable importance for international conflict as a whole, and for a socialist evaluation of the contemporary world, the Middle East remains the site of violent local conflicts that are to a considerable extent independent of broader international patterns.

Historical Formation

The Middle East, a region of 21 states with a combined population of around 260 millions, is the only area of the Third World geographically contiguous with Europe. Conflict between it and Europe, taking military, economic and religious-ideological forms, has been in train for centuries, reaching far back beyond the era of contemporary imperialism into the epoch of feudalism and the Crusader wars. The modern period of interaction between Europe and the Middle East began in the late eighteenth century, first with the Russian assaults upon the Ottoman Empire from the late 1770s onwards, and then with Napoleon's invasion of Egypt in 1798.

European interest in the region was, until this century, mainly strategic. Throughout the nineteenth century, inter-imperialist contradiction took the form of the 'eastern question', the competition of rival powers, especially Russia and its competitor Britain, for influence at the expense of the Ottoman Empire and over communications between Europe and the east. Until 1914 the Ottoman Empire survived, but in the preceding decades various imperial powers were able to establish themselves on its periphery – France in Algeria (1830), Tunisia (1881) and Morocco (1912), Italy in Libya (1911), Britain in Egypt (1882), in Sudan (1898), in South Arabia (1839) and in the string of coastal Persian Gulf states (late nineteenth century to 1914).

With the end of World War I the eastern question was dramatically transformed. On the one hand, the Ottoman Empire was dismembered, its heartland becoming the nation state of Turkey, and its former Arab dominions being divided into seven separate states or colonial entities: two of these new entities were now ruled by France (Lebanon and Syria), three by Britain (Iraq, Jordan and Palestine) and two became independent Arab monarchies (Saudi Arabia and North Yemen). But while the territory of the Ottoman Empire was thus divided, the very coordinates of strategic rivalry in the region were also simultaneously redefined by new developments: by the discovery, just prior to World War I, of substantial quantities of oil in and near the Persian Gulf, by the entry of a rival imperial power into the Middle Eastern arena for the first time, namely the USA, and most importantly of all by the transformation of the political character of one of the powers that had been central to the eastern question, namely Russia, in the 1917 revolution. Thus, if the old order, and its eastern question, were dissolved by World War I, new problems simultaneously emerged: the region, hitherto of *geostrategic* importance, became of *intrinsic economic* significance, with the discovery of oil; the pre-existing inter-European imperialist rivalry of the region, between France, Britain, Italy, Germany and Czarist Russia, was now complicated by the entrance of the American challenger – albeit, at this stage, mainly in the form of oil companies; and, superimposed upon these economic and inter-capitalist concerns, there emerged a new global contradiction, between the Bolshevik revolution and the capitalist powers as a whole, which impinged directly on the Middle East. One of the first acts of Bolshevik revolutionaries was to publish the secret agreements on the Middle East between Britain, France and the Czarist government.[4]

In addition to these changes, the decline of the Ottoman Empire and the events accompanying and succeeding World War I had produced two other major changes *within* the Middle East itself, one being the entry into the political arena for the first time of a hitherto neglected actor, popular forces, the other being the consolidation of Zionist settlers in Palestine. A combination of factors stimulated the former of these processes – the increased economic impact of the industrialized world, foreign occupation, the spread of new ideas of religious and national radicalism, peasant resistance to agricultural change, urban resistance by traditional bazaar forces to imports. Together these produced a wave of resistance and revolt across the region in the decades after 1880. In Egypt it was nationalist military forces under Urabi Pasha who resisted the Anglo-French invasion of 1882, while in 1919, as Britain was preparing to deny Egyptian nationalists their right to attend the Versailles Conference and demand independence, a major peasant revolt broke out in the villages of the Nile Delta. To the south, in the Sudan, a mass revolt led by the Mahdi wiped out the expeditionary force of General Gordon in 1886 and prevented Britain from establishing control for more than a decade. In the

Arab lands of the Ottoman Empire World War I was preceded by substantial political organization against Turkish rule, and in the war itself Arab nationalists and officers rose up to join the British in driving the Ottomans northwards.[5] The imposition of colonial rule in the territories freed from Ottoman rule was itself followed by a series of uprisings – in Iraq in 1920, in Syria in 1926 and in Palestine in 1936–9. In Iran there had been a major urban rising against the Shah, in the Constitutional Revolution of 1906–8, and in the aftermath of World War I communists and nationalists established a distinct revolutionary regime in the northern, Gilan, province.[6] The complex new strategic situation in the Middle East was, therefore, underpinned by a situation in which popular dissent and resistance to foreign domination had become major forces.

Parallel to this mobilization of parts of the indigenous populations of the Arab countries and of Iran, there developed the colonization of Palestine by Zionist settlers. This movement had begun with the first emigration or *aliya* in the 1870s, and by World War I there existed a substantial, but still minoritarian, Jewish community in Palestine.[7] The world war dramatically altered the conditions under which this settlement took place: it provided in Britain an administrative power that was more favourable to such settlement, a favour enunciated as policy in the 1917 Balfour Declaration, which promised Jews a 'national home' in Palestine; and it laid the basis in Europe of the political and social conditions that were to impel many of those Jews able to survive Nazism towards the comparatively safer haven of the Middle East. Substantial Jewish migration to Palestine continued between the wars, and by the end of World War II the Jewish community there was strong enough to demand, and establish, an independent state.[8] Britain purported to be even-handed as between the two nationalities, Palestinian and Jewish; but it had itself opened the door to the new settlers in Palestine (while closing the door to them in Britain itself) and by the end of World War II it was so vulnerable to American pressure, by then firmly pro-Zionist, that it in effect abdicated in the face of mounting pressure for an Israeli state. The result was that in 1948 a third non-Arab state emerged in the Middle East, one that the Arab states long refused to accept and which was to provide the focus for nationalist and religious resentment for decades to come. If the modern history of the Middle East cannot be *reduced* to the conflict between Israelis and Arabs, it was nonetheless *dominated, enflamed* and *warped* by it to a remarkable extent.[9]

The World War I settlement was, for all its contradictions, the one that established the state system of the Middle East as it has emerged today.[10] Immediately after the war, there were only four fully independent states in the region. Saudi Arabia and North Yemen were conservative monarchies: these arose in those parts of the Arabian Peninsula that the Ottomans abandoned but where no colonial power sought to exercise its domination and where new tribal coalitions seized power. The two others were non-Arab states that had escaped colonial rule after World War I, partly because of their size and partly because of the need felt by all outside powers to create buffers on the south of the USSR: these were Turkey and Iran. Both had been the sites of major resistance to the victors of World War I – in Turkey this took the form of Kemal Pasha's military revolt of 1920–2, in Iran it led to a popular mobilization that forced Britain to abandon its 1919 plan to turn Iran into a Protectorate.

The remaining 17 Arab states all now fell under colonial rule, and divided up into three main groups. The states of the Maghreb, or North Africa, all already dominated before World War I, comprised three French colonies (Morocco, Algeria and Tunisia), one Italian (Libya) and two British colonies (Egypt and Sudan). In the Arabian Peninsula, Britain maintained control over six distinct administrative entities around the coast (Kuwait, Bahrain, Qatar, the Trucial Oman States, Oman and South Arabia). It was in the third Arab region, the east, or Mashrik, that the territories taken from the Turks were parcelled out as five distinct entities between Britain and France.

Imperial control of the Middle East was to prove relatively transient, and the decolonization process began in the inter-war years. By the end of World War II, Egypt, Syria, Lebanon and Iraq were all formally independent: but the process of decolonization then became a much more bloody and conflictual affair. In Palestine, the process of decolonization led to the open conflict between Jewish settlers and Palestinians; while in 1948 the predominantly Jewish state was established, half the Palestinian population became refugees.[11] British troops only finally left Egypt's Suez Canal zone in 1954, in the face of nationalist opposition, and then tried to return in the Suez invasion of 1956. France hung on in the Maghreb: it took the deaths of over one million Algerians, out of 14 millions, for the nationalists to prevail in the war of independence that lasted from 1954 to 1962.[12] In South Yemen, Britain's plans to establish a strategic pivot for its east of Suez policy at Aden was only thwarted by the nationalist, and increasingly radical, guerrilla-led revolution of 1963-7.[13] British Rule elsewhere in Arabia lasted until 1971, when the last of the Persian Gulf colonies acceded to independence: the transition in the Gulf involved substantial repression, of the worker's movement in Bahrain and the guerrilla resistance in the Dhofar province of Oman.[14] Short as it had been, imperial rule in the Middle East was only established and terminated amidst substantial resistance and conflict. These conflicts over decolonization did not usher in a new more quiescent period. The outbreak of the first Cold War over Iran in 1946 set the scene.[15] The tensions of the Middle East since decolonization have been of far more than local interest.

The 'Conformity' of the Middle East:
Six Third World Characteristics

Recognition of the international importance of developments in the Middle East tends to coexist with a markedly uncertain, and persistently mystified, approach to the internal character of these societies. One central aspect of the countries of the Middle East is their great diversity, a factor often ignored in generic statements about them. The modern history of the Middle East, and the decisions of the World War I victors, have produced a region of great variety and instability. Of the 21 states in the region, 18 are Arab, and three non-Arab – Israel, Iran and Turkey. This ethnic diversity is matched by that of demography. The total population of around 260 millions is divided up most unevenly between these states, three of them – Egypt, Turkey and Iran – having near 50 millions each, and some having populations of under one million – Bahrain, Qatar and Oman. The salience of certain shared characteristics – strategic position, Islamic culture, arid geography and, for most, Arabic language – is offset by great differences and conflicts between them. As much as any other area of the Third World, the Middle East is a diverse and internally divided area, united by some common features and relations to the outside world, but convulsed by contradictions and distinguished by variations within.

Before analysing what is specific about the Middle East, it is useful to recognize a number of characteristics of Middle Eastern societies that, in general terms, they share with other regions of the Third World:

1. The Middle East has for a century or more been subjected to domination by the developed capitalist world, through direct colonialism in some areas, and through indirect control in others. This experience of domination forms the fundamental context in which Middle Eastern politics and society have been formed and has given rise in this region to the features visible in other societies of the Third World: nationalist resistance, unstable post-colonial states, extremes of economic distribution, manipulation by metropolitan states, penetration by metropolitan economies. For all its apparent eccentricity, the Middle East has *not* escaped the colonial and post-colonial experiences characteristic of the rest of the Third World.

2. In common with parts of Sub-Saharan Africa and the whole of the Americas and the Antipodes, the Middle East has also endured, for a period, *direct* colonial settlement. In general, colonial settlement took three broad forms: settlement followed by long-term accommodation to the local population (Kenya and Morocco) or later departure (Egypt, Vietnam and Zimbabwe); settlement and elimination of the local population (the majority of the Americas); and, an inter-mediate model, where neither accommodation nor elimination were possible, and where an unstable situation, one of post-colonial conflict, therefore continued (South Africa). In the majority of the Middle Eastern cases, the settlers were either assimilated or later expelled (Algeria, Libya and Egypt). The first option prevailed. But in one case, that of Palestine, there was precisely that intermediate and unresolved situation found also in South Africa.

3. In common with all the others of the post-colonial world, the state structures and inter-state boundaries of the Middle East reflect not long-established divisions, but the decisions of colonial administrators that cut across pre-existing regional linkages. This is as true for North Africa as it is for the Arab states of the Mashrik (Iraq, Syria, Lebanon and Jordan) and for the states of the Arabian Peninsula. Yet, arbitrary as they were in origin, Middle Eastern state boundaries have survived beyond the departure of the colonial powers: these states have neither disintegrated nor have they merged. Rather they have endured, under the control of ruling groups established in the colonial period. These groups have seen their best interests as being served by the preservation of this state system inherited from colonialism.

4. In their conflictual relationship with the metropolitan states, the countries of the Middle East have followed the pattern of other Third World states and developed forms of nationalism that exalt their specificity and distinct historical origins, while at the same time maintaining and developing economic relations with the metropolitan countries. The figure of Sheikh Yamani, the Saudi oil minister, negotiating over OPEC prices from beneath his Arab headdress, summed up the two sides of this attitude. The exaltation of the Islamic past, or of the supposed greatness of the Arabs and their component individual nations, is part of a much wider Third World pattern of simultaneous rejection and acceptance of the international system dominated by western states. The rejection focuses on the symbolic, the acceptance on the material.

5.   Again in common with the Third World as a whole, the violent relationship with the metropolitan countries, and the tensions generated within these societies by this contact, have led to recurrent waves of popular unrest and mobilization against external domination as well as against those within these societies who cooperate with it. The history of the modern Middle East has been punctuated time and again by uprisings, riots, demonstrations, revolts and protests, in cities, villages and oases, against the influence, real and imagined, of foreign powers. The uprisings in Egypt (1919 and 1952), the Iranian revolutions (1906 and 1979), the Yemeni revolutions of North (1962) and South (1963), the Algerian revolution (1954–62), the repeated popular upheavals of the Sudan (1964, 1985), and a host of other resistance movements testify to this recurrent pattern of uprising and mobilization. The energies of the Middle Eastern peoples may have too often been misdirected: but they have been recurrently rebellious and intransigent.

6.   The Middle East shares with other Third World regions the character of its local ruling classes. In the post-1945 period they have seized control of the state structures inherited from colonialism, and the economic opportunities offered by the integration of their countries into the world economy, in order to consolidate their own domestic position against their subjects and regional rivals. For all the rhetoric of Islamic or national communality, uniting rulers and subjects, the tenures of these ruling classes have been marked by a persistent and ruthless use of the instruments of class rule – repression, massacre, demagogy, censorship, bribery. Moreover, while the maintenance of political power over subjugated classes has been the predominant and most general concern of these ruling groups, they have demonstrated equally their concern to maintain other forms of power – over subject ethnic groups, such as the Kurds in Turkey, Iran and Iraq, over subject confessional groups, such as the Shi'ites in Lebanon, and over women, whose subordinate position throughout the Middle East has been maintained by a ferocious combination of violence, law and ideology. When it comes to maintaining the mechanisms of domination, on class, ethnic and gender bases, Middle Eastern rulers have resorted to all too characteristic practices in order to sustain their position.[16]

Regional Anomalies? Islam, Palestine, Arab Unity, Oil

The six dimensions of Third World societies listed above can underline the degree to which the Middle East has not escaped the common experience of other regions of the Third World in the epochs of imperialism and post-colonial independence. They can also serve to place what may appear to be the particularities of the Middle East in another, less anamolous, context. Indeed what are often taken as being events or trends that distinguish the Middle East from other parts of the Third World can, in this comparative light, appear far less particular. This can be illustrated by reference to what are most commonly held to be four distinctive examples of this particularity: the hold of Islam, the Palestine question, the devotion to Arab unity, and the rise of the oil states. Far from relativizing the region, these four prominent features of the modern Middle East can in fact illustrate the analytic universality of its politics and society.

The Islamic religion, which originated in the Arabian Peninsula in the seventh century, is, first of all, no preserve of the Middle East. The majority of the world's 700 million or so Muslims are not only not Arabs, but do not live in the Middle East: the largest Islamic countries lie elsewhere – Indonesia, Bangladesh, Pakistan, Nigeria. At the same time, significant numbers of Arabs – in Lebanon, Palestine, Egypt and Iraq – are Christians. By definition, therefore, an *Islamic* political or social character can hardly define what is *specific* to the Middle East; generalizations about politics' or 'society' deployed to explain the Middle East would have to apply to these other societies as well, and exclude the behaviour of the region's Christians. Examination of what Muslims *do* reveals the fact that Islam cannot dictate a politics: it itself is politically and socially contingent. While the Islamic religion does have certain specific implications in theory for social and even political practice, and legislates for areas some other religions do not, these doctrinal specifications are meagre and partial; they tell us very little about how Muslims will or do act in any society or political situation. The very variety of behaviour in Muslim societies bears this out. To explain the *particular* social forms and political beliefs of people in Muslim societies, *other* factors, external and additional to Islam, have to be examined – the patterns of class rule, the relation to external forces, the historical formation of the country. Certainly, the Iranian revolution of 1979 took the form it did in part because of the belief systems of the Iranian people and the presence of a clergy committed to a course of political action: but the particular version of political Islam espoused by Khomeini, the willingness of the population to follow him, the inability of the state to defeat its unarmed opponents, and the failure of the Shah's allies to help him – none of these can be explained by reference to the Koran.[17] In a comparative perspective, the Iranian revolution, which took place in the major cities of Iran after a decade of rapid socio-economic change, has much in common with urban-based populist movements in other Third World countries, from Peronism and Getulism in Latin America to the mass movements of the Hindu right in India.[18] It had an Islamic ideological character, yet it cannot be explained by Islam – any more than an abstracted Christianity can explain the peasant movements of Germany in the early sixteenth century, or *Solidarnosc*.

Many in the Middle East, and outside, consider the region to be unique because of another feature, the Arab-Israeli question – the refusal of the Arabs to accept Israel, the continued struggle of the Palestinians and the resistance of Israelis to compromise with the Palestinians. In some ways, this dispute *is* unique; but it is not *so* anomalous. For as has already been suggested, the Palestine question is, in its origin, a product of a colonial situation, part of the outward expansion of European-based settlers in the nineteenth century; trans-Mediterranean colonialism was by no means specific to Palestine – it encompassed every country on the southern Mediterranean shore from Morocco to Palestine. What *was* specific to Palestine was first, the particular ideological and religious character of that settlement movement, embodied in Zionism; secondly, the fact that the Zionist settlers evolved into a separate Israeli nation while neither of the two conventional resolutions of colonialism occurred – the local inhabitants were not eliminated or definitely crushed, nor were they able to resist the establishment of a settler state; thirdly the very intense and ultimately decisive support which this settler community obtained from the metropolitan countries, and in particular from the USA. The peculiar additional character of this colonial experience, one in its origins and essence nonetheless similar to dozens of other colonial settler processes, produced the conflict now seen as the Arab-Israeli dispute. That the immigrants should have become a distinct nation is by no means unique: many of the current nations of the Americans and Antipodes were so formed.[19]

Of equal importance in the panorama of Middle East politics, and ideologically linked to that of the Palestine issue, is a third special feature, the drive for Arab unity.[20] The Middle East contains 18 states which consider themselves to be Arab; they are formally committed both to Arab unity and to 'solidarity' on the Palestine issue. They are members of a regional body, the Arab League, founded in 1945. In the post-1945 period there have been several attempts by Arab states to merge, most notably that by Egypt and Syria in the period 1958–61. The failure of such attempts at unity has not apparently lessened the formal commitment of Arab states to this goal. On closer examination, however, this anomaly is not quite as peculiar as it may appear. Commitments to unity are not specific to the Middle East: in some cases they have succeeded (German and Italian unifications of the nineteenth century), in others they have faded, after initial enthusiasm (that of the Latin American revolutionaries in the 1820s, briefly revived by Che Guevara, and that of the African states in the early 1960s, as advocated by Nkrumah). The European states have, in the past decade or two, also proclaimed an interest in greater unity and, short of that, coordination. Arab unity is one of those unificatory movements.

If the *reality* of Arab unity is examined more closely then it appears even less surprising. First, there is *a* reality of unity – at the economic and cultural levels. The growth of economic ties within the Arab world, as a result of the oil boom, is substantial; this can be measured in terms of migration and financial flows. But these linkages are not in any way unique, being comparable to other flows of labour and capital in the contemporary world economy. They have, moreover, created a new hierarchy between Arab societies, not fraternity or equality. The sense of *cultural* unity which Arabs have, based on language, but extending to music, poetry, film and humour, is certainy stronger than that within most parts of Asia and Africa: but that of Spanish-speaking Latin America is certainly comparable, and that of the English-speaking world is becoming so. On the other hand, when we come to the political, the reality is one of Arab *disunity*. Abstracting from the rhetoric, the post-colonial states of the Middle East have remained as separate and as jealous of their state and ruler's interests as any other. After decades of demagogy about unity, the post-colonial divisions have endured in the Arab world, just as they have in Africa and Latin America. Nor has the Palestine question in reality provided a transcendent, unificatory, cause: it has led to little common action, or sacrifice, except where states have actually had common frontiers with Israel, and here the conflict has taken the form of a border war, something by no means unique to the Middle East. Solidarity with the *Palestinians* themselves has been largely rhetorical: the practice has been one of seeking to use the issue of Palestine for domestic legitimacy, while avoiding confrontation with Israel, and of trying to manipulate the Palestinian resistance movement itself for partisan purposes. The zenith of Palestinian activity, from 1967 until the mid-1970s, to a considerable extent concealed this. However, from 1948 until 1967, the Palestinians were permitted no independent political presence in the Arab world, and afforded scant attention. Developments since the mid-1970s – Sadat's independent initiative towards Israel in 1977, the division of the Arab world into several camps, and then, in 1983, Syria and Libya's direct attack upon the Arafat leadership in the PLO – have helped to strip away the mythology about a unificatory Palestinian commitment. These events reveal the separate, self-regarding interests of Arab states lying beneath their supposedly common position on Palestine.

The issue of oil has been a fourth issue that has, for many, come in recent years to symbolize the uniqueness of Middle Eastern societies. Yet, as with Islam, so with oil:

1. The majority of OPEC producers are not Arabs, and many are outside the Middle East – Venezuela, Ecuador, Nigeria and Indonesia amongst them.
2. The impact of oil upon producer states varies greatly depending upon the character of the society in question. Only a few Arab producers have enjoyed substantial oil surpluses in the post-1973 period – Saudi Arabia, Kuwait, Qatar and the Emirates. The rest remain capital-hungry and with large populations: they are beset by many of the problems of other developing countries.
3. The reality of 'oil power' is far more restricted than was thought in the 1970s: in political terms, the Arab states have not been able to any significant extent to alter metropolitan policies on Palestine – the 'oil weapon' has been a chimera: economically, the producers were able for a number of years to raise the price and their real incomes by combining to enforce a near-monopoly position in a favourable market – but it is the law of supply and demand, not any Middle Eastern specificity, that explains this success. About all the Arabs achieved politically were some increased arms sales by the USA to Saudi Arabia and a few anodyne utterances by the EEC: only one OECD country – Japan – recognized the PLO. Moreover, even in economic terms OPEC's power proved to be a temporary one, as in the early 1980s OPEC's share of the world market declined.

The uniqueness of oil is something that resides quite elsewhere, in the peculiar form of payment resulting from it, namely a rent to producer states, without the forward and backward linkages within the local economy characteristic of other primary production in the Third World.[21] This enables the state, and those controlling it, to amass enormous sums of money without engaging in production; it is this which has generated such social tensions within the producer states. These tensions – growing income inequality, rampant corruption in the state, grandiose development projects, neglect of productive activity and skills, especially in agriculture – have been seen as much in Lagos and Jakarta as in Tehran and Riyadh. Islam, the Palestine question, Arab unity and oil do not, therefore, define a *sui generis* Middle East. Neither the determination of the geological substructure nor those of the religious-ideological superstructure can establish a Middle East exempt from analytic universality.

The Discriminations of History

Such are the historical origins of the contemporary Middle East and those formative characteristics which it shares with the colonial, and post-colonial worlds, as a whole. It now becomes possible to identify with greater accuracy where the real particularities of the region do lie. These are particularities not born of the workings of a socially abstracted religion, or the timeless workings of 'Arabism', but out of the specific history of the Middle Eastern region, and of its component societies.

1.   The Middle East in the post-colonial period continues to be markedly influenced by the individual character of its pre-colonial societies.[22] Modern forms of communication, and ideas of nationalism, obviously did not exist prior to the impact of imperialism: but, in the context of the great Muslim empires, the Middle East was to a considerable degree bound together by ties of trade, administration, religion and migration in a way that gave it a certain cultural and social unity. The current ideology of its unity as a region, or of the Arabs as one people, for all that is imaginary in it, also reflects the endurance of some elements of this *pre-colonial* cohesion. Of equal import are many of the specific features of pre-colonial social structure: the prevalence of tribal forms of organization, not only amongst nomads, but amongst settled agricultural populations in the Peninsula and in some other countries, such as Libya; the adherence of much of the population to Islamic values which, for all their political contingency, provided a common demotic culture in the face of imperial domination; the presence in the cities of trading and financial sectors opposed to central government and able, under propitious circumstances, to express political opposition to them, as in Syria and Iran. These, among other features of the pre-colonial Middle East, have substantially affected the politics and society of the more recent decades.
2.   The influence of these pre-colonial factors has been all the more because of the comparatively superficial impact of colonial rule itself, the limited transformation of society by imperialism in the region. In North Africa imperial rule did take the form of colonial settlement and agricultural transformation: the former was particularly strong in Algeria, the latter in Egypt. But in the rest of the region – in Turkey, Iran, the Arabian Peninsula and, with the exception of Palestine, the Mashrik, no comparable transformations of the pre-colonial society were affected. Four of the states escaped colonial domination altogether; in the remaining four Mashrik and six peninsular Arab states, colonial rule was effected through local social and political forces – either ones inherited from the pre-imperial period, as in Kuwait and Oman, or monarchies and local administrations installed by Britain and France in the wake of the Ottoman retreat. This relative abstention was partly for reasons of colonial parsimony, and partly because there was little to attract metropolitan economic transformations in these arid lands, apart from oil, a mineral whose production requires little social or economic linkage. The result of this superficial impact was that in contrast to most of Africa, to Latin America and to the rest of Asia, the Middle East states of the Peninsula and the Mashrik acquired independence with many archaic social and political

structures intact. Many retained their pre-colonial ruling classes. Even in the Maghrib the degree of continuity was striking, as the survival of the kings of Morocco and, up to 1969, Libya demonstrated.[23]

3. Another distinctive feature of Middle Eastern societies has been the virulence of ethnic and confessional differences. Like elsewhere in the Third World, the current force of these divisions derives from a combination of pre-colonial historical legacy with later colonial and contemporary social and political division. Historical evidence shows that the relations between different religions and ethnic groups in the pre-colonial period were *certainly not* wholly harmonious or egalitarian: the idea that they were and that current divisions are *solely* the work of imperialism is part of contemporary nationalist mythology. But colonial rule often did much to worsen them, by playing one group against another, by provoking forms of nationalism that exalted one group's past and so antagonized the other, and by stimulating the divisive search for 'genuine' national values. The pattern of confessional conflict in Lebanon and Egypt has in this way much in common with that of Cyprus and India, Sri Lanka and Indonesia. That over Palestine has additional elements, combining as it does settler-native conflicts, rearoused but in some measure traditional Jewish-Muslim enmities, and a comprehensive inter-state rivalry between Israel and the Arab states.

The greatest tragedy of the modern Middle East has been the way in which popular movements, social in origin, have been warped and diverted by sectarian and confessional forces. Time and again social, inter-class contradictions have developed in Middle Eastern societies but have taken a confessional, religious or even chauvinist form. The Lebanese civil war that began in 1975 was a result of the long maturing of social contradictions within the country, as the power bloc established in the 1940s came under increasing pressure from underprivileged groups. Similarly, the Islamic fervour of the Iranian revolution reflected the sharp tensions within Iranian society created by the oil boom and the Shah's autocracy. The sense of outrage and solidarity of Arabs at the plight of the Palestinians has often cascaded into an anti-Jewish demagogy and chauvinism as retrograde as it is ineffective, while large sections of the Israeli population, including the more deprived social groups, have recently swung behind the semi-religious bigotry of the Likud and its overtly religious satellites.

4. The Middle East is characterized by what *is* peculiar to oil, the anomolous economic and social consequences of its production. Less than half of the Middle Eastern states are oil producers, and the majority of those have small populations. The majority of states with large populations do not not have oil. This assymetry of population and oil resources provoked substantial migration from oil-less to oil-producing states, while at the same time enabling the oil producers to use their wealth for individual political purposes in the region. The ability of these oil-producing states to use their wealth in this way, has, however, been compounded by the peculiar economies of oil production itself, which has a minimal linkage with the society in which it is taking place. The main, indeed sole significant, effect of oil is that the producer state is provided with a substantial rent from overseas sales. Inputs of labour, capital or agricultural goods are very small: hence oil production has an enclave character. Taken together, these two features of oil production – its asymmetrical distribution, its provision of rent rather than generation of national income – mean that some of the states most marked by

precolonial continuities have been the very ones endowed with substantial quantities of surplus capital. This they have deployed to promote not only their particular political values but also their social values as well, a form of conservative Islam whether in its Saudi or Qaddafi-ite varieties.

5.   Finally, the politics of the Middle East have been characterized by a combination of popular mobilization and political regression unique in the Third World. For all the west's anxiety about Soviet influence, the facts that the region borders the Soviet Union, and that the USSR has played a role there in support of states allied to it, have had little impact on the character of politics within that region. Egypt's ability to manipulate Soviet aid and, under Sadat, to expel Soviet advisers is a case in point. So too is the denunciation heaped upon Moscow by the leaders of the Islamic Republic of Iran. The USSR's role in the Middle East has been a strategic and military rather than a political one. The forces of the left that have merged have in some cases been substantial: communist parties have, at certain times, been powerful in Iran, Sudan and Iraq. But these parties have been subjected to severe repression and, increasingly, to competition from rival Islamic radicalisms. In other cases where groups of an 'anti-imperialist' and allegedly socialist character have emerged these have taken the form of military dictatorships of a most repressive and chauvinist kind, as in the Ba'thisms of Syria and Iraq. Those left-wing regimes that have survived and have avoided the degenerations of the Ba'th, as in Algeria and South Yemen, have been comparatively isolated from the mainstream of Middle Eastern politics. The left in the Middle East has had to operate in a very difficult situation, one of international isolation, sustained state repression and religious and ethnic chauvinism.

International Orientations: the Left and the Middle East

The Middle East has long aroused the interest and support of socialists in other countries. The risings in Iran and Egypt in the first decades of this century were supported by European socialists. In the 1950s and early 1960s some of the French left adopted policies of support for Algeria. The greatest single division in post-war British politics was over Suez, while an active minority in the Labour Party gave attention in the 1950s, 1960s and 1970s to the liberation movements in the Arabian Peninsula, South Arabia and Oman. The struggle of the Kurds in Iran, Iraq and Turkey has also drawn considerable sympathy from a wide range of opinion, socialist and liberal.[24] There is clearly an imperative need to maintain and increase the concern of the left for the manifold struggles of the region, as there is in regard to other areas of the Third World. Two special problems present themselves, however: one of analysis, the other of stance.

Coverage of this region, both academic and journalistic, reveals a tendency towards a suspension of analytic rigour in the face of what appear to be impenetrable, or at least *sui generis*, political and social developments. Somehow, it is implied, the Middle East is simply *not* like other parts of the Third World: its dynamics, conflicts and patterns of behaviour are different. One version of this particularist approach is what has come to be termed 'orientalism' – the assertion of a special, Islam-dominated, area, where canons of rationality and comparative judgement are not applicable.[25] It is asserted that the only way to understand the behaviour of Middle Eastern societies is through analysis of Islam: or that class politics, or revolutions, or even class consciousness do not arise there. Or that democracy, in either its liberal or revolutionary socialist senses, is not possible in such countries. But the temptations of particularism are not confined to 'orientalists': for, in suitably altered form, they constitute much of the self-image of Middle Eastern peoples themselves. No one could be more 'orientalist' than the Arab nationalist vaunting the uniqueness and specificity of the 'Arabs', and arguing that forms of oppression found elsewhere – based on class, gender or ethnicity – do not operate in the Arab world. Equally, the vision of Islamic radicals of the 1970s and 1980s, epitomized in, but not confined to, Khomeini, stresses the different social and moral character of Middle Eastern peoples. It denies, explicitly, the relevance of what are seen as alien, secular, criteria of assessment to the Muslim world. Since the early 1970s, as part of the wide disillusion with earlier forms of socialist and secular thought, large numbers of Arab intellectuals have also focused their work upon a search for Arab identity, and the unearthing of what are presented as *al-turath*, the 'roots' of Arab culture and history. Even ex-Marxists and Arabs of Christian origin can be found extolling the virtues of the Arabs' Islamic culture. Essentialism and relativism of many stripes therefore pervade a wide section of discussion of the Middle East, both within the region and beyond.

In reaction against this there has, predictably, arisen a contrary current, persistent if still subordinate. This dispenses with the apparent exceptionalism of the Middle East and instead seeks to assimilate, without major qualification, developments in the Middle East with those of Europe and/or other regions of the Third World. Thus in the nineteenth and early twentieth centuries, much liberal writing, Arab, Turkish, Persian and European, saw the region as progressing along an increasingly enlightened and optimistic path towards more acceptable democratic norms. In the 1940s, 1950s and 1960s a body of Marxist writing, some orthodox pro-Soviet, others independent, or Maoist, which developed with historical materialist panache, portrayed the region in class terms, without almost any apparent need to refer to factors of tribe, nationality, religion or faction. It seemed that here the complexes of orientalism and colonial essentialism had been well and truly overcome. In these class analyses the petty bourgeoisie, the proletariat and the semi-feudal forces, among others, were moved firmly to the centre of the analysis. As the OPEC-led boom of the 1970s took shape, and led to the spectacular increase in producer-state incomes, it seemed also to many more orthodox economic and social analysts as if the pattern of Middle Eastern economic growth could be tidily assimilated to that of other states and models. This was the view some took of Egypt's economic liberalization: nowhere was this optimism more common than in writing on Iran, where virtually all the literature of the 1970s colluded in some degree with unilinear and apologetic illusions of the Shah's modernization programme. Yet each of these universalist approaches, as others, has faced an apparent rebuff by history: neither liberal progress, nor rigorous class politics, nor orthodox capitalist modernization have come about.

Both these approaches, the particularist and the universalist, have profound problems associated with them: both have to some extent foundered on the rocks of empirical reality, both rest on questionable theoretical assumptions, and both have, evidently, served ideological functions. But study of their competing ideological approaches is of more than discursive interest: for these ideologies have been those of groups, within and beyond the region, who have been striving to gain power over these societies and economies. The particularism of the colonialist, as much as the universalism of the capitalist modernizers, reflects a material interest of those who hold these beliefs in dominating the region. The relativism of Arab nationalists or Islamic revolutionaries serves comparable ideological functions. The ideologies of Middle Eastern society, exceptionalist and universalist, are therefore themselves part of the overall pattern of conflict and tension within Middle Eastern societies.

A preliminary solution to this problem can, however, be suggested, and has informed the preceding analysis. The particularist approach to the Middle East, and its universalist antimony, contain two distinct arguments as to the character of Middle Eastern societies. One is what can be termed an *analytic particularism*, according to which the very categories used to describe these societies must themselves be specific to this region – the nationalist who rejects Weberian sociology or Marxism in the name of 'authentic' national or Islamic concepts, or some revised version of the thought of Ibn Khaldun, being a case of such analytic relativism. The other can be termed a *historical particularism*, according to which the specificities of the contemporary Middle East can only be comprehended in the light of the particular historical formation of the societies and politics of the region. In terms of this second particularism the Middle East is peculiar, not because the categories of analysis applicable elsewhere do not apply, but because of the specific processes of historical formation through which Middle Eastern states have gone. The particularity of the Middle East is therefore to be seen in the manner in which its contemporary social formations have emerged: these particularities are, however, to be grasped in terms of analytic categories that are universal, and that may be all the more revelatory precisely because they *are* of general and comparative application. This approach, matching an analytic universalism with a historical particularity, can provide a means of avoiding both the rampant relativism that has dominated discussion of the Middle East in recent years, and that bland universalism that applies to the Middle East general schemata for the Third World, without taking its special character into account.

The problems of solidarity with the Middle East are not, however, only questions of analysis: nor are they just questions of degree, of mobilizing more support for causes generally held to be just – as in Vietnam or Central America. For there are other difficulties of stance that have complicated, and continue to complicate any work of publicity or active support in regard to this region:

1.   There is a problem of information and focus. While events surrounding oil and the Arab-Israeli question are well reported in the major journals of the metropolitan countries, the same cannot be said for the undergrounds in other countries – the trade unions, the writers, the women, the ethnic minorities. Not only is it difficult to obtain accurate information on these, but the very meagreness of the material available makes it all the more difficult to establish the initial interest and audience. The majority of what is produced by groups within the Middle East is itself deficient for this purpose – often rhetorical, lacking in empirical content, dogmatic and tailored to a local rather than an international audience.

2. There is the record of anti-imperialist and revolutionary governments in the Middle East itself. The Shah of Iran was a tyrant, who murdered many of his subjects. His replacement, Khomeini, killed many more Iranians in a much shorter period. The Islamic Republic carried out torture, social repression and discrimination against women to a far higher degree than the Pahlavi monarchy. The Ba'th Party in Iraq has massacred many thousands of its subjects and rules with an iron fist. Too often socialists and solidarity groups in the west have avoided comment upon or indulged the crimes of the self-proclaimed revolutionaries, either out of genuine doubt, or for tactical reasons. The silence of much of the left during the earlier years of the Khomeini regime was a case in point. The left can win no credit, nor make any impact, if it selects its indignation in this way.

3. There is the problem of relativism, of those who argue that it is wrong to criticize Middle Eastern societies in terms of what are termed 'our values' – be these on political rights, women or even torture. The argument raised earlier in the discussion can be restated here: that the criteria for such judgements must be universally applied, even if it is possible to comprehend the specific historical forces that led to a particular Middle Eastern abomination. Some of the grotesque positions of western socialists in recent years, of 'anti-imperialists' defending the firing squads of Khomeini's *pasdaran*, or the cliterodectomy of some Arab Muslim societies, show where such relativism and 'understanding' can lead.

4. Finally, and most evidently, there are the national questions themselves. The left has historically been divided on these, and nowhere more so than on the Arab-Israeli dispute. If in the period since the mid-1960s the majority of the western left has sided with the Palestinians, the majority before that, and a significant minority since, has sided with Israel. There have been all too few who have taken up clear, critical and independent, positions on this issue. Two who did, and who were repeatedly denounced for so doing, were Isaac Deutscher and Maxime Rodinson.[26] Both denounced the chauvinism and repression of the Israeli state, and declared their support for Palestinian statehood. But both also named and opposed the chauvinism of many Arab politicians, a chauvinism meekly reproduced in much metropolitan anti-imperialism, which simply called for the abolition of an Israeli state. The clear, democratic position both Deutscher and Rodinson adopted was that *each* nation should have its own state in a partitioned Palestine. Such a position required both a detailed study of the issues involved and a political willingness to distance themselves from two political camps that have managed virtually to monopolize the terms of discussion. The great tragedy of so much solidarity with the Middle East is that it has taken the form of support for one or other chauvinism in the Arab–Israeli dispute, and in other conflicts.

These four problems of stance – information, repression, relativism and chauvinism –provide what may be termed the final specificity of the Middle East, namely the attitude of the western left toward it. Neither homogenous analysis, nor simple application of class terminology, nor enthusiastic but uncritical solidarity are possible in regard to this region. The peoples of the Middle East have long suffered from the depradations of their own rulers from within. The least they can expect from those concerned with their condition elsewhere is an interest and solidarity that is as informed, and politically balanced, as it is tenacious.

Notes

1 The term 'Middle East' has no precise definition, in that its boundaries are flexible from one usage to the other. In this analysis I use it to cover Iran, Turkey, Israel and 18 of the members of the Arab League including some from North Africa (Morocco, Algeria, Tunisia, Libya, Sudan, Egypt, Syria, Lebanon, Jordan, Iraq, Kuwait, Bahrain, Qatar, the United Arab Emirates, Oman, South Yemen, North Yemen and Saudi Arabia). The Arab League has four other members, three of whom are not strictly speaking Arab states, i.e. states in which the majority of the population speak Arabic, but which for reasons of political convenience have joined the League (Mauritania, Jibuti, Somalia), while a fourth member represents an Arab people but does not have a state (the Palestine Liberation Organization).

2 For good background studies see David Gilmour, *Lebanon: The Fractured Country* (Oxford, Martin Robertson, 1983), and Helena Cobban, *The Making of Modern Lebanon*, (London, Hutchinson, 1985).

3 For greater detail on the question of the origins of the war, see Fred Halliday, 'The Iranian Revolution and International Relations: Programme and Practice', *Millennium*, Spring 1981.

4 See E. H. Carr, *The Bolshevik Revolution* (London, Macmillan, 1952), vol. 3, for a survey of early Bolshevik policy in the region.

5 George Antonius, *The Arab Awakening*, (London, H. Hamilton, 1938) provides the standard Arab nationalist account of this period.

6 See Fred Halliday, 'Revolution in Iran: Was it Possible in 1921?' *Khamsin*, no. 7 (1980).

7 From the large literature on this subject see Maxime Rodinson, *Israel and the Arabs* (Harmondsworth, Penguin, 1982), Pamela Ann Smith, *Palestine and the Palestinians: 1876–1983* (Croom Helm, 1984), and, for an alternative account, Walter Laqueur, *A History of Zionism* (London, Weidenfeld and Nicolson, 1972).

8 For a British liberal history of this relationship, see Christopher Sykes, *Cross-Roads to Israel* (London/Bloomington, Indiana University Press, 1965).

9 See Maxime Rodinson, 'Arab Views of the Arab–Israeli Conflict', in *Cult, Ghetto and State* (London, Al Saqi Books, 1983).

10 For background on the individual states of the region see Peter Mansfield, *The Middle East, A Political and Economic Survey*, 5th edn (London, Oxford University Press, 1980).

11 On the social effects of the conflict see Smith, *Palestine and the Palestinians*.

12 A. Horne, *A Savage War of Peace*, (Harmondsworth, Penguin, 1978).

13 See Fred Halliday, *Arabia without Sultans* (Harmondsworth, Penguin, 1974), for a history of the nationalist revolution in South Yemen.

14 Details ibid.

15 Britain and the USSR had jointly occupied Iran in 1941, as part of their anti-Nazi alliance, and in the course of this occupation autonomous Kurdish and Azerbaijani Turkish republics were established in the Soviet zone. The USSR did finally withdraw its forces in March 1946, leaving its Iranian allies to face the repression of the Shah's forces.

16 See the excellent collection from *Khamsin* journal, edited by Jon Rotschild, *Forbidden Agendas: Intolerance and Deviance in the Middle East* (London, Al Saqi Books, 1984).

17 The best analysis of the revolution is given in Ervand Abrahamian, *Iran Between Two Revolutions* (Princeton, Princeton University Press, 1982).

18 This argument on the social contingency of Khomeini's movement is well developed in Sami Zubeida, 'The Ideological Conditions for Khomeini's doctine of government', *Economy and Society* 11, no. 2 (May 1982).

19 That Israel has colonial origins and retains a colonial relationship with the Palestinians does not entail, as most Arab nationalism purports, that therefore the Israelis have no right to their own state. As Rodinson among others has clearly shown, the Israelis now constitute a distinct nationality, with the right to their own state: but this does not legitimate the denial of Palestinian statehood.

20 Roger Owen, 'Arab Nationalism, Arab Unity and Arab Solidarity', in Talal Asad and Roger Owen (eds), *The Middle East* (London, Macmillan, 1983).

21 Hossein Mahdavy, 'Patterns and Problems of Economic Development in Rentier States: the Case of Iran', in M. A. Cook (ed.), *Studies in the Economic History of the Middle East* (London, Oxford University Press, 1970).

22 See Asad and Owen, *The Middle East*, for discussion of these dimensions.

23 The Arab world has retained a greater number of monarchies than any other region of the world. Eight of the 22 Arab League rulers are still monarchs.

24 See Gerard Chaliand (ed.), *People Without a Country; the Kurds and Kurdistan* (London, Zed Press, 1982).

25 See the classic analysis of this phenomenon in Edward Said, *Orientalism* (London, Routledge and Kegan Paul, 1978).

26 Isaac Deutscher, 'The Arab–Israeli War: June 1967', in *The Non-Jewish Jew, and other essays*. Edited with an introduction by Tamara Deutscher (London, Oxford University Press, 1968); Rodinson, *Israel and the Arabs*.

9

The United States and Central America

NORA HAMILTON

The Changing Context

The most important of the current challenges to US hegemony in Latin America comes from an area in which this hegemony has traditionally been most direct and unequivocal: the small, impoverished countries of Central America. And the way in which US control has been exercised is largely responsible for evoking this challenge. In short, while the revolutions of Nicaragua, El Salvador and Guatemala respond to internal conditions in each of these countries, these conditions have been directly or indirectly shaped by the overpowering presence of the United States, particularly during the twentieth century, and by domestic efforts to respond to this presence.

The Central American revolutions are not the only challenge confronting the United States in its traditional sphere of influence. A major shock to the inter-American system was delivered by the Cuban revolution in 1959. Cuba's subsequent rejection of US capitalism and efforts to implement a socialist model, and the presence of the Soviet Union in the region as economic and military guarantor of the revolutions's continuity against US efforts to destroy it, have implications for the current revolutions in Central America.

There are other potential challenges to US political and economic hegemony in Latin America. The post-war economic expansion of Western Europe and Japan was reflected in Latin America during the 1960s and 1970s by a growth in European and Japanese investments, loans and technology transfers. In the case of Europe, there has also been a growing, if still attenuated, European political presence in the region, expressed less in formal relations between countries than in informal links between political parties, unions, and churches.[1] Since at least the early post-war period, there have been links between European (and especially German) Christian democracy and the Christian democratic parties of Chile and Venezuela, and between the social democratic parties of Europe and parties such as Acción Democrática of Venezuela, the American Revolutionary Popular Alliance (APRA) in Peru, and Mexico's Institutional Revolutionary Party (PRI). However, during the 1970s there developed an increased European consciousness of Latin America and the Third World in general, expressed in the 1976 conference of the Socialist International (the international coordinating body of the social democratic parties and parties having social democratic tendencies) which emphasized the greater participation of Southern Hemisphere countries in a new international order and led to renewed interest in closer cooperation with Latin American political groups.[2]

Another development has been the growing economic and political importance of regional actors – particularly Mexico, Brazil, Venezuela and Argentina. It can be argued that the spectacular economic growth of the Mexican and Brazilian economies during the 1960s and 1970s was largely based on foreign investments and loans and in fact increased their economic dependence and integration with international capital. The governments of these and other Latin American countries, however, have succeeded in placing restrictions on foreign capital through limitations on ownership, through domestic sourcing of inputs, through restrictions on fees for technological transfers and through other measures. Several countries have also taken foreign policy positions independent of and, in some cases, antagonistic to those of the United States. Venezuela was a founding member of the Organization of Petroleum Exporting Countries (OPEC), and Brazil has developed ties with the socialist states of Angola and Mozambique in southern Africa. Mexico's independence in foreign policy is part of its revolutionary tradition; it was the only Latin American country to continue relations with Cuba throughout the post-revolutionary period and has consistently opposed US intervention in the region, including in Guatemala in 1954, Cuba in 1961, and the Dominican Republic in 1965. Beginning in the 1970s with the Echeverria administration, Mexico began to play a more prominent leadership role, taking the initiative in the establishment of regional economic organizations which specifically excluded the United States, and in efforts to build the new international economic order to promote the economic interests of Third World countries.

More recently, the economic importance of the larger Latin American countries was forcefully brought home to the governments and banks of the United States, Europe and Japan with the debt crisis and the sudden recognition that a default by any one of the major debtor states, and certainly by any combination of them, could have a devastating effect on the international financial system. Efforts of the banks at 'crisis management' and debt-rescheduling have failed to resolve the problem. The implementation of International Monetary Fund (IMF) austerity programmes in the debtor countries have only aggravated the recession they are experiencing and worsened the conditions of the impoverished sectors of the population, raising the prospect of prolonged political instability and social upheaval.

The changing context of US–Latin American relations, and particularly the emergence of revolutionary movements in Central America, raise several questions. How has US economic and political penetration of Latin America shaped the development of these countries, specifically the Central American countries? How can the emergence of revolutionary movements in the taken-for-granted client states of Central America be explained? What are the goals and implications of US policy in response to these revolutions? What role, if any do the new European and Latin American regional actors have in the resolution of the crises? And what are the goals and strategies of left and other progressive groups in the United States with respect to Central America?

US–Central American Relations in Historical Perspective

US intervention in the Caribbean region and more generally in Latin America has been motivated by strategic and economic concerns: to prevent foreign powers not in the region from establishing a foothold in the area and to preserve the hemisphere for US economic expansion. While US strategic concerns were officially expressed in the Monroe doctrine in 1823, it was with US economic expansion in the late nineteenth century that the Central American and Caribbean countries came under the economic and political domination of the United States. The unequal relationship between the United States and Central America has never been in question, but the effects of US penetration of the region have varied over time in response to changing conditions in the United States and to the distinct economic and political structures which have emerged in each country.

Spanish colonization and the hacienda economy

The area which today comprises the countries of Central America (Guatemala, El Salvador, Honduras, Nicaragua and Costa Rica)[3] was gradually incorporated into the Spanish colonial empire through military expeditions south from Mexico and north from South America and Panama. These met with considerable resistance by the Indian populations, particularly in areas of high population density such as Guatemala, a major centre of Mayan civilization, and parts of El Salvador, which had been settled by Pipil Indians migrating from the central valley of Mexico. As elsewhere, conquest and colonization had a devastating effect on these populations, which were decimated through war, disease and economic exploitation, but many Indian communities survived into the nineteenth century and, in the case of Guatemala, to the present.

The dominant economic structure which emerged in the colonial period was the hacienda, the large estate controlled by the Spanish and their creole descendants, and dependent upon various forms of coerced labour from the Indian population. While the haciendas produced indigo, cacao and other products for export to Europe, they were chiefly oriented to subsistence cultivation and were only partially and intermittently linked to the world economy. The haciendas continued to encroach on the Indian communities throughout the colonial period, but a large number of the communities remained untouched and continued to coexist with the haciendas after three centuries of colonial rule. Livestock haciendas were introduced in the more sparsely populated colonies of Honduras and Nicaragua, and in Costa Rica, where the Indian population was virtually non-existent (having been sent as slaves to other colonies), the European settlers and their descendants worked their own land in small family plots.

Independence, wars and the coffee economy

The Central American provinces achieved independence in 1823, in the wake of the independence movements in other parts of the Spanish Empire, followed by a struggle with Mexico, which had wanted to include the Central American provinces in its own empire. An effort at unification in the United Provinces of Central America disintegrated in 1838 in a war between conservatives (representing

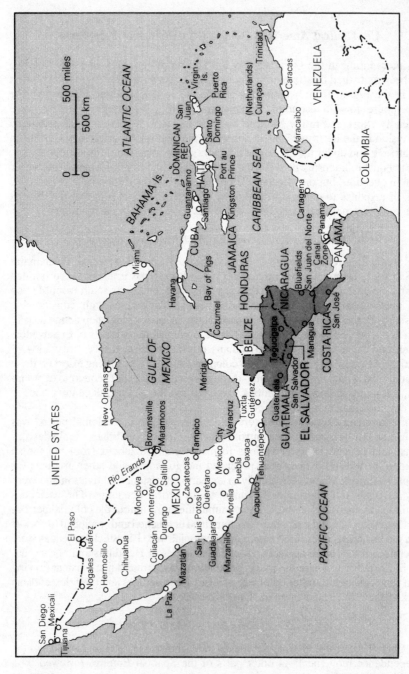

Map 9.1 The five original countries of Central America

landowning elites who favoured a continuation of colonial traditions, including a
strong church role) and liberals (who favoured restrictions on clerical power and
privileges, elimination of taxes on trade, development of roads and ports, and in
some cases, egalitarianism, public education and similar measures).[4] Throughout
the nineteenth century, conflicts between liberals and conservatives – representing
personalities as often as ideas – led to frequent civil wars in the Central American
nations. These often crossed borders, developing into wars between countries.

The independence of the Latin American countries brought a renewed interest
from the US government. The Monroe doctrine stated that any attempt by
European powers to intervene in the newly independent Latin American countries
would be looked upon as an unfriendly act toward the United States. Strategic
concerns were paramount, given British interest in the new Latin American
republic, but even at this point US officials visualized economic and geographic
expansion into Latin America. Such expansion was to be facilitated by the
instability and civil war following independence in many of these nations.[5] The
United States however at this time was not in a military position to enforce even
its strategic interests, and Britain succeeded in establishing a foothold in Central
America through colonizing Belize, which in turn became a commercial outlet
for other Central American countries. Britain also seized the Miskito province
on the Caribbean coast of Nicaragua. In the meantime, the US expansionist drive
concentrated on the west, which was sparsely settled, for the most part by
indigenous populations.

The war with Mexico and the annexation of half of Mexico's territory in 1848
extended United States territory to the Pacific. It also raised the question of whether
the new territory would be incorporated in the form of slave or free states. This
issue, combined with the discovery of gold in California that same year, led to
renewed interest in the Caribbean area and the countries of the region. On the
one hand, the southern states looked to the Caribbean countries as possible targets
for incorporation as additional slave states. On the other, the discovery of gold
in California increased the desirability of a quicker route from the Atlantic to
the Pacific than the cumbersome land route. The most obvious site for such a
route was the narrow strip of land which connected the mainland of North America
with that of South America, a fact which had not been lost on the Central American
governments themselves, who regarded their strategic position as a potential source
of future prosperity.

These issues were linked in a bizarre series of events which took place in
Nicaragua in the 1850s – the William Walker episode – in which a US private
adventurer (filibusterer) joined the liberals in their war against the conservatives
then in power in Nicaragua, and had himself proclaimed president of the country,
whereupon he legalized slavery, made English the official language, and attempted
to have Nicaragua annexed to the United States as a slave state. Walker was
supported by the Morgan interests of New York and the Garrison interests of
San Francisco, who were seeking to undercut Cornelius Vanderbilt's control of
inter-oceanic transit lines in Nicaragua and Panama. Walker was however, finally
defeated by a Central American army led by Costa Rican president Juan Rafael
Mora and supported by the British and several South American countries.[6] The
episode discredited the Nicaraguan liberals who would not return to power for
several decades and thus delayed the development of Nicaragua's export economy.

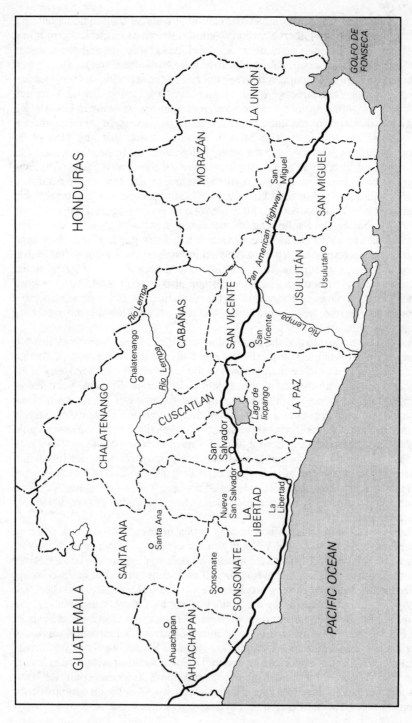

Map 9.2 El Salvador

It was the production of coffeee for the growing markets of Europe which incorporated the Central American countries into the world market as commodity producers. The process began in Costa Rica, the smallest and poorest of the Central American countries, during the first half of the nineteenth century; coffee production expanded to Guatemala and El Salvador during the 1850s and 1860s and to Nicaragua toward the end of the century. By the 1880s coffee had become the major export of Costa Rica, El Salvador and Guatemala.[7]

The introduction of coffee production for export was accompanied by substantial internal changes. The emerging coffee interests gained control of the government (usually through a struggle with conservative groups representing landowners and the Church) and used it to introduce liberal reforms which would 'free' land and labour from traditional restrictions and make them available for coffee production. The liberal state also secured foreign capital and technology, chiefly from Europe, for coffee processing and the construction of the infrastructure needed for an export economy, especially roads, ports and railroads.

In El Salvador, the introduction of coffee production for export shaped the economic and social structure which, with some modifications, has endured to the present. The most desirable areas for coffee production were the highlands of the western provinces where the remaining Indian communities were concentrated. With the takeover of these lands for coffee production the indigenous communities virtually disappeared, their inhabitants forced to more marginal lands or transformed into a permanent or seasonal labour force for the coffee growers. The emergence of a small but powerful oligarchy with undisputed economic and political control distinguished El Salvador from the other Central American countries and may be a factor in the relative economic independence of El Salvador well into the twentieth century.[8]

In Nicaragua a somewhat similar process occurred under the liberal government of José Santos Zelaya (1897–1909), but it was on a smaller scale and ultimately frustrated by the conservative wars and US interventions of the early twentieth century. In Guatemala, Church holdings were extensive and their expropriation became a major source of land for coffee producers; although some indigenous communities were expropriated, most of them remained untouched. Partly as a consequence, there was a scarcity of landless labour and laws were enacted to force Indians from highland communities to work on the coffee plantations part of the year. The new coffee oligarchy was drawn in part from traditional landowners and in part from immigrants, expecially Germans, and continued to share political power with the traditional *hacendados*.

Yet another situation emerged in Costa Rica, where idle land was relatively plentiful and the population sparse, and coffee was grown on family farms. Small coffee farmers were in turn dependent on a dominant group of large estate owners who controlled credit and marketing. But because of the labour scarcity, and the fact that many of the workers were also smallholders, they obtained high wages and benefits relative to workers in other Central American countries.

While the production of coffee was controlled by nationals (and in some cases by immigrants), the credit, technology and infrastructure needed for its processing and export came under foreign domination. Credit houses in England and Germany provided advance payments for harvests; only in El Salvador were national landowners and exporters able to establish a national bank to finance coffee

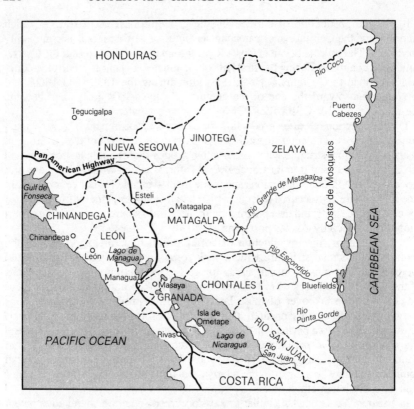

Map 9.3 Nicaragua

production. Coffee processing equipment was also exported from Europe or brought in by immigrants. Railroad construction financed by British and US capital included an Atlantic railroad linking the central mesa of Costa Rica to the Atlantic port of Puerto Limón, a line giving El Salvador an outlet to the Atlantic at Pto Barrios in Guatemala and the railroad system of Guatemala was financed by British and US capital, with the latter increasing in importance toward the end of the century. The high costs of building railroads in difficult terrain, combined with the speculative and often fraudulent practices of railroad contractors, left the Central Americans with a heavy foreign debt and in many cases little to show for it.[9]

US expansion, military intervention and enclave economies

Following the William Walker episode, US intervention in Central America declined. This was partly because of the civil war and later because of the building of railroads spanning the United States, which temporarily lessened interest in a trans-isthian route in Central America. But the spectacular economic growth which occurred in the post-war period, including the growth of finance capital and trusts, laid the groundwork for the expansion into the Caribbean basin in the late nineteenth century. US expansionism ceased to be a sporadic practice of

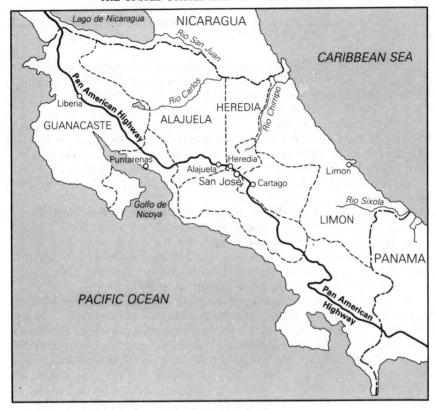

Map 9.4 Costa Rica

individual adventurers or specific corporations and banks, and became a concerted, conscious and broadly promoted policy. Senator Lodge was able to state in 1895, 'We have a record of conquest, colonization and expansion unequaled in the nineteenth century...We are not about to be curbed now.'[10]

US interests had now developed extensive enclaves centred in the production of bananas in Central America as well as sugar production in the Caribbean Islands. Bananas had been produced locally in Central America since the mid-nineteenth century. In the 1880s, two US railroad contractors, Miner Cooper Keith and Henry Meiggs Keith, began to export this crop from Costa Rica to the Gulf Coast areas of the United States. They established the Tropical Trading and Transport Corporation, which later merged with the Boston Fruit Company (established in the 1880s to ship bananas from Jamaica to Boston) to form the United Fruit Company. United Fruit received generous government concessions, acquiring extensive holdings on the Caribbean coast of Central America, and eventually expanded its banana plantations to include holdings in Costa Rica, Panama, Nicaragua, Honduras and Guatemala, as well as islands of the Caribbean. It also built railroads in Nicaragua. Panama and El Salvador, and by 1912 it controlled the Atlantic railway network through the International Railways of Central America. The Standard Fruit and Steamship Company was formed in 1924 and by 1929 United Fruit and Standard

Fruit dominated banana production in Central America, which they continued to control until the 1970s when Del Monte took over many of the operations of United Fruit.

In contrast to coffee production, which was controlled by nationals or immigrants, all phases of banana production – including plantations, transport, refrigeration, marketing and finance – were controlled by the US companies. They enjoyed a near monopoly on transportation in the region, both railroads and steamships.[11] Although banana exports brought foreign exchange and increasing government revenues (as the Central American governments began to levy taxes on banana export and production), the production of bananas constituted a virtual enclave, more closely linked to the US than to their own economies. With the exception of the railroad linking El Salvador with the Barrios port of Guatemala, none of the countries were connected by railways.

The absence of a national dominant class in Honduras enabled the corporations virtually to control the government. In Guatemala and Costa Rica, politics remained formally under national control, but the coffee oligarchy (and in Guatemala traditional landowners) were forced to share power with the US fruit companies, and only with the approval of North American diplomats and company management did presidents maintain themselves in office.[12]

The consolidation of the banana enclaves coincided with the struggle between the United States, Great Britain and Germany for hegemony in the region. During this period US dominance expanded in the Caribbean basin as a whole. The United States intervened in the Spanish American War in 1898, creating US protectorates in Cuba, Puerto Rica and the Philippines. It subsequently took advantage of a succession movement in Panama, then a province of Colombia, supporting Panamanian independence and in turn securing an agreement for the building of the Panama canal. In 1905 President Theodore Roosevelt added a corollary to the Monroe doctrine stating that the United States had the right to act to insure order and stability in the hemisphere – i.e. to play the role of policeman. The next 30 years were marked by frequent US military, political and economic intervention in the Central American and Caribbean countries, including long-term occupation in some cases, to protect US economic and strategic interests.

At the same time concern for stability led to US efforts to control the frequent civil wars and regional conflicts among the Central American states. The United' States was instrumental in the establishment of a Central American court which had jurisdiction in cases of conflict among Central American nations, and during the next few years the Court was indeed successful in adjudicating conflicts.[13] Ironically, it was the US refusal to abide by the Court's decisions which weakened the Court and ultimately caused its demise.

The occasion was US intervention in the protracted struggle between liberals and conservatives in Nicaragua following the defeat of William Walker in 1857. After an extended period of conservative rule, José Santos Zelaya had seized power in 1897 and established conditions for the coffee economy, decades after it had been introduced in Costa Rica, Guatemala and El Salvador. Zelaya attempted to lessen foreign domination of Nicaragua by placing restrictions on foreign investment and refused to grant canal rights to the United States, which feared that a second interoceanic canal might be built in Nicaragua controlled by other foreign powers. Zelaya was defeated in 1909 in a US-backed conservative coup but the conservatives, once in power, were unable to retain it and again called on the United States for help. The US marines landed in 1912 and stayed until 1926. A US-sponsored truce, followed by an American-supervised election in 1928, was agreed to by conservatives and liberals with the exception of liberal Colonel Cesar Augusto Sandino, who formed a guerrilla army in the mountains of Nueva Segovia and Matagalpa (in the north central section of the country) and vowed to fight all vestiges of US intervention. The marines returned in 1927 and carried on an unsuccessful struggle against Sandino until they left in 1933, by which time they had trained a National Guard commanded by General Anastasio Somoza Garcia. Although Sandino had agreed to negotiate once the marines left, Somoza had him assassinated in 1934; in 1936 he staged a coup against the elected president, Juan B. Sacasa, and made himself president of Nicaragua. For the next 42 years the Somoza family controlled political power (and an increasing proportion of the economic wealth) in Nicaragua, with US support. In turn, the Somozas were dependable allies of the United States, consistently promoting its economic and strategic interests in the region.

While Sandino and his followers were fighting the marines and the newly created National Guard in Nicaragua, workers on the coffee estates of western El Salvador were organizing with the support of the recently formed Communist Party. The rapid decline in coffee exports in the wake of the 1929 depression led to layoffs and wage cutbacks for coffee workers, worsening their already destitute conditions and accelerating the process of mobilization. When peaceful demonstrations had no effect, and the government refused to recognize the election victories of sympathetic (often Communist Party) candidates, the organized rural workers decided to revolt and, armed with machetes, they staged an uprising in the western provinces in January 1932. The uprising was quickly crushed by General Maximiliano Hernández Martínez, who had come to power a month before through a miliary coup. Not satisfied with crushing the rebellion, Hernández Martínez unleashed a reign of terror in the western provinces in which an estimated 20,000 to 30,000 peasants and rural workers were killed. The success of Hernández Martínez in crushing the revolt convinced the coffee oligarchy to entrust the military with direct control of the government (formerly controlled by the oligarchy), which it has continued to exercise, in the interests of the oligarchy, to the 1980s.

After 120 years of political independence, the incorporation of the Central American economies in the informal empire of the United States was complete. US corporations controlled the banana enclaves, railroads and shipping of Guatemala, Honduras and Costa Rica and exercised direct or indirect domination of the governments of those countries. The Panama Canal was secured and the threat of an alternative canal route in Nicaragua controlled by powers outside the Western Hemisphere had been eliminated. US economic and strategic hegemony was backed by military power, which could be used to control recalcitrant workers or hostile governments, to shore up weak allies, or to prevent interference by other foreign powers. By the mid-1930s, however, much of the US policing of Central America could be entrusted to local governments which had fallen under the control of long-term dictators in most of the Central American countries: Jorge Ubico (1931–44) in Guatemala, Hernández Martínez (1931–44) in El Salvador, Tuburcio Carías Andino (1932–49) in Honduras and Anastasio Somoza (1936–57) in Nicaragua.

From Modernization to Revolution

The turning point: Guatemala 1954

Each of the three revolutionary Central American countries experienced a crisis which stamped the character and direction of its modern history. In El Salvador, it was the peasant uprising of 1932 and its brutal repression, which institutionalized the political control by the military in defence of the economic hegemony of the Salvadoran oligarchy. In Nicaragua it was the struggle of Sandino against the US marine occupation, the assassination of Sandino by Somoza and the subsequent seizure of power by Somoza which established the character of the US-supported Somoza dynasty as well as of the Sandinista movement which ultimately overthrew it. And in Guatemala it was the democratic revolution of 1944–54 and its suppression by a US-sponsored coup which eliminated hopes for democratic reform and established a context in which revolution was seen as the only means to bring about social and economic change. In many respects, the sequence of events leading and following the overthrow of the Arbenz government in Guatemala was a turning point for Central America as a whole.

The mid-1940s brought an end to the long dictatorships in El Salvador, Guatemala and Honduras, and in several countries a process of economic diversification and modernization was undertaken with the expansion of agriculture into new export crops, such as cotton and sugar, and the development of light industry. The most far-reaching experiments of democratization and modernization took place in Guatemala, where a coalition of workers, university students, professionals and military officers ousted the dictator Jorge Ubico in 1944. Subsequent elections brought an intellectual, Juan José Arévalo to the presidency and he initiated a series of reforms: the extension of democratic reform which included the extension of voting rights, freedom of the press, a literacy campaign, a public health programme, social security legislation and a labour code providing for a minimum wage, the right to organize unions, and the right to strike. Arévalo's elected successor, Colonel Jacobo Arbenz, sought to build on these reforms and establish the basis for capitalist development in Guatemala through industrialization based on imports and the transformation of 'feudal' agricultural structures. Arbenz was probably influenced in part by the Communist party (the Guatemalan Workers' Party) of which his wife and some officials of his cabinet were members; to some extent his programme reflected a primary assumption of Latin American communist parties that the elimination of feudalism and the development of capitalism constituted a necessary pre-condition to the transition to socialism in Latin America. His most controversial measure was an agrarian reform which expropriated all land holdings over 223 acres, affecting not only the estates of traditional landowners but also those of military officers who owned land and those holdings of the United Fruit Company which were not being utilized. Arbenz's policies aroused the antagonism of the US government, which through various stratagems sought to destabilize the Arbenz government and orchestrated its overthrow through a CIA-trained exile army.[14] In the context of the Cold War, US antagonism toward the Arbenz administration was justified on the basis of anti-communism, but there is little doubt that Arbenz's treatment of United

Fruit, which was accustomed to wielding political as well as economic power in Guatemala, and had connections with the Eisenhower administration through the Dulles brothers, was a main factor.

The overthrow of the Arbenz government in 1954, following the coup against the Moussadeq regime in Iran the year before, was viewed as a major US foreign policy success. Many of its tactics were incorporated in subsequent US efforts to destabilize and ultimately eliminate 'unfriendly' governments in Latin America, including current efforts against the government of Nicaragua: among them; diplomatic isolation of the target government, trade and credit blockades, CIA-planted stories in the media, the training of exile invasion forces, efforts to secure the cooperation of other countries of the region, and US air force bombing missions accompanying the invasion force. The language justifying US intervention in Guatemala in 1954 has been incorporated in current pronouncements of the Reagan administration, including references to Soviet weapons, Guatemala as a beachhead of international communism, and even the domino theory.

The 1954 coup ushered in a period of unprecedented repression against any signs of opposition in Guatemala, implemented by a succession of military or military-controlled governments often with US support.[15] It also led to recognition among the more well-informed US policymakers that forces for change in the region could not be stifled indefinitely, a recognition which was reinforced by the Cuban revolution. In the meantime, US corporations had begun to look to Central America as a new market for investment in manufacturing and mining, particularly with the creation of the Central American common market.

The Central American common market: the costs of modernization

The formation of the Central American common market and the impetus given it by US aid and investment marked a new phase in the economic history of the region.[16] The common market resulted from several factors: the response of economists and technicians in several Central American countries to the periodic crises resulting from world market fluctuations due to economic dependence on commodity exports (coffee, cotton and bananas); the push by new industrial groups to expand markets for industrial products, especially in El Salvador; the interest of officials of the UN Economic Commission on Latin America (ECLA) in combining the Central American markets in order to implement ECLA's import substitution programme; and concern among US officials, in the wake of the Cuban revolution, to eliminate conditions for revolution in Central America through modernization and reform, as well as recognition that the integration of the Central American markets would make it the fifth largest market for US investment and trade in Latin America.

During the 1950s El Salvador and Guatemala signed bilateral agreements with each other and with other Central American countries lowering or eliminating tariffs on certain products. The five Central American governments reached agreement with ECLA to proceed toward economic integration through a gradual reduction of tariffs, and an equal distribution of 'integration industries' among the five countries – those in which, for reasons of size, one plant could produce for the entire region. Regional planning was to ensure balanced development, and related restrictions were agreed on foreign investment. But little headway was made in industrial investment due to limited financial resources: governments were unwilling or unable to tax the landowners, and restrictions on the free operation of the market had limited interest on the part of the US or other foreign investors.

By the late 1950s the US government recognized the potential of the Central American common market once it had been divested of the 'statist' characteristics of the ECLA plan, and the financial needs of the Central American governments facilitated agreement to make the required changes. Internal tariffs among the five central American countries would be abolished immediately rather than by degrees, and the concept of integration industries and restrictions on foreign trade and investment would be to all effects eliminated. After the Kennedy administration launched the Alliance for Progress, a special agency, the Regional Office for Central America and Panama (ROCAP) was set up within the newly created US Agency for International Development to administer US aid to the Central American common market.

As noted above, the Alliance for Progress was an ambitious programme of modernization, reform and counter-insurgency which attempted to respond to the challenge of the Cuban revolution. The visible part of the Alliance – promotion of reform-oriented governments and modernization through government and multilateral loans and private (including foreign) investment – would attack the root cause of revolution – poverty and social injustice. These two elements would reinforce each other: reform, particularly of antiquated agrarian structures, would remove obstacles to capitalist development; capitalism in turn would generate the 'middle sectors' which would continue to promote social and political reforms from which they benefited; and the 'trickle-down' effect would spread the benefits of development to the impoverished masses, thus attenuating the vast inequalities which characterized the Latin American social structures and diminishing the likelihood of social revolution.

The less visible part of the alliance, the counter-insurgency programme, would deal with any revolutionary movements which did emerge. This involved the equipping and training of Latin American military officers in their home countries, in Panama or in the United States. An Office for Public Safety was set up within the Agency for International Development for the training of Latin American police forces; one of its major targets was Guatemala, where the United States spent $4.4 million on police training and where the police force grew from 3,000 to 11,000 members, the second largest (after Brazil) in Latin America. Both the reform and counter-insurgency components of the Alliance were a response to the Cuban revolution and aimed to prevent similar occurrences elsewhere in the region – through premptive reform if possible, through military repression if necessary or through a judicious combination of the two.

Although the reform component of the Alliance had little impact in Central America, US support for modernization via the common market provided the financial impetus needed to spur its growth. Between 1960 and 1969 the US provided $1 billion in aid and loans to the common-market countries, much of it through the newly created Central American Bank for Economic Integration (BCIE), the major lending agency for infrastructure and major industrial projects in the region. Foreign investment from the United States had also reached $1 billion by 1980, primarily focused on manufacturing (approximately 60 per cent of the total) for export to other common-market countries. Initially this investment came from two sources: the fruit companies (now United Brands and Standard Brands) which diversified into such areas as plastics, soap, cement, steel, electronic data processing systems, communications, banking and real estate; and corporations such as Borden, Phelps Dodge, Westinghouse, Alcoa, Kimberly Clark and Atlas Chemical, which set up subsidiaries for food processing, chemicals (pharmaceuticals, plastics and cosmetics), textiles, paper products, auto assembly, electronics and other products.

By the second half of the 1960s the Central American common market was widely regarded as one of Latin America's success stories: there had been a substantial increase in economic integration with trade among the five countries increasing 700% – from approximately 4% to 35% of their total trade between 1960 and 1969; and economic growth rates, though uneven, had been impressive in each of the five countries, particularly in the manufacturing industry. By the early 1970s, however, the expectations of the 1960s had dimmed. A war between Honduras and El Salvador had ended trade relations between the two countries and resulted in Honduras withdrawing from the common market. A decline in international commodity prices in the early 1970s and its effects on the domestic economies demonstrated that the growth of the previous decade had not lessened Central America's economic dependence on commodity exports. The drop in commodity export prices prompted a new emphasis on export diversification. This coincided with the growth of fast food franchises in the United States, and investments in Central America by agribusiness supplied cheap beef to the new hamburger and restaurant chains in the United States. The firms involved included LAAD (Latin American Agribusiness Development Corporation, a conglomerate owned by a variety of US banks and agricultural firms including Bank of America, Caterpiller Tractor Companies and Border, Inc.), and United Brands (which by 1978 made twice as much in meat sales as in bananas). Beef exports from Central America increased from 13.7 thousand tons in 1960 to 114 thousand in 1979. By the mid-1970s, several garment and electronics firms, which had formerly established export platform industries in Mexico and the Caribbean (but had been running into labour problems) were attracted to Central America, especially El Salvador, where labour was plentiful, cheap and, it was believed, relatively compliant. Tourism was also an attractive investment, particularly for 'Sunbelt' investors whose fortunes had been made in electronics, real estate and defence industry contracts; in Central America they formed alliances with the state and military bourgeoisie (especially President Arana of Guatemala and the Somozas of Nicaragua) and invested in casinos, hotels and other tourist services.

By the 1970s, US investors were joined by European and Japanese interests, which had begun to expand into the larger Latin American countries by the 1960s, particularly in manufacturing. During the 1970s Japanese firms began to set up export platform industries in El Salvador and Costa Rica. European banks also provided loans to the BCIE, and to banks, development companies and corporations in individual Central American countries.

The economic growth resulting from the creation of the common market and the influx of foreign capital strengthened dominant sectors of the bourgeoisie and in some cases fomented the creation of new bourgeois fractions. Joint investments by foreign corporations with national capitalists gave the latter a definite stake in foreign-induced growth. In El Salvador, the major beneficiaries were 'modernizing' groups within the coffee oligarchy, such as the de Sola family, which invested with Unilever in detergents, soap and margarine.

In Nicaragua, foreign investment and foreign aid – particularly following the 1972 earthquake – primarily benfited the Somoza interests, which expanded to include new common-market industries. In 1978 the wealth of the Somoza family was estimated at $400 to $500 million, including 25–30 per cent of all cultivable land, in tobacco, sugar, coffee and rice estates; processing industries such as dairy, meat packing, salt, fishing, refining and distilleries; industrial firms including cement, construction materials, textiles and cooking oil; communications including newpapers, radio stations and the only television station; transportation; banking and insurance. Links with corporations such as Consolidated Food, Booth Fisheries, Pepsi Cola, United Fruit, General Mills and ABC Television, as well as with the US Agency for International Development, also strengthened a relatively new group which emerged with the post-war cotton boom and was organized around the Banco Nicaraguense (BANIC) as a major economic group. During the 1960s the older livestock interests from the southern city of Granada, associates with the Banco de America (Banamerica, no relation to the Bank of America), also benefited. Both the Banco Nicaraguense and the Banco de America received funding from foreign banks (Chase Manhattan and the First National Bank of Boston, respectively); the latter was 33 per cent owned by Wells Fargo.[17]

In Guatemala, the most striking change within the bourgeoisie was the emergence of the military as a caste, and specific military officers in particular, as the dominant bourgeois fraction. Their geographic base was the Franja Transversal del Norte (the northern transversal strip), a wide swath of land approximately 3,500 square miles crossing the northern states of Huehuetanango, El Quiche, Alta Verapaz and Izabal – a region marked by the generals as a new area of development (see map 9.5). The Franja was the location of oil and nickel production by transnationals as well as the construction of hydroelectric plants; during the 1970s the generals in power handed out land titles to their cohorts for ranching, rubber and chicle farming for export. The properties of General Lucas Garcia, head of the Franja development project during the 1970's and president from 1978 to 1982, were estimated at 81,000 to 135,000 acreas and included 14 large farms.[18] Military officers were often junior partners of foreign corporations which invested in industry, commerce and finance during the 1960s. Right-wing policial organizations such as Amigos del Pais and the Guatemalan Freedom Foundation linked Guatemalan businesses with military and government officials, on the one hand, and the US business community on the other.[19]

But the benefits of economic growth did not 'trickle down' to the poorer sectors of the population, and two decades of economic growth increased rather than lessened the susceptibility of the Central American economies to external pressures. Many of the new industries were in fact last-stage assembly or processing plants, which imported most of their inputs as well as machinery. By 1978, US exports to Central America, at $1.57 billion, were greater than its total fixed investment. The elimination of restrictions on investment led to numerous inefficiencies: while a single firm could provide for the entire regions's needs in areas such as auto assembly and oil refining, there were six firms in each of these sectors by 1969. For the first time, inflation became a problem for Central

Map 9.5 Guatemala

American countries in the mid-1970s. High-cost imports of fertilizers, pesticides and other agricultural inputs raised the cost of production, which was passed along to consumers in higher food prices; the increased cost for oil imports affected the prices of both manufactures and agricultural products. The costs of new infrastructure needed for agricultural and industrial expansion – roads, ports, hydroelectric plants, communications systems – were covered through loans from the United States and other foreign governments, international lending agencies and foreign banks; Central American governments could not raise taxes to help finance these costs without risking an abrupt termination of their regime. With the decline in international prices for commodity exports in the 1980s, each of the Central American countries is faced with escalating debts.

Most important, the process of modernization also led to massive dislocations which increased the vulnerability of large sectors of the population to the recession which followed. The expansion of agricultural estates and ranches, as in the past, forced much of the rural population off the land. In Guatemala, during the 1970s small peasant holdings lost 26 per cent of their acreage.[20] In some cases, small farmers were shifted from subsistence production to cooperatives producing for the export market, dependent upon agribusiness firms for loans for new expensive inputs such as seeds, fertilizers and insecticides. Investments in nickel production and the construction of a highway and an oil pipeline across the Transversal Strip in the northern part of the country resulted in a massive dislocation of the Kekchi and Pokoman Indian communities of the region, as high-level military officers lay claim to extensive land tracts for plantations, ranches or land speculation. In El Salvador the number of landless workers in the rural section increased from 12 to 40 per cent between 1960 and 1975; those with two hectares or less increased from 72 to 90 per cent. By the 1970s in Nicaragua, approximately half of the economically active population in the agricultural section were seasonal cotton workers who had employment two to three months a year. In some areas agricultural estates were transformed into ranches requiring less labour, therefore increasing rural unemployment.

The net effect of these changes was to increase the dependence on the cash economy of large sectors of the population, which had formerly supplied all or part of their needs through subsistence farming. Many were pushed to marginal lands; others flocked to the capital cities, swelling the slum population.[21] In El Salvador, the situation was exacerbated when the Honduran government forced the Salvadorans who had settled there (estimated at 350,000) to return to El Salvador, where unemployment was 20 per cent and underemployment 40 per cent. When agricultural unemployment increased, as it did in most countries, or when supermarkets refused to purchase cash crops grown on peasant cooperatives, as occurred in Guatemala, or when inflation raised the price of such staples as beans and corn, the situation of large sectors of the population became desperate.

Reform and revolution

The dramatic economic transformations of the 1960s and 1970s were accompanied by intense political change.

1.   As noted above, the dislocations produced by the rapid incorporation of large numbers of people into the market economy increased incentives to mobilization around protests against increases in food prices and bus fares or around demands for wage increases and access to land and jobs.
2.   Such mobilization was facilitated in some cases by industrialization, which brought workers together in factories, and rural-urban migration, which expanded the population of working-class communities and urban slums.
3.   While the reform element of the Alliance was definitely limited in Central America, there were political openings in each of the three countries for the creation of organizations representing workers, peasants and other sectors of the population, including the establishment and/or expansion of moderately reformist political parties.
4.   Reforms within the Catholic Church in Latin America encouraged progressive sectors within the Church to promote the organization and mobilization of the economically and politically repressed population groups.

Any possibility that these developments might have led to peaceful resolution of the contradictions resulting from the process of modernization was precluded in

Guatemala, El Salvador and Nicaragua by the reactions of the military and oligarchy. Military and security forces as well as right-wing death squads carried out massive assaults against organized peasants and selectively kidnapped, tortured and assassinated leaders of unions, political parties and other urban groups. By the second half of the 1970s, broad sectors of the population in each country were convinced that social justice could not be achieved by peaceful means but only by revolution.

For some, the defeat of the Arbenz government and the success of the Cuban revolution demonstrated that the model of peaceful, democratic change was already outmoded by the beginning of this period. Partly inspired by the Cuban experience, partly motivated by conditions within their respective countries, revolutionary movements emerged in Guatemala and Nicaragua in the early 1960s. The Guatemalan guerrilla movement had its origins in a November 1960 revolt by nationalist army officers protesting against an agreement between the United States and Guatemalan president Ydigoras (without the consent of the military) to use Guatemala as a training and staging area for the CIA-sponsored Bay of Pigs invasion of Cuba. Although the officers' revolt was crushed with US support, several of its leaders went underground, establishing contact with exile groups and winning the support of the peasants in the eastern provinces of Izabal and Zacapa. Guerrilla activities became the excuse for a brutal US supported counter-insurgency programme resulting in the decimation of the guerrilla forces and the death of thousands of their supporters. But the guerrilla experience of the 1960s was incorporated in the revolutionary movement which emerged in the 1970s on a much broader population base.[22]

In Nicaragua in 1961 a group of university students influenced by the writings of Sandino and the Cuban revolution formed the FSLN (Sandinista Front for National Liberation). Gradually the Sandinistas established a rural base, beginning in the mountainous area around Matagalpa which had been a stronghold of the peasant guerrillas under Sandino, and established contacts with the still small industrial working class and university students.[23]

In the meantime, events of the 1960s demonstrated the ineffectiveness of civilian opposition to the Somoza regime. Following the assassination of Anastasio Somoza Garcia in 1957, Nicaragua had experienced a brief period of moderate reform under his son, Luis Somoza (1957–65) and under Luis Somoza's hand-picked successor René Schick (1963–7), including some degree of press freedom and relatively lenient treatment of opponents. This period was marked by the struggle between Luis Somoza and his brother Anastasio Somoza Debrayle. They fought over the question of control by the civilian bureaucracy which was favoured by Luis, or the military which was favoured by Anastasio who was then head of the National Guard. This period was also characterized by development of opposition parties, several of which – Christian Democrats, Conservatives and Independent Liberals – formed a coalition (National Union of Opposition – UNO) to contest the 1967 elections.

Recognizing that Anastasio Somoza, the government candidate, would not permit a fair election, the leaders of the new coalition led a protest march of 60,000 to the National Palace. The National Guard fired into the crowd, killing an estimated 600. The victory of Anastasio Somoza in the subsequent elections (which was followed by the death of his brother Luis later that year) reintroduced the model of government by military repression.

The failure of the reformist coalition led to a space in the opposition which the FSLN was gradually able to fill. Military confrontations between the FSLN and Somoza's National Guard beginning in 1967 resulted in the death of several FSLN militants and leaders but also set-backs to the National Guard, and by the end of the decade the FSLN was known nationally. These and the following years were devoted to intensive organizing, including the formation of urban cells, the creation of front organizations within the universities and working class neighbourhoods, the circulation of documents denouncing both National Guard repression and the electoral strategies of the opposition, and the formulation of long-term goals and strategies. The 1970s were characterized by increased mobilization, including strikes, demonstrations and marches and land invasions, many of them led by the Sandinista organization.

The 1972 earthquake, which left 20,000 dead and leveled the capital city of Managua, exposed the corruption of the Somoza clan, who channeled international aid funds to their construction, real estate and building supply companies. The corruption of the regime antagonized Church leaders and even sectors of the bourgeoisie as Somoza took advantage of his political position to increase his wealth by closing off opportunities to other bourgeois fractions. As a result, the Sandinistas were able to establish broad alliances which included these groups in the final stages of the war against Somoza.

The reformist interlude had a different trajectory in El Salvador, where the United States encouraged the opening of the electoral process to opposition parties and promoted the development of the Christian Democratic Party, established in 1961 with support by the Christian Democratic parties of Germany and Italy. By 1968, the Christian Democrats won 42 per cent of the popular vote, 19 (of 52) National Assembly seats, and 76 mayors (including those of San Salvador, Santa Ana and San Miguel, the three largest cities of the country). During the 1960s other opposition parties were also formed, including the National Revolutionary Movement (MNR), a social democratic party headed by lawyer Guillermo Ungo, which was linked to the Socialist International. In 1971 the PDC and MNR formed a coalition with the National Democratic Union (UDN), a front for the Communist party which (like the CD–Conservative–Independent Liberal coalition formed earlier in Nicaragua) took the name National Opposition Union (UNO).

But electoral fraud prevented the opposition candidate of the UNO, Christian Democrat José Napoleon Duarte, from coming to power in 1972. An aborted uprising following the 1972 elections led to Duarte's imprisonment and subsequent exile. Electoral fraud also prevented opposition candidates from winning in the 1974 parliamentary elections and in the presidential elections of 1977.[24]

Urban and rural workers, slumdwellers, teachers and students also took advantage of the limited political opening of the 1960s, organizing into unions, peasant associations and other organizations. Efforts were made to neutralize growing labour and peasant militance through the establishment of government-controlled unions. AIFLD (American Institute for Free Labor Development), established in 1962 under the auspices of the AFL to promote 'free' trade unionism in Latin America, organized training seminars for Salvadoran peasants and helped to finance the UCS (Salvadoran Communal Union), formed in 1968. Nevertheless, the level of mobilization increased throughout the 1970s as organized groups took part in strikes, factory sit-ins, land invasions, marches and demonstrations.

A new and unexpected ally of the reform movements of the late 1960s and 1970s was found among sectors of the Catholic Church. The Second Vatican Council, called by Pope John XXIII in 1962, had challenged the traditional concerns and hierarchical structure of the Church and urged it to take an active role in the pursuit of social justice. In Latin America this orientation was reinforced at the Conference of Bishops held in Medellín, Colombia in 1968, which called on the Church 'to defend the rights of the oppressed', to foster grassroots organizations, and 'to denounce the unjust action of world powers that works against self-determination of weaker nations.²⁵ The call for an identification with the poor gave a new legitimacy to progressive sectors within the Latin American Church, including foreign missionaries as well as local clergy. One result was the dramatic growth of Christian base communities in Central America (as well as other Latin American countries), particularly in poor *barrios* and rural villages, which combined religious and social concerns and focused on the injustice of economic exploitation. Organized efforts to change conditions of exploitation included land invasions, the incorporation of members of the communities into existing trade unions, peasant associations and neighbourhood organizations in poor urban *barrios* and similar movements. Priests such as José Alas of Suchitoto, El Salvador began to call for agrarian reform; in Nicaragua members of the clergy and ultimately the Church hierarchy openly denounced the corruption and repression of the Somoza regime.²⁶

By the early 1970s, government repression and electoral fraud had become the accepted mode of dealing with the Salvadoran opposition. In 1968 a rural paramilitary force, ORDEN (Organización Democrática Nacionalista) was formed to cooperate with the military and security forces by informing on peasants involved in peasant organization, land invasions, and other 'subversive' activities. Following a 1968 strike by the newly formed teachers' union ANDES (National Association of Salvadoran Teachers), two of its leaders were kidnapped; several days later their mutilated bodies were found. This pattern of 'disappearance', torture, mutilation and death became familiar in the following decade, when death squads such as the White Warriors League and the Mano Blanco, composed in many cases of members of the military and security forces, began to target union and peasant leaders, students, teachers and members of the clergy.

The repression of efforts at peaceful reform in El Salvador had a radicalizing effect and led more and more groups to seek change through revolution. The guerrilla movements in El Salvador had their origins in political parties. In 1969, a group led by Cayetano Carpio broke off from the Communist party and subsequently formed the Farabundo Marti Popular Liberation Forces (FPL) (named after a leader in the 1932 peasant uprising). In 1971 dissidents from the Christian Democratic Party formed the Popular Revolutionary Army (ERP) and in 1975 a split within the ERP led to the formation of the Armed Forces of National Resistance (FARN). At the same time the groups which had organized during the 1960s and the early 1970s united to form heterogeneous mass organizations which by the end of the decade were linked to the guerrilla movements. Through the end of the decade resistance to exploitation and repression took numerous forms – military and non-military, legal and illegal.

Following the victory of the Nicaraguan revolution in July 1979, junior officers in the Salvadoran armed forces carried out a coup and established a civilian–military junta which for many represented the last chance for a peaceful resolution to the Salvadoran crisis. But the blocking of reforms by the upper levels within the military and the continued repression by the military, security forces and death squads led to the resignation of progressive members of the government, many of whom later joined the Democratic Revolutionary Front (FDR) formed in April 1980, which became the political and diplomatic arm of the revolutionary forces (later united as the FMLN, the Farabundo Marti Forces for National Liberation).[27] The facade of a 'centrist' government was maintained through the presence of Christian Democrat, José Napoleon Duarte as leader of the ruling junta (from March to December 1980) and as provisional president (December 1980 – March 1982). But many of the Christian Democrats refused to support the Duarte government, which, despite belated efforts to carry out an agrarian reform and other measures, marked a period of growing conflict and unprecedented violence against the civilian population.

In Guatemala, the 'reformist interlude' was later and of even shorter duration than elsewhere in Central America. With the exception of the presidency of Julio Cesar Mendez Montenegro (1966–70) the government was directly controlled by the military; by 1970 a pattern was established whereby each president was succeeded by his minister of defence. The years 1966–68 and 1970–3, in which thousands were killed, were characterized by waves of violence against civilians previously linked with the Arévalo and Arbenz government, as well as students, union leaders, intellectuals and any others who opposed social injustice. Protests by the Kekchi and Quiche Indians at the takeover of their lands in the Franja Transversal del Norte for land speculation by military officials were brutally repressed.

During the 1970s there was a resurgence of the Guatemalan labour movement, beginning with the 1973 strike by 20,000 teachers whose wages had been frozen for eleven years, followed by strikes of railroad, tobacco and electrical workers in 1974 and the organization of several previously unorganized sectors, including bank employees, municipal workers and university staff. The dismissal of workers in the Coca Cola plant and other factories following the 1976 earthquake led to the formation of CNUS (the National Confederation of Trade-Union Unity), and the next few years were marked by strike activities and growing solidarity among different sectors of the working class. An outstanding example was the mobilization in November 1977, beginning with a march of mineworkers who had been dismissed, from the north west to Guatemala City. En route they were offered food and other forms of support by Quiche and Calchiquel Indians and Ladino peasants, while mineworkers at Oxec and construction workers at hydroelectric plants staged sympathy strikes. Even after the demands of the mineworkers had been met, they continued their march in support of sugar-mill workers then on strike at the Panteleon mill, who were also supported by industrial workers. In all, 100,000 people – workers and peasants, Indians and Ladinos – were mobilized.

The collaboration of Indian and Ladino peasants from different economic sectors was also a feature of the revolutionary movements which emerged or resurfaced in the 1970s. Both the Guerrilla Army of the Poor (EGP) and the Organization of the People in Arms (ORPA) were concentrated in the highland communities and had strong support among the peasantry. The Rebel Armed Forces (FAR), a descendant of one of the guerrilla movements of the 1960s which resurfaced in

1978, and the Guatemalan Labour Party (PGT), the traditional Communist Party, were strong in the labour movement. In 1982 the four guerrilla organizations united in the URNG (Guatemalan National Revolutionary Unity).

The 1979 victory of the Sandinistas and the growth of the revolutionary movements of El Salvador and Guatemala raised hopes that the oppressed majorities of these countries would at last liberate themselves from centuries of exploitation and repression. But the path of revolution has not been smooth. In addition to numerous military set-backs and the imprisonment or death of many of its leaders, the FSLN in Nicaragua experienced a split in its own ranks, as well as contradictions in its broader alliance with other population groups including sectors of the bourgeoisie and the Church hierarchy. The 1974 split divided the FSLN into three tendencies: those who visualized the revolution as a long-term process of organization and education with particular emphasis on the peasantry and rural workers, who constituted the largest population group (i.e. the prolonged people's war tendency, partly drawn from the Vietnam experience), those who advocated a greater concentration on the urban sectors and particularly the urban proletariat (the proletarian tendency) and the *tercistas*, who pushed for broad alliances with other anti-Somoza factions and for a broadly based popular insurrection against Somoza. The three tendencies were not necessarily mutually exclusive, and were reunited in 1978. The contradictions within the broader alliance with the bourgeoisie, however, have intensified since the 1979 Sandinista victory. This has resulted in an increasing polarization between the Sandinistas and their supporters, on the one hand, for whom the defeat of Somoza and the National Guard is but a first step toward a radical restructuring of society in the interests of the formerly excluded majority, and bourgeois factions and their followers on the other, who had opposed Somoza but not the existing economic order and resented their loss of political control to the Sandinistas; many of these have now joined, or provide support to, the armed counter-revolutionary forces (*contras*).

In El Salvador efforts at unity among the different guerrilla organizations have been frustrated by differences over such issues as the possibility and terms of negotiation with the Salvadoran government, and internal conflicts among factions have on two occasions had tragic results: the assassination of Salvadoran poet Raque Dalton by a militarist faction of the ERP in 1975 (which led to a split and the formation of the FARN), and the assassination of Melida Anaya Montes, second in command of the FPL, followed by the suicide of FPL leader, Cayetano Carpio, in 1983.

In both Guatemala and El Salvador, the assassination by security forces and death squads of opposition political party leaders, union militants, peasant organizers, professors and priests, teachers and students has accelerated in the late 1970s and 1980s with two purposes: to destroy the political centre and thus eliminate any option except the leftish guerrillas and the right wing, and to destroy the political base of the guerrilla forces. This latter includes military efforts to eliminate the guerrillas' rural bases in both countries, a goal which has been pursued with unprecendented savagery in the Indian highlands of Guatemala, entailing the murder of thousands and the flight of hundreds of thousands into refugee camps in Mexico. In the case of El Salvador, an estimated 50,000 persons have been killed since the 1979 coup, and it is estimated that one million – 20 per cent of the population – are internal refugees in El Salvador, in refugee camps in Honduras and other neighbouring countries, or have migrated to the United States. In Guatemala, the result has been a temporary set-back to the forces of the URNG. In El Salvador, the FMLN is strong militarily but its political infrastructure has been weakened by the assassination or imprisonment of urban-sector leaders.

In spite of contradictions, internal conflicts and persecution, the achievements of the revolutions in Central America have already been remarkable. In the five years following the victory over Somoza, the lives of the majority of Nicaraguans are being transformed through literacy, education and health programmes, agrarian reform and new forms of political involvement. Behind the FMLN lines in El Salvador, a rudimentary prototype of a revolutionary society is emerging. In Guatemala, traditional barriers between the Indian majority and other oppressed sectors have been broken down, and the cultural integrity of Guatemala's Indians has been incorporated as a principle of the revolution.

Today the major threat to the revolutionary movements of Central America is not internal but external – the resurgence of the Cold War as the dominant perspective of US policy makers and the threat of direct US military involvement in Central American conflicts.

The Neo-Conservative Project for Central America: A Return to US Hegemony?

The Reagan offensive

The Vietnam experience and the 'economic shocks' which signaled the erosion of US hegemony in the late 1960s and early 1970s also initiated the decline of liberalism as the prevailing ideology of the Democratic Party and to a large extent of the American post-war consensus. The economic contradictions eroded the economy base of the welfare-warfare state, which was no longer able to respond to the needs and demands of a broad range of domestic groups. The Democrats were also deeply implicated in the Vietnam war and thus in the moral crisis resulting from US involvement as well as the crisis of confidence resulting from the US defeat. The right was able to take advantage of the moral vacuum resulting from the decline of liberalism, and the election of Reagan brought to power what had previously been a fringe element of the political establishment. Right-wing interests of the west and south are allied around a new ideological pole which skilfully blends justifications for the privileges of a minority with new-right populist appeals to groups victimized by the economic recession.[28]

The foreign policy consensus which had characterized both Republican and Democratic administrations during the Cold War had also broken down as a result of the Vietnam experience. During the 1970s US policymakers and corporate executives, in conjunction with their counterparts in Western Europe and Japan, sought to design a new consensus for an era of declining US hegemony through détente with the Soviet Union and a new emphasis on north–south relations. The Carter election in 1976 brought several trilateralists into prominent positions in government.[29] But the contradiction inherent in trilateralism became evident toward the end of the Carter administration: the militaristic, geostrategic policies or trilateralist Zbigniew Brzezinski, as National Security Adviser, began to take precedence over the policies of accommodation, negotiation and détente advocated by trilateralist Cyrus Vance as Secretary of State.

The foreign policy shift under Carter and the introduction of the neo-conservative model under Reagan were reflected in the change in US policy on Central America. This policy can be explained in terms of conflicts and adjustments among three positions:

1. The confrontationist views the revolutionary movements of Central America as an extension of the global struggle with the Soviet Union and focuses on support for military efforts of right-wing, pro-US regimes to defeat them.
2. The liberal interventionist to a large extent shares the policy goals of the confrontationist but prefers economic and diplomatic pressures to military intervention and seeks a 'centrist' alternative to right-wing regimes and leftist revolutionaries.
3. The neo-realist advocates a more flexible response to Third World revolutions, and specifically those of Central America, as the only alternative to right-wing dictatorships, at the same time advocating restrictions on revolutionary governments in power, including limitations on their relations with socialist-bloc countries.[30]

The confrontationist and liberal interventionist positions have clear affinities with policy positions of the past; the confrontationist perspective was dominant in the case of the 1954 coup in Guatemala, while the liberal interventionist approach was evident in the Alliance for Progress. The neo-realist position is relatively recent and became important only in the Carter administration, which was characterized by conflicts between the liberal interventionist and neo-realist tendencies with the former clearly dominant in the last months.

The contradictions between these tendencies were evident in Carter's policies toward the revolutionary movements in Central America. Having failed in its efforts to prevent the Sandinistas from coming to power in Nicaragua (e.g. through a last-minute proposal to send an Organization of American States (OAS) peace-keeping force to Nicaragua prior to the fall of Somoza, which was rejected), the Carter administration sought to control the revolution through economic aid (important not in terms of amount but as a signal to banks and multi-lateral lending agencies) and cultivating factions of the bourgeoisie whose uneasy alliance with the Sandinistas was rapidly disintegrating in the year following the fall of Somoza. In El Salvador, the United States sought to neutralize the revolutionary movement by supporting the reformist civilian–military junta which came to power through a military coup in October 1979, and continued to support it long after it had been abandoned by progressive elements, many of whom declared their support for the revolution as the only means to reform in El Salvador. Thus, in both Nicaragua and El Salvador, the policy of the Carter administration was characterized by a search for a 'centrist' alternative to revolution as an answer to repressive right-wing regimes. The failure of the centrist alternative in Nicaragua led to a compromise between the liberal interventionist and neo-realist approaches, while the liberal interventionist position prevailed for El Salvador.

The confrontationist position became dominant with the Reagan administration. Convinced that the challenges to US hegemony reflected nothing more than a loss of will on the part of US policymakers, the Reagan administration determined

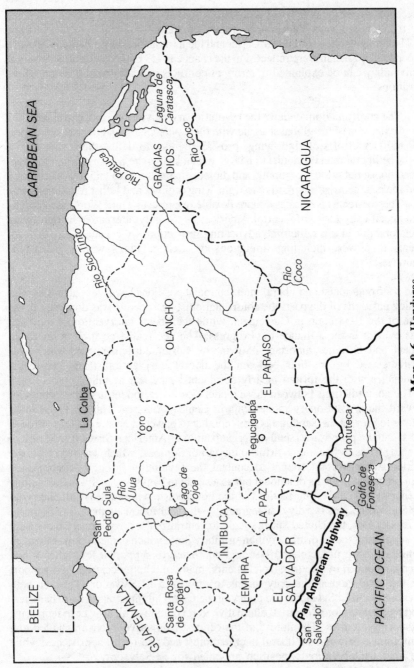

Map 9.6 Honduras

to 'draw the line' in El Salvador and subsequently to 'roll back' the revolution in Nicaragua, which was accused of shipping arms to the Salvadoran guerillas.[31] His chief ideologue for Latin America, US Ambassador to the United Nations, Jeane Kirkpatrick, justified support for 'authoritarian' Central American regimes allied to the United States on the grounds that they were preferable to 'totalitarian' regimes which would be the inevitable result of victory by the revolutionary forces.[32] El Salvador and Nicaragua, and by implication Guatemala, were the battleground for confrontation between the east and west. The endorsement of a military option in Central America is the extension of the Reagan administration's militaristic policy elsewhere and the logical consequence of its interpretation of US loss of control.

However, 'rolling back' the revolutionary process was not so easy as administration policymakers initially assumed. The resilience of the FMLN, the continued popularity of the Sandinistas, opposition by Latin American and European governments to the militarization of Central America, and the growing opposition to US policy within the United States itself led the administration to pursue a dual policy: on the one hand, the continued pursuit of military victory over the revolutionary forces in El Salvador and Guatemala and the destabilization and/or overthrow of the Sandinista government in Nicaragua, and on the other an intense propaganda effort directed at liberal congressional critics and the American public.

In the four years of the first Reagan administration neo-realists and many of the liberal interventionists in the State Department were replaced, neutralized or transformed. Between 1980 and 1984 US military aid to El Salvador increased from $6 million to nearly $200 million (not including economic support funds, which cannot be used for weapons but are often used for military-related purposes). Aid to Honduras, which was slated for the role of US proxy in the region, has increased to $77 million. Beginning in December 1981, the CIA has financed and trained an army of Nicaraguan exiles, including former members of Somoza's National Guard, who attack Nicaragua from camps in Honduras in an effort to overthrow the revolutionary government. The CIA has participated in bombing raids against fuel storage tanks and other strategic economic targets in Nicaragua as well as the mining of Nicaragua's harbours. Honduras has been completely militarized, with at least six new military air bases and several more projected. There are 1,700 to 3,000 permanent US forces in Honduras, plus up to 30,000 additional combat-ready US troops in the region during frequent military manoeuvres. In April 1984 US Pentagon officials announced that the United States was now in a position to take on a combat role in Central America.[33]

The cost of Reagan's military policy is extremely high for the people of the region: thousands killed, wounded and mutilated by the CIA-financed *contra* forces in Nicaragua, an estimated 50,000 civilians dead in El Salvador and Honduras transformed into a vast military camp. Despite these horrific figures Reagan is not winning the war in Central America. The *contras* have failed to establish a foothold in Nicaragua, and the Nicaraguans have responded to the US offensive by building up their defence system, increasing the number within the armed forces and mobilizing the population through an expansion of the militia. After four years of escalating US military aid to the Salvadoran armed forces, the FMLN appears stronger and more unified than ever, not only maintaining its control in liberated zones but capable of inflicting serious losses on the government forces and of shifting its tactics in response to changes in those of the Salvadoran army. The inability of the Reagan Administration to achieve its goals in Central America through military aid increases the likelihood of more direct US military intervention.

The constraints on Reagan's militaristic policy in Central America have diminished in the past four years. During the early 1980s the renewed European interest in Latin America and the growing economic and political importance of the largest Latin American countries led to efforts by several Latin American and European governments to promote an alternative perspective on the Central American crisis as a basis for a negotiated solution. Among these was the French--Mexican resolution of August 1981 recognizing the Salvadoran FDR; the Mexican–Venezuelan proposal for negotiations between Nicaragua and Honduras; and the formation of the Contadora group (composed of the foreign ministers of Mexico, Venezuela, Colombia and Panama) in January 1983, which has been dedicated since then to establishing a basis for negotiations among the five Central American countries. Nicaragua also received substantial aid from the European countries; as of spring 1982 the amount of aid from Western Europe surpassed the amount from the Soviet Union, Eastern Europe and Cuba combined.

But Reagan has clearly signaled his disregard for international opinion; and the European governments, while still indicating their disapproval of Reagan's Central American policy, have partly withdrawn from involvement in Central America, to some extent as a consequence of the shift from a Social Democratic to a Christian Democratic government in West Germany, which is more closely aligned to the US foreign policy position. European governments share a general unwillingness to seriously challenge US policy in an area that is not of primary interest to Europe. The Contadora countries have continued their efforts on behalf of regional peace and negotiations, but the Latin American countries are in a weakened position in relation to the US due to their debt problems and their desperate need for foreign exchange. The Reagan administration has given lip service to the Contadora process but has disregarded it in practice. This was most blatant in the rejection of a proposed Contadora treaty in the autumn of 1984 after it had been endorsed by several European governments and signed by the Nicaraguans.

Major constraints upon the Reagan administration have been US public opinion and Congress. These have been the target of Reagan administration propaganda efforts to erase the Vietnam syndrome and to reorient the focus of the Central American debate to issues of national security. The goal is to convince the American public and Congress of the dangers of communist penetration in Central American with particular emphasis on depicting the Nicaraguan government as totalitarian and as a willing partner in Soviet and Cuban subversion of the region. The Kissinger Commission, formed by President Reagan in 1983, represented an effort to re-establish a bipartisan consensus on US policy in Central America. In January 1984 it issued a lengthy report providing a rationale for a continuation of current policy and an escalation of US military aid, which the Administration subsequently used to secure increases in the Central American aid package.

The promotion of a democratic facade in El Salvador through elections has also been geared to US public consumption as well as to the liberal interventionist tendency in Congress. The victory of Christian Democrat José Napoleon Duarte in the 1984 presidential election in El Salvador (apparently with CIA support) had the desired effect of reassuring Congressional critics in the United States, who responded with a $70 million increase in US aid to El Salvador. The July 1984 elections in Guatemala for a constituent assembly and the presidential elections of 1985 have been used to justify a resumption of military aid to that country. The skills of the Reagan administration in manipulating public opinion were graphically demonstrated when the United States invaded Grenada in October 1983. Widely condemned in the rest of the world, the Grenada invasion was a propaganda coup in the United States, providing the American public with a quick, easy military success which restored US confidence in itself as a military power and weakened resistance to military intervention elsewhere.

Although the Reagan administration has not yet achieved a bipartisan consensus on Central America, its ideological offensive has benefited from the disarray among the liberals in the Democratic Party. Caught between their fears of being labeled pro-communist and their unwillingness to support either left-wing revolution or right-wing repression in Central America, the liberals have been unable to come up with an alternative policy and are reduced to responding to the Reagan initiatives on an *ad hoc* basis. This dilemma is reflected in the inconsistencies and vacillations evident in Congressional voting on Central America. By the 1984 election campaign, the Reagan administration had to a large extent succeeeded in its efforts to shift the terms of the debate on Central America to issues of national security and anti-communism.[34] While the American public would still oppose a commitment of US troops to Central America, the reinforcement of the ideological realignment, evident in the 1980 elections, over the subsequent four years suggests increasing receptiveness to the Reagan administration's policy goals in Central America.

The anti-intervention movement

Central America has become an important focus of activity by left and progressive groups in the United States, in part due to identification with the revolutionary movements of Central America and in part because US policy in the region is seen as closely linked to other major issues, both foreign and domestic. Support for the revolutionary movements is centred in the solidarity organizations, of which the Committee in Solidarity with the People of El Salvador (CISPES) is the largest, with some 400 chapters around the country. As the militarization of the region proceeds and US military involvement accelerates, however, activities of solidarity groups as well as other organizations have focused increasingly on non-intervention. These activities include efforts to educate both the general public and targeted groups on Central America and US policy through talks, panels, demonstrations, teach-ins, media events and other activities, and for some groups through extensive lobbying of Congress. An important element of non-intervention movements has been efforts to build coalitions among progressive sectors, including peace activists, church organizations, women's groups, human rights and civil rights advocates, and to some extent labour and minority groups, around alternatives to current US policy in the region. This is linked to other elements of the neo-conservative programmes such as the military build-up and social services cuts.

Despite Reagan administration efforts to 'bury' the Vietnam syndrome, it has been an important impetus to organization against US policy in Central America, and many of the current activists are in fact 'veterans' of the Vietnam anti-war movement. Partly as a result of the Vietnam experience, the level of organization and mobilization around Central America is much higher than at a similar stage of the Vietnam war.

At the same time, mobilization around Central America differs from the Vietnam anti-war movement in several important respects. On the one hand, participation by college and university students is low compared to the Vietnam years, reflecting the fact that the draft has not become an issue in the case of Central America and reflecting as well the growing conservatism of college youth. This conservatism is in turn a function of the closing of economic opportunities and of the rightward ideological shift. On the other hand, the Central American movement has been distinguished by the early and intense involvement of church organizations, to some extent influenced by their counterparts in Central America.

A third distinction has been the close and continuing contact with Central Americans themselves. The large number of refugees fleeing repressive and chaotic conditions in Central America have brought the war home to the United States in a distinct manner that was impossible during the Vietnam war. By 1984 an estimated 500,000 Salvadorans had gone to the United States (over 10 per cent of the Salvadoran population). Estimates of the number of Salvadorans in southern California range from 200,000 to over 350,000; there are probably at least 100,000 Guatemalans in the area, including 4,000 Konjabal Indians from a highland village in western Guatemala. For the most part without documents they find work in proliferating low-wage service jobs: as maids or gardeners in middle- and upper-class neighbourhoods, as bus boys or dishwashers in restaurants, as janitors or cleaning personnel in institutional buildings or as workers in garment factories. In constant danger of being picked up by the INS (Immigration and Naturalization Service) and deported back to an uncertain future in their home countries, they have become the focus of a range of activities such as demonstrations and lobbying against airlines which assist in deportation (resulting in the decision of three airlines to cease deportation of Salvadorans from Los Angeles), legal counselling for refugees seeking asylum and other services, lobbying for congressional action to enforce legislation on asylum and refugee status; and the Sanctuary movement, whereby church congregations and other groups provide asylum and transportation for aliens without documents.

The proximity of Central America and the increasing presence of Central Americans in the United States has also facilitated communication between the revolutionary movements in Central America and the solidarity groups in the United States. US-based representatives of the FDR-FMLN participate in events in the United States, as do Sandinista officials and representatives of the revolutionary movement in Guatemala. US tours by priests, nuns, labour activists, medical personnel, university professors, artists, professionals and students from Central America provide a constant source of information and analysis. Thousands of North Americans have travelled to Central America in delegations sponsored by church, human rights, educational and other organizations. This interaction has vitalized the US movement and raised the level of consciousness and awareness of the struggles in Central America in a way which was not possible in the case of Vietnam.

One form of interaction between Central Americans and the United States has been collaborative efforts of scholars. In 1982 several US and Central American academics and policy analysts formed PACCA (Policy Alternatives for the

Caribbean and Central America) to carry out research which would be relevant for activists concerned about Central America. Its first effort responded to the need to do more than oppose Reagan administration policy, by proposing an alternative policy on the Caribbean and Central America. This was intended to go beyond the neo-realist approach and to initiate a constructive dialogue on policy alternatives among activist groups, policymakers and other interested and concerned individuals and groups. Beginning with a critique of existing policy and an historical overview of US–Central American relations, the PACCA proposal (*Changing Course: Blueprint for Peace in Central America*) establishes a framework for a progressive policy toward Central America, including a positive response to the revolutionary movements in the region and taking into account both the 'legitimate interests' of the United States and those of the Central American countries.[35] In assuming compatibility between US interests and Central American revolutions, the PACCA report has been accused by leftist critics of failing to carry its analysis to its logical conclusion. This illustrates a dilemma of left activists in the non-intervention movement: while their analysis indicates that US policy in Central America is rooted in the system of imperialist hegemony (in turn a function of US capitalism) which must be fundamentally restructured if that policy is to change, the urgency of the need to mobilize large sectors of the population around a non-intervention position has led to an emphasis on pragmatic, short-term goals. In the case of the PACCA report, its purpose was to present a rational alternative to existing militarism in Central America which can appeal to a broad range of population groups in the United States and at the same time be more progressive than previous policy conceptions. In this it has largely succeeded: the *Blueprint* was endorsed by a large number of church, academic, peace and human rights activists and has been widely distributed among grassroots groups throughout the country. It became the basis of Jesse Jackson's primary campaign position on Central America and was circulated among delegates to the Democratic party convention and partly incorporated into the Democratic Party platform position on Central America. The PACCA *Blueprint* has also become an important tool for lobbying Congress by church and other activist organizations.

PACCA has also worked with scholars from Central America, Latin America and Europe in efforts to outline economic alternatives for the Central American and Caribbean region, and is sponsoring a conference on transition to socialism in small, peripheral societies. PACCA also sees its role as providing analysis which will link domestic and foreign policy issues, a concern which will be addressed in an upcoming project on the domestic roots of foreign policy.

Differences among left activists regarding the validity of working with established political institutions, including Congress, the Democratic Party and the electoral process surfaced during the 1984 presidential campaign. In the Democratic Party primaries Jesse Jackson became a forceful spokesperson for many of the domestic and foreign policy positions of concern to leftists, including Central America, and thus a catalyst for uniting a broad range of groups around a left alternative to both the Republicans and mainstream Democrats. Groups on the left disagreed regarding the nature of the 'rainbow coalition', some seeing it as a relatively durable alliance that could be institutionalized beyond the elections, others regarding it as a tool for the political ambitions of Jackson, organized from the top and lacking a grassroots base to give it any continuity.[37] Despite these criticisms, the Jackson campaign was significant in articulating a progressive position and in its ability to mobilize the vote of blacks and other minority groups.

With the selection of Mondale as the Democratic Party nominee, the issue became whether to support the Democrats at all. Those opposed pointed to the continuity in US foreign policy between Democratic and Republican administrations, the record of Mondale himself as a Cold War liberal, and the assumption that the best that could be hoped for under a Mondale administration would be an attempted reconstitution of the liberal welfare–warfare state. Others supported the Democrats on the grounds that Reagan represented not a continuation of previous policy but a confirmation of a radical realignment toward the extreme right. Thus a restoration of the liberal project under Mondale was preferable to the continued assault on the working class, minorities and other domestic groups, as well as a dangerous swerve to the right in foreign policy, which could be anticipated under Reagan. Central American activists also assumed that a Mondale government would at least provide an environment in which it would be possible to work for more progressive policies on Central America. Efforts of left activists centred on registering new voters, particularly among minorities, unemployed and other disadvantaged groups who are the chief victims of the right-wing assault on domestic social programmes. The effectiveness of the registration drive was undermined by Mondale's campaign strategy of attempting to draw voters from the Reagan camp rather than appealing to potential new voters, and while it is not clear that anyone could have stopped Reagan, Mondale's unimaginative campaign was undoubtedly a factor in Reagan's sweeping victory.

Reagan's Second Term

The direction of the Administration's policies for the next four years was evident in the proposed 1986 budget – a bloated $974 billion with a projected deficit of $180 billion – which includes a $29 billion increase in defence expenditures (to $277 billion) and a cut of $39 billion in domestic programmes, including cutbacks or freezes on Medicare payments, student loans, public transportation and several programmes aimed at low income groups.[38]

With respect to Central America, the Administration lost no time in fanning the flames of counter-revolution. A calculated 'leak' to the press on the night of the election that Soviet MIGS *might* be on their way to Nicaragua led to several days of agitated speculation in the press and media on the necessity and form of US retaliation, should Nicargua indeed accept MIGS from the Soviet Union. The rumour, of course, proved false, but not before the American public had been given one more 'justification' for the Administration's hard line against Nicaragua. Central America activists fear that Reagan's 1984 victory has lessened any existing constraints on his policy for the region. Reagan is pushing for a resumption of aid to the *contras* in Nicaragua, and has asked for large increases in military aid to El Salvador and Honduras as well as $35 million in military aid to Guatemala.

In January 1985 the government launched a surprise attack against the Sanctuary movement, indicting 16 Sanctuary activists in Tuscon, Arizona, for planning and implementing the 'smuggling' of Central American refugees into the United States, charges that could bring five years in prison and fines of up to $10,000. Although

Sanctuary workers in Texas had been previously indicted on charges of transporting refugees, the numbers indicted in the present case, the detention of 50 refugees to appear as witnesses against the Sanctuary activists, and the revelation that government agents had infiltrated the movement, using secret recording devices to obtain information, reinforced fears that the second Reagan administration would mean a concerted attack on organizations and activists involved in Central American work. For the moment, however, the indictments have failed to deter the Sanctuary movement: over a thousand Sanctuary workers and supporters attended a previously scheduled conference in Tuscon the following week, well over the few hundred anticipated prior to the indictment; Sanctuary workers have pledged to continue their activities and report that the number of volunteers has increased substantially since the indictment.

Despite a generalized depression caused by four more years of Reagan, there are further indications of sustained and increased resistance by left and progressive groups to the current direction of US politics, including policies toward Central America. Church and solidarity activists have collected over 40,000 signatures to pledges to engage in or support civil disobedience should the United States invade Nicaragua or escalate military intervention in Central America. The number, cohesiveness and extent of support for organizations devoted to work concerning Central America increased substantially in the four years of the first Reagan administration. While the population at large is uninformed or misinformed regarding Central America and thus easily manipulable by a popular president, the education and efforts of Central America activists have raised the level of awareness and commitment of significant sectors of the US public. So too has the recent public exposure of Reagan's secret funding of the Contra rebels. The remaining years of the Reagan administration will be critical for both the military struggle in Central America and the ideological struggle in the United States.

Notes

1 Wolf Grabendorf, 'Latin America and Western Europe: Towards a New International System', in *The European Challenge: Europe's New Role in Latin America* (London, Latin American Bureau, 1982), p. 51.

2 Ibid., p. 54.

3 Panama, which was a province of Colombia until 1903, has had a somewhat different historical trajectory from the five countries mentioned, as has Belize, which was controlled by Britain and became independent only recently.

4 Ralph Lee Woodward, *Central America: A Nation Divided* (New York, Oxford University Press, 1976), pp. 93–4.

5 Walter La Feber, *Inevitable Revolutions: The United States in Central America* (New York, W. W. Norton & Company, 1984).

6 Woodward, *Central America*, pp. 134–44.

7 Most of the following material is from Cardoso Santana, 'Historia Economica del cafe en Centroamerica (Siglo XIX): Estudios Comparativo', *Estudio Sociales Centroamericanos* IV, 10 (1975).

8 La Feber, *Inevitable Revolutions*, p. 70.

9 This was particularly true of Honduras, which contracted four British loans between 1867 and 1870 amounting to £6 million. By 1916 Honduras had only 50 miles of track

and an accumulated debt of $125 million. See Steven Volk, 'Honduras: On the Border of War', *NACLA Report on the Americas* XV, 6 (November–December, 1981).

10 Quoted in William Appleman Williams, *The Tragedy of American Diplomacy* (New York, Dell Publishing Company, 1959).

11 See Edelberto Torres Rivas, 'Poder nacional y Sociedad dependiente. Notas sobre las clases y el Estado en Centroamerica', in Rafael Menjvar (ed.), *La Invastion Extianjera en Centroamerica*, (San Jose, Costa Rica, EDUCA, 1974); and Woodward, *Central America*, p. 182.

12 Rivas, 'Poder nacional y Sociedad dependiente', p. 265.

13 Woodward, *Central America*, pp. 193–4.

14 Stephen Schlesinger and Stephen Kinser, *Bitter Fruit: The Untold Story of the American Coup in Guatemala* (Garden City, New York, Anchor Books, 1983).

15 Ibid. and also George Black et al., 'Garrison Guatemala', *NACLA Report on the Americas* XVII, 1 (January–February 1983); see also G. Black et al., 'Guatemala: The War is not Over', *NACLA Report on the Americas* XVII, 1 (March–April 1983).

16 Much of what follows is based on Norma Chincilla and Nora Hamilton, 'Prelude to Revolution: US Investment in Central America', in R. Burbach and P. Flynn (eds), *The Politics of Intervention: The United States in Central America* (New York, Monthly Review Press, 1984).

17 George Black, *Triumph of the People: The Sandinista Revolution in Nicaragua* (London, Zed Press, 1981).

18 Black, 'Garrison Guatemala', pp. 11–16.

19 Jenny Pearce, *Under the Eagle: US Intervention in Central America and the Caribbean* (London, Latin American Bureau, 1981).

20 Black, 'Garrison Guatemala', p. 17.

21 Black, 'The War is not Over', p. 6.

22 Schlesinger and Kinser, *Bitter Fruit*.

23 Black, *Triumph of the People*, pp. 75–82.

24 Tommie Sue Montgomery, *Revolution in El Salvador* (Boulder, Colorado, Westwood Press, 1982).

25 Michael Dodson and Tommie Sue Montgomery, 'The Churches in the Nicarguan Revolution', in Thomas W. Walker (ed.) *Nicaragua in Revolution* (New York, Praeger, 1982), p. 164.

26 Philip Berryman, *The Religious Roots of Rebellion* (Maryknoll, New York, Orbis Books, 1984).

27 Montgomery, *Revolution in El Salvador*.

28 Robert Armstrong, 'Are the Democrats Really Different?', *NACLA Report on the Americas* XVIII, 5, (September–October 1984); and Roger Burbach 'US Policy: Crisis and Conflict', in Burbach and Flynn, *The Politics of Intervention*.

29 For a discussion of Trilateralism see chapter 5.

30 Burbach, 'US Policy'; and Richard E. Feinberg, *The Intemporate Zone: The Third World Challenge to US Foreign Policy* (New York, W. W. Norton & Company, 1983).

31 Among many see, William Leo Grande, 'The Revolution in Nicaragua: Another Cuba?' *Foreign Affairs* 58, 1 (Fall 1979), and Feinbereg, *The Intemporate Zone*, p. 16.

32 Jeanne Kirkpatrick, 'Dictatorships and Double Standards' *Commentary* 68, 5 (November 1979), pp. 34–45.

33 Hedrick Smith, 'US Latin Forces in Place if Needed, Official Report', *New York Times*, 23 April 1984.

34 William Bollinger, 'Central America, National Security and the 1984 US Elections', Occasional Papers Series, no. 6, (Los Angeles, Interamerican Research Center, November 16 1984).

35 PACCA, *Changing Course: Blueprint for Peace in Central America and the Caribbean* (Washington, Institute for Policy Studies, 1984).

36 Kim Moody, 'Is there a Peaceful Alternative to Imperialism?', *Changes*, January–February 1985.
37 Armstrong, 'Are the Democrats Really Different?', and Anthony Thigpin 'Jesse Jackson and the Black Movement', *Against the Current* 3, 1 (Fall 1984).
38 Tom Redburn, 'Reagan Budget to Ask $974 Billion', *Los Angeles Times*, (2 February 1985).

10

Southern Africa
The Struggle Ahead

RAY BUSH and LIONEL CLIFFE

Southern Africa has been a 'cause' for the left for over 25 years: since the first
boycott campaigns, the massacre at Sharpeville, and South Africa's withdrawal
from the Commonwealth. During a quiescent period inside South Africa in the
late 1960s and 1970s, liberation struggles in Mozambique and Angola then later
in Zimbabwe captured radical imaginations – although they did not always command much effective solidarity. Today, questions of who and what to support
in South Africa itself are again dramatically posed, and it is instructive to remember
past mistakes on the left: the fact that some groups gave support to Jonas Savimbi's
UNITA (Union for the Total Independence of Angola), so clearly shown now
as a South African puppet; the fact that, unable to agree who the 'good guys'
were, there was no effective solidarity in the west for the courageous struggle
of the people of Zimbabwe.

As we write, trying to stay ahead of a rapidly changing scene, not only is South
Africa clearly centre stage, but it has undoubtedly reached a turning point. Pressure
has steadily mounted since the widespread strikes of the early 1970s and the Soweto
uprising of 1976. The apartheid regime is now assailed by a similar but higher
stage of resistance, through protests, school and consumer boycotts, since 1984,
as well as the mushrooming black trade-union movement and its considerable
militancy. New, open, mass political organizations have emerged and liberation
movements wait in the wings and underground. Increased repression and censorship following the State of Emergency declared in June 1985 have not deterred
this resistance. Not coincidentally, the apartheid society is also facing a long,
belated economic crisis, and the regime finds itself under pressure even from
those circles – right-wing English-speaking governments and international
investors – from whom it has been used to receiving sustenance.

So we are now beginning to witness the death throes of apartheid. To be sure,
it may be long-drawn, but even State President P. W. Botha has now belatedly
acknowledged in his speech opening Parliament early in 1986, that apartheid in
its present form cannot be maintained. Some of its main elements – the pass laws
which control movement of Africans; the myth that urban blacks are citizens of
other countries, the Bantustans – are being removed and some vague promise
is held out for political representation of Africans. These measures show that

the reform strategy of 1984 is now acknowledged as non-viable – attempts to divide the blacks by giving some political representation to Asians and Coloureds but not Africans, and by giving residence rights and improved living conditions to black middle-class and skilled workers but not to the unskilled, the migrants and those dumped in the homelands. Whether the new measures represent an alternative that the regime can make stick, and indeed whether they do constitute a meaningful dismantling of apartheid, remain doubtful – but these vital questions posed by the present events need to be clarified.

They in turn prompt further questions: if there are to be further policy changes beyond what the regime seems to be promising (and there must be, for not even the western bankers are satisfied with this current package), what further changes in the political and socio-economic terrain will be offered to the black majority? And as a result of what pressures from within ruling circles and the dominant white community inside South Africa and from outside will these changes be offered? This latter question is the more crucial to ask now that establishment groups in the west have stolen a little of the left's clothes, now that the US Congress and all western governments except the British are calling for some sanctions. In these circumstances, when at least the *ideology* of apartheid is no longer officially proclaimed and the South African regime is even saying it was 'colonial' and 'paternal' and has to be ended, campaigns that have been based on a slogan of 'anti-apartheid' must reassess their stance if they are not to be out-flanked.

Another issue, now very much a question for solidarity movements, concerns the southern Africa region as a whole. Reagan is announcing sanctions of a limited sort against South Africa. At the same time he is flushed with success at interfering in Grenada and Nicaragua. He proselytizes a gospel of backing 'freedom fighters' in Central America. He receives the arch-puppet Jonas Savimbi of the South African-backed Angolan dissident movement, UNITA, in Washington and seeks funds for military intervention in Angola. In Botha's speech offering concessions and a dialogue to blacks in South Africa, the South African president reiterates his threats against the surrounding countries if they don't sign 'non-aggression pacts' with him. And to underline his government's intention to dominate the region as a pre-condition for any internal 'dialogue', he was able in 1986 to put such a stranglehold on Lesotho as to induce a coup which installed a government even more slavishly subordinate than the one in place. It is clear, therefore, that whatever further upheavals occur in South Africa, and they are likely to be intense and long-drawn-out, they will have massive impact on the surrounding countries. South Africa's neighbours will undoubtedly take the stick for any imposed sanctions as they have done for the internal challenge to apartheid. Their economic and political subordination to South Africa and the end to any 'socialist pretensions' may well be pre-conditions for the kind of 'solution' that South African and western ruling groups would like to concoct inside South Africa. At the same time, the outcome of the internal struggle in South Africa may well determine new possibilities for the further development and transformation of all the societies of southern Africa. Why the South African crisis has such serious overspill effects and what they might be, and how these regional dimensions need to be kept in mind in solidarity efforts, will all be major concerns of this chapter.

As southern Africa explodes, the reverberations may well be felt even further afield. These events will hold the key to much that will happen in the whole of

Africa south of the Sahara. There is a further danger that the conflicts may amplify, and in turn be amplified, by east–west conflicts, particularly with a United States administration that sees events in simplistic Cold War terms – an acute danger, given South Africa's nuclear capability, of a frightening escalation of these conflicts. For the corporations and national economies of most advanced capitalist countries, any changes that denied them access to South African raw materials and shipping lanes, or to the highly profitable investment opportunities in that region, would be marginally upsetting. But for some sectors of British capital, given the high level of investment and history of superprofits, the effect would be very considerable. The left in the United Kingdom is thus required to shoulder a more considerable burden of solidarity: of trying to minimize the die-hard resistance of British capital and the Thatcher government to meaningful change in southern Africa. The British left must also seek to understand the likely implications of changes that may occur in the British economy, and the effects of these on political options in Britain. That is in turn part of a broader international responsibility: to reduce at least by some small degree the price the upholders of apartheid will exact from the people of the region before they concede.

In order to come to grips with this situation it is necessary to understand South Africa, the broader region with which it interacts and the region's interplay, through an interlocking set of systems, with advanced capitalist societies. South Africa boasts that it is an outpost of western civilization – to what extent is there truth in that? It is clearly a capitalist society: western capital has an enormous stake there; it is in practice integrated into NATO networks; indeed there has always been an 'imperial factor' at work there. But that is not the whole truth. South Africa has the power, as a heavily militarized state and a powerful economy, to dominate the southern African region and to do so in terms of its own calculations, not necessarily at western bidding. Conflicts between South Africa and western interests do in fact arise. We shall thus trace the main dimensions of the international setting of southern Africa, and the position of South Africa within that region.

It is, however, with the internal system of apartheid that we shall begin our analysis. And in order to understand not only how it works but also the enormous cleavages that are rending it apart, plus the alternatives to it, we have to ask: what kind of beast is it? As we shall see, this last question has raised arguments. In particular there has been a body of opinion (of all ideological hues) that has stressed its racist character, seeing this mainly as an ideological factor that operates 'irrationally' from an economic point of view – a racism that is destined to fade away as capitalist industry develops and imposes its own logic. A contrary view that has gained weight in recent years sees apartheid as essentially a form of 'racial capitalism' that operates to generate a black section of the workforce that can be super-exploited – a perspective that sees the need for structural change and not just changes of attitude, but that also raises the prospect that in the process of uprooting apartheid an alternative to capitalism is on the agenda. We need to come to some conclusion about the relation between apartheid and capitalism to establish a starting point for discussing the future prospects for change. For if South Africa is indeed at a turning point, in very broad terms what is now at stake are three alternative tendencies: 'apartheid' might continue in some modified but still recognizable form, although not in name; some multi-racial or Africanized capitalist economy and society might emerge; or some more fundamental social revolution may be possible or likely – and this could be what is variously called 'socialism', 'national democracy' or 'national liberation'.

The prospects for these various solutions will depend not only on how inextricable the links are between apartheid and capitalism, but also on the strengths and purposes of the social and political forces pushing for change. The classes and the particular position and contradictions in which they are caught up in South Africa (and in the region), and the political organizations and forms through which these interests are mediated, will form the final item on our agenda.

These are the possibilities for the region which will be explored in what follows. We will not attempt to offer a possible scenario but will try to sketch in the background of the existing national and regional structures that are now subject to such strains, and try to identify the social forces that are contesting these different futures. This way we hope to offer readers a perspective through which they can get some purchase on these earth-shaking events. We can't tell you what is going to happen, but we can point you to some factors and forces to keep your eye on.

The Nature of Apartheid Society

One day soon, the rulers of South Africa, or of the western powers, or both are going to turn to us and say: 'Why still this anti-apartheid campaigning? Apartheid is no more.' Indeed both Reagan and Thatcher have taken this public stance at times since 1984, and have then had to admit the announcement of its demise was premature. So that we can judge when victory against apartheid has been won, or when the struggle has turned into a struggle for 'genuine liberation' or 'socialism', we have to have some measure of the beast.

Literally translated from the Afrikaans, *apartheid* means 'separateness'. The term came into vogue after the Nationalist Party, mainly identified with the Afrikaans-speaking part of the white population, came to power in 1948.It refers in part to an *ideology*, the defiant attempt to justify racial discrimination on scriptural and cultural grounds – and clearly in that sense it has taken a blow; the Nationalist Party and most of its supporters being no longer prepared to assert it. But it meant something concrete as well, an institutionalized structure of racial discrimination that went beyond the pre-1948 practices and those that existed elsewhere in white-dominated Africa, where jobs, residential areas, farmland and access to public places were also made exclusive. In South Africa what was new and different was the formalization of control of almost all aspects of where blacks lived, worked and moved. People were legally classified on a register as either 'white', 'coloured' (i.e. of mixed ancestry), 'Asian' or 'Bantu' by the Population Registration Act. The land was zoned into racial categories by the Group Areas Act – restricting property ownership, residence and work in them. Then movement between the areas was restricted in pursuance of a policy of 'influx control' whose chief mode of implementation were the Pass Laws, which required Africans to carry a Reference Book. This Pass was carried by all Africans over the age of 16 who moved outside the Bantustans. It revealed to any official the holder's right to be where he or she was; whether the holder had a job, had paid his or her taxes and what his or her ethnic classification was. Pass book information was computerized in Pretoria and could be accessed in any main centre. Each Pass book, moreover, contained the fingerprints of the holder and these were copied in a central registry also in Pretoria.

The Pass (recently substituted by an identification card held by all racial groups, but which still contains the above information) was the mechanism through which the state sought to limit the number of Africans allowed, on sufferance, into the 'white areas' (i.e. the towns and the large farms) and the terms on which they were allowed entry – in theory, having a job for a specified contract period. Male Africans were thus supposed to be restricted to being migrants leaving their 'unproductive dependants' behind in the African areas. However, there were already many blacks resident in towns and white rural areas when this system was introduced and when in 1960 the legal fiction was promulgated that the African rural areas constituted 'homelands', that could in fact become self-governing 'Bantustans'. To package this racial separatism neatly then involved making a 'partition', removing from white areas people without the proper residence or work rights recorded in their Pass. According to the Surplus Peoples Project, a monitoring agency, over 3,500,000 removals have taken place since 1960: this figure is in addition to removals within the homelands, Pass Law enforcement and 'betterment planning'.

Despite recent claims that apartheid is being demolished, removals quickened in the 1980s. In 1982, a total of 206,022 people were arrested for Pass Law offences: this was a 28.3 per cent increase over the 1981 figure of 160,000 and meant that 564 people a day or 23 per hour were being arrested for their 'unlawful' presence in a white area.[1] Between 1948 and 1981 at least 12.5 million people were arrested or prosecuted under Pass Law regulations.[2]

It is important to recognize that apartheid is in essence a system of *labour regulation* as well as of residential segregation. Patterns of labour recruitment, of types of job, of terms of service, of residence and social provision for workers are regulated by law.

The working of South African society has recently involved another *de facto* exception to this legalized system of racial separateness. The changed demands of business, especially of industry, for more skilled, more permanently resident, workers generated a category of semi-permanent African urban dwellers, even though they were technically citizens of some Bantustan. Section 10 (1) of the Black (Urban Areas) Act specifies the exemptions under which an African may reside – or simply be present – in a white area. The condition for this 'privilege' is birth or continuous residence for 15 years. He or she must have been in lawful employment for one employer without a break for 10 years. However, many migrant workers renew their contracts annually, and this is considered a break in continuous employment. The rights under this Act do not extend even to the dependants of those who qualify for urban residence. Those dependants or others who contravene are not only jailed or fined but rounded up to be 'removed' to what is supposed to be their Bantustan 'homeland'.

The first 'reforms' introduced into the apartheid system at the end of the 1970s affected these more permanent urban dwellers. They were extended some rights of residence and property ownership outside the Bantustan – within the white 'country' of South Africa, but still in African townships. At the same time these professional, middle-class and skilled workers, needed by the white-dominated economy in increasing numbers, were freed from some of the 'petty apartheid' regulations governing access to public places and also allowed to join trade unions and to elect local government bodies in the townships. What Botha's February 1986 speech seemed to be offering are some further removal of restrictions on this group. The fiction that they are citizens of a Bantustan will be dropped, and they will no longer be subject to the infamous Pass Laws. These reforms had in fact been presaged for a year by recommendations of the President's Council and had been urged by certain sections of industrial capital for years before. It was generally agreed, as Botha said, that policing the Pass Laws was too expensive, in straight financial costs to the regime, as well as political and social costs.

We shall go on in the next section to consider whether the repeal of the Pass Laws and changes in the citizenship laws constitute in any sense an end to the apartheid system, and that in turn will require us to delve more analytically below the legal *forms* of apartheid to grasp its underlying patterns, and the way these interact with capitalism. Before attempting to explore their significance, we should first underscore the direct and obvious limits of these promised reforms, for on reading the fine print it is clear that they are not by any means on offer to *all* Africans.

The first set of 'reforms' introduced in 1978/9 in fact made some concessions – residence and trade-union rights – to those whose permanence in the towns was required by further development of modern industry. But what has often been overlooked in discussions as to whether these were 'real' changes or just 'cosmetic', was the fact that they were accompanied simultaneously by measures, in the so-called Kornhoof Acts for instance, which tightened restrictions on work-seekers from the Bantustans. Those who did not qualify for the new dispensation were now confirmed in their migrant status, as temporary sojourners in the towns, and restrictions on their movement from the Bantustans was made tighter, even if they had a job. This at a time when unskilled jobs have been getting even scarcer, especially for residents in the distant Bantustans who have to be recruited through a labour bureau at home and whose range of jobs is narrowing.

These intensified restrictions on prospects for migrants are occurring against a background of ever-deteriorating conditions in the Bantustans. The Bantustans represent only 17 per cent of the land area of South Africa, although they contain perhaps half the African population. They are made up, artificially in most cases, of many small pockets of the poorest land with the least potential, in which there has been persistent environmental deterioration because of overcrowding and over-use and their being starved of agricultural resources. Now, with removals and natural population increase, many of the families resident there are denied access to land and thus are totally dependent on the remittances of some family member earning something in the white areas. Some still migrate on contract, but the flow of cash back to wives and dependants is not regular and women are often abandoned; others are close enough to commute daily or weekly to town or white farms; yet others seek something from the pettiest of trade. But for increasing numbers their very survival in the Bantustans is called into question: infant mortality, declining health and all the other signs of absolute impoverishment are rising. So far reforms have benefited *some* blacks, but the measures have in turn *worsened* the living conditions and life prospects of others – the migrants from, and the would-be-migrants in, the Bantustans. These measures, in turn, are intended to create a divide between the permanent urban-dwellers and the migrants and their dependants.

The same kind of distinction seems to be part of Botha's new promises. The further residence and regulations concessions – the ending of Pass Law regulations and granting of citizenship – seem to be on offer only to the permanent urban residents. 'Influx control' is to give way to some unspecified new system of organizing 'orderly urbanization'. The clear implication is that two categories of Africans will be created – the urban 'South Africans' and the 'Bantustan citizens' – if these proposals are made law.

There is, at first reading, another very significant retention of the apartheid structure in the present proposals. If some pillars like the Pass Laws are to go (or to be replaced), others are still considered sacrosanct, notably the Group Areas Act under which a black may be a South African citizen free to come and go, and even to own a house, but can still only buy it or work freely in a 'black township'. And of course underlying all is the fact that some political *voice* may be conceded to Africans, but no political *power*.

Apartheid as a Social System:
Ideological Distortion or 'Racial Capitalism'?

If these then are the obvious, legal limits to what changes are being made in the institutional framework of apartheid, we must now try to understand what deeper significance these and perhaps other future changes have on the shape of South African society. What we hope to have conveyed already is a realization that it is too simplistic to ask, 'Do these particular reforms constitute the "real" end of apartheid, or if not what further minimum package would?' Rather, we feel that the reforms of a few years ago and those now on offer do represent a shift in South African society. Even though they were 'limited', what is even more crucial is to ask limiting for *whom*? They in fact represented a departure from the basic pattern of the last 60 years or so, where the basic *economic divide*, in terms of who benefited, and the *political divide*, in terms of how people were organized in support or opposition to these structures, were both *racial*. What has been seen in the last decade, and not just through government's legislative actions, are changes that are having a differential impact on different classes among blacks. In short, then, the inter-play between racial, national and class groups in South Africa is in flux and may come to take on different configurations from those that have characterized the last two generations or more. It is with those configurations, with which the world has become familiar as 'apartheid', that we now must start our deeper-level analysis.

The origins can of course be traced back to the first Dutch settlers who established a small trading post for the Dutch East India Company at the Cape of Good Hope in 1652. Over the next 150 years as they gradually moved out north and east from the Cape and from subordination to the Company, they savagely put down fierce opposition from the indigenous Koikhoi and San who gradually lost their existence as separate peoples, being partly decimated, and partly enslaved and mixed with Malays and with whites to become the 'Coloureds' of today. By the 1800s the settlers were coming into contact and confrontation with Bantu-speaking peoples in the northeastern half of South Africa. Some of these, like the Zulu and Xhosa, were becoming centrally organized into powerful militarized kingdoms. As these peoples were conquered in the many 'border wars', they were not subordinated as slaves but were either confined to small pockets from which those that survived came to make up the Bantustans, or their lands were incorporated as parts of large estates that the settlers carved out for themselves, the inhabitants becoming tenants cum serfs. The African population on the 'white farms' is today over 3 million, and elements of 'labour tenancy' still survive, despite being legally abolished in the 1960s.

It was in this kind of milieu that what we would recognize as capitalist forms of production appeared in the late nineteenth century with the discovery of minerals in what were by then the Boer Republics of the Transvaal and the Orange Free State. This wealth also brought in the 'imperial factor' more openly, which in turn led to the incorporation of these republics into the Union (later Republic) of South Africa formed after the British victory in the Boer War. The mining of diamonds at Kimberley and gold around Johannesburg was eventually built up on a system of labour recruitment which became characteristic of the apartheid society generally. Independent small miners were gobbled up in Cecil Rhodes' monopoly, and large-scale mining found it could not, profitably, depend just on a white labour force that was experienced, organized, in short supply and expensive. African labour was recruited from far and near to do the heavy manual work and was housed in compounds without their families. The latter remained in the rural areas not only of South Africa but as far afield as Malawi and even southern Tanzania, where they had access to land and subsistence production. Mine employers were thus able to keep wages to an absolute minimum, just enough for the immediate upkeep of hostelized menfolk during the period they were there. A two-tier system of labour developed in the mines, where much of the work today continues to be manual, unskilled and performed by black migrant labour, while white workers became technicians and supervisors.[3]

The mining boom fostered a demand for food. This was at first met by African peasants producing a surplus for the market, but after the turn of the century white farming became more market-oriented and the farmers' powerful lobby ensured that political measures gradually eliminated African competition – by monopolizing the market and support for agriculture and by reducing African access to land. Over a long period these processes have gradually transformed African tenants who were subservient to their white landowners, but did at least have some security, into paid labourers. Many of the two million farm workers today are migrants or casual workers, the latter often female. At the same time almost all African peasants in what are now the Bantustans have been reduced to sub-subsistence producers.

The third dimension of capitalist enterprise to get off the ground was manufacturing industry. It was after 1920 that a concerted effort was made, spearheaded by the state, to have local industry replace imported manufactures. Basic industries like power, iron, steel and railways were built up, as well as a range of consumer goods industries, which were later to include durables. With this industrialization and the rapid urbanization that took place, many blacks came to town and found jobs, where, despite discrimination in residence and in jobs, they were better off, less subservient and less controlled than in the mines and on the farms.

Their circumstances all began to change with the Nationalist government of 1948. Over the next years the apartheid measures against urban blacks – demolition

of mixed or black neighbourhood and the building of distant townships, population removals, the myth of Bantustan citizenship, etc. – sought to reduce all
urban blacks to the status of temporary migrant workers.

As we have indicated, one explanation of these changes is that once united
politically, the Afrikaner's political party was elected to power with a significant,
and as it has turned out, permanent majority over the successive, mainly English-
speaking opposition parties and proceeded to apply the crude logic of their national
philosophy, that had emerged from their warped, calvinistic religiosity and their
history as an itinerant people fighting for its survival. On this view, apartheid,
in the literal and extreme sense to which their absurd beliefs were taking them
– the total physical separation of races – was always an impossibility that flew
in the face of the modern capitalist economy that was developing. From this
perspective, the problem was a racial and irrational ideological commitment; so
the bigger part of the battle is now over: the Nationalist Party leaders having
given up these beliefs, the problem that remains becomes one of merely over-
coming the die-hard white opinion, and of actually implementing reform.

We would like to present an alternative explanation of the patterns of the recent
past, which embodies a different view of how capitalism and apartheid are interrelated. What distinguishes capitalism in one setting from another is, at root, the
way that labour is reproduced, day by day and generationally. It is the conditions
abroad in society, often orchestrated by the state, rather than just what happens at
the 'point of production', which determines the level and form of exploitation in a
society. From this perspective it is possible to see institutionalized apartheid as
a modification of a distinctive pattern of labour organization, recruitment and
reproduction. We have seen how the patterns in mining and agriculture were
distinctive. In mining a two-tier labour system developed, with white workers
living entirely off their high wages and a migrant class of African males barely
surviving in compounds on their wages while their families lived off their peasant
holdings – often, as we shall explore below, outside South Africa. In agriculture
some degree of unfree labour persisted and kept wages low, so that even today
this is one sector not being unionized in South Africa. These patterns influenced
the terms of labour in other sectors, cheapening the wage to the level where it
only met the short-run needs of the menfolk, assuming that family and long-term
subsistence were met by people's own labours outside the system, and thus
increasing the profitability of production, so long as it was largely labour-intensive.
But no such system remains static. Contradictions arose from a half century or
more of intervention into peasant areas to recruit, inhibit cash crop production
and prevent a drift to towns. Conditions were created in which it was no longer
possible for the African reserves to provide 'subsistence' for the surplus population, thus fuelling a drift to the towns. The rapid urbanization in the 1940s,
involving whole families, could in turn have eroded both the cheap labour system
and discriminatory job practices, and indeed farmers were already concerned that
other sectors were attracting their labour away.

The apartheid initiatives can be seen as geared to resolving such matters:
protecting white farmers against competition, reasserting the principle of temporary
residence and thus the migrancy of labour. At the same time, increasingly
impoverished 'reserves' could not on the basis of their 'natural' abundance absorb
their increasing, dependent populations and those who had been 'removed'.

Draconian laws of a much more institutionalized population control rather than the prospect of gaining a livelihood would have to be the mechanism for keeping Africans in place in the countryside. In recent years the Bantustans and the fiction of their citizenship has further served to reduce the overall burden on employers or the state of keeping alive the waiting migrants and their dependants. In this view, apartheid, and the practices it was built on, represent a structure where the seemingly expensive irrationality (e.g. of maintaining influx control, of a shortage of skilled workers, white wages, etc.) in fact generated an ultra-cheap and super-exploited black workforce. The shifting connections between capitalism and racism have been neatly summed up in these terms:

> Capital did not invent racism, but it has certainly been able to live with it, more or less comfortably. Racism has indeed been built into South Africa's industrial revolution. While not always necessarily functional to economic growth there has at least been a certain reciprocity between South Africa's racist practices and its industrialisation.[4]

What is now in process is a set of changes from the two-tier labour force divided according to race. The attempt to give effect to a belief that all blacks could be reduced to temporary *Gästarbeiter* whose reproduction could in part be external-ized has finally been given up. The state envisages that black labour in large numbers will have to be trained and become skilled, and thus will become fully proletarianized. But although the divide will no longer be racial, nothing has been done or said by the regime to suggest that there will be an end to a two-tier labour system; or that they will not try to continue to exclude, even if by other mechanisms, a large proportion of blacks from any political or other rights and from having to rely on migrant or casual low-paid work plus what little they can eke out of the Bantustans. But before we begin to explore what *might* happen, as we shall in the next section, our picture of apartheid as embodying a particular system of labour reproduction needs to be filled out in one or two further dimensions.

If the key to understanding the basic structure of South African society and the changes within it is to see it as a particular pattern of structuring labour, changing in form at different stages, we must also recognize that a central ingre-dient for the maintenance of these patterns was the *state*. Indeed with the apartheid stage of this 'racial capitalism', the state's role became even more central – and of course this role has not been confined to labour and population control. In particular, its external activity has been important.

The state has had to mediate between different would-be dominant classes within South Africa and the 'imperial factor', and itself has been both the object and arena for such conflicts: whether the new Dutch settlers' interests or those of the Dutch East India Company would be dominant; in the late nineteenth century, whether Boer settlers could secure a place for themselves beyond British imperial-ism; and whether international mining and later manufacturing interests would subordinate farming and other indigenous capital. In recent years, too, we have seen multinationals and western governments, sometimes happy to go along with existing structures, sometimes pressuring for some change. Precisely what to expect from these forces in the present conjuncture will be explored below.

A later section will be devoted to another complicating feature of apartheid – the regional dimension. But here we should note that in so far as it was a system of labour recruitment and reproduction of much of that labour, especially in the key sector of mining, apartheid has affected not only South Africa but several neighbouring countries for most of this century. As a result of this and other ties, often the subject of explicit South African government policy, the countries of the region have been structured into complex and dependent relationships within a regional political economy dominated by South Africa. They have also been the site of their own struggles, but these have and will continue to have repercussions on and from South Africa.

We need briefly to explore the character of the state that has played these roles. Since the Boer War the state has found a place for the interests of all fractions of capital – mining and manufacturing, foreign and local, Afrikaner and English – even as they jockeyed for dominance. Since 1948 Afrikaner capital, in farming but increasingly in finance and industry, has had a bigger say and been officially promoted by the state. But there has always been a degree of incorporation of other classes – white workers and petty bourgeoisie. The European workers' position as part of a ruling bloc was strengthened in the mid-1920s and in the 1940s as part of the buying off of their militancy and a bid for their vote in return for guarantees of a privileged and protected economic status. In this sense the state has been a 'white' state but not in some straightforward, reflexive sense of race being the dominant, indeed sole, factor. Rather it is white as the historical outcome of a particular set of (shifting) alliances which have thus far led to compromises between the interests of different classes and fractions of capital, all of them white. To be sure, a racist ideology has provided cement for such an alliance, but, seen in this light, it is not automatically the case that, after this particular turning point, the state will continue to represent all or only white classes. So our final balance sheet, when we try to assess what is happening and is likely to happen in South Africa, must review changes in the form and social character of the state.

The Contradictions of Apartheid Surface

To understand what is happening to the apartheid system and what is likely to happen, we need to assess the contending political forces: in particular, the ruling Nationalist Party, and the state structures through which it rules, and the various expressions of African nationalism, black protest and workers' action. As well as their different organizations and their relative strengths, we need to assess their programmes of action – in particular the 'reform package' the power-holders may be working out, as well as the various programmes for a future South Africa put forward by different opposition groups. The gap between these two views also helps to reveal whether there is any chance for change through some negotiated political process or other 'peaceful' transition, or whether the resolution of the present crisis will be as a result of conflict of some sort. But the prospects for change are not just a matter of the aspirations and manifestos of political groups. None of them has complete freedom of action to pursue their ideals; they have to operate in a given situation. Even a powerful state like South Africa's has its choices in part shaped for it – by the underlying shifts in the structure of society that are occurring, as well as by the strength of organized opposition. Indeed the latter is shaped by and in turn helps to reshape the social structure. At the same time, for the last ten years the political scene in South Africa has been marked by eruptions of social forces, more spontaneous than a result of the conscious implementation of the programme of action of any organization.

Fundamental processes have been at work in South Africa, as in all societies. The social system has gone through a number of stages where the form it takes and the way it operates changes, although these have been variations around a common theme of racial domination. 'Apartheid' itself can be seen as representing one phase and form in this history, one of a much more institutionalized racism, following the Nationalist Party's coming to power in 1948. Its present crisis, we have argued, represents a moment when this particular system of domination must reform or be transformed. But it is important in assessing these prospects to recognize that they are posed against a background in which significant shifts have been occurring anyway since the late 1970s – albeit trends that have affected only the *form* of racial dominance, and that have heralded some worsening conditions as well as some improvements for blacks. These changes can be seen operating at a number of levels: in the system of reproduction of labour; in the nature of the ruling alliance of classes and in the formal organization of the state; and in the forms of subordination of the black population. These trends, some a result of conscious policy, others a result of forces to which policy is trying to respond, are occurring against a backcloth of changes in the economic framework.

Underlying economic trends have been significant in a number of ways. The 30 years up to 1980 saw consistent growth in the economy and, in particular, significant continued industrialization. However, there were structural limits to this growth process, limits which have a defining effect on the economic dimension of the current crisis. We have seen how industrialization included a wide range of consumer, consumer durable and basic industries. But despite the fact that South Africa is the one part of the continent that can claim to have an industrial base, it has relied, and continues to do so, on foreign investment as the basis of this growth – not so much because of a shortage of finance or even foreign exchange, but rather in the form of the presence of multinationals and in turn access to advanced technology and equipment. A second feature of South Africa's industrialization is that, compared with other relatively advanced industrializing economies like Brazil, it has been characterized by only a very limited export of manufactures. It has remained at the stage of import substitution, even if the substitution is of things like Mercedes and air conditioners. Thus, for all its technical sophistication, the South African economy remains 'underdeveloped', in the sense that it relies on exports of primary products and imports manufactures, especially technology.

Now that economy is beset by a particular set of pressures as it feels the pinch, in its own particular way, of the world economic crisis. In many ways, South Africa has experienced a delayed impact. During most of the 1970s it was partially cushioned by the rise in the price of its main export, gold – first, with the ending of the fixed price of gold in the early 1970s and then through the usual depression phenomenon of a rising gold price. The first round of intensive black worker pressure, beginning with the strikes in 1973, could be partly absorbed by wage increases. But as this trend in gold prices has been reversed in the 1980s and worker pressure has continued unabated, the former super-profitability of South African investments has turned to crisis. The flight of foreign capital and even of corporate South African capital has now intensified as the escalating political disturbances have shaken long-term confidence of international capital in South Africa in the last months. The regime thus faces direct pressure from foreign capital, and the indirect imperative of restoring profitability and confidence, to make changes that can defuse the situation – although we should be clear that the pressure is not as yet overwhelming: witness the IMF and the private banks' comparative amenability to rescheduling the country's international debt. Nevertheless these immediate pressures reinforce the more fundamental underlying need, as in all economies, for some economic restructuring to make possible renewed long-term growth to take it out of crisis.

It is possible to isolate the requirements of such a further stage of renewed capitalist growth; indeed, South African capital has spelled them out. It is clear that the prospects of renewed industrialization on the basis of catering for the expensive consumerism of a small internal, white population are very limited. What are needed are different types of industries, catering for different markets, requiring imports of technology and needing therefore a growing section of the workforce with a high-level of technical capability. In part, capital must be looking to export manufactures, and that obviously means penetrating the regional market in Africa; the possibilities in the wider world seem remote, but the immediate market too has so far been limited because of South Africa's political unacceptability. But the corporate planners also have their sights very much set on the internal market – among blacks. In 1985 one Afrikaner bank, Merca Bank, pointed to the expansion of black consumer spending power since 1970, at 5 per cent per annum and projects that it will be R30 billion by 2000 AD, almost equal to that among whites.[5] Such market calculations reinforce the 'supply-side' logic for training, and in some way incorporating into the South African economy, substantial numbers of black workers.

If the search for markets and skilled labour are some of the economic pressures orienting sections of capital toward reform, these considerations also help to define the difficulties inherent in achieving these prerequisites. Industrial regeneration oriented toward a black and not so well-off market would require emphasis on a different range of industries and not necessarily the high-tech ones that many producers are poised to go into. Whatever choice of product is made, it will require foreign technology, equipment and funding, and whether this will be forthcoming, given political circumstances, is open to question. Finally, the offer of consumerism and secure employment plus residential security and some political concessions to some black workers, professionals and businessmen has to be premised upon a political deal which would buy off their demands at the expense of unskilled workers and would-be migrants. The prospects of such a cleavage being opened up will be considered below.

Similar doubts must exist as to whether enough open access and the undisrupted conditions required for stable trade in the neighbouring economies is compatible with continued South African assertion of dominance. Beyond the doubt whether the state can effectively meditate on behalf of such ambitions of capital to achieve any of these objectives, internally or externally, there is the overall issue as to whether all of these several conditions for growth can be simultaneously met.

But, this review of the prospects for further advance under a reforming capitalism, difficult as they might be to achieve in practice, does not automatically rule out the possibility of such reform under capitalism. If apartheid can be characterized as a form of 'racial capitalism' in the sense that South African capitalism has wrought advantage from the racist structures, it does not follow that the racism is so embedded a factor that reform of South African capitalism can be dismissed. Unfortunate as it might seem, the alternatives are not apartheid or socialism.

The Politics of the Total Strategy

The options defined by underlying economic realities do in fact signify the bounds which mark the freedom of action of the various political actors, whether those associated with the state or the black opposition. What is clear, however, is that the present holders of state power have had an overall programme for achieving some of their goals, the so-called 'total strategy'. But their objectives and thus their methods must be seen as couched in terms not just of aiming to fulfil the conditions that can guarantee these economic imperatives of renewed internal growth and a more integrated and amenable regional economic system. They have political *ends*, as well as political means for ensuring economic ends, and sometimes the two conflict. Notably, internally, while there might be some logic for capital to want to foster and thus politically incorporate black middle classes and sections of the black working class, this incorporation has to be on limited terms which do not offer the prospect of 'black power' and the possibility of more basic changes in the economic system. Externally, the prospect of neighbouring economies open to South African trade, investment and overall economic management is a goal that would also provide a lever for asserting control over their policies, especially as regards support for liberation movements. But so far, the more immediate imperative of enforcing this latter kind of political subordination has put the emphasis on destroying local economies rather than peacably managing them. And, as we have suggested, regional policies which combine both disruption and economic manipulation of front line states, as a combination of tactics would give the greatest leverage. But in the long run the two can be contradictory – and certainly the managers of the international economy may well feel so.

One characteristic of state structures in South Africa has been the paraphenalia of parliamentarism, of elections between parties competing for power bestowed by adult suffrage – by whites only, of course. This was what necessitated the concession of a privileged socio-economic status to the white working class as junior partners in a ruling alliance, and it was simultaneously a reflection of that kind of class alliance. The corollary of this form of racially exclusive state, was that the black population was held in place by direct political control, by repression as a feature of everyday life, not just an ultimate weapon of last resort. But still some few blacks were always incorporated by degrees into the political sphere. Up to the 1950s this incorporation was limited to chiefs, who were offered little in status or power, except that their power to allocate land under a 'traditional' system of tenure was a powerful instrument of social control.

Thereafter, by the creation of Bantustans, the state gave greater powers and social and economic status not only directly to the larger group of homeland politicians but to a wider group of local bureaucrats, professionals and even to some better-off farmers. The very obvious puppet status of such officials should not blind us to the realities of the power they exercise. They have often shown an appetite for repression that the white repressive mechanisms would envy – all too ready to detain without trial and ban trade unions. There is thus a small group with a stake in the system able to wield some power in protection of their interests. The Bantustan system has thus far 'worked' to some extent as both a divide-and-rule mechanism – promoting ethnic consciousness and promoting conflict over access to jobs, land, etc. – and one for oppression and exploitation through the 'citizenship' device, weakening the position of Africans in towns and diverting costs of social welfare provisions.

As the need for a permanent black economic presence in white areas was conceded in the late 1970s, one would expect that this would have some political repercussions. But political forms are not automatically and immediately reshaped in response to underlying socio-economic changes. In fact it has taken until 1986 for the announcement that such black urban residents would have citizenship, although there is still no readiness to equate this with the fundamental right to vote. Earlier the 'Kornhof' measures had set up elected black local authorities, particularly in the townships – but the position of those black elites ready to climb aboard this particular bandwagon has been weak. As administrators of services in dormitory areas without any productive activities and thus without a tax base, they have been dependent on, and thus susceptible to control by, central authorities; and yet at the same time they have been unable to deliver improved living conditions and were thus unpopular, and in recent months have become a prime target for attack.

The other avenue for political incorporation has been the provisions under the new Constitution of separate legislatures for Asian and Coloured populations. But the signs were, in the elections for these two new chambers in 1984, that many of these new voters were not ready to be satisfied with this kind of manipulative device, nor were they prepared to go along with Botha's efforts to seek to ally these two minority communities with whites against the African majority. The boycott campaigns during these elections were very successful; only some 20 per cent of those eligible to vote actually polled. The other purpose involved in the racial tricameral legislative system and the other constitutional changes was not only to grant some political concessions to Asians and Coloureds but to have them available to ruling circles as possible allies to fend off the extreme right wing. The creation of an executive presidency was also seen as a way of enabling the Nationalist Party leadership to withstand pressure from the right – and as a device, therefore, for dispensing with some degree of support from white workers. Thus Botha sought room for manoeuvre as he began to unpick the alliance of classes that had held power for 50 years. Clearly though, Botha still has to keep one eye open for the white right, and when announcing his 'reform' package in early 1986, his government announced a 10 per cent increase in wages of government employees, who account for 60 per cent of white workers.

There remains the question of political rights for Africans. Up to 1985 the intention was clearly to build up a 'racial confederal' arrangement. The tricameral structure for the minorities was to be associated with self-ruling Bantustans, which would be the sole avenue for African 'national' citizenship and representation. The setting up of black township local authorities, part of the Kornhof package, was a concession within such a framework, reflecting recognition of the permanence of an 'insider' group of Africans resident in the towns, who would have some corresponding social and economic rights. But although it was vaguely mooted, there was to be no offer of a fourth chamber for Africans. The limited social privileges and local government voting rights for residents was another divisive tactic, aiming to make sharp distinctions between the status of resident Africans and that of migrants and of Bantustan residents. Indeed the Kornhof package included the imposition of even more stringent influx control against the Bantustan dwellers under an Orderly Movement and Settlement of Black Persons Act. The concessions announced in 1986 mark a shift. Citizenship and presumably political rights in a combined South Africa will be offered to Africans. But, although the Pass Laws and other influx control measures are reputedly to be repealed, these are to be replaced by some unspecified measures for 'orderly urbanization' of blacks; and as the citizenship offer is held out only to permanent townspeople, the division between them and migrants is still part of the regime's strategy. It is in these respects, in particular, that it is premature to talk about the full dismantling of apartheid. An effective and united black mobilization has arisen against these attempts to divide and rule, together with an insistent demand for rights within a single South Africa. These social movements and the growing ungovernability of the black-run townships are forcing the regime to continually amend its formula for political representation of Africans.

The dilemma facing South African rulers throughout the 1980s is to find a formula that would answer pressures for political rights for blacks and end formal racialism politically without, in their terms, 'capitulating to majoritarianism'. How is it possible to concede political rights without handing over the power to redistribute resources in the society, let alone herald in socialism? Bantustan independence and a tricameral legislature, even with black local authorities, was not enough. In now announcing citizenship rights for (some) Africans, South African leaders are still simply casting around for a device that does not concede majority rule. The most likely formula is one based on some federal formula. Until very recently such ideas were associated with white opposition groups like the Progressive Federal Party and were given some point by the Buthelezi Commission in 1982 which outlined the basis for a multi-racial structure integrating the Bantustan of KwaZulu and the rest of the Province of Natal. Now the Nationalist Party seems to be picking up the approach, and has in fact set up eight Development Regions which are about to have their own Councils combining white provincial councils and black urban authorities. These might presage a package which the Nationalists might see as a way of solving their problem of African representation and offer the semblance, to the outside world especially, of a unified (federal) state in which all its residents have political rights, but in which the white minority still enjoys special guarantees. At the lowest level, residential segregation remains – the Group Areas Act remains intact according to Botha – and is the basis for what will be *de facto* racial local authorities, maintaining the 'insider'–migrant divide. Then at a second level the Regional Councils can provide a bridge between white and black areas. What the government may have in mind, when saying they will grant citizenship to non-Bantustan Africans, is some indirect form of representation in these regions, rather than a fourth chamber. If the details are not clear, it is already obvious what such a formula might mean in political and social terms. Politically, a structure could be worked out that is acceptable to a coalition embracing the Nationalist Party, the white liberal opposition, Coloured and Asian parliamentary parties and the Inkatha movement of Gatsha Buthelezi. The chances of such an offering will depend on the strength of these groups and on whether it may be acceptable to any broader grouping.

The Forces of Black Struggle

African resistance to the racist structures in South Africa have taken many forms and have been articulated by a variety of movements. Today the apartheid system is assailed by one main and three smaller national liberation movements operating from exile and underground. Two broad new umbrella 'fronts' operate legally within the country. The labour movement is increasingly organized. Widespread protest, and occasional rebellion by black youth, and township organization and action challenge the state.

By far the longest-established and best-known liberation movement is the African National Congress (ANC). Its earliest operations, from 1912, were based on an emerging class of educated Africans and were couched in terms of legal representations. After 1948, young activists of Mandela's generation injected more broad-based mass action through the civil disobedience campaigns of the 1950s. The non-violence of approach did not prevent a large group of leaders being tried for treason nor the eventual banning of the ANC in 1960, and of the breakaway Pan African Congress (PAC) after the massacre at Sharpeville following a PAC rally. Thereafter, both movements opted for armed struggle and formed military wings, Umkhonto we Sizwe (Spear of the Nation) for the ANC, and Poqo for the PAC. At the time, they launched sabotage operations; then in the 1970s the ANC trained guerillas for some kind of 'people's war'.

Implicitly, their model was similar to that of the successful struggles, in Mozambique, Angola and Zimbabwe: rural-based guerilla forces gradually liberating pockets of territory. Some action in border areas in the late 1970s and early 1980s pointed in this direction, but the terrain of large white farms or game parks was not condusive to that type of struggle, so it has been combined with urban sabotage. In recent years, a new strategy has evolved, adopted by an important consultative conference of the ANC in Zambia in July 1985. It seeks a more mass-based and urban-oriented mobilization to make the country ungovernable. The circumstances and prospects of this approach we shall consider below, but before exploring methods further it is important to consider the broader political strategy for revolution put forward by different groups.

The same manipulative efforts at cooptation and division by the state considered above have generated in response attempts to weld broad alliances and to resist incorporation, and in particular have stimulated the formation of profoundly influential, broad-based movements like the United Democratic Front (UDF) and unparalleled levels of protest. But, as in all periods of acute political conflict, debates about the nature of the struggle and its potential social basis have greatly intensified. Of course, such issues have been part of the currency of South African politics for almost 60 years – since the birth of the South African Communist Party. The SACP originally made the mistake, which some rivals still use as a stick to beat it, of looking to the only proletariat that existed in the 1920s, the white workers. In the 1930s it shifted to supporting the common struggle of black and white workers and then moved to association with the ANC. With the adoption of the Freedom Charter in 1955 it became absorbed in the Congress Alliance, which brought together the (white) Congress of Democrats, the Indian Congress, the Coloured People's Congress, the ANC and the South African Congress of Trade Unions (SACTU). The SACP's perspective on this alliance was that it was part of a strategy for a classic 'two-stage' revolution – a prescription based on an analysis of South Africa as an 'internal colony' as well as a capitalist state. A national democratic revolution would precede a move to socialism, and would be fashioned on the basis of a broad front of classes, welded together in a nationalist movement which would be open to 'democrats' of all races. This kind of formulation was taken up by the ANC as a whole in later policy statements, like the 'Strategy and Tactics' adopted at a 1969 conference in Morogoro, Tanzania, in which a commitment to socialism was explicit. Very generally, and with exceptions, the groups now banded together in the UDF represent this kind of 'congress position' – a national alliance of classes, with workers (it is to be hoped) in the vanguard, but with the broadest coalition of all classes that can be mobilized for an initial stage of a democratic alternative to apartheid.

Other movements have emerged over the years, differing with some aspects of this position. PAC, for instance, originally articulated a more African nationalist stance objecting to the 'leftists, whites and Indians of the Congress Alliance'. The black consciousness movement in general that grew up in the early 1970s inside South Africa, and the actual organization called BCM, mainly in exile, plus the Azania People's Organization (AZAPO) that emerged as an openly operating political movement in the 1970s, and now the National Forum, all broadly speaking take a similar position, although for these more recent bodies 'black' is defined to include Asians and Coloureds as well as Africans. But they would exclude white democrats from their conception of the 'nation' and thus their movements. Within this tradition, some analysts distinguish a right wing that stresses the ideological component of black nationalism, from a left whose analysis does relate racial oppression to capitalism and refers to the 'historic task of black working class', to quote the AZAPO manifesto.

An earlier liberation movement, with a separate history going back to the 1940s, is the Unity Movement. This never won widespread backing outside the Cape nor recognition from the Organization of African Unity but it articulated an interesting and sophisticated ideological position. Its espousal of a unity of all non-white activists and its attacks on the communists early won it the label 'Trotskyist' and yet this movement put more emphasis on the potential revolutionary role of the peasantry than others. As an external group its influence is now minimal, but there are some, though only some, connections between its analysis and another current discernible among activist groups in South Africa today, especially among trades unions – that of an 'independent workerist' position.

On such a basis, some unions have not joined the UDF and National Forum, which are umbrella bodies with many affiliates, and they even call for a 'workers' political movement'.

What matters, of course, is not only the formal stance of different movements but the measure of support they can effectively mobilize. In this connection, one of the most heartening and significant dimensions of resistance in the last decade has been the emergence of trade unions for they have taken an increasing role in the struggle against apartheid. Although only 15 per cent of all black workers are unionized, blocs of trades unions like FOSATU (Federation of South African Trade Unions), – the first among blacks since SACTU went into exile in the 1960s – were formed in recent years. Then, at the end of 1985 a new 'centre', COSATU (Confederation of South African Trade Unions), brought together unions representing half a million workers. Industrial unrest has been significant ever since the key strikes in the Durban area in the early 1970s. 1984 and 1985 saw the highest level of disputes ever, and these spread to include not just manufacturing but the mineworkers, most of them still migrants. Since 1984 trade unions have increasingly combined with community groups or youth associations to mobilize 'stay aways' around 'political' issues of detention (one such involved the Congress of South African Students (COSAS) in the Transvaal in November 1984), although there are still some constraints, chiefly the quite different structures of these organizations, that inhibit such collaboration. In the particular circumstances of urban South Africa – with segregated and sealed-off residential areas originally an instrument of state control now backfiring on the state as no-go areas are created – both community-based and work-oriented actions are important. Spontaneous protests, stay-aways, school boycotts, pressure on 'collaborators' and attacks on all government symbols first escalated during the Soweto uprisings in 1976 and have reached a dramatic new crescendo in the uninterrupted ground-swell of black resistance since 1984. These now constitute the most immediate and dramatic force against the apartheid regime.

Massive discontent is ringing out from the black townships. Trade-union militancy and organizational effectiveness are escalating and new mass political movements are emerging. A new strategy for struggle has evolved and is now articulated by the ANC since its 1985 gathering – a shift of emphasis from guerila struggle and urban sabotage to the creation of a state of ungovernability. This strategy has been compared with the actions that led to the overthrow of the Shah's regime in Iran in 1979 – although one difference is in the nature of the ruling groups and classes. The new approach also involves a counter to the regime's divide-and-rule measures that seeks to build the widest possible political alliance against apartheid. We see the ANC involved in a dialogue with some Bantustan leaders, with disaffected church and other white groups, and with representatives of internal and foreign capital. In this kind of scenario the maverick leader of the KwaZulu Bantustan, Gatsha Buthelezi, no doubt aspires to a pivotal role. He has refused independence and the grosser forms of collaboration with apartheid, but is no enemy of capitalism and condemns the campaign for economic sanctions. He is wedded too to a tribal and thuggish form of political organization that does not auger well for future nationalist politics, but this has undoubtedly given him enough clout that he cannot be ignored by the ANC. Buthelezi also stands invitingly ready to be brought into a state-orchestrated plan for regionalism and federalism that will seek a political settlement some way short of black majority rule, let alone a sustained transformation of capitalism.

Southern Africa in the World Context

In pondering likely outcomes of the present crisis in southern Africa, calculations have also to be made about the involvement of external social forces, in particular the western powers and the specific corporate actors with interests in the area. The significant western stake in the area has been documented ever since Kissinger commissioned an evaluation of his strategic options in 1970 (the famous National Security Memorandum no. 39). There are very considerable (and hitherto profitable) investments in South Africa, both bank loans and other portfolio investment as well as subsidiaries of multinational corporations. The latter are keen to exploit further their South African operations as a springboard to the region. The Republic, and to some extent other countries like Namibia, Zambia and Zimbabwe, are suppliers of key minerals to the world economy, though South Africa clearly overestimates the degree to which, during economic stagnation, this gives it leverage. The whole region, especially the sea lanes to the Gulf and Asia around the Indian and Atlantic Ocean shores, are of undoubted strategic significance in global terms, although again the South African regime has found it a useful ploy to inflate the degree of their importance to the West.

It is, however, one thing to calculate these linkages, it is quite another to read off from them the kind of political intervention that can be expected. What can be said generally is that western interests do care about what happens in the region certainly more than in an area like West Africa, and will take action to try to ensure that the outcome suits them. What is also clear, is that while the USSR will no doubt be ready to seize what advantages it can from the situation, events in the region are not such as to make the Soviet Union stick its neck out as far as it might be prepared to in areas of more strategic significance to it, such as the Horn of Africa.

Indeed even the most visible sign of communist bloc involvement, the presence of some thousands of Cuban troops in Angola for the last ten years, since the so-called 'civil' war at independence, needs to be seen in context – especially now that Reagan has given public backing to the UNITA forces opposing the MPLA (Popular Movement for the Liberation of Angola) government. In fact, it has been precisely the continued invasions, hundreds of miles into Angola, of the South African military, and their logistical and other support to Jonas Savimbi's UNITA, that have ensured the need for Angola's continued reliance on the Cuban troops. Given this obvious cause and effect, doubt must surround the seriousness of South African, and now US, stated intentions that they want to see the Cubans leave southern Africa. It is equally plausible to interpret South African military involvement over the last few years as a policy to sustain the visible reality of a 'communist menace', as a ploy to draw in the US as the guarantor against any external threat to South Africa. Certainly South African strategy has always recognized the limits to the country's own considerable military and economic muscle and thus aims to have the west more decisively involved.

The US clearly has been drawn in, and, as President Kaunda of Zambia, whose own stance on South African and US involvement in Angola has been equivocal in the past, remarked: there is the obvious contradiction in US policy of support for UNITA which 'has made it impossible for its own conditions [of Cuban troop withdrawal] to be met'. It is unlikely that this contradiction is a result of an oversight or miscalculation only obvious to Kaunda and not to US policymakers. This US commitment is significant in that it marks a stepping-up of US involvement in the whole region, which has been growing in the 1980s. The earlier 'cease-fire' between Angola and South Africa brought in US military observers, and there is a US liaison mission in Windhoek, capital of Namibia. But if the stepped-up US presence is what Pretoria has wanted all along, what still has to be explained are what forces determined that the US went along with this. The shift in policy is significant in that it was against the wishes and advice of certain US corporations with interests in the area. Indeed, when Reagan sought three years ago to lift the Clark Amendment which forbade covert US involvement in the region, it was the lobbying of Gulf Oil, with its oil wells in the Cabinda enclave in the north of Angola and of a few other old-established, eastern seaboard corporate interests that steeled Congress to resist. The latter interests could be seen as representative not so much of a fraction of US capital but of a certain approach to the political strategy of US empire. This position was best summarized in relation to southern Africa in the late 1970s by Andrew Young, then President Carter's UN Ambassador, who argued that even 'Marxist–Leninist' regimes like Angola's could be brought round, using indirect, 'neo-colonial' leverage because of their underlying economic dependence. Now in many world arenas, and particularly over Angola, a hard-nosed lobby who believe the best safeguard for US interests and the continuation of capitalism is direct political intervention, is clearly more influential in Washington.

South Africa in Southern Africa

Labour recruitment has been a central feature of South Africa's involvement in the region. In fact the Republic dominates the southern African region economically, politically and militarily. This still remains very much the case today even after the successful struggle for national liberation from Portuguese colonialism in Angola, Mozambique and from settler colonialism in Zimbabwe in the 1970s, and even after the formation of an alliance designed to free nine countries from such reliance – the Southern African Development Coordination Conference (SADCC). Granted there is a degree of *inter*dependence in southern Africa: South Africa was once dependent upon large numbers of migrant workers from its neighbouring states to work in the mines and on white farms at even lower wages than South Africans – although even that has changed. (Table 10.1 gives figures of increased recruitment within South Africa.) And the same debilitation of local peasant agriculture, which everywhere is a characteristic of any area that becomes a 'labour reserve', has occurred in most of these states – thereby underlining their dependence on jobs in the Republic. South Africa is also increasingly dependent upon Angola and Mozambique for hydro-electric energy. It uses the Mozambican port of Maputo which serves the area around Johannesburg. It looks to neighbouring states as a potential market – possibly a vital ingredient

Table 10.1 Estimated extent of migrant labour from South Africa's 'homelands' 1977–82 (thousands)

	1977	1978	1979	1980	1981	1982
KwaZulu	244	244	245	261	280	294
QwaQwa	34	37	38	43	51	60
Lebowa	155	159	163	175	186	180
Gazankulu	43	45	46	50	58	64
KaNgwane	34	37	44	48	57	67
KwaNdebele	27	33	35	44	63	52
Transkei	301	302	302	308	336	346
Bophuthatswana	175	178	185	197	197	236
Venda	28	29	33	35	41	37
Ciskei	54	54	54	56	60	59
Total	1,095	1,118	1,145	1,217	1,329	1,395

Source:
Race Relations Survey, 1983 & 1984, S.A. Institute of Race Relations, Johannesburg 1984 & 1985.

Table 10.2 Registered workers in South Africa from neighbouring states.

	Botswana	Lesotho	Malawi	Mozambique	Swaziland	Zimbabwe	Other
1983	25,967	145,797	29,622	61,218	16,773	7,742	70,906
1985	29,169	150,422	30,603	59,391	13,418	16,965	n.a.

in economic recovery, as we have seen. But the net effect of the historical pattern of economic integration in the region places South Africa in the driving seat. Its neighbours are dependent upon the Republic for jobs (see table 10.2) and earnings in a variety of ways and for vital imports such as food and machinery. The securing of electric power and markets is one reason for South Africa seeking to dominate politically.

Just because of these interconnections we would expect the manner in which the internal crisis is resolved in South Africa to have profound repercussions for other countries in the region. However, as we shall see, South Africa uses its position as a regional power in southern Africa to externalize the crisis within South Africa itself, so that the struggle to overthrow the racist system is having an even more traumatic impact on these neighbouring countries.

South Africa's economic and infrastructural dominance of the region is extensive. Of an estimated 90,000 km of railways in the whole of sub-Saharan Africa, more than 25 per cent are to be found in the Republic, more than in all of the surrounding region put together. Map 10.1 shows that rail links in the region are crucial for the neighbouring land-locked states to transport goods in and out and for export overseas – thus giving the Republic a powerful blackmailing weapon. At the moment, even Zambia, which has no common border with South Africa, receives 45 per cent of its imports from there and sends one-third of its exports through South Africa's ports. In addition, Botswana, Lesotho and Swaziland (often called the BLS states) are almost totally integrated into South Africa, as part of the South African Customs Union and the Rand currency area. In fact, Botswana imports 88 per cent of its needs from South Africa, and although little more than 8 per cent of its exports go there, all go through; Swaziland imports 90 per cent of its goods from South Africa and at least 20 per cent of its exports go to South Africa. Small wonder then that South Africa only had to stop the flow of goods and people – including food aid sent by the international community and fuel – for a few days, in order to topple the Lesotho government.

From the 1960s South Africa sought actively to build on its inherited dominance in the region, espousing an 'outward-oriented' strategy, but this involved mainly close ties with colonial authorities, and pliant states like Malawi, that were simultaneously economic satellites and buffers. The political and military climate changed with the collapse of Portuguese colonialism in the 1970s. In 1974 South Africa was no longer ringed by a *cordon sanitaire* of friendly regimes. Although it had a buffer with Angola, because it had illegally occupied Namibia since 1966, it was more vulnerable than it had ever been. At the moment when it was having to combat more persistant opposition from within to apartheid, it was denied political friends in the region. Once Ian Smith and Abel Muzorewa lost power in Zimbabwe/Rhodesia in 1980, South Africa's only friends were Mobutu in distant Zaire, Banda in Malawi and the monarchy in tiny Swaziland. It was in these circumstances that the project for a 'constellation of Southern African States' (CONSAS) was launched to try to bind some of the independent states and the Bantustans (thus seeking to gain them recognition in the process) more firmly to South Africa.

In seeking this new kind of security and dominance, South Africa has pursued a carrot-and-stick strategy against its neighbours. The carrot was the opportunity to have access to a steady supply of scarce goods, to accept loans and investment

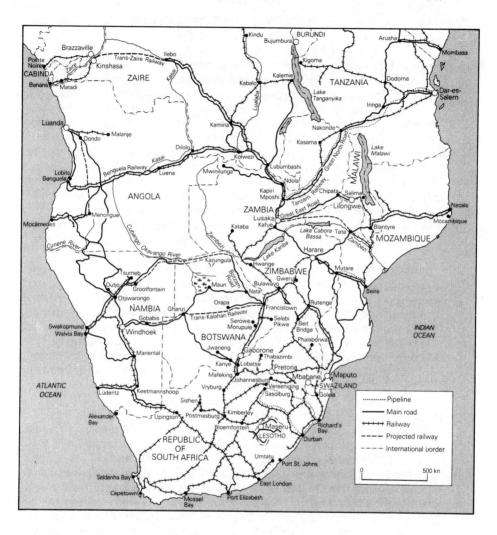

Map 10.1 Southern Africa

which would of course tie in neighbours even tighter and increase their dependency, and thus make available yet another stick – withdrawal of these benefits. Otherwise, the stick included a whole range of methods of destabilization of regimes from outright invasion, covert deployment of or support for armed dissident movements, to economic blockades and more subtle political and diplomatic pressures. This systematic campaign of destruction has occurred on a scale not always realized in the west, and has cost thousands of lives and billions of pounds in damage. Then after such a softening up, the carrot of a let-up in the attacks and renewed supplies of goods is offered again – for a price. All this is part of South Africa's 'total strategy' a sustained onslaught against its neighbours. As the 1977 South African White Paper on Defence and Armaments Production stated: 'The resolution of a conflict in the times which we live demands interdependent and co-ordinated action in all fields – military, psychological and political, sociological.' Because of this combination of tactics it is not always clear what the policy objectives are in any one area: to replace the regime (as in Lesotho), to bring about more economic and political incorporation or to maintain a broken-backed state.

Mozambique and Angola have perhaps taken the brunt of direct and covert acts of destabilization by South African forces and of its support of dissident organizations – specifically the Union for the Total Liberation of Angola (UNITA) and the Mozambique National Resistance (MNR or Renamo). After South Africa's humiliating defeat in Angola in 1975–6 when MPLA formed the new independent government, South African Defence Forces have invaded the southern part of the country on at least six different occasions and have caused massive destruction over vast areas. They still, despite the Lusaka agreements of 1983 agreeing to withdrawal, occupy the southern part of that country. At the same time, their support – in terms of mobility, logistics and arms – is what has made possible the widespread operations of Savimbi's UNITA.

South African forces have undertaken many covert actions against the Mozambique government. It has also imposed a partial economic boycott of the port of Maputo, and South African traffic in 1983 fell to one half that of 1982 and only 16 per cent of the 1973 level, after earlier systematic destruction of the port of Beira, the oil pipeline, roads and railways which were Zimbabwe's (and to some extent other SADCC countries like Zambia's) main arteries to the outside world. However the main instrument of destabilization of the Mozambican economy and society has been South Africa's support for Renamo: a resistance movement opposed to FRELIMO (Mozambican Liberation Front), originally spawned by the Rhodesian government after Mozambique's independence from the Portuguese in 1975. Indeed, it was initially formed from members of the Portuguese secret police and others who had lost land and property appropriated during the takeover from the colonial government. Between 1982 and 1983, after it had passed under South African tutelage, official figures estimate that Renamo activities had destroyed 140 villages, 840 schools, 900 rural shops and more than 200 public health installations. Apart from this physical destruction, whose financial cost was put at $US3.8 billion, the most horrific of the atrocities perpetrated by the South African-backed Mozambique National Resistance Movement (MNR) in Mozambique was the widespread and systematic sabotage of roads, depots and convoys that were seeking to get food relief to drought-stricken areas, especially in the south. These deliberate acts turned food shortage into a famine that claimed perhaps 200,000 needless deaths. In comparison to that, South Africa's bombing raids, its support for dissidents and its assassinations of opponents of apartheid in Lesotho, Swaziland, Zimbabwe and Botswana seem minor.

South Africa's Strategy for the Region

By 1983 these measures had reduced most of the countries of the region to a broken-backed and pliable state; but this seemingly was not enough. Despite the signing of the Nkomati Accord in 1984, which the Mozambique government hailed as a 'victory', thinking it would at least give them a breathing space wherein they could rebuild their massively disrupted economy, there has in fact been no peace for Mozambique. Attacks, sabotage and terrorizing of the population have continued unabated; the only change has been a partial northward shift in their location, as though the MNR were not operating from South Africa. Likewise the withdrawal of South African troops from Angola, agreed in the Lusaka accords of early 1984, has been only partial, and disruptions by the South African-backed UNITA also continue. Indeed now 'big brother' Reagan has stepped in to give it his blessing and covert support in undermining of the Angolan government. Unlike Mozambique, where there has been a real threat to running any semblance of a national economy and even to the maintenance of a viable state, Angola's international security has been more guaranteed, partly by the continued presence of Cuban troops.

Now as we write, the Lesotho regime of Chief Jonathan, which may have said things Pretoria didn't like, but whose actions were always susceptible to economic pressure, has been toppled. These acts of destabilization are not without some costs to South Africa. Internally, the extra economic burden at a time of crisis is heightened by the loss of 'boys at the front'; externally it earns condemnation just when the international bandwagon for sanctions is gaining momentum. If even 'Marxist–Leninist' Mozambique has shown itself compliant and open to economic ties, why then does the reliance of tactics of disruption go on? Why aren't the levers of economic penetration (which are anyway inhibited by instability) enough? It is important that we are not content just to condemn South Africa's immediate actions; we need to understand its long-run purposes, if we are to fathom what lies ahead.

South Africa's continued acts of destabilization and incursions into Angola would seem designed to ensure the Cuban's stay – despite the oft-stated aim of the Republic and the United States that they want them out. There are no economic levers South Africa can use against Angola, which makes a difference in relations with that country. However, Pretoria could also be determined to make a reality of scare tactics over a 'communist threat' that it uses to draw in the west to its side. This is perhaps so in the case of Angola, but this scarcely explains continued destabilizing of Mozambique, where there are no foreign troops, where the government has now expelled the ANC and is openly looking for economic investment. It could be that the Renamo has just got out of hand, or in the hands of ex-Portuguese colonial interests, as South Africa seems to want us to believe. Far less tenable is the view that some elements of the South African Defence Forces are out of control and independently assisting Renamo. Clearly it could not continue to operate without at least arms supplies from the South African Defence Forces, and equally clearly this is a deliberate act, not a mistake or an act of rebellion by the military. And clearly, too, there are reasons why South Africa should not live up to its side of an unequal treaty: it may be suspicious of Mozambique back-sliding, and anyway in its dealings with other countries, e.g. Zambia since 1974, it has never seen economic blandishments and leverage as a *substitute* for disruption. The puppeteer aims to pull on two strings.

Another aspect of the 'total strategy', which may shed light on present actions, is that South Africa realizes that not even its own considerable military might can provide a long-run guarantee of the stability of the restructured system within and outside South Africa that it is trying to put into place. Only the involvement of the west, and especially of the United States, can do that. And certainly one consequence of recent aggressions, and of the agreements that they have extracted, has been to provide, for the first time, a significant United States political and military presence in the region. The United States has set up a mission in Namibia ostensibly to monitor the cease-fire in Angola. The Reagan administration has also a foot in the door in Mozambique, to which it has given military aid. And Reagan has now literally embraced Savimbi.

Another perspective would see South Africa's external actions as primarily a reaction to the *internal* threat to the apartheid system. Unable to contain mounting military operations within the Republic, it seeks to undermine the ANC's platform in surrounding countries – and even, to get them to collaborate in curtailing the ANC, as Botha said was his aim in Mozambique. But faced as it is with manifold and new forms of opposition which owe nothing to outside forces, which have escalated in the 1980s and which the regime can't contain, it turns, partly in desperation, to its considerable armoury and to the only places where it can unleash its destructive capacity – the front-line states. Thus, predictably, when in late 1985 the outside world eventually moves to impose some sanctions, President Botha responds with a promise to wreak havoc on the SADCC countries. To 'take others down with her' may be one of the few cards South Africa can play to respond to an increasingly uncontrollable internal situation and to scare off international pressures for change. These internal challenges to the system represent the crucial dynamic, and we will return to them in this chapter's conclusion.

Front-Line States and South Africa

If this kind of line of 'rolling back' of radical regimes is in part an extension of a globalist perspective to this particular region, it may well also be a response to shifting tides within southern Africa. For several years South Africa has pursued a strategy of undermining and also incorporating its neighbours, the emphasis between these two dimensions shifting over time and between countries which were faced with destabilization. Western powers and particular capitalist interests were faced with the choice of mild protest or silent acquiescence. In general these interests might have preferred to see South Africa using its economic ties to dominate and extend the regional economic grid rather than to engage in too overt a destabilization; they perhaps generally supported those infrastructural and other aspects of the SADCC project that extended the regional network, but not in so far as they posed an alternative to eventual integration within South Africa. But, up to now, such calculations were made in terms of how they would like to see, (and how the South African state in practice sought), the structuring of relations between the independent, 'peripheral' countries of the region and a South Africa that was, whatever else, stable. Now the main issue for South African and imperialist states alike is not the regional relationship but the restructuring of a now *unstable* South Africa. One new calculation may thus well be to ensure that the front-line states are least able to put some weight behind a more progressive resolution of contradictions internal to South Africa. This would be a prescription, if the analysis is correct, for continued softening-up operations against all the neighbouring countries, as a prelude to restructuring the internal South African situation – an imperative as much for western and US as for South African policymakers.

Tension was heightened on 19 October 1986. In circumstances indicating South African complicity the aircraft carrying President Samora Machel, returning to Maputo from a mission to Lusaka, crashed in South African territory. Thirty-four of the delegation were killed – including President Machel.

Such a possible response to the internal upheavals in the Republic may go some way to explain why there is still no let-up in the destabilization of Mozambique; why the Lesotho government has been undermined; and why the US with its support for UNITA and, apparently, its covert role in support of the MNR in Mozambique has come more into the picture. It may also explain why there has been no progress toward negotiated independence in Namibia, despite the long initiative of the five-member western-nation contact group, and why South Africa is now going ahead with its own 'internal solution'. If this is so, it offers a grave prognosis for these countries and for Zimbabwe, Botswana and Zambia as well. It is no longer the radicalism of their internal policies, their attempts to distance themselves from South Africa, nor their specific support for the ANC that renders them targets, but the survival of any capability for political or economic coherence at all. Paralysed states and economies, severely weakened and entirely dependent on South Africa, would make it possible to concentrate on internal events without having to consider the peripheral areas seriously in their calculations. Any such tendency will be reinforced by South Africa's stated intention to make the surrounding economies suffer in the event of sanctions being imposed against the Republic – a form of blackmail by South Africa to reduce western pressures on them for concessions.

Such possible calculations do not augur well for the further implementation of the SADCC project of mutual development and reduction of dependence on South Africa. There has, in fact, always been an ambiguity about the way these objectives have been pursued in practice. Certain infrastructural projects do enhance linkages between the countries, but often in such ways that they also add to the grid linking these areas into the regional networks, and in turn to South Africa. Only some initiatives, certain alternative transport routes, the search for regional food security, etc. have a potential for developing a capability for independence from South Africa. In the present circumstances, these latter projects are likely to come under greater threat. They are likely to be even less popular as recipients of aid. And such measures as building up food stocks in surplus countries to meet needs of deficit countries, while feasible economically given Zimbabwe's and Malawi's levels of production, will have to contend with the real possibility of South African destruction of facilities and transport networks. Should there be any doubt about this, one has only to recall recent history: the destruction of food conveys and supplies by the South African-backed MNR in southern Mozambique in 1983 which turned drought into mass starvation. Moreover, in 1979 during the final negotiations over Zimbabwe's independence, similar destruction of transport links and food denial against Zambia and Mozambique was an effective tactic by the Rhodesians, also backed by South Africa, in wrenching concessions out of the front-line states and, in turn, the Zimbabwe liberation movements.

It is likely, therefore, that South African destabilization, perhaps backed actively by the US, will be a feature of efforts to cope with internal restructuring and pressures for more fundamental change in South Africa; that South Africa will attempt to spoil, by economic and military means, the SADCC countries' efforts to protect their economies, through food-security programmes for instance. It also seems reasonable to conclude that such pressures may well continue into any period of negotiation over South Africa's future – i.e. even while there is a *de facto* 'cease-fire' inside the Republic.

If the immediate prospects for the front-line states are disturbing, the longer term holds out some intriguing possibilities to them for redefining their present relations with racist South Africa. Even the immediate period ahead may hold out positive as well as negative possibilities. There are those in Zimbabwe, for instance, who see the possibility of their country being forced into another period of self-sustained industrial innovation and growth as occurred during the sanctions imposed against Smith's Rhodesia in the 1960s and 1970s. Beyond this, the prospect of pursuing their own regional and national programmes, without the enormous costs, disruptions and thus distortions imposed by South African interventions, must seem an encouraging light at the end of the tunnel, and will indeed make some different futures available to these countries. One thinks of Mozambique especially. Of course those futures might also induce problems for those regimes, like Zambia's or Mozambique's in recent years, that have been inclined to foist all the blame for the straits they are in on the external factor. But the more basic question that is prompted concerns the fate of the various 'socialisms' that have been attempted in the region.

In many international circles, solidarity has been geared largely to identification with and support for the left-wing strategies pursued by some of the liberated countries – both as a legacy of support for earlier struggles but also as an element in strengthening these countries as a support base for the struggle in South Africa and Namibia. In the 1980s, the destabilization efforts of South Africa and enforced agreements, like Nkomati, and the necessarily changed strategy of revolution in South Africa, have meant that the neighbouring states have ceased to be 'front line' – except in the sense of being on the receiving end. But equally the prospect for any socialist transformation in these countries has taken a blow. Nor, if we are to be candid, can all the blame be laid at South Africa's door. While the process of national liberation struggle did leave a legacy of ideologically committed leaderships – in the form of avowedly Marxist–Leninist parties in Angola and Mozambique, and in a more ambiguous, but not yet definitely neo-colonial way in Zimbabwe, the extent to which there was a radicalization and mobilization of workers, migrants and peasants was, it now must be admitted, exaggerated and/or that awakening has been left to atrophy. If the political capabilities for

socialist transformation were not all in place, some of the strategic choices of
the road to be followed were clearly ill-conceived – especially the penchant for
gigantismo in development, with emphasis on the large scale and mechanization,
so expensive in money and import terms. But what is also clear now, with
hindsight, is the utopian element in strategies that assumed any significant transformation would be viable in the teeth of the heavy political threat from South
Africa, coupled with economies so structurally intertwined with and dependent
on South Africa. Such transformations will only be on the agenda once major
change has occurred in South Africa. One hopes that the political will and capability
will not by then have eroded.

Looking ahead to those possible futures, it must also be recognized that a change
from the racist character of the South African state, even progressive social and
economic policies in the Republic, will not automatically reduce the neighbours'
overwhelming reliance on imports of food and manufactures, on transport routes,
on jobs for migrants, on a market for power and other supplies, that South Africa
represents. For that reason the SADCC project, in so far as it has developed their
economic capacities, may allow these countries to re-engage with a liberated South
Africa on a slightly more equal footing. But for the same reason it can also be
said that the period where it was seen as necessary for the SADCC countries
to seek economic independence may be coming to an end, even while that independence will be needed and be tested to the full in the short-term crisis period
immediately ahead.

Conclusions

As we earlier warned, we are not offering a prediction of what will happen in
southern Africa. The possible outcomes are finite but there are many combinations
of possibilities – of the new or not so new social structure that might emerge
in South Africa, of the process whereby it emerges, and of repercussions for the
surroundings regimes.

We have contented ourselves with trying to put forward a view of the task ahead
in South Africa and the region – that it is not solely a matter of changing attitudes
or even just social practices but of fundamentally altering social, economic and
political structures both within the Republic and in relationships within the region.
Beyond that, we have pointed to the range of outcomes and to the various set
of social forces – powerholders of the regime and external powers, and the
opposition movements: the various already privileged (white) classes, the potentially advantaged (black) classes, i.e. the petty bourgeoisie and (to a degree) the
skilled workers, and the disadvantaged migrant workers and Bantustan womenfolk
– that are locked in struggle and whose interests and effectiveness in defending
them will shape that outcome. The one conclusion from our caution in the face
of these complexities is to urge against any too simplistic posing of the alternatives
or specifying prescriptions of what should be done.

We feel this caution is warranted in the teeth of the many ready-made analyses
of the southern African situation that are on offer on the left internationally, some
of which have a pre-packaged answer to the question of what will inevitably occur,
or (more often) narrow the alternatives down to two starkly opposed alternatives.

One such approach that could be generally derived from a too historical application of the view of apartheid as 'racial capitalism' would conclude that apartheid cannot therefore be reformed: the alternatives are purely superficial changes or socialism. One concrete political example of such thinking is a line put forward by a breakaway group that calls itself the Marxist Workers Tendency of the ANC, which believes that the capitalist rationale of apartheid precludes the possibility of majority rule that does not imply socialism. While not rejecting the 'racial capitalist' characterization, thus far we have tended to argue that the particular set of conjunctures – of emphasis on super-exploitation of unskilled manual labour plus a cross-class alliance based on race – in which apartheid emerged are not givens. A third set of alternatives, some sort of 'reformed', non-racist (or not primarily racist) capitalism is not an impossibility, and is being actively probed by interests around the South African state and in the west, although the political prerequisites of such a deal will be difficult to achieve and their possible form is as yet unclear; perhaps there might be some kind of federation – although the time for that may already be passed.

Our cautions would also extend to other analyses that have tried not to predict outcomes but to identify the pre-conditions for certain desired changes. Some formulae suggest certain methods of struggle will bring certain social forces to the fore that will herald in certain types of changes. One such view is the 'radicalization' thesis that emerged from the successful struggle for liberation in Angola, Mozambique and Zimbabwe: that where armed struggle occurs, often out of necessity militants will more closely identify with the people (i.e. peasants and to some extent workers) and thus the movement will put socialism (or national democracy, at least) on the agenda. However useful, an understanding of earlier events elsewhere (and that we have questioned), the actual evolution of the struggle in South Africa in the 1980s has ruled out that kind of guerilla war scenario.

Another 'model' is offered by the 'workerist' view that preaches the need for struggle 'at the point of production', which would bring out the working class's vanguard position in the struggle and thus, in turn, also put socialism on the agenda. Consideration of such issues is vital, precisely because the struggle is entering a phase where it has not only to be a struggle against an unchanged status quo but a struggle with South Africa's version of neo-colonialism – of incorporation of some blacks, while retaining the basic structures of capitalism, even of a capitalism based on cheap, migrant labour. But to move from the recognition of this issue to the call for a specifically workers' political organization – as do some trade-union circles inside, plus some groups outside with a reflexive Trotskyist formulae for all seasons, is too simplistic.

Indeed the actual dynamics of the struggle may have already transcendended the simple dichotomy between 'workerist' and 'nationalist or populist' tendencies. This is evident in the joint 1985 statement of COSATU and ANC, and the joint action of unions, student and community organizations in the townships. The issues of what role workers should play within a broader 'nationalist' struggle and what constitutes the post-apartheid phase of struggle are precisely the issues that engage the emerging opposition groups in South Africa. These are again complex issues. What is a 'worker' in this context? Those obviously urbanized and proletarianized? And migrants? And women and families of the migrants in the Bantustans? What then of the 'peasantry'? Is there such a class? What also needs to be considered is the possible content of what we have termed, deliberately vaguely, the post-apartheid phase of struggle. Majority rule must clearly be an element. But so is some form of land reform, some working out of a long-term alternative to migrant labour (for South Africa and the whole region) and some decision on how to handle the vast mining sector.

It is urgent that consideration of such complexities and the ultimate definition of more clear-cut strategies take place within South Africa. But it is also important that the left outside delve into such matters. The particular difficulty to be faced now, internationally, is how to combine a preparedness to respond to support for a post-apartheid phase of struggle without prematurely undermining those coalitions which are likely to guarantee the success of the struggle against apartheid.

Notes

1 *Survey of Race Relations In South Africa 1983* (Johannesburg, Institute of Race Relations, 1983), pp. 262–3.
2 *Apartheid, The Facts* (London, International Defence and Aid Fund for Southern Africa, in cooperation with UN Centre Against Apartheid, June 1983), p. 44.
3 For more detail on this process of racial segregation at work see, S. Marks and R. Rathbone (eds), *Industrialisation and Social Change in South Africa: African Class Formation, culture and consciousness 1870–1930* (London, Longman, 1982), and Charles van Onselen, *Studies in the Social and Economic History of the Witwatersrand 1886–1914*, 2 vols (Johannesburg, Raven Press, 1982).
4 Introduction to Marks and Rathbone, *Industrialisation and Social Change in South Africa*.
5 *Business Daily*, Johannesburg, 14 May 1985.

Bibliography

1 From Fordism to Reaganism

For a fuller statement of the arguments in this chaper, see; M. Davis, *Prisoners of the American Dream* (London, Verso, 1986).

See also, on the international context, K. van der Pilj, *The Making of an Atlantic Ruling Class*, (London, Verso, 1985).

Trends in political economy can also be followed by reading M. Aglietta, *A Theory of Capitalist Regulation* (London, New Left Books, 1979), A. Lipietz, 'Towards Global Fordism', *New Left Review*, 132 (March–April 1982), and, M. Aglietta 'World Capitalism in the 1980's', *New Left Review*, 136 Nov.–Dec. 1982).

2 The Soviet Bloc

For an extended discussion of the issues raised in this chapter see E. Mandel, *Revolutionary Marxism Today* (London, New Left Books, 1979).

Alternative assessments of the Soviet Union and the Eastern Bloc can be found in C. Harman *Class Struggles In Eastern Europe* (London, Pluto Press, 1983); R. Bahro, *The Alternative in Eastern Europe* (London, New Left Books, 1978); M. Rakovski, *Towards An East European Marxism* (London, Allison & Busby, 1978); F. Fehér, A. Heller & G. Márkus, *Dictatorship Over Needs* (Oxford, Basil Blackwell, 1983); and A. Westoby, *Communism Since World War II* (Brighton, Harvester, 1981). *The Making of the Second Cold War* (London, Verso Editions & New Left Books, 1983) by Fred Halliday contains a judicious assessment of the role of the Soviet Union in international affairs.

The Stalinist Legacy (Harmondsworth, Penguin Books, 1984) edited by Tariq Ali contains useful chapters on Stalinism and political opposition in Eastern Europe.

Some sense of the character and complexity of political opposition in the Eastern Bloc can be found in B. Lomax, *Hungary 1956* (London, Allison & Busby 1976); B. Lomax (ed.), *Eyewitness in Hungary: The Soviet Invasion of 1956* (Nottingham, Spokesman, 1980); J. Pelikan, *Socialist Opposition in Eastern Europe: The Czechoslovak Example* (London, Allison & Busby, 1976); M. Simecka *The Restoration Of Order: The Normalization Of Czechoslovakia 1969–1976* (London, Verso, 1984); V. Havel *et al.*, *The Power of the Powerless* (London, Hutchinson, 1985); M. Haraszti, *A Worker In a Worker's State* (Harmondsworth, Penguin, 1977); C. Barker, *Festival Of The Oppressed: Solidarity, Reform And Revolution In Poland 1980–81* (London, Bookmarks, 1986); N. Ascherson, *The Polish August* (Harmondsworth, Penguin, 1981); M. Myant, *Poland: A Crisis For Socialism* (London, Lawrence & Wishart, 1982); and G. Konrád, *The Loser* (Harmondsworth, Penguin, 1984).

3 Ups and Downs

A general survey of European conditions at the end of the war is provided by R. Mayne, *Postwar* (London, Weidenfeld & Nicolson, 1983).

A good account of the US and international relations in the immediate post-war period is offered by G. Kolko and J. Kolko, *The Limits of Power: the World and US Foreign Policy* (New York, Harper & Row, 1972). A good account of the reconstruction of the international monetary system can be found in R. Gardiner, *Sterling Dollar Diplomacy* (Oxford, Oxford University Press, 1956). Distinctive explanations for the scale of the long boom and its demise are attempted by A. Maddison, *Phases of Capitalist Development* (Oxford, Oxford University Press, 1982), J. Cornwall, *Modern Capitalism: its Growth and Transformation* (Oxford, Basil Blackwell, 1977) and E. Mandel, *Late Capitalism* (London, New Left Books, 1975). For a detailed account of the break-up of the long boom and an alternative explanation, see P. McCracken, *Towards Full Employment and Price Stability* (Paris, OECD, 1977). An alternative analysis of the causes and effects of the break-up of the international monetary system in the late 1960s and early 1970s is given by R. Parboni, *The Dollar and its Rivals* (London, New Left Books, 1981). For detailed analyses of labour relations in western Europe see R. Flanagan, D. Soskice and L. Ulman, *Unionism, Economic Stabilization and Incomes Policies* (Washington, Brookings, 1983). The most coherent outline and defence of 'the left alternative' is provided by The London CSE Group, *The Alternative Economic Strategy* (London, CSE Books, 1980).

4 The New International Division of Labour

There are several good, mainstream economics texts which assess the empirical record of industrialization in the Third World and the effects of the growth of new industrial centres on the old: B. Balassa, *The Newly Industrializing Countries in the World Economy* (Oxford, Pergamon, 1981). L. T. Turner and N. McMullen, *The Newly Industrializing countries, trends and adjustment* (London, Allen and Unwin, 1982); OECD, *The Impact of the Newly Industrialising Countries on production and trade in manufactures*, Report by the Secretary General (Paris, OECD, 1979); R. H. Balance, J. A. Ansari and H. W. Singer, *The International Economy and Industrial Development* (Brighton, Wheatsheaf Books, 1982).

Particularly of relevance to the 'adjustment' problems of British manufacturing are the contributions in Rubin Riddell (ed.) *Adjustment or Protectionism: The Challenge to Britain of Third World Industrialisation* (London, CIIR, 1980). This collection of essays includes a balanced review of S. Korea as a major emerging industrial nation.

The first comprehensive critique of the new interational division of labour from within a neo-Marxist perspective, and substantiated with empirical case studies of the German textile industry in Southeast Asia, was F. Frobel, J. Heinrichs and O. Kreye, *The New International Division of Labour* (Cambridge, Cambridge University Press, 1980).

The 'dependent' nature of industrialization in the NICs forms the focus the voluminous collection of essays in D. Ernst, *The New International Division of Labour, Technology and Underdevelopment: consequences for the Third World* (Frankfurt, Campus Verlag, 1980).

Within the Marxist tradition, there have also been positive appraisals of Third World industrialization, attributing to it the potential for 'independent' national development. See Bill Warren, *Imperialism, Pioneer of Capitalism* (London, New Left Books, 1980).

A good review of the debate within Marxism on the dependent or independent nature of Third World industrialization is Rhys Jenkins, 'Divisions over the international division of labour', *Capital and Class*, no. 22 (Spring 1984). See also the contributions by Andreff and Lipietz, in the same volume which deal especially with the restructuring of world capitalism.

Finally, a useful student text on the nature of contemporary imperialism and the world system is A. Portes and J. Walton, *Labor, Class and the International System* (New York, Academic Press, 1981).

5 The Crisis In The Third World

There is a vast and disparate literature on the Third World. Much of what sets out to be of general interest and scope is necessarily bound by the area of expertise of its authors and, indeed, the best work is often the detailed area case study rather than the general text.

The debates concerning the influence of capitalist expansion into the Third World are presented best in Anthony Brewer, *Marxist Theories of Imperialism: A Critical Survey* (London, Routledge & Kegan Paul, 1980). Paul Baran's *The Political Economy of Growth* (Harmondsworth, Penguin, 1973) sets much of the agenda of debate for the last thirty years and is worth examination – if only to remind the reader that his arguments are more complex and sophisticated than has been represented by proponents and critics alike.

Hamza Alavi and Teodor Shanin, (eds), *Introduction to the Sociology of 'Developing Societies'* (London, Macmillan, 1982) and Charles K. Wilber, ed., *The Political Economy of Development and Underdevelopment* (New York, Random House, 1973 and 1979 edns) are excellent collections of readings on issues and structures of underdevelopment, dependency, peripheral capitalism, etc.

A useful introduction to multinational corporations and the impact of the international order on the Third World, is provided by Ronald Muller, 'The multi-national corporation and the underdevelopment of the Third World' in the Wilber collection cited above and by Norman Girvan, *Corporate Imperialism: Conflict and Expropriation* (Monthly Review, 1976).

On aid and aid agencies, see Teresa Hayter and Catherine Watson, *Aid: Rhetoric and Reality* (London, Pluto Press, 1985) and on the role of the IMF in regulating the Third World, see the special issue of *Development Dialogue* (no. 2 of 1980).

The reader seeking a set of texts linking the Third World to general issues of corporate expansion and international capital flows, could do a lot worse than start with Hugo Radice, (ed.), *International Firms and Modern Imperialism* (Harmondsworth, Penguin, 1975), an excellent collection.

On the general context of the current crisis, see Yann Fitt, Alexandre Faire and Jean-Pierre Vigier, *The World Economic Crisis* (London, Zed Press, 1980); Samir Amin, Giovanni Arrighi, Andre Gundar Frank and Immanuel Wallerstein, *Dynamics of Global Crisis* (London, Macmillan, 1982).

The literature on the post-colonial state is badly in need of development itself. For a critical survey of the issues it raises, see Carolyn L. Baylies, 'State and class in postcolonial Africa' in Maurice Zeitlin, (ed), *Political Power and Social Theory*, vol. 5 (London, Jai Press, 1985). An important attempt to build a theory of the postcolonial state is found in Clive Y. Thomas, *The Rise of the Authoritarian State in Peripheral Societies* (London, Heinemann, 1984).

Issues of class and state and of class formation and class struggle in the Third World are necessarily area or case-study based. See, among many, James Petras, *Critical Pespectives on Imperialism and Social Class in the Third World* (New York, Monthly Review, 1978); Robin Cohen, P. Gutkind and P. Brazier, (eds), *Peasants and Proletarians* (New York, Monthly Review 1979); Carolyn L. Baylies and Morris Szeftel, 'The rise of a Zambian capitalist class in the 1970s', *The Journal of Southern African Studies* 8 (2) 1982.

Work which is area-focused and which raises a variety of the issues under discussion includes: Peter Evans, *Dependent Development: the alliance of multinational, state and local capital in Brazil* (Princeton, NJ, 1979); Anupam Sen, *The State, Industrialization and Class Formations in India* (London, Routledge and Kegan Paul, 1982); Hamza Alavi, 'India and the Colonial Mode of Production', *The Socialist Register* (1975) Patnaik Rudra, Banaji et al, *Studies in the Development of Capitalism in India* (Lahore, Pakistan, Vanguard Books, 1978); Latin American Bureau, *The Poverty Brokers: The IMF and Latin America*

(London, LAB, 1983); Roger Burbach and Patricia Flynn, *Agribusiness in the Americas* (New York, Monthly Review, 1980); Special Issue on 'Dependency and Marxism', *Latin American Perspectives*, 8 (3/4) 1981; and Martin Fransman, ed., *Industry and Accumulation in Africa* (London, Heinemann, 1982).

6 The Arms Race and Cold War

For discussion of the Cold War see G. Kolko and J. Kolko, *The Limits of Power: The World and US Foreign Policy* (New York, Harper & Row, 1972); D. Horowitz, *From Yalta to Vietnam* (Harmondsworth, Penguin, 1967); D. Yergin, *Shattered Peace* (Boston, Houghton Mifflin Co. 1977); and V. Mastny, *Russia's Road to the Cold War* (New York, Columbia University Press, 1979).

On the character and dynamics of the new Cold War, see F. Halliday, *The Making of the Second Cold War* (London, Verso & New Left Books, 1983); N. Chomsky, J. Steele and J. Gittings, *Superpowers in Collison: The New Cold War* (Harmondsworth, Penguin 1982); New Left Review (ed.) *Exterminism and Cold War* (London, Verso, 1982); and J. Steele, *The Limits of Soviet Power* (Harmondsworth, Penguin, 1984).

The most reliable source on military capacity and expenditure is The Stockholm International Peace Research Institute (SIPRI) in their SIPRI yearbook, *World Armaments and Disarmament* (London, Taylor & Francis, annual); see also P. Rogers, *Guide to Nuclear Weapons 1984–5* (Bradford, Bradford School of Peace Studies, 1984).

7 The Third Great Revolution

Chen Erjin, *China Crossroads Socialism: An Unofficial Manifesto for Proletarian Democracy* (London, Verso, 1984) – a critical analysis of contemporary Chinese politics published in China during the Democracy Movement in 1979 with a programme for radical democratic reform.

On post-Mao policies, see: Stephan Feuchtwang and Athar Hussain (eds), *The Chinese Economic Reforms* (Kent, Croom Helm, 1983); John Gardner, *Chinese Politics and the Succession to Mao* (London, Macmillan, 1982) – for analyses of the politics of leadership conflict in the Chinese Communist Party in the aftermath of Mao's death; and Jack Gray and Gordon White (eds), *China's New Development Strategy*, (London, Academic Press, 1982) – on the changes in Chinese development policies in the immediate aftermath of Mao's death in the late 1970s.

A personal history of everyday life and political struggles during the Cultural Revolution decade is given by Liang Heng and Judith Shapiro, *Son of the Revolution* (London: Fontana, 1984). A classic study of land reform in a Chinese village on the eve of nationwide revolutionary victory is provided by William Hinton, *Fanshen: A Documentary of Revolution in a Chinese Village* (New York, Monthly Review Press, 1966). For a comprehensive review and evaluation of China's politics and economics in the early 1980s see Neville Maxwell and Bruce McFarlane (eds), *China's Changed Road to Development* (Oxford, Pergamon, 1984). A very useful textbook on Chinese politics after 1949 is Tony Saich, *China: Politics and Government* (London, Macmillan, 1981). A classic study by US sociologists of Chinese government and society before the Cultural Revolution can be found in Franz Schurmann, *Ideology and Organisation in communist China* (Berkeley, University of California Press, 1966). A comprehensive analysis of recent developments by a group of international experts is provided by Gerard Segal and William T. Tow (eds), *Chinese Defence Policy* (London, Macmillan, 1984). For a study of the Yenan base area and its influence on Chinese revolutionary politics and ideology, see Mark Selden, *The Yenan Way in Revolutionary China* (Cambridge, Mass., Harvard University Press, 1971). On

Chinese socialism, see: Mark Selden and Victor Lippit (eds), *The Transition to Socialism in China* (New York, Sharpe, 1982) for a review and evaluation of Chinese development performance by North American scholars; Su Shaozhi, *Democracy and Socialism in China* (Nottingham, Spokesman Books, 1982), which features a leading official Chinese Marxist scholar in conversation with East European and western scholars, including Polish economist Wlodzimierz Brus; and Xue Muqiao, *China's Socialist Economy* (Peking, Foreign Languages Press, 1981), which gives a valuable analysis by a senior Chinese economist of the central problems of socialist political economy. A very useful analysis of changes in foreign policy in the 1970s and early 1980s is provided by Michael Yahuda, *China's Foreign Policy after Mao* (London, Macmillan, 1983). For a comprehensive analysis of the post-Mao economic reforms edited by a noted Chinese economist, see Yu Guangyuan (ed.), *China's Socialist Modernization* (Peking, Foreign Languages Press, 1984).

8 The Middle East in International Perspective

An excellent general introduction, covering politics, sociology and economics, with a comprehensive bibliography, is provided by Talal Asad and Roger Owen (eds), *The Middle East* (Macmillan, London, 1983).

The best book on the Iranian revolution and its aftermath, and particularly good on the politics and ideas of the regime, is Shaul Bakhash, *The Reign of the Ayatollahs* (London, I. B. Tauris, 1985).

For a brilliant anthropological study of Islam in practice, far from the abstract analyses of theology and holy texts, see Michael Gilsenan, *Recognizing Islam* (London, Croom Helm, 1983).

A history of the revolutionary movements in Arabia, and of the role of imperialism in the Gulf region is provided by Fred Halliday, *Arabia without Sultans* (London, Penguin, 1974).

A succinct historical overview and balanced introduction to the contemporary situation can be found in Bernard Lewis, *The Arabs in History* (London, Longman, 1968).

A persuasive account of the development of the problem, critical of Arab and Israeli nationalism, is Maxime Rodinson, *Israel and the Arabs* (2nd edn) (London, Penguin, 1982).

On the history and politics of the Jews, Maxime Rodinson, *Cult, Ghetto and State: The Persistence of the Jewish Question* (London, Al Saqi Books, 1983) provides a set of interlocking essays.

For an erudite, measured and incisive analysis of the development of Arab nationalism from the 1950s onwards, see Maxime Rodinson. *Marxism and the Muslim World* (London, Zed Press, 1979).

Jon Rotschild (ed.) *Forbidden Agendas: Intolerance and Defiance in the Middle East* (London, Al Saqi books, 1984) is a collection of texts on oppressed groups in the Middle East, including women, ethnic minorities and workers.

The classic study of the implantation of the oil companies in the Middle East and of their place in the economics of the world market is Joe Stork, *Middle East Oil and the Energy Crisis* (New York, Monthly Review Press, 1975).

9 The United States and Central America

On Central America, see The Stanford Central America Action Network (ed.), *Revolution in Central America* (Boulder, Westview Press, 1983); Jenny Pearce, *Under The Eagle* (London, Latin American Bureau, 1982); G. Black, *Triumph of the People: the Sandinista Revolution in Nicaragua,* (London, Zed Press, 1982); James Dunkerley, *The Long War: Dictatorship and Revolution in El Salvador* (London, Zed Press 1985); Roger Burback and Patricia Flynn (eds), *The Politics of Intervention: The United States in Central America* (New York, Monthly Review, 1984); Timothy Harding and Nora Hmilton (eds), *Modern Mexico* (London, Sage, 1986).

10 Southern Africa

On the background and the growth of the Apartheid State, and South African capitalism see: H. J. Simons and R. E. Simons, *Class and Colour in South Africa 1850–1950* (London, International Defense and Aid Fund for Southern Africa, 1976); Dan O'Meara, *Volkskapitalisme: Class and Ideology in the Development of Afrikaner Nationalism, 1930–48* (Cambridge, Cambridge University Press, 1983), Shula Marks and Richard Rathbone (eds), *Industrialisation and Social Change in South Africa: African class formation, culture and consciousness 1876–1930* (London, Longman, 1982); Charles van Onselen, *Studies in the Social and Economic History of the Witwatersrand 1886–1914*, vol. 1 *New Babylon*, vol. 2 *New Nineveh* (Johannesburg, Ravan Press, 1982); Duncan Innes, *Anglo-American and the Rise of Modern South Africa* (London, Heinemann Educational Books, 1984), *Review of African Political Economy*, no. 7 'Special Issue on South Africa'; Merle Lipton, *Capitalism and Apartheid: South Africa, 1910–1986*, (London, Wildwood House, 1985) and Robin Cohen, *Endgame in South Africa?* (London & Paris, James Currey and Unesco Press 1986), E. Webster, *Cast in a Racial Mould* (Cape Town, Raven Press, 1986), the most detailed recent work on trade unions.

For a factual guide to South Africa's everyday racial policies, see: Roger Omond, *The Apartheid Handbook* (Harmondsworth, Penguin, 1985) and the *Survey of Race Relations in South Africa* (Johannesburg, South African Institute of Race Relations annual).

On the liberation movements, see the comprehensive two-volume work, Rob Davies, Dan O'Meara, Sipho Dlamini, *The Struggle for South Africa, A Reference Guide to Movements, Organisations and Institutions* (London, Zed Press, 1984), and Tom Lodge, *Black Politics in South Africa since 1945*, (London, Longman, 1983).

On South African terrorism in the region see: Phyllis Johnson and David Martin (eds), *Destructive Engagement, Southern Africa at War* (Harare, Zimbabwe Publishing House, 1986), and Joseph Hanlon, *Beggar Your Neighbours, Apartheid Power in Southern Africa* (London, Catholic Institute for International Relations with James Currey, 1986) and for introductions to the region, Joseph Hanlon, *Mozambique: the Revolution Under Fire* (London, Zed Press, 1984), Jane Bergerol and Michael Wolfers, *Angola in the Front Line* (London, Zed Press, 1984) and C. Stoneman, *Zimbabwe's Inheritance*, (London, Macmillan, 1980).

Index

Aden, 207
Adenauer, 9, 51
Afghanistan, 41, 153, 159, 164, 191, 201
Africa, 87, 88, 90, 92, 96, 101, 103, 105, 108, 109, 128, 171, 211, 213; and coups, 124; and multinationals, 113
Albania, 30; Doce, 32
Alcoa, 235
Algeria, 40, 91, 205, 207, 213, 215
Alliance for Progress, 14, 15, 16, 23, 234, 245
American Federation of Labor, 9, 240
American Institute for Free Labor Development, 240
Andino, Turburcio Carias, 231
Andropov, 158
Angola, 4, 122, 130, 153, 176, 222, 257, 272, 275, 276, 278, 280, 285; and Lusaka Accords, 280, 281; and MPLA, 275; and UNITA, 256, 275, 281, 283; see also Savimbi, Jonas
apartheid, see South Africa
Arab League, 210
Arbenz, Colonel Jacobo, 232, 233, 239, 242
Arevalo, Juan Jose, 232, 242
Argentina, 71, 80, 124, 222; and debt, 101, 196; and nuclear weapons, 143; and Peronism, 210
arms race, 142–4 see also 141–68
Arrafat, Yasir, 212
Asia, 87, 88, 92, 101, 105, 109, 111, 171, 211, 275; and multinationals, 113, 116

Asian Productivity Organization, 72
Atlas Chemical Company, 235
Austria, 27
Australia, 91

Bahamas, 75
Bahrain, 207
Balfour Declaration, 206
Banda, Hastings, 278
Bangladesh, 74, 210
Bank of America, 235
Baran, Paul, 108
Belgium, 58, 65, 151
Belize, 225
Bermuda, 75
Beveridge Report 1942, 51
Biao, Lim, 184
Bismarck, 51
Bolivia, 40
Borden Inc., 235
Bosch, 15
Boston Fruit Company, 229
Botha, P. W., 256, 261, 270, 271, 281
Botswana, 278, 280, 282
bourgeoisie, Muslim, 202; national, 71, 123, 173; Nicaragua, 240, 245; Third World, 122, 124, 126; US, 23
Brandt, Willy, 23, 51, 127, 153
Brazil, 40, 71, 72, 80, 89, 222, 234, 267; and debt, 95, 96, 101, 105, 106; and famine, 112, 117; and growth, 91, 94; and multinationals, 116; and nuclear weapons, 143
Breshnev, L., 30, 142, 158, 162, 164; and doctrine, 30
Bretton Woods, 77, 79

Brezezinki, 202, 244
Bukharin, No. 29
Bulgaria, 32, 36, 37, 38
Business Roundtable, 22
Business Week, 157, 158
Butler, R., 51

Canada, 65, 193
Caribbean, 16, 19
Carpio, Cayetano, 243
Carter, Jimmy, 22, 23, 129, 157, 201, 245, 276
Castro, Fidel, 15, 39, 105
Caterpillar Tractor Companies, 235
Ceausescu, 31
Central America, 3, 116, 122, 150, 157, 158, 217, 221–55; and Reform and revolution, 238, 244; and Spanish colonisation, 223
Central Intelligence Agency, 128, 131, 143, 232, 233, 247, 248; see also United States; Reagan, Ronald
Chamoun, Camille, 202
Chernenko, 158
Chile, 40, 80, 91, 124, 221; and debt, 105, 106
Christian Democracy, 9, 17, 221
Churchill, Winston, 29
Clark Amendment, 276
class struggle, 23, 82; and India, 124, 125; and People's Republic of China, 183; and Third World, 132; and United States, 18, 19; and Western Europe, 43–64, 54, 62
Coca Cola, 192, 242
Cold War, 2, 4, 8, 9, 14, 20, 22, 23, 24, 141, 148–59, 202, 252; and central America, 232, 244; and functions and dysfunctions, 159–62; and South Africa, 258
Comecon, 31, 36, 37; see also Soviet Union
Cominform, 47
Comintern, 28, 29
Committee in Solidarity with the People of El Salvador, 249
Committee on the Present Danger, 129
Confédération Générale du Travail, 47; see also, France
Confederazione Generale Italiane del Lavoro, 47; see also Italy
Congress of Industrial Organizations, 9, 16

Costa Rica, 223; and bananas, 229; and coffee production, 227, 228
Council on Foreign Relations, 128
Cranston, 22
Cuba, 4, 15, 39, 40, 201, 222, 248; and Angola, 275, 280; and Bay of Pigs, 14; and revolution, 124, 221, 233
Cyprus, 214
Czechoslovakia, 28, 30, 31, 33, 35, 37, 39, 41, 159; and Communist Party, 151; and Slansky, 32

Dawes Plan, 8
De Gasperi, 9
De Gaulle, General, 51, 153
Del Monte, 116, 230; see also, agribussiness
Democratic Party, see United States of America
détente, 35; 152–5
Deutscher, Isaac, 218
Dominican Republic, 15, 222
Duarte, José Napoleon, 240, 248
Dubček, A., 31
Dulles, J., 6, 14, 233
Dutch East India Company, 262
Duvalier, 130

East India Company, 110, 111, 136n.
East Timor, 105
Eastern Europe, 2, 3, 31, 32, 37, 38, 40, 41, 65, 67, 188; and cold war, 150, 151, 152, 164; and disarmament, 162, 164, 166; see also, Soviet Union
Egypt, 15, 40, 124, 204, 207, 208, 209, 210, 211, 213, 215
Eisenhower, D., 14, 152, 233
El Salvador, 105, 124, 130, 176, 221, 223, 230, 232, 233, 240, 245, 247; and Catholic Church, 241; coffee production, 227, 228, 231; and communist and opposition parties, 231, 240, 241; and death squads, 129; and landlessness, 238; ORDEN, 241; United Fruit Company, 229
Equador, 212
Ethiopia, 94, 129, 201
Eurocurrency markets, see, Eurodollar markets
Eurodollar markets, 77
European Nuclear Disarmament, 141–68

Export Processing Zones, *see* free trade zones

Fair Deal, 22
famine, 94, 107, 108, 112, 125, 129, 136n.; and China, 182; Mozambique, 280; relief, 117
Fanon, Franz, 123
Federal Republic of Germany, 8, 9, 17, 27, 41, 44, 51, 53, 65, 221, 248; and anti fascist committees, 45; and arms industry, 144; and detente, 153; and post-war reconstruction, 43–64; and Trades Unions 52–3
Fiat, 76
Finland, 27, 30, 65
Force Ouvrière, 47; *see also*, France
Fordism, 7, 10, 11, 12, 13, 14, 15, 16, 23
Fourth World, 83
France, 9, 27, 30, 40, 41, 45, 51, 151, 164, 171, 202, 207, 213, 215; and class structure, 17; and cold war, 150; and general strike, 47; and Middle East, 205; and nuclear weapons
free trade zones, 72, 82

Gaitskell, Hugh, 51
Galbraith, John Kenneth, 24
Gambia, 96
Gandhi, Rajiv, 125
Garcia, General Lucas, 236
GATT, 14
General Motors, 18
German Democratic Republic, 28, 34, 36, 37, 38, 154
Getulism, 210
Ghana, 103
Gierek, 35
Gomulka, 31
Gorbachev, M., 162
Gordon, General, 205
Gramsci, Antonio, 23
Greece, 30, 91, 158
Green Revolution, 89, 92
Grenada, 249, 257
Guatemala, 124, 129, 221, 222, 223, 230, 232–4, 236, 247; and bananas, 229; and cotton production, 227, 228; and Freedom Association, 236; and trade union movement, 242, 243; and Workers' Party, 232
Guinea-Bissau, 96
Gulf Oil, 276

Habib, Philip, 130
Heritage Foundation, 129
Herman, Edward, 124, 125
Hitachi, 192
Holland, 158
Honduras, 223; and bananas, 229, 230
Hong Kong, 72, 91, 132n., 172, 189, 193
Hoover, J. Edgar, 20
Hungary, 27, 33, 34, 37, 38, 39, 67, 159
Huntington, 122, 123
Husák, G., 39
Hussein, Saddam, 203

imperialism, 44, 81, 118, 119, 125, 145; and arms race, 41; and inter-imperialist conflict, 29, 81, 86n., and Middle East, 201, 204; and Soviet Union, 40; and sub-imperialism, 72, 83; and super-imperialism, 81, 86n.; and United Kingdom, 265; and US, 7, 14, 126
Import Substitution Industrialization, 70, 71, 89, 90; *see also*, 65–86
India, 40, 65, 67, 69, 70, 71, 111, 112, 121, 188, 214; and Congress Party, 121, 123, 124; and debt, 105; and growth, 89, 94; and Hindu, 210; and nuclear weapons, 143
Indonesia, 15, 40, 105, 132n., 210, 212, 214
Inter-American Development Bank, 101
International Business Week, 116
International Labour Office, 82
International Monetary Fund, 3, 15, 23, 34, 67, 81, 82, 109, 121, 222, 268; and conditionality, 80, 103–5, 117, 120, 126–7; and dominance by US, 126
International Power Systems Ltd, 79, 80
Iran, 3, 129, 131, 147, 209, 213, 215, 216, 274; and nuclear weapons, 143; and US hostages, 157; and war with Iraq, 201, 202, 203, 204
Iraq, 3, 40, 206, 207, 208, 210, 215; and Ba'th party, 215, 218
Islam, 202, 209, 210, 212, 215, 216, 217; and Shiite muslims, 202; and Sunni muslims, 202
Israel, 67, 214; and Arab war, 201, 202, 210, 218; and Lebanon, 203; and nuclear weapons, 143

Italy, 17, 27, 30, 40, 65, 151, 207, 211; and arms industry, 144; and Middle East, 205; and trade unions, 47
Ivory Coast, 103

Jackson, Jessie, 22, 251
Jamaica, 121, 126–7
Japan, 1, 2, 8, 10, 65, 66, 91, 128, 154, 158, 171, 172, 186, 190, 191, 193, 212, 221, 222, 235, 244; and boom 50; and class structure, 17; and communist party, 41; and crises, 54; and economy, 43, 44; and Hiroshima, 7, 142; and Japanese League of employment, 47; and Ministry of trade and industry, 53; Nagasaki, 142; and post-war reconstruction, 43–4; and Sino-war, 172, 173; and welfare provision and trade unions, 47, 48;
Jonathan, Chief, 280
Jordan, 91, 205, 208

Kádár, Janos, 31, 39
Kai-shek, Chiang, 172, 173, 175
Kamenev, L., 29
Kampuchea, 191
Kaunda, Kenneth, 275
Kautsky, Karl, 26
Kennedy, Edward, 22
Kennedy, John, F., 13, 14, 57, 152, 234
Kenya, 119, 208
Keynesianism, 14, 51, 63, 127
Khaldun, Ibn, 217
Khomeini, Ayatollah, 40, 203, 210, 216, 218
Khruschev, Nikita, 35, 142, 152
Kimberley Clark, 235
Kirkpatrick, Jeane, 247
Kissinger, Henry, 248, 275; and Commission on Central America, 248
Korean War, 10
Kornai, Janos, 188
Kumintang, 171, 172, 173, 176
Kurds, 203, 209, 215; see also Iran; Iraq
Kuwait, 207, 213; and oil, 212

Laclau, Ernesto, 109, 136n.
Latin America, 14, 15, 19, 20, 65, 71, 82, 87, 88, 90, 113, 118, 124, 125, 129, 130, 171; and Catholic Church, 238; and debt, 101, 109; and multinational subsidiaries, 113

Latin America Agribussiness Development Corporation, 235
League of Nations, 65
Lebanon, 3, 201, 207, 210; and war, 202, 203, 214
Lenin, V. I., 28
Lesotho, 257, 278, 281, 283
Lever, Lord, 96
Liberia, 96
Libya, 143, 204, 207, 212, 213, 214
Lodge, Senator, 229
Luxembourg, Rosa, 26

Macmillan, Harold, 51
Mahdi, 205
Malawi, 278, 263, 283
Malaysia, 72, 91, 132n.
Mali, 96
Malta, 67
Manchukuo, 172
Mandela, Nelson, 272
Manley, Michael, 121, 126
Marcos, F., 130
Marshall Plan, 9, 13, 14, 15, 23, 47
Martinez, General, Maximiliano, Hernandez, 231
Marx, Karl, 177, 198; see also, Marxism
Marxism, 172, 216, 217; Marxist-Leninism, 175, 180, 195
Mauritania, 96
McGovern, Goerge, 22
McNamara, Robert, 14
Merchant Capital, 109, 110
Mexico, 13, 15, 19, 80, 82, 83, 91, 222, 235; and debt, 96, 101; and Institutional Revolutionary Party, 221
Middle East, 3, 20, 125, 158, 201–20
Mitterand, François, 158
Mobuto, 278
Mondale, Walter, 252
Monroe Doctrine, 129, 223, 225, 230
Montes, Melida, Anaya, 243
Mora, Juan, Rafael, 225
Morocco, 205, 207, 208, 210, 214
Mossadeq, 131, 233
Mozambique, 85, 94, 122, 129, 131, 133n., 176, 222, 256, 272, 276, 283; and FRELIMO, 279; and MNR, 280, 282, 283, 284; and Nkomati, 281, 284

multinational corporations, 13, 71, 72,
126; and agribussiness, 116, 120,
124, 131, 235, 236; and bauxite,
127; and corporate growth, 113–17;
and industrial relocation, 73–81; and
international finance, 77; and
internalization theory, 74–5; and new
international division of labor 65–81;
and South Africa, 267, 275, 286; and
transfer pricing, 75–6, 194
Muzorewa, Abel, 275

Namibia, 4, 275, 276, 282; and Angola,
276
Napoleon, 204
Nasser 40, 124
National Security Council, 149
nationalism, 117, 118, 121, 124, 127,
129, 214, 216; Arab, 202, 206, 208,
213, 217; and South Africa, 267,
273, 274
Nazism, 206
New Deal, 16, 21, 22
New International Division of Labor, 2,
13, 65–86, 67, 80, 81, 83, 88
New Zealand, 91
newly industrialized countries, 65, 66,
69, 72, 73, 82, 154
Nicaragua, 225, 257; and bananas, 229;
and contras, 130, 243, 252; and
opposition movements, 241; and
revolution, 39, 40, 119, 122, 157,
176, 191, 221, 243; and Sandinista
Front for National Liberation, 239,
240; and United Fruit Company, 229;
and US intervention, 247; see also,
Sandino; Somoza
Nigeria, 72, 106, 124, 210, 212
Nissan, 81
Nixon, Richard, 146, 153, 191; and
Nixon doctrine, 147
non-proliferation treaty, 144
North Atlantic Treaty Organization, 9,
10, 145, 147, 148, 158, 166, 258
North Korea, 39, 204
North Yemen, 205, 206, 209
nuclear disarmament, 141–68
Nuclear Freeze Movement, 24
Numeiri, 105
Nyerere, Julius, 96

Oman, 91, 207, 213, 215
Organization of African Unity, 273

Organization of American States, 245
Organization for Economic Co-operation
and Development, 10, 15, 66, 67,
73, 193, 194, 212
Organization of Petroleum Exporting
Countries, 12, 13, 106, 107, 201,
208, 212, 216, 222
Ottoman Empire, 204, 205, 206

Pahlavi Monarch, 218; see also, Iran
Pakistan, 69, 124, 210; and nuclear
weapons, 143
Palau, 79, 80
Palestine, 3, 202, 205, 206, 207, 208,
209, 210, 212, 214, 218; and PLO,
212
Panama, 129, 223, 234; and bananas,
229; and canal, 231; and United Fruit
Company, 229
Pasha, Kemal, 206
Pasha, Urabi, 205
Peace Corps, 14; see also United States
of America
peasantry, 11, 88, 92, 112, 131, 173,
176, 177, 184, 204, 205, 231, 242,
263, 273, 276, 284, 286
People's Republic of China, 3, 28, 30
39, 41, 67, 69, 108, 171–200; and
building socialism, 176–89; and
communist party, 172, 183, 186,
192, 194, 195, 197; and cultural
revolution, 182, 184; and democracy
movement, 197, 198, 199; and
democratization, 195–200; and
foreign policy, 189–95; and great
leap forward, 180–6; and nuclear
weapons, 143, 144; and revolution,
171, 176–89; and rural peoples
communes; and socialist market
economies, 186–9; and special
economic zones, 192, 194; and
Yenan, 174, 175, 180
permanent revolution, 26
Peru, 101, 105, 121, 176; and American
Revolutionary Popular Alliance, 221
petit bourgeoisie: and China, 177; and
Eastern Europe, 34; and
independence movements in the Third
World, 119, 126; and Middle East,
216; and South Africa, 266, 284; and
state in Third World, 119, 120, 122;
and United States, 10, 17
Petras, James, 124, 125

Phelps Dodge, 235
Philippines, 3, 15, 72, 105, 132n., 176
Poland, 28, 32, 37, 38, 67, 198; and
    Solidarnosc, 32–3, 35, 159, 210
Pol Pot, 191; Policy Alternatives for the
    Caribbean and Central America, 251
Portugal, 91, 128; and colonialism, 276,
    278, 280
post-colonial state, see Third World
Pretoria, 3, 260, 276, 281; see also,
    South Africa
Puerto Rico, 24

Qaddafi, 215
Qatar, 207, 212

Reagan, Ronald, 3, 7, 16, 20, 22, 23,
    24, 129, 157, 158, 164, 191; and
    Central America, 233, 244–53; and
    imperialism, 128; and nuclear
    weapons, 144, 148; and southern
    Africa, 257, 259, 280, 281
Red Army, 29
Republican Party, see United States of
    America
Rodinson, Maxime, 218
Romania, 37, 39, 67
Roosevelt, Theodore, 29, 39, 230
Russia, 26; and revolution, 27, 89; see
    also, Soviet Union

Sacasa, Juan, B., 231
Sadat, Anwar, 212, 215
Samuelson, Paul, 44
Sandino, Colonel Cesar Augusto, 231
Sanyo, 82
Saudi Arabia, 91, 205, 208, 215; and
    oil, 212
Savimbi, Jonas, 4, 256, 267, 275, 280,
    282; see also, Angola
Schick, Rene, 239
Schumann, 9
Schumpeter, J., 44
Seaga, Edward, 126
Selden, Mark, 175
Shaoqi, Liu, 183
Singapore, 72, 132n.
Smith, Ian, 278
Socialism, 3, 26, 82, 84, 113, 118, 121,
    152, 164, 166, 171, 172, 191, 195,
    204, 215, 218; and China, 176–89;
    international conference 1976, 189;
    and South Africa, 257, 259, 269,
    271, 273, 284, 286

Sokolovsky Doctrine, 41
Somalia, 94, 96
Somoza, General Anastasio, 231, 236,
    239, 240, 243, 244, 245
South Africa: and ANC, 272, 273, 274,
    283; and apartheid, 256, 257, 258,
    259–86; AZAPO, 273; and
    Bantustans, 259, 260, 261, 263, 264,
    265, 269, 271; Black consciousness,
    273; and Buthelezi, Chief Gatsha,
    271, 274; and Congress Alliance,
    273; CONSAS, 278; and constructive
    engagement, 130; and COSAS, 274;
    COSATU, 274; and FOSATU, 274;
    and group areas act, 259, 262, 271;
    Inkatha movement, 272; Koornhoof
    act, 261, 270, 271; and Kwa Zulu,
    271, 274; and Marxist workers
    tendency of ANC, 286; and migrant
    labour, 232, 263, 266, 267, 271,
    287; and national forum, 273, 274;
    and nationalist party, 259, 263, 270,
    271; and nuclear weapons, 143, 258;
    and PAC, 272; and Pass laws, 259,
    260, 261; and population registration
    act, 259; Progressive Federal Party,
    271; and region, 276; and SACP,
    273; and SACTU, 273, 274, 278;
    and state of emergency, 256; and
    total strategy, 269–72, 280, 281; and
    trade unions, 270; and UDF, 272,
    274; and unity movement, 273; and
    white working class, 269, 273; and
    workers' unrest, 267, 268, 272, 274
South East Asian Treaty Organization, 8
South Korea, 13, 80, 92, 95, 132n.; and
    nuclear weapons, 143
South Yemen, 201, 207, 209, 215
southern Africa, 113, 266, 256–86; see
    also, South Africa
southern African Development Co-
    ordination Conference, 276, 280,
    282, 283, 284, 285
Soviet Bloc, see Eastern Europe
Soviet Union, 1, 3, 26–42, 44, 65, 121,
    128, 129, 190, 191, 201, 204, 215,
    221, 244, 245, 248, 275; and arms
    race, 142, 144; and bureaucracy, 28,
    39, 41; and cold war, 141, 148–59;
    and comecon, 31; and communist
    party, 27; and Eastern bloc trade,
    35–9; and new economic policy, 27;
    and nuclear disarmament, 162–6; and

nuclear strategy, 145–8; and nuclear weapons, 144–5; and opposition within Eastern Europe, 31; and revolution, 27, 205; and Sino conflict, 29; socialism in one country, 29, 32, 40; and thermidor, 27, 28, 29

Soweto, 256

Spain, 40; and colonialism, 223; and Spanish-American War, 230

Sri Lanka, 214

Stalin, Joseph, 28, 36, 146, 149, 151, 152; and Stalinism, 175

Standard Brands, 235

Star wars, 148

Sudan, 94, 103, 134n., 135n., 205, 209, 215; and debt, 105

Surplus Peoples Project, 260; see also South Africa

Swaziland, 278, 281

Sweden, 17

Switzerland, 120

Syria, 91, 202, 204, 206, 207, 208, 211, 212, 215

Taiwan, 3, 67, 72, 95, 132n., 172, 190, 199; and nuclear weapons, 143

Tanzania, 96, 263, 273

Thailand, 15

Thatcher, Margaret, 63, 64, 153, 191, 239, 258

Thermidor, see Soviet Union

Third World, 4, 17, 23, 37, 40, 65, 66, 67, 73, 79, 84, 87, 88, 90, 94, 107, 112, 120, 121, 141, 142, 147, 151, 153, 154, 155, 157, 162, 166, 176, 184, 188, 190, 191, 192, 193, 194, 201, 204, 207, 215, 221, 245; and arms expenditure, 105, 144; and crises, 87–139; and debt, 81, 82, 87, 94–105, 156; and economic exchange, 70; and export-oriented industrialization, 72; and industrialization, 67–73, 70, 117; and labour absorption rate, 69; and military coups, 105, 159; and multinational corporations, 113; and new international economic order, 65–86; and state, 119–25; and structural transformation, 69; and uneven development, 109–13

Thomas, Clive, 119, 122

Thompson, E. P., 156, 160

Togo, 96

Toshiba, 82

Trade Expansion Act 1963, 14; see also, United States of America

Transnational Corporations, see multinational corporations

Trilateral Commission, 128; and Trilateralists, 245

Trinidad, 91

Tropical Trading and Transport Corporation of USA, 229

Trotsky, Leon, 26, 27, 28, 29

Truman, Harry, 14; and Doctrine, 150

Tudeh party, 40

Tunisia, 205, 207

Turkey, 15, 62, 71, 205, 206, 207, 209, 213

Ubico, Jorge, 231, 232

Unilever, 236; and de Sola family, 236

United Arab Emirates, 91; and oil, 212

United Brands, 235

United Fruit Company, 229, 232

United Kingdom, 27, 81, 156, 159, 206, 207, 213, 215; and Boer War, 263; and China, 189; and cold war, 150; and disarmament, 164; and 1945 Labour Government, 46, 47, 51; and Latin America, 225; and Middle East, 205; and nuclear weapons, 143, 144

United Nations, 89

United Nations Commission for Trade and Development, 69

United Nations Economic Commission for Latin America, 233

United Nations Industrial Development Organization, 66

United States of America, 1, 2, 3, 4, 7–25, 65, 121, 173, 176, 189, 190, 191, 193, 196, 210; and Agency for International Development, 236; and Angola, 265–6, 281; and arms race, 142–4; and Central America, 221–55; and cold war, 141, 144, 148–59; and Democrats, 14, 22, 23, 24, 244, 251; and economic crises, 54; and franchise, 120; and imperialism, 126; and multinational capital, 113; and nuclear disarmament, 162–6; and nuclear weapons, 144–5; and oil, 85; and opposition to policy in central America, 250–3; and peace corp, 14;

and post-World War II recovery, 44, 46, 47, 49; and rates of profitability; and refugees from Central America, 250; and Republicans, 14, 20, 22, 23, 240; and strategy, 145–8; and sunbelt, 16, 19; and tertiary sector, 17, 19
Uruguay, 130
Ustinov, 142

Vance, Cyrus, 245
Vanderbelt, Cornelius, 225
Venezuela, 15, 91, 212, 222; and Accion Democratica, 221
Vietnam, 39, 159, 190, 208, 217, 243, 249, 250; and revolution, 39; and Tet Offensive, 14; and war, 11, 12, 128, 131, 146, 152, 154, 156, 158, 162, 176
Volkswagen, 192

Walker, William, 225, 228, 230
West Berlin, 30
Western Europe, 1, 2, 8, 9, 14, 150, 221, 248; and crises, 54; and détente, 153; and disarmament, 141, 163, 166; and economies, 43–64; and post-war reconstruction, 43–64; and rates of profitability, 56–64; and trades unions, 52; and unemployment, 57–60
Westinghouse, 235
Wilson, Harold, 51
Wilson, Woodrow, 8

women, 16, 24, 94, 113, 217, 218; and franchise, 120; and landlessness, 120; and southern Africa, 261, 285; and US labour participation, 16; and waged work, 44, 57
Wood, Robert, E., 96, 107, 134, 135
working class, 12; and eastern Europe, 32, 41, 47; and southern Africa, 113, 209, 273; and Third World, 111, 122, 124; and US, 11, 17, 21, 22, 24
World Bank, 3, 66, 67, 69, 80, 81, 96, 101, 128
World War I, 8, 26, 29, 205, 206, 207
World War II, 2, 10, 16, 29, 39, 40, 41, 43, 44, 74, 149, 154, 163, 173, 204, 206, 207

Xhosa, 262
Xiaoping, Deng, 183, 186, 190, 197

Yalta, 29
Yamani, Sheikh, 208
Young, Andrew, 129, 276
Yugoslavia, 30, 31, 38, 39, 196, 199

Zaire, 95, 96, 103, 278
Zambia, 87, 95, 96, 103, 104, 121, 122, 272, 275, 278, 282, 283
Zedong, Mao, 40, 173, 216; and Maoism, 179–95
Zelaya, Jose, Santos, 227, 230
Zimbabwe, 119, 208, 256, 272, 275, 276, 281, 283, 284, 286
Zinoviev, 28, 29
Zulu, 262